THE COLLECTED POEMS OF CHRISTOPHER MARLOWE

THE COLLECTED POEMS OF CHRISTOPHER MARLOWE

EDITED BY

Patrick Cheney
Pennsylvania State University

Brian J. Striar
University of North Florida

New York   Oxford
OXFORD UNIVERSITY PRESS
2006

Oxford University Press, Inc., publishes works that further Oxford University's
objective of excellence in research, scholarship, and education.

Oxford   New York
Auckland   Cape Town   Dar es Salaam   Hong Kong   Karachi
Kuala Lumpur   Madrid   Melbourne   Mexico City   Nairobi
New Delhi   Shanghai   Taipei   Toronto

With offices in
Argentina Austria Brazil Chile Czech Republic France Greece
Guatemala Hungary Italy Japan Poland Portugal Singapore
South Korea Switzerland Thailand Turkey Ukraine Vietnam

Published by Oxford University Press, Inc.
198 Madison Avenue, New York, New York 10016
http://www.oup.com

Oxford is a registered trademark of Oxford University Press

Library of Congress Cataloging-in-Publication Data
Marlowe, Christopher, 1564–1593.
  [Poems]
  The collected poems of Christopher Marlowe / edited by Patrick Cheney, Brian J. Striar.
    p. cm.
  Includes bibliographical references (p.) and index.
  ISBN-13: 978-0-19-514777-3
  ISBN 0-19-514777-4 (pbk. : alk. paper)
   I. Cheney, Patrick Gerard, 1949-   II. Striar, Brian J.   III. Title.

PR 2662.C47 2005
821'.3—dc22

                                                                2005040458

Printing number: 9 8 7 6 5 4 3 2

Printed in the United States of America
on acid-free paper

In memory of Millar MacLure
Victoria College, University of Toronto
P. C.

For Alan Levitan
Brandeis University
B. J. S.

CONTENTS

PREFACE

The Collected Poems of Christopher Marlowe is designed primarily for use in the class-room, including as a supplement to an edition of Marlowe's plays. We print all five of Marlowe's known poems, together with a prose letter in Latin that bears on them (addressed to Mary Sidney Herbert, Countess of Pembroke, and presented here in a new English translation). Additionally, we include a series of subsidiary works that help place Marlowe's poems in their original historical context: for *Ovid's Elegies,* Sir John Davies' *Epigrams,* because these two poems were originally printed together in the same volume; for "The Passionate Shepherd to His Love," a series of response poems, by Sir Walter Raleigh, John Donne, William Shakespeare, and others; and for *Hero and Leander,* the 1598 continuations by both George Chapman and Henry Petowe.

By printing all of Marlowe's poems alongside the works that bear most directly on them, we hope students will have further access to Marlowe's role as a pioneer author of the Elizabethan age. Not merely a great dramatist who precedes and rivals Shakespeare, he is also an inventive author of important English poems, spread across the genres of love elegy, pastoral lyric, Lucanian counter-imperial epic, and Ovidian narrative verse.

In this way, *The Collected Poems* aims to present Christopher Marlowe to students of English literature as an innovative author of both poems and plays important to the twenty-first century.

ACKNOWLEDGMENTS

The editors are grateful to Tony English, former editor at Oxford University Press in New York, for proposing the idea of this edition and for shepherding it through the planning phase. We are also grateful to Jan Beatty, executive editor at OUP, for her subsequent help with the project; to her associate editor, Talia Krohn, for serving as liaison; to Lisa Grzan, for serving as project editor; and to Michele Kornegay, for copyediting the manuscript. The Press supplied six readers' reports on the edition, and we are grateful for the support the readers lent and for the criticisms they provided. We hope that the final product is much improved because of their efforts.

We would also like to thank Professor David Lee Miller and his students at the University of South Carolina for trying parts of the edition out in the fall of 2004, and for making invaluable suggestions for revision.

Patrick Cheney would like to thank three research assistants who contributed to the edition: David Goldfarb, who supplied help early on, Thomas Bassinger, who helped in the final stages, especially with assembling the text, and Nicholas Repsher, who prepared the index. Cheney would also like to thank Robert R. Edwards, Garrett A. Sullivan, and Mark Thornton Burnett for support and guidance over the course of the project.

Brian Striar would like to thank J. C. McKeown for advice on some of Ovid's Latin, Mary Baron for advice on sixteenth-century psalms, and G. W. Pigman III and Eric Robinson for help with locating the commentary of Beroaldo.

Dedications

Patrick Cheney:
I would like to dedicate this edition to the memory of Millar MacLure, Victoria College, University of Toronto. Professor MacLure was a distinguished Marlovian, the editor of the Revels Plays edition of Marlowe's *Poems* and of the Critical Heritage volume on Marlowe. In the academic year 1974–75, I took Professor MacLure's graduate seminar on Marlowe—an unusual and illuminating yearlong experience, for we read the whole canon of poems and plays under the watchful eye of a great scholar and teacher. When I left residency in May 1977, Professor MacLure kindly took me for a drink on Bloor Street. When we exited, the wind was howling, and I remember the last time I saw Millar MacLure and heard him speak: "Remember me, Patrick. Don't forget."

I do not forget you, Professor MacLure, and present this volume to you with affection.

Brian J. Striar:
It is a special pleasure to dedicate this book to Alan Levitan, and it is supremely appropriate that I do so. My interest in Renaissance translation generally, and in Ovid and Marlowe specifically, began with an undergraduate paper I wrote for Professor Levitan in a junior-level class in Renaissance poetry at Brandeis University in 1974. Prior to that class I had also taken two years earlier—as a first-semester freshman—his class in Shakespeare. Both these classes proved to be the two most enjoyable classes I took throughout my entire undergraduate experience. They were also the most important, and he the most important professor. He imparted to me a deep understanding of and love for Renaissance literature, and I would never have come upon Marlowe's poetry in those years but for him. Professor Levitan's influence runs throughout all my work in this volume.

ABBREVIATIONS

Barsby	John Barsby, ed. and trans. *Ovid "Amores" I.* Bristol: Bristol Classical P, 1979.
Beroaldo	Filippo Beroaldo, commentary, along with Sulpitius, etc. *M. Annei Lucani {. . .} Pharsalia diligentissime per G. Versellanum recognita cum commentariis.* Paris, 1514.
Booth	Joan Booth, ed. and trans. *Ovid: The Second Book of "Amores."* Warminster, England: Aris, 1991.
Bowers	Fredson Bowers, ed. *The Complete Works of Christopher Marlowe.* 2nd ed. Cambridge: Cambridge UP, 1981.
Brooke	C. F. Tucker Brooke, ed. *The Works of Christopher Marlowe.* Oxford: Clarendon P, 1925.
Bullen	A. H. Bullen, ed. *The Works of Christopher Marlowe.* New York: AMS P, 1970.
Burnett	Mark Thornton Burnett, ed. *Christopher Marlowe: The Complete Poems.* Everyman's Poetry. London: Dent; and Rutland, VT: Tuttle, 2000.
Cheney	Patrick Cheney. *Marlowe's Counterfeit Profession: Ovid, Spenser, Counter-Nationhood.* Toronto: U of Toronto P, 1997.
Cooper	Thomas Cooper. *Thesaurus Linguae Romanae & Britannicae.* London, 1584.
Cunningham	F. Cunningham, ed. *The Works of Christopher Marlowe.* London, 1870.
DF	*Doctor Faustus*
Dido	*Dido, Queen of Carthage*
Duff	J. D. Duff, ed. and trans. *Lucan: The Civil War.* Cambridge, MA: Harvard UP; and London: Heinemann, 1988.
Dyce	Alexander Dyce, ed. *The Works of Christopher Marlowe.* London, 1850.
EII	*Edward II*

Gill   Roma Gill, ed. *"All Ovid's Elegies," "Lucans First Booke,"*
                                  "Dido Queene of Carthage," "Hero and Leander." Oxford:
                                  Clarendon P, 1987.

Green   Peter Green, ed. and trans. *Ovid: The Erotic Poems.* New
                                  York: Penguin, 1982.

Herbert Dedication   Dedicatory Epistle to Mary Sidney Herbert

HL   *Hero and Leander*

JM   *The Jew of Malta*

Kenney   E. J. Kenney, ed. *P. Ovidi Nasonis Amores, Medicina Faciei*
                                  Femineae, Ars Amatoria, Remedia Amoris. Oxford: Claren-
                                  don P, 1994.

Krueger   Robert Krueger, ed. *The Poems of Sir John Davies.* Oxford:
                                  Clarendon P, 1975.

LFB   *Lucan's First Book*

MacLure   Miller Maclure, ed. *The Poems: Christopher Marlowe.*
                                  London: Methuen, 1968.

MacLure *CH*   Millar MacLure, ed. *Christopher Marlowe: The Critical*
                                  Heritage, 1588–1896. London: Routledge and Kegan
                                  Paul, 1979.

Manwood   Epitaph on Sir Roger Manwood

Martin   L. C. Martin, ed. *Marlowe's Poems.* London: Methuen,
                                  1931.

McKeown   J. C. McKeown, ed. *Ovid: "Amores": Text, Prolegomena and*
                                  Commentary. 4 vols. London: Cairns, 1987–.

McKerrow   Ronald B. McKerrow, ed. *The Works of Thomas Nashe.* Ed.
                                  F. P. Wilson. 5 vols. Oxford: Basil Blackwell, 1958.

MP   *The Massacre at Paris*

Niger   Marius Dominicus Niger, comm. (1) *P. Ovidii nasonis*
                                  amorum Libri Tres {. . .}. Venice, 1518. (2) *P. Ovidii Naso-*
                                  nis poetae Sulmonensis Opera quae vocantur Amatoria: cum doc-
                                  torum virorum commentariis partim hucusque etiam alibi edi-
                                  tis, partim iam primum adiectis {. . .}: his accesserunt Iacobi
                                  Micylli annotationes longe doctissimae {. . .}: eiusdem Iacobi
                                  Micylli locorum aliquot ex Ovidiana Metamorphosi retractatio.
                                  Basle, 1549.

OE   *Ovid's Elegies*

OED   *Oxford English Dictionary*

Orgel   Stephen Orgel, ed. *Christopher Marlowe: The Complete Po-*
                                  ems and Translations. Harmondsworth: Penguin, 1971.

Ovid   Ovid. *Ovid.* 2nd ed. Trans. Frank Justus Miller; rev. G. P.
                                  Goold. Loeb Classical Library. 6 vols. Cambridge, MA:
                                  Harvard UP; and London: Heinemann, 1984.

"PS"   "The Passionate Shepherd to His Love"

Shepherd   Richard Herne Shepherd, ed. *The Works of George Chapman*. 3 vols. London: Chatto and Windus, 1911–24.

Shakespeare   *The Riverside Shakespeare*. Ed. G. Blakemore Evans et al. Boston: Houghton, 1997.

Showerman   Grant Showerman, ed. and trans. *Heroides and Amores*. Cambridge, MA: Harvard UP; and London: Heinemann, 1986.

Spenser   *The Poetical Works of Edmund Spenser*. Ed. J. C. Smith and Ernest de Selincourt. 3 vols. Oxford: Clarendon P, 1909–10.

Starnes and   DeWitt T. Starnes and Ernest William Talbert. *Classical
Talbert   Myth and Legend in Renaissance Dictionaries*. Chapel Hill: U of North Carolina P, 1955.

Sulpitius   See Beroaldo.

1 Tamb   *Tamburlaine, Part One*

2 Tamb   *Tamburlaine, Part Two*

CHRONOLOGY

1564	Marlowe born in Canterbury. Son of John Marlowe and Katherine Arthur Marlowe. *26 Feb.* Christened at St. George the Martyr. *26 Apr.* William Shakespeare baptized at Holy Trinity Church, Stratford-upon-Avon.
1576	Opening of The Theatre, Shoreditch, first regular commercial playhouse in London, built by James Burbage.
1579–80	Holds scholarship at the King's School, Canterbury
1580	Begins residence at Corpus Christi College, Cambridge.
1581	Matriculates as a "pensioner" at Corpus Christi. Thomas Watson's *Antigone* published. *7–11 May.* Elected to a Mathew Parker scholarship at Corpus Christi.
1584	Completes the BA degree at Cambridge University.
1585	Probably composes *Ovid's Elegies*. *Dido, Queen of Carthage* probably first written while Marlowe is at Cambridge. Watson's *Aminta* published. *31 Mar.* Admitted to candidacy for the MA degree at Cambridge. *Nov.* Witnesses the will of Katherine Benchkin of Canterbury.
1586	Death of Sir Philip Sidney. Babington Plot to assassinate Queen Elizabeth exposed.
1587–88	*Tamburlaine, Parts One* and *Two* performed in London; Marlowe works for the Admiral's Men, Edward Alleyn its leading actor. Possibly composes "The Passionate Shepherd to His Love."
1587	*29 June.* The Privy Council writes a letter to the Cambridge authorities exonerating Marlowe for his absences and supporting his candidacy for the MA degree. Marlowe probably doing secret service work for the Queen's Privy Council. The Rose Theatre built in Bankside (Southwark) by Philip Henslowe. Execution of Mary, Queen of Scots, mother of James VI of Scotland, future king of England (James I).
1588	England defeats the Spanish armada. Robert Greene charges Marlowe with atheism in his epistle to *Perimedes the Blacksmith*.

1588–92   Writes *Doctor Faustus, The Jew of Malta, The Massacre at Paris, Edward II,* although the order of composition and the precise dates remain uncertain.

1589   *Sept.–Dec.* Engages in swordfight in Hog Lane, London, with William Bradley, who is killed by Thomas Watson, Marlowe's friend and fellow poet-playwright. Watson and Marlowe are jailed on suspicion of murder in Newgate Prison but eventually released by Sir Roger Manwood, Canterbury jurist.

1590   *Tamburlaine, Parts One* and *Two* published, without Marlowe's name on the title page. Edmund Spenser's epic poem, *The Faerie Queene* (Books 1–3), also published. Death of Sir Francis Walsingham.

1591   Shares room with Thomas Kyd, author of *The Spanish Tragedy.* Seeks patronage from Ferdinando Stanley, Lord Strange, whose acting company, Lord Strange's Men, performs his plays.

1592–93   Plague breaks out in London, closing the theaters.

1592   *26 Jan.* Accused of counterfeiting by Richard Baines in Flushing, the Netherlands, and sent back to London by Sir Robert Sidney, governor of Flushing, to be examined by the treasurer, William Cecil, Lord Burleigh, but is evidently released. According to Sidney, Marlowe admitted to counterfeiting, but claimed he was prompted by curiosity.
            9 May. Bound to keep the peace by the constable and subconstable of Holywell Street, Shoreditch.
            3 Sept. Robert Greene dies. The posthumously published *Greene's Groatsworth of Wit,* perhaps coauthored by Henry Chettle, again accuses Marlowe of atheism.
            15 Sept. Fights with William Corkine in Canterbury. Corkine's suit against Marlowe is dismissed (or perhaps settled out of court).
            26 Sept. Watson buried at St. Bartholomew the Less, London, perhaps a victim of plague. Watson's *Amintae Gaudia* published posthumously, with Marlowe contributing the Latin Dedicatory Epistle to Mary Sidney Herbert, countess of Pembroke.
            14 Dec. Death of Sir Roger Manwood, Canterbury jurist. Marlowe writes Manwood's epitaph sometime during the next few months.

1593   Perhaps under the patronage of Thomas Walsingham, of Scadbury, Kent, translates *Lucan's First Book* and writes *Hero and Leander.* Shakespeare's *Venus and Adonis* published.
            5 May. Libel attacking Protestant immigrants is posted on the wall of the Dutch Church in London. It is signed "per Tamberlaine" and contains several allusions to Marlowe's plays.
            11 May. The Privy Council orders the lord mayor to arrest and examine persons suspected in connection with the Dutch Church libel.
            12 May. Thomas Kyd arrested on suspicion of libel, imprisoned, and tortured. Investigators discover a heretical document in Kyd's room, but he claims it was Marlowe's.

?12–27 May. An unnamed spy writes "Remembrances of words & matter against Richard Cholmeley," which reports that Marlowe has been lecturing on behalf of atheism.

18 May. The Privy Council issues a warrant for Marlowe's arrest.

20 May. Appears before the Privy Council and is instructed to give his "daily attendance"; released on his own recognizance.

27 May. Possible delivery of the Baines Note accusing Marlowe of atheism.

30 May. Killed by Ingram Frizer at the house of Eleanor Bull, Deptford. Witnesses in the room are Robert Poley and Nicholas Skeres. The official coroner's report says that Marlowe attacked Frizer over a dispute about who would pay the "reckoning," or bill.

1 June. A jury determines that Frizer acted in self-defense for the killing of Christopher Marlowe. Buried in a nameless grave at St. Nicholas's Church, Deptford. Soon afterward, Kyd writes two documents to the lord keeper, Sir John Puckering, accusing Marlowe of atheism and of being an injurious person.

29 June. Richard Cholmeley admits he has been influenced by Marlowe's atheism.

28 Sept. Lucan's First Book and Hero and Leander entered together in the Stationers' Register.

1594 Publication of Dido, Queen of Carthage and Edward II, the first works bearing Marlowe's name on the title page, although Thomas Nashe's name also appears on Dido. Possible publication of The Massacre of Paris. Publication of Shakespeare's The Rape of Lucrece and Titus Andronicus. Nashe's The Unfortunate Traveler also published.

1597 Thomas Beard's The Theatre of God's Judgments published.

1598 Hero and Leander published later in the year, first as an 818-line poem and later as an expanded epic, divided into "sestiads," and completed by George Chapman. (Reprinted in 1606, 1609, 1613, 1617, 1629, and 1637.) Henry Petowe's The Second Part of "Hero and Leander" also published.

1599 The bishop of London and archbishop of Canterbury ban Ovid's Elegies (probably published in mid- to late-1590s), along with Sir John Davies's Epigrams, and have them burned in public. The Passionate Pilgrim published, with Shakespeare's name on the title page, and including versions of "The Passionate Shepherd" and Raleigh's "The Nymph's Reply."

1600 Lucan's First Book published with Marlowe's name on the title page. England's Helicon published, including versions of "The Passionate Shepherd" and Raleigh's "The Nymph's Reply."

1602 Philip Henslowe, manager of the Admiral's Men, pays William Birde and Samuel Rowley £4 for additions to Doctor Faustus.

1603 Death of Queen Elizabeth I. Succession of James VI of Scotland as James I.

1604   The A text of *Doctor Faustus* published, with Marlowe's name on the title page.

1616   The B text of *Doctor Faustus* published, with Marlowe's name on the title page.

1633   Thomas Heywood publishes *The Jew of Malta*, identifying Marlowe as the author.

INTRODUCTION: AUTHORSHIP IN MARLOWE'S POEMS

Patrick Cheney

THE EDITION

Christopher Marlowe (1564–93) is famous today as an inventor of both modern English drama and modern English poetry. In this edition, Brian J. Striar and I aim to present Marlowe's achievement as a poet within the context of his dramatic career. He is Renaissance England's first great poet-playwright, the author of seven extant plays (*Dido, Queen of Carthage, Tamburlaine, Parts One* and *Two, The Jew of Malta; Edward II; The Massacre at Paris; Doctor Faustus*) and five extant poems: *Ovid's Elegies,* "The Passionate Shepherd to His Love," *Lucan's First Book, Hero and Leander,* and a Latin epitaph on the jurist Sir Roger Manwood.[1] Because so many editions of Marlowe's plays are in print, Oxford University Press has commissioned us to concentrate on the poems. At the time of writing, Mark Thornton Burnett's Everyman edition of *The Complete Poems* (2000) is the primary alternative available.[2] In his inexpensive paperback edition, Burnett prints all five of Marlowe's poems, along with a useful, albeit modest, editorial apparatus: a "Chronology of Marlowe's Life and Times," a seven-page "Introduction," and ten pages of "Notes" at the back. The need for a fuller edition of Marlowe's poems underlies the Oxford *Collected Poems of Christopher Marlowe.*

While today Marlowe's plays are more often singled out and studied as a group, we believe that Marlowe's poems constitute a historically important corpus in their own right and deserve to be read as such. Only by putting the poems together with the plays can we form an accurate, composite view of Marlowe's English authorship. In this edition, we present the poems not as an isolated series of works scattered through Elizabethan England's manuscript and print culture, but as a set of poems collaboratively produced in that culture.

What we notice about Marlowe's poems is how embedded they are in the works of other authors, individuals, and institutions. We recall the ways in which the four major poems originally emerge from the complexities of a nascent print culture (the

---

[1] On Marlowe as an English poet-playwright, see Patrick Cheney, "Introduction," *Cambridge Companion to Christopher Marlowe* (Cambridge: Cambridge UP, 2004) 1–23.

[2] Burnett, *Christopher Marlowe: The Complete Poems,* Everyman's Poetry (London: Dent; Rutland, VT: Tuttle, 2000). After we completed our edition, another edition emerged: *Christopher Marlowe's Complete Poems,* ed. Drew Silver (Mineola, NY: Dover P, 2003).

fifth poem, the Manwood epitaph, appears originally only in manuscript). None of the poems is published in Marlowe's lifetime.[3]

While the author himself had been killed on May 30, 1593, his first poem with a verifiable printing date is *Hero and Leander,* which appears in 1598—not in one edition but in two different ones. The first prints Marlowe's 818-line Ovidian narrative poem by itself; the second turns this poem into an English and European minor epic, dividing the 818 lines into two "Sestiads" and completing the well-known myth of the tragic principals with four new Sestiads, written by George Chapman.

Then, in 1599 "The Passionate Shepherd" appears, without Marlowe's name attached to it, in a little volume of verse called *The Passionate Pilgrim,* which the printer, William Jaggard, falsely ascribes to William Shakespeare.[4] Jaggard's version of "The Passionate Shepherd" consists of only four of the known six stanzas, and it is followed by an abbreviated version of an anonymously printed poem known today as "The Nymph's Reply," believed to be written by Sir Walter Raleigh. By 1653, when Izaak Walton included both poems in *The Compleat Angler,* four different versions of Marlowe's lyric become available, creating an even more complex textual problem than that for *Hero and Leander.*[5]

In 1600, *Lucan's First Book* appears in print, but again, there are textual problems. Not merely does this poem show up back-to-back with *Hero and Leander* in the Stationers' Register on September 28, 1593 (a few months after Marlowe's death), but in 1600 as well another edition of *Hero and Leander* appears with a title page identifying *Lucan's First Book* as a companion poem, even though the edition itself does not include it.

As for *Ovid's Elegies,* we possess three editions—two printing a selection of ten poems, the third "all" forty-eight—but for none do we know the date of publication, and all the title pages list the place of publication as Middlebourgh, Holland (perhaps spuriously).[6] Scholars believe that the three editions were printed between about 1595 and the early years of the seventeenth century, and all print Sir John Davies's *Epigrams* as a companion poem, for reasons to which we are not privy. In 1599, this volume was publicly burned by order of the Bishops' Ban.[7]

---

[3] Full information on the texts of Marlowe's poems can be found in the major scholarly editions: Brooke; Martin; MacLure; Bowers; and Gill. The following discussion is indebted to these editions and to other works cited later.

[4] For the most recent discussion, see Patrick Cheney, *Shakespeare, National Poet-Playwright* (Cambridge: Cambridge UP, 2004) ch. 5.

[5] See Susanne Woods, "'The Passionate Shepherd' and 'The Nimphs Reply': A Study of Transmission," *Huntington Library Quarterly* 34 (1970): 25–33.

[6] See Charles Nicholl, "'At Middleborough': Some Reflections on Marlowe's Visit to the Low Countries in 1592," in *Christopher Marlowe and English Renaissance Culture,* ed. Darryll Grantley and Peter Roberts (Aldershot, Hants, England: Scolar P; Brookfield, VT: Ashgate, 1996) 38–50.

[7] On the Bishops' Ban, see Richard McCabe, "Elizabethan Satire and the Bishops' Ban of 1599," *Yearbook of English Studies* 11 (1981): 188–93; and Ian Frederick Moulton, "'Printed Abroad and Uncastrated': Marlowe's *Elegies* and Davies' *Epigrams,*" in *Marlowe, History, and Sexuality: New Critical Essays on Christopher Marlowe,* ed. Paul Whitfield White (New York: AMS P, 1998) 77–90. For further detail on the texts and dating of *Ovid's Elegies,* see Roma Gill and Robert Krueger, "The Early Editions of Marlowe's Elegies and Davies's Epigrams: Sequence and Authority," *Library,* 5th

All of this uncertainty about Marlowe's poems has led some recent critics to reject the "Romantic" notion of Marlowe as an author and to speak rather of a "Marlowe effect."[8] This poststructuralist principle objects to the idea of the author as an autonomous creator and puts in its place an individual who is "socially constructed" by political and economic institutions.[9] Yet this binary opposition is simplistic. While accurately emphasizing the pressures that institutions place on authors, it fails to allow agency to the author. Accordingly, postrevisionist theorists now posit a principle of reciprocity between authors and institutions, including between Marlowe and Elizabethan institutions of power, performance, and print.[10]

For this reason, we here present Marlowe as an author in relation with other voices and hands and try to suggest that his intertextual relations constitute a visible form of his poetic signature. All four of the printed poems appear in dialogue with other poets. *Ovid's Elegies* and *Lucan's First Book* are themselves translations from Latin authors, and thus formalize Marlowe's dialogue with Ovid and Lucan, classical Rome's two most influential counter-Virgilian poets.[11] *Hero and Leander* responds to Ovid's two verse letters about the tragic lovers in the *Heroides* (*Heroical Epistles*): poem 18, "Leander to Hero," and poem 19, "Hero to Leander." Yet Marlowe also knew of the Greek poem titled *Hero and Leander,* written by Musaeus, a fifth-century CE Greek grammarian, whom Renaissance scholars mistook for the "primeval poet" Musaeus, regarded as a founder of poetry, along with Orpheus.[12] "The Passionate Shepherd" responds to invitational poetry in the pastoral works of Theocritus, Virgil, Ovid, and Edmund Spenser (Cheney, *MCP* 68–87). But Marlowe's poem itself had the immedi-

---

ser. 26 (1971): 243–49; Fredson Bowers, "The Early Editions of Marlowe's *Ovid's Elegies,*" *Studies in Bibliography* 25 (1972): 149–72; J. M. Nosworthy, "The Publication of Marlowe's Elegies and Davies's Epigrams," *Review of English Studies* 4 (1953): 260–01, and "Marlowe's Ovid and Davies's Epigrams—A Postscript," *Review of English Studies* 15 (1965): 397–98.

[8] See Leah S. Marcus, "Textual Indeterminacy and Ideological Difference: The Case of *Dr. Faustus,*" *Renaissance Drama* 20 (1989): 1–29; and Thomas Healy, *Christopher Marlowe* (Plymouth, England: Northcote House in Association with the British Council, 1994) 1–9.

[9] This is the project of *Constructing Christopher Marlowe,* ed. J. A. Downie and J. T. Parnell (Cambridge: Cambridge UP, 2000). See also Stephen Greenblatt, "Marlowe and the Will to Absolute Play," in *Renaissance Self-Fashioning: More to Shakespeare* (Chicago: U of Chicago P, 1980) 193–221.

[10] On this principle in such authors as Shakespeare and Spenser, see Richard Helgerson, *Forms of Nationhood: The Elizabethan Writing of England* (Chicago: U of Chicago P, 1992) 215; Michael Bristol, *Big Time Shakespeare* (New York: Routledge, 1996) 49–58; and Louis Montrose, "Spenser's Domestic Domain: Poetry, Property, and the Early Modern Subject," in *Subject and Object in Renaissance Culture,* ed. Margreta de Grazia, Maureen Quilligan, and Peter Stallybrass (Cambridge: Cambridge UP, 1996) 83–130 (esp. 92). On Marlowe, see Richard Dutton, "Marlowe: Censorship and Construction," in *Licensing, Censorship and Authorship in Early Modern England: Buggeswords* (Basingstoke: Palgrave, 2000) 62–89; Simon Shepherd, "A Bit of Ruff: Criticism, Fantasy, Marlowe," in *Constructing Christopher Marlowe* 102–15; and Richard Wilson, "'Writ in blood': Marlowe and the New Historicists," in *Constructing Christopher Marlowe* 116–32.

[11] On this topic, see Philip Hardie, *The Epic Successors to Virgil: A Study in the Dynamics of a Tradition* (Cambridge: Cambridge UP, 1993).

[12] See Clarke Hulse, "Marlowe, The Primeval Poet," in *Metamorphic Verse: The Elizabethan Minor Epic* (Princeton: Princeton UP, 1981) 93–140. Marlowe refers to Musaeus at lines 51–52: "Amorous Leander, beautiful and young / (Whose tragedy divine Musaeus sung)."

ate effect of inviting a series of response poems. We have spoken of Raleigh's "The Nymph's Reply," but during the period several others emerge: "Another of the Same Nature, Made Since," which appears in another Elizabethan miscellany printing Marlowe's lyric, *England's Helicon* (1600); John Donne's "The Bait," which emerges in the same miscellany; J. Paulin's "Love's Contentment," which appears in a manuscript collection of miscellaneous poems dating from the early 1640s; and Robert Herrick's "To Phillis to Love," which is printed in his 1648 collection of verse, *Hesperides*.[13]

To complicate the situation, Marlowe imitates his own poem in his plays. In *The Jew of Malta*, the slave Ithamore provides a detailed parody of "The Passionate Shepherd" (4.2.101–11), while nearly all of Marlowe's other plays include shorter self-quotations. In short, Marlowe writes in dialogue with himself and with other authors, while poets during his own lifetime begin a process of bringing themselves into dialogue with him, including on the stage. For instance, in *The Merry Wives of Windsor* Shakespeare presents Sir Hugh Evans parodying "The Passionate Shepherd." Perhaps no other English poem, before or since, has had such magnetic power.

The present edition prints Marlowe's poems alongside works by other authors important to the original moment of publication or the process of early modern reception. In particular, we follow Burnett's edition in printing Marlowe's poems in the order of a three-part Ovidian career model or *cursus*, invented in response to the famed Virgilian progression from pastoral to georgic to epic.[14] Ovid begins with amatory verse: the *Amores* (*Loves*), *Ars amatoria* (*Art of Love*), and *Heroides*. Then, using the *Fasti* (*Rituals*) as a bridge, Ovid progresses to the high genres: tragedy (*Medea*, extant in two lines) and epic (*Metamorphoses*).[15] Virgil's developmental model of three genres operates by a principle of typology, through which pastoral predicts epic, georgic encloses pastoral and predicts epic, and epic encloses both georgic and pastoral.[16] Ovid replaces this Virgilian typology by knitting together the three-phase career with a principle of oscillation. Thus, Ovid begins with amatory poetry, but even as he concludes the *Amores* by announcing his move to tragedy (3.15; *OE* 3.14), he tells us he has already written a tragedy (2.18.13–14). As such, Ovid does not merely change the genres of the literary career; he scrambles the maturational model of Virgil's career idea.

Like Ovid, Marlowe inaugurates his career with amatory poetry, represented by *Ovid's Elegies* and "The Passionate Shepherd." Then he intertwines this lower form with the genre of tragedy, represented by his seven extant plays. Finally, he intertwines

---

[13] See R. S. Forsythe, "*The Passionate Shepherd;* and English Poetry," *PMLA* 40 (1925): 692–742. See also Douglas Bruster, "'Come to the Tent Again': 'The Passionate Shepherd,' Dramatic Rape and Lyric Time," *Criticism* 33 (1991): 49–72; and Diana Henderson, "'Unhappy Dido': Marlowe's Lyric Strains," in *Passion Made Public: Elizabethan Lyric, Gender, and Performance* (Urbana: U of Illinois P, 1995) 120–66.

[14] Burnett follows Cheney, *MCP* (see Burnett, ed. xiv).

[15] On Ovid's *Medea*, see A. G. Nikolaidis, "Some Observations on Ovid's Lost *Medea*," *Latomus* 44 (1985): 383–87; and Cheney, *MCP* 42–46, 91–96. On Ovid's *Metamorphoses* as an epic, see Brooks Otis, *Ovid as an Epic Poet*, 2nd ed. (Cambridge: Cambridge UP, 1970); for its reception in England, see Raphael Lyne, *Ovid's Changing Worlds: English "Metamorphoses," 1567–1632* (Oxford: Oxford UP, 2001).

[16] See John S. Coolidge, "Great Things and Small: The Virgilian Progression," *Comparative Literature* 17 (1965): 1–23.

tragedy and elegy with epic, represented by *Lucan's First Book*, an "Englishing" of book 1 of Lucan's counter-Virgilian epic, the *Pharsalia*, and by *Hero and Leander*, an Elizabethan epyllion or "minor epic." In Marlowe's Ovidian *cursus*, the first and the third phases are distinctly "poetic" and are thus printed here, while the second phase, the "dramatic," is widely available in other editions.[17] By reading Marlowe's poems within an Ovidian rubric, students may acquire a historical frame for a canon that might otherwise look like simply a haphazard series of scattered exercises.

For three of the four printed poems, early editions authorize us to include ancillary texts. Hence, we print Davies's *Epigrams* with *Ovid's Elegies*—the first edition to do so since Tucker Brooke's in 1910. We also print versions of "The Passionate Shepherd" from both *The Passionate Pilgrim* and *England's Helicon*, together with Ithamore's parody in *The Jew*, and we add six response poems: those by Raleigh, the anonymous poet of "Another of the Same Nature," Shakespeare, Donne, Paulin, and Herrick. By making these poems available together, we aim to suggest the ways in which Marlowe's lyric emerged through the printing of two quite different Elizabethan media: the verse miscellany and the quarto play. Moreover, *Lucan's First Book* puts Marlowe into dialogue with Lucan himself, and Lucan's epic project also generically matches Marlowe's other poem in this register, *Hero and Leander*. Further, this last epyllion enters into dialogue with two contemporary "continuations": Chapman's and one made by Henry Petowe, also in 1598.

The epitaph on Manwood is something of a special case, and we print it both in the original Latin and in a new translation by Striar. Marlowe's poem thus appears double-voiced, even as it puts the poet into conversation with the Canterbury jurist.

Our edition prints one final document, also newly translated by Striar: Marlowe's Dedicatory Epistle to Mary Sidney Herbert, countess of Pembroke, author, literary patron, and sister to Sir Philip Sidney. This prose letter in Latin prefaces *Amintae Gaudia*, a Latin poem composed by Thomas Watson and published posthumously in 1592, probably by his friend, fellow poet-playwright Christopher Marlowe. (Watson and Marlowe were arrested, imprisoned, and finally freed for their roles in the 1589 killing of William Bradley in Hog Lane, London—freed by Sir Roger Manwood.) Marlowe's *Dedicatory Epistle* is often produced in editions of Marlowe's poems (e.g., Martin, MacLure, Gill) because it appears as part of a verse edition but also because it bears valuably on Marlowe's role as a poet toward the end of his life.

MARLOWE AS AN ELIZABETHAN POET

Marlowe's brief corpus of poems is of historic importance in the development of English poetry. The nineteenth-century poet and critic Algernon Charles Swinburne may be exaggerating when he calls "The Passionate Shepherd" "one of the most

---

[17] See, e.g., Mark Thornton Burnett, ed., *Christopher Marlowe: The Complete Plays*, Everyman Library (London: Dent; Rutland, VT: Tuttle, 1999); David Bevington and Eric Rasmussen, eds., *Christopher Marlowe: "Tamburlaine, Parts I and II," "Doctor Faustus," A- and B-Texts, "The Jew of Malta," "Edward II"* (Oxford: Clarendon P, 1995); E. D. Pendry and J. C. Maxwell, eds., *Christopher Marlowe: Complete Plays and Poems* (London: Dent, 1976).

faultless lyrics [. . .] in the whole range of descriptive and fanciful poetry" (MacLure *CH* 183), but today we might still find Swinburne's rhapsody captivating. Millar MacLure is more circumspect when he recalls that "The Passionate Shepherd" was simply "the most popular of all Elizabethan lyrics" (xxxvii). Similarly, C. S. Lewis says of *Hero and Leander:* "I do not know that any other poet has rivaled its peculiar excellence"; he means William Shakespeare, who tried his hand at the Ovidian epyllion twice, first in *Venus and Adonis* (1593) and then in *The Rape of Lucrece* (1594), yet could not match the Canterbury youth.[18] Lewis goes on to judge *Lucan's First Book* "of very great merit," so much so that he was tempted to deny Marlowe's authorship of it (86). Today, Marlowe's authorship is not in dispute, and recently the classicist Charles Martindale calls *Lucan's First Book* "arguably one of the underrated masterpieces of Elizabethan literature."[19] In fact, Marlowe's translation of Lucan is "the only sustained sixteenth-century heroic poem in blank verse after Surrey's [translation of Books 2 and 4 the *Aeneid*]," writes O. B. Hardison Jr.[20] MacLure goes even further: Marlowe's "*Lucan* remains the chief monument in undramatic unrhymed English pentameters between Surrey and Milton" (xxxvi). While few scholars would designate *Ovid's Elegies* a masterpiece, critics routinely single out its historical importance: it is the very first translation of the *Amores* not merely into English but into any European vernacular, and it is the first early modern English poem in sustained heroic couplets.[21]

Moreover, Marlowe is usually credited with perfecting the Ovidian epyllion and making the blank verse line the gold standard for English verse, as Shakespeare later perfected it on the stage (e.g., *Hamlet*) and Milton in epic poetry (*Paradise Lost*).[22] Marlowe's influence on English poetry is indeed paramount, and once again we might wish to recall the exaltation of Swinburne: Marlowe is

> alone [. . .] the true Apollo of our dawn, the bright and morning star of the full midsummer day of English poetry at its highest. [. . .] The first great English poet was the father of English tragedy and the creator of English blank verse [. . .] the first English poet whose powers can be called sublime. [. . .] He is the greatest discoverer, the most daring and inspired pioneer, in all our poetic literature.
>
> *(MacLure CH 175–84)*

---

[18] Lewis, *English Literature in the Sixteenth Century Excluding Drama* (1954; London: Oxford UP, 1973) 488.

[19] Martindale, *Redeeming the Text: Latin Poetry and the Hermeneutics of Reception* (Cambridge: Cambridge UP, 1993) 97.

[20] Hardison, "Blank Verse Before Milton," *Studies in Philology* 81 (1984): 253–74, 265. J. B. Steane, in *Marlowe: A Critical Study* (Cambridge: Cambridge UP, 1964), observes: "In this poem blank verse has already, virtually before Shakespeare, become the Shakespearean instrument" (276–77).

[21] On the first European translation, see Brian J. Striar, "Theories and Practices of Renaissance Verse Translation" (Diss. Claremont Graduate School, 1984) 187; and Cheney, *MCP* 49, 282n1. For a full study of the *Amores'* reception, with chapters on Marlowe and Shakespeare, see M. L. Stapleton, *Harmful Eloquence: Ovid's "Amores" from Antiquity to Shakespeare* (Ann Arbor: U of Michigan P, 1996). On heroic couplets in Marlowe's translation, see Georgia Brown, "Marlowe and Classicism," in *Cambridge Companion* 106–26.

[22] See Roma Gill, "Christopher Marlowe," in vol. 62 of Fredson Bowers, ed., *The Dictionary of Literary Biography: Elizabethan Dramatists* (Detroit: Gale Research Group, 1987) 212–31.

Although the claim may seem exaggerated, Marlowe has always provoked such "high-astounding terms" (to quote his own Prologue to *1 Tamb*). His fellow poet-playwright Michael Drayton imagines Marlowe "bath[ing] [. . .] in the Thespian springs":

> [He] Had in him those brave translunary things
> That the first Poets had, his raptures were,
> All Ayre, and fire, which made his verses cleere,
> For that fine madnes still he did retaine,
> Which rightly should possesse a Poets braine.
>
> *(Drayton, in MacLure CH 47)*

OVID'S ELEGIES

In addition to being a historic translation, *Ovid's Elegies* is a valuable Elizabethan poem in its own right, notable for two features worth underscoring here: its presentation of the poet as an author with a literary career and its portrait of Corinna as a young woman. The twin features of poetry and desire lend support to Stephen Orgel's suggestion that "In a sense, this is Marlowe's sonnet sequence, the psychomachia of a poet-lover whose love is both his creation and his ultimate monomania, frustration and despair" (233). When viewed as a sexy Elizabethan sequence, *Ovid's Elegies* becomes more than simply a scholarly translation; it lines up with such Petrarchan poems as Sidney's *Astrophil and Stella,* Spenser's *Amoretti,* and Shakespeare's sonnets, all of which present their poet-figures caught in the throes of desire. However flawed Marlowe's translation may sometimes be, students may profit by reading Marlowe's portraits of the Ovidian author and the Ovidian female against portraits in these more familiar Elizabethan poems.

Ovid's Elegies is indeed structured around a set of poems introducing the speaker as a poet. Classicists call this set the "programmatic" poems because it foregrounds a professional program for the poet. The volume's forty-eight poems divide into three carefully structured books. Books 1 and 3 both consist of fifteen poems, although the edition Marlowe used contains only fourteen for book 3.[23] Both books 1 and 3 begin and end with poems foregrounding the speaker's role as a poet (1.1 and 1.15; 3.1 and 3.15[14]). Like books 1 and 3, book 2 begins with a programmatic poem (2.1), but it veers from the pattern in two ways. First, it includes nineteen rather than fifteen poems; and second, it slots its last programmatic poem into the penultimate position (2.18 rather than 2.19). This principle—setting up a pattern of expectation only to foil it—forms part of Ovid's playful technique of oscillation, a counter to Virgilian order.

Indeed, the six programmatic poems present the poet as a counter-Virgilian author with a new model for a literary career. Together, the poems tell a story about a young poet who tries to write both Virgilian epic and Roman tragedy; who abandons that high calling when he falls in love, turning instead to the lower form of love

---

[23] The Loeb edition includes a dream vision poem as 3.5, and this makes its numbering of the subsequent poems differ from those in Marlowe's translation (e.g., the Loeb's 3.15 is Marlowe's 3.14).

elegy; and who finally bids farewell to Venus, her son, and elegy in order to write his first tragedy. While today we rarely remember Ovid as a tragedian, we might speculate that Marlowe, himself a pioneer of English tragedy, would have been especially interested in this feature of Ovid's literary career. One way to view the sequence, then, is as a narrative about the poet's struggle to turn from the writing of poems to the writing of plays.

The Ovidian poet's professional relationship with Venus—and with such figures as Dame Tragedy and Dame Elegy in elegy 3.1—coheres with his erotic relationship with Corinna. Thus, Ovid names this mistress after the Greek poetess Corinna, so that even his friends suspected she was merely a figure for his poetic inspiration. Yet Marlowe's translation produces something unexpected: Corinna becomes one of our most detailed masculine portraits of a woman during the Elizabethan era. Taking Orgel's cue, we may see her as a counter to the late-sixteenth-century vogue for Petrarchan ladies, including Petrarch's Laura herself, Sidney's Stella, Spenser's Elizabeth Boyle, and Shakespeare's Dark Lady.

Unlike Elizabeth Boyle or Stella, and anticipating the Dark Lady, Corinna is no "lady." For starters, she is fond of adultery (1.4, 2.12). Sometimes to our dismay (sometimes to our delight), we become privy to the remarkable details of her character. She enjoys sports: horse racing in particular (3.2). She dyes her hair, only to lose it (1.14), and she has an abortion (2.13, 2.14). She not only enjoys sex but also famously visits the poet in his bedroom on a hot summer's day, dressed for the occasion: "Then came Corinna in a long loose gown, / Her white neck hid with tresses hanging down" (1.5.9–10). When the poet snatches her gown off—"being thin, the harm was small" (13)—she coyly struggles, "as one who would be cast, / Betrayed herself, and yielded at the last" (15–16). Her naked body is without blemish, primed for love-making, especially (but not exclusively) with the poet: "What arms and shoulders did I touch and see, / How apt her breasts were to be pressed by me!" (19–20). This girl has a "smooth" belly, a "large" leg, and a "lusty thigh" (22). Later, when Corinna grows "tired," she does not slacken her gyrations but bids her lover to continue "kiss[ing]" (25).

Ovid's Elegies may be a sexy poem, but it is never pornographic. Since the poet sees sexiness, the female body, and Corinna's character as a fountain for masculine poetry, his sequence exhibits a bold, unashamed representation of male–female relations. In ways that might compel us today, *Ovid's Elegies* refuses to *idealize* desire, the relations between men and women, human sexuality, and the body. Instead, the sequence candidly registers the cultural need to display desire in all its ardor, confusion, and violence. From the display, two figures emerge that make the sequence historically valuable: the male poet with his playful counter-Virgilian career of changing literary forms and Corinna with her bold sexuality and ever-changing body.

Davies's *Epigrams*

Clearly, the bishops in 1599 who banned and publicly burned the volume containing *Ovid's Elegies* and Davies's *Epigrams* had different ideas. Together, these two works mounted a subversive attack on "social norms of gender identity and behavior" (Moulton 86). According to Ian Frederick Moulton, "although epigrams can be seen to have a conservative, regulatory function—mocking vice and folly in order to encourage conformity to a 'rational' and 'natural' social order—Davies' epigrams, like much satire in the 1590s, were seen by the Bishops and others concerned with policing public morals as provoking the vices they condemned" (85). This public use of a literary form has its origins in funeral monument inscriptions, but from the *Greek Anthology* onward an epigram was a short, pithy verse with an astringent moral. In Roman antiquity, Catullus (c. 84–c. 54 BCE) contributed to the early development of the Latin epigram, while Martial (CE 40–103) polished and elevated it into its most effective, pithy, and pointed form. The evolution of the Latin epigram bears close comparison with the evolution of the Roman elegy, one of the earliest fashioners of which was again Catullus yet whose greatest artificer was Ovid. Such a comparative evolution helps contextualize the appearance of Davies's *Epigrams* in a volume alongside *Ovid's Elegies*.

The sixteenth-century poet Edward Guilpin called Davies "our English Martial" (*Skialetheia*, epigram 20; rpt. Krueger 1). Effectively, Davies transposes Martial's Roman scenes to downtown 1590s London. According to Robert Krueger,

> In an address on epigrams and epitaphs to the Society of Antiquaries in 1600, Davies states that the only rules governing the epigram are that it must be brief and witty; this leaves the writer free to choose form and content. Probably, therefore, Davies's choice of genre and of specific content represents his natural inclination to write poetry as a display-case for wit, humour, and mastery of form, directed towards arousing laughter and admiration in the audience. The epigrams embody also one of the poet's ideals, revealed in the subject-matter and in the implied character of the observer; between the subject and the observer is set a great gap in sophistication.
>
> *(lix)*

Davies's epigrammatic wit and urbane sophistication make him a natural companion of Marlowe's Ovid, and readers can benefit a great deal from putting the two poems into dialogue with each other. Like *Ovid's Elegies,* the *Epigrams* focus on the role of the poet as a man about town. The work begins and ends with epigrams addressed to the Muse, and throughout Davies showcases his art for its satiric social content: "Oft in my laughing rhymes, I name a gull" (2.1). What might be surprising, though, is the space these laughing rhymes devote to the new Elizabethan theater: "Rufus the Courtier, at the theater, / Leaving the best and most conspicuous place, / Doth either to the stage himself transfer, / Or through a grate, doth show his doubtful face" (3.1–4). While Davies was not a poet-playwright like Marlowe, we may discover in his work a compelling fusion of poetry and theater that once more lines up with *Ovid's Elegies.*

As to be expected of one frequenting the theater district, Davies spends sufficient time browsing at the "common stews and brothels of the town" (3.10), where we find a lot of "drinking, thriving, wenching, war" (17.9). In fact, we see a lot of London and its environs, to the extent that Davies's *Epigrams* offers an entirely robust visit to an Elizabethan city. Often we find ourselves in the shadows of such familiar landmarks as St. Paul's Cathedral (7.5) or the Inns of Court (3.5). Yet Davies is careful to locate London on a European map that includes such countries as Ireland, Scotland, France, Spain, Italy, Holland, Belgium, and Turkey. There are splendid character types— most notably the "gull" and the "gallant"—but also references to such historical figures as King Philip of Macedon, Cicero, Henry VIII, Sir Thomas More, Mary I, Sir

Christopher Hatton, Sir Francis Vere, and Sir John Norris, including contemporary writers Raphael Holinshed, George Gascoigne, and Davies's predecessor in the English epigram, John Heywood. We meet "Jove" and "Pallas [Athene]" (17.2) alongside "Puritans" and "Protestants" (13.1, 8), Homer and his Helen alongside the contemporary performer Banks and such equally famous performing animals as horses and elephants. Like Publius in epigram 43, we might wish to "Leav[e] old Ployden, Dyer and Broke alone, / To see old Harry Hunks and Sacarson" (13–14).

"THE PASSIONATE SHEPHERD TO HIS LOVE"

If, like Davies's *Epigrams, Ovid's Elegies* does not idealize but processes desire, inviting our response, "The Passionate Shepherd" virtually turns this Ovidian poetics into a separate form. Both Marlowe poems mine two principal erotic genres forming the lower end of the Renaissance hierarchy of genres: elegy and pastoral. Like elegy, pastoral traces to classical culture: to the Greek Alexandrian poet Theocritus, who invents it in his *Idylls,* a collection of pastoral eclogues written in response to Homeric epic; and to the Roman Virgil, who innovatively places the pastoral in his three-part career as an inaugural form, the *Eclogues,* a collection of ten pastoral poems. Both Theocritus and Virgil include pastorals of invitation that underlie Marlowe's lyric (see Cheney, *MCP* 69–71).

In his counter-Virgilian epic, the *Metamorphoses,* Ovid responds to the invitational pastorals of Virgil and Theocritus when he inserts the story of the one-eyed Cyclops Polyphemus and the beautiful nymph Galatea into his retelling of Aeneas's voyage from Troy to Rome (13.623–968).[24] In Ovid's hands, the invitational pastoral mode interrupts the epic quest for empire, pausing to sound the lover's complaint, not simply against Galatea, who prefers to lie in the arms of her lover, Acis, but against Virgil's poetics at large.

In antiquity, the intertextual channel may flow from Homer to Theocritus to Virgil to Ovid, but in 1579 Spenser re-routes it into his English collection of Virgilian pastoral eclogues, *The Shepheardes Calender.* In the *Januarye* eclogue, England's New Poet (as he is called in this work) presents his authorial persona, Colin Clout, relying on the invitational mode. Colin tells how his friend, Hobbinol, had given him (homoerotic) gifts but how Colin then gave the gifts to his Petarchan mistress, Rosalind, who in turn has rejected them (55–60). In this economy of gift-giving, Spenser re-routes the flow of homoerotic desire, surfacing especially in Theocritan and Virgilian pastoral, to the heterosexual desire foregrounded in Ovid's nonpastoral poem, the *Metamorphoses.*

Marlowe's sophisticated strategy linking the pastoral modes of Spenser, Ovid, Virgil, and Theocritus is belied by the poem's "shallow" surface:

And we will sit upon the rocks,
Seeing the shepherds feed their flocks

---

[24]See Joseph Farrell, "Dialogue of Genres in Ovid's 'Lovesong of Polyphemus' (*Metamorphoses* 13.719–897)," *American Journal of Philology* 113 (1992): 235–68.

By shallow rivers, to whose falls
Melodious birds sing madrigals.
                    ("PS" 5–8)

On the surface of the text, a passionate shepherd invites a shepherdess to "Come live with [him]. [. . .], and be [his] [. . .] love" (1); together, they "all the pleasures prove." The word "pleasure" seems a natural goal for erotic desire, but the following scientific word, "prove" (meaning *experience*), introduces a philosophical edge. The shepherd invites his love to engage in an epicurean or hedonistic way of life. In Elizabethan England, however, epicureanism could signal the educated goal of materialist philosophy (quite literally, *a philosophy of matter*), which historically opposed essentialist philosophy (a philosophy of essence), especially as the Roman poet Lucretius (96?–55 BCE) counters Plato in his epic poem, *De rerum natura* (*On the Nature of Things*).[25] Marlowe has been hailed as "the Lucretius of the English language," and nowhere is this designation on more concentrated display than in "The Passionate Shepherd."[26]

Not merely does the shepherd strive for "pleasure," but he uses material gifts to persuade his beloved to engage in erotic play:

And I will make thee beds of roses,
And a thousand fragrant posies,
A cap of flowers, and a kirtle,
Embroidered all with leaves of myrtle.
                    ("PS" 9–12)

Like everything else in this poem, the shepherd's offer of gifts is ambiguous, subject to romantic and cynical interpretations. Does he use his masculine voice to address the desires of his shepherdess with an endearing reciprocity, or does he aim simply to seduce her with material rewards, the contents of which (we may speculate) are empty? Are we witnessing here a genuine expression to a beloved or a rhetorical ploy to a pretty girl? The poem is justly famous precisely because Marlowe manages to invent a "shallow" poetry that cuts deeply along this interpretive divide.

While generations of readers have absorbed themselves in "that smooth song" that Izaak Walton said "was made by Kit Marlow, now at least fifty years ago,"[27] even the earliest recorded readers found something as alarming as they did beautiful. Raleigh was evidently the first to discern the depth of Marlowe's shallow invitation. In "The Nymph's Reply," he cross-dresses his masculine voice to offer the passionate shepherd a feminine rejoinder. Briefly, Raleigh's nymph rejects the shepherd's carpe diem philosophy, which imagines lovers entering a timeless world through intense entry into the transcendence of sensual pleasure.

---

[25] Briefly, materialist philosophy posits matter, in the form of the atom, as the underlying building block of the universe. Such materialist (or atomic) theory challenges the essentialist philosophy of Plato, who held that matter is an illusion of truth, a mere thing that participates in a divine form or idea existing in the heavens. Essentialism and materialism form the two large-scale philosophies of Western thought and culture.

[26] U. M. Ellis-Fermor, *Christopher Marlowe* (1927; Hamden, CT: Archon Books, 1967) xi.

[27] Qtd. in John Bakeless, *The Tragicall History of Christopher Marlowe*, 2 vols. (1942; Hamden, CT: Archon Books, 1964) 2: 149–50. The Walton quotation comes from *The Compleat Angler* (1653, 1655), qtd. by Thomas Warton in his 1781 "History of English Poetry," rpt. in MacLure *CH* 60.

The philosophical stakes of "The Passionate Shepherd" do not shatter the illusion of the poem's innocent beauty but intensify it. Such complexity helps explain something that contemporaries also found here: not merely a philosophy of desire but a "politics of mirth." [28] Critics have long recognized the May Day festivity rite underlying Marlowe's poem, but only recently have they relied on M. M. Bakhtin's theory of *carnival* to sort out its ideological program (Cheney, *MCP* 78–87). Marlowe's carnival festivity enacts Queen Elizabeth's government policy, which allows such rites of flower as May Day to include "both normative and revisionary impulses," a "seemingly lawless topsy-turvydom" that could "both undermine and reinforce" (Marcus 7). In other words, Marlowe's lyric engages simultaneously in a "normative" carnival rite and a more subversive political act. The political undertones of Marlowe's poem appear immediately, in the anonymous "Another of the Same Nature, Made Since": "And all the woods to be a screen, / Lest Phoebus kiss my summer's queen" (7–8). During the English Civil War, J. Paulin makes the political dynamic explicit: "For if Contentment wears a crown / Which never tyrant could assail, / How many monarchs put we down / In our Utopian commonweal" (4–8). Effectively, Paulin finds in Marlowe what Marlowe himself found in Lucan and his republican (or antimonarchical) poetics. But it is Marlowe himself who invents the political dynamics of his invitational mode, when he puts "Come live with me" into the voice of such monarchical figures as Jupiter, king of the gods, in *Dido;* the mighty monarch of the east, Tamburlaine; and the English King Edward II (see Forsythe).

While response poems by Donne, Herrick, and others further intensify the complexity of Marlowe's poem, "The Passionate Shepherd" remains endlessly rich, four hundred years later. The smooth pastoral has a lyrical music and philosophical voice that resound as vitally today as they did in the sixteenth and seventeenth centuries.

LUCAN'S FIRST BOOK

Remarkably, the author of "The Passionate Shepherd" is also the first English translator of the counter-imperial Latin epic of empire, Lucan's *Pharsalia.* The poet who begins his lovely lyric "Come live with me, and be my love" opens his epic,

> Wars worse than civil on Thessalian plains,
> And outrage strangling law, and people strong
> We sing, whose conquering swords their own breasts launched.
> *(LFB 1–3)*

Civil war replaces erotic monologue, politics rather than eros define human desire, the nation overrules the individual, and mass suicide tramples the tender intercourse of shepherd and nymph. Pastoral gives way to epic, private speech to public voice: "we sing."

---

[28] Leah S. Marcus, *The Politics of Mirth: Jonson, Herrick, Milton, Marvel, and the Defense of Old Holiday Pastimes* (Chicago: U of Chicago P, 1986).

As Philip Hardie reminds us, Lucan follows Ovid in de-authorizing Virgil, the great Roman poet of empire (*Epic Successors*). Thus the *Pharsalia* joins the *Metamorphoses* as a counter-epic of empire, using the genre of epic to rewrite the *Aeneid*. Ovid's counter-epic strings together a vast encyclopedia of epyllia or little epics, drawn from classical mythology, to foreground the immortality not of the emperor but of the poet, revealing the metamorphosing power of erotic desire to be the defining feature of the Roman nation.

> And now my work is done, which neither the wrath of Jove, nor fire, nor sword, nor the gnawing tooth of time shall ever be able to undo. [. . .] I shall be borne immortal far beyond the lofty stars and I shall have an undying name. Wherever Rome's power extends over the conquered world, I shall have mention on men's lips, and, if the prophecies of the bards have any truth, through the ages shall I live in fame.
>
> *(Ovid, Metamorphoses 15.871–79)*

In contrast, Lucan tells a historical narrative about the battle for political control of Rome in 48 BCE, when Julius Caesar defeated Pompey the Great on the field of Pharsalus in Thessaly, Greece. Whereas Ovid had inscribed his relation with the emperor in such stories as Diana's punishment of Actaeon (*Metamorphoses* 3.138–252) or Minerva's punishment of Arachne (*Metamorphoses* 6.1–145), Lucan uses his first-person voice to tell the story of how Caesar turned the Roman Republic into the Empire, a government run by a group of aristocratic men practicing the principle of freedom into a dictatorship.

Lucan's epic is known for its political boldness, because Nero was not merely the poet's emperor but his companion. In book 1, Lucan announces that he draws his inspiration from Nero, but the passage is so charged with dissent one wonders how the emperor himself could have missed it. Whether he did or not, in 65 CE he ordered the twenty-six-year-old Lucan to commit suicide along with Lucan's uncle, Seneca, who was Nero's chief advisor, a Stoic philosopher, and our only extant Roman tragedian, for their role in the Pisonian conspiracy. No one but Lucan could address the most famous madman of antiquity as the inspiration for a poem so obviously attacking his dictatorship. Sadly, Lucan's premature death left us with only ten books of (at least) a planned twelve.

Fragmentation is not merely the state of Lucan's text but virtually its topic. Following Ovid, Lucan breaks the Homeric and Virgilian convention of presenting a single epic hero. Instead of an Achilles or an Aeneas, we meet two gigantic men dividing the civilized world between them. Julius Caesar relentlessly attacks the Roman Republic to create the Roman Empire, while Pompey the Great tries to hold the Republic together. We might expect the pro-republican poet to support the republican hero, but Lucan's method is hardly so straightforward. Without question, he despises Caesar and sides with Pompey, but he ends up turning the mighty Julius into one of literature's most intriguing villains, and he hauntingly diminishes Pompey's greatness. As such, Lucan holds both principals to account; as Marlowe brilliantly puts it, capturing Lucan's savage irony, "Pompey could abide no equal, / Nor Caesar no superior" (125–26).

This principle in characterization helps explain why Caesar energizes Lucan, becoming the poem's grandest achievement; the principle also helps explain why

Pompey cannot compete for the poet's attention. Historically speaking, these men were not simply kin, linked in marriage when Caesar's daughter, Julia, married Pompey; they shared a mind-set that sacrifices the public good to personal desire.

Students may have trouble following the narrative of *Lucan's First Book*, impeded by references to alien people, places, and events. They might wish to be patient, however, not least because of some stunning verse moments, which hopefully will whet their appetite for reading more of the *Pharsalia*—an experience found rewarding by many notable literary figures, from Statius, Dante, Chaucer, and Shakespeare to Milton, Doctor Johnson, and Lord Byron.

Book 1 assumes some knowledge of Roman history, which conveniently divides into the following phases and events:

1. *BCE 753–BCE 509:* the foundation of Rome and the establishment of the monarchy under the Tarquin family
2. *BCE 509–82:* the suicide of Lucretia after her rape by Sextus Tarquinius, the subsequent consulship of Lucius Junius Brutus, and thus the foundation of the Roman Republic
3. *BCE 88–86:* the bitter military struggle between Marius and Sulla for control of Rome (until the death of Marius in BCE 86): a precursor to the Roman Civil War between Caesar and Pompey
4. *BCE 82–79:* the brutal dictatorship of Sulla
5. *BCE 53:* the death of Crassus, one of the First Triumvirite (with Julius Caesar and Pompey the Great)
6. *BCE 49:* the inaugural moment of the Roman Civil War, when Caesar crosses the Rubicon, a small river in northern Italy flowing into the Adriatic Sea (near modern Rimini) and forming the boundary between one of his provinces, Gallia Cisalpina, in which he was allowed to travel, and Italy, in which he was not
7. *BCE 48:* battle of Pharsalus, in Thessaly, Greece, where Caesar defeats Pompey in the decisive battle of the Civil War
8. *BCE 48:* assassination of Pompey in Egypt
9. *BCE 44:* assassination of Caesar in Rome by Marcus Brutus and other conspirators

Book 1 may not be the best book of the ten, but during the English Renaissance it was the arch-republican book.[29] Although we do not know why Marlowe translated only book 1, or whether he would have translated the remaining books had he lived longer, we may recall another historic achievement: he pens an Elizabethan

[29] According to David Norbrook, *Writing the English Republic: Poetry, Rhetoric, and Politics, 1627–1660* (Cambridge: Cambridge University Press, 1999), the "first book of the *Pharsalia* was in fact much cited by two of the leading seventeenth-century theorists of republicanism, James Harrington and Algernon Sidney" (36–37). Norbrook defines republicanism as "'a state which was not headed by a king and in which the hereditary principle did not prevail in whole or in part in determining the headship'" (17), quoting Zera S. Fink, *The Classical Republicans: An Essay in the Recovery of a Pattern of Thought in Seventeenth Century England* (Evanston: Northwestern UP, 1945) x.

minor epic in the republican mode.[30] By viewing *Lucan's First Book* as a republican poem that darkens empire, we may begin to reimagine Marlowe as an *epic poet*. Not simply a lyricist with a smooth song or a tragedian with a mighty line, he is a budding epicist writing a heroic poem about Roman history, government, and politics. He takes the nation as his topic and the republican value of liberty as his center.[31]

When a poet's primary reader happens to be a tyrant, we should expect an armed poetics:

> Thou, Caesar, at this instant art my god:
> Thee if I invocate, I shall not need
> To crave Apollo's aid or Bacchus' help,
> Thy power inspires the Muse that sings this war.
>
> (LFB 63–66)

Every detail exudes ambiguity. "[A]t this instant" suggests the immediacy of the poet's need for Nero to be his god but also *the god's own ephemeral nature;* he is bound by time, by the shortest of temporal spans indeed: "this instant." The word "if" introduces an innocent condition to the invocation but catches the poet hesitating. Apollo is the god of the lyre, of lyric and epic poetry, while Bacchus is the god of the vine, of tragedy. By telling Nero he does not need either deity, the poet pays tribute to the emperor's divine status but locates the despot outside the boundary of these high genres. Nero is the demonic inspiration for a tragic epic about the suicide of the nation. But it is the last line that looks especially damning, for the poet suggests something worse: Nero "inspires" the madness of Lucan's civil "war" itself.

In lines 185 forward, the poet narrates the most famous historical event of book 1: Caesar's crossing of the Rubicon in 49 BCE. By crossing, Caesar enters Italian territory illegally, inaugurating the Civil War. For the poet, this momentous action provides occasion for a dark, visionary poetics: the origin of Caesar's decision to cross the Rubicon lies in his "dreadful vision" (188). During a daytime dream, "fearful Rome" appears to him; she is in "Mourning," her hair "torn," her "arms all naked" (189–90), and even though she warns Caesar not to cross, he sees only a sign that he should: "O Rome, / My thought's sole goddess, aid mine enterprise! / I hate thee not, to thee my conquests stoop; / Caesar is thine" (201–04). Here we glean something else important about Lucan to Marlowe: the Roman poet's absolute absorption in "thought"—in subjectivity, inwardness, the working of the human mind. Like nearly everything in this poem, it is hard to determine where Lucan locates final authority for the operation of the cosmos: is it in the gods, or in the minds of men? While one finds repeated evidence for the latter, the larger design of the Lucanian universe is clear: we are all "Predestinate to ruin!" (251: "O tristi damnata loco!": "doomed by its unlucky site to misfortune!"). Marlowe's use here of the premier term of Calvinism, *predestination,*

---

[30] See Patrick Cheney, "'Defend his freedom 'gainst a monarchy': Marlowe's Republican Authorship," in *Renaissance Conversations: Literature, Politics, and History in Dialogue,* ed. Zachary Lesser and Benedict Robinson, forthcoming.

[31] On Lucan as the champion of liberty, see W. R. Johnson, *Momentary Monsters: Lucan and His Heroes* (Ithaca: Cornell UP, 1987) 30, 88, 133.

turns the great Reformer's providentialism against itself: the Christian divine comedy of Scripture metamorphoses into a dark pagan tragedy; the cosmos is bent on destroying humanity.

The *Pharsalia* may be an epic poem about the tragedy of two men bringing the civilized world to its knees, but Caesar's vision of Rome as a female introduces perhaps a less well-known feature of Lucanism: its recurrent representation of women, female identity, and especially females who respond to males traumatizing the domestic domain. In later books, Lucan lends considerable space and authority to Cornelia, Pompey's second wife, a heroic woman of integrity whose life is ruined by her husband's military enterprise.

In Book 1, the poet begins and ends with portraits of the female. Near the beginning, we learn of Julia, who "restrain[s]" the "rage" of both her "headstrong husband" and her "father" (116–17) before dying in 54 BCE while giving birth to Pompey's child. The ghost of Julia, an icon of female anger against male stupidity, will haunt the entire *Pharsalia,* but here at the outset the poet pauses to mourn her death, for she is the last bulwark against civil war. Only when this young woman dies do the two huge men in her life seek to destroy each other: "Julia, / Snatched hence by cruel fates with ominous howls, / Bare down to hell her son, the pledge of peace" (111–13). With this Lucanian edge, the birthing mother becomes Rome's only hope; when she passes to the beyond, the nation passes with her.

At the end of book 1, an unnamed Roman matron runs through the streets in a state of frenzy, delivering a prophecy of outcome to the civil war: " 'This headless trunk that lies on Nilus' sand, / I know.[. . .] / I have seen Philippi.' / This said, being tired with fury she sunk down" (684, 693–94). In other words, the matron envisions not merely Augustus Caesar and Mark Antony's defeat of Brutus and Cassius at Philippi, but also Julius Caesar's defeat of Pompey at Pharsalus, two battles that occurred on the same battlefield in Greece (Orgel 259). The "headless trunk" lying on the beach is that of Pompey, who is to be beheaded by a lone assassin in book 8. As such, book 1 typologically predicts the structure of the poem itself, revealing perhaps why seventeenth-century English republicans could see it as an arch-republican document.

In book 1 as well, the poet reveals his purpose, to "unfold" the "causes" of the civil war (66). In lines 72–84, Marlowe uses his blank verse line to thunder Lucan's dark picture of universal chaos. Indeed, line 81, one of the most famous in the *Pharsalia,* is often understood to function as a motto for the entire Marlovian canon: "All great things crush themselves." For Lucan, as for his English transcriber, the gods conspire with men to perform a grand annihilation, complete with self-butchery, civil broil, and cosmic disintegration. While Lucan's catastrophic vision appears exaggerated, we might wish to recall that this was an epiphanic era. While he was imagining the dissolution of the universe in Rome, St. Paul was on the road preaching the Gospel and St. John of Patmos was undergoing his apocalyptic vision in the Book of Revelation.

If the Roman and Elizabethan poets see the universal "engines of the broken world" (80), time ending, stars colliding, the four elements mixing, and everything turning to chaos, they can see something else, and it is also characteristically Lucanian: the origin of dissolution lies in the dark underside of physiology—the swirling blood of the human body. Toward the end of book 1, an augurer named Arruns sacrifices a bull, tears out its entrails, and reads the future of civic and cosmic annihilation in the butchered animal's organs:

> A dead blackness
> Ran through the blood, that turned it all to jelly,
> And stained the bowels with dark loathsome spots.
> The liver swelled with filth, and every vein
> Did threaten horror from the host of Caesar:
> A small thin skin contained the vital parts;
> The heart stirred not, and from the gaping liver
> Squeezed matter; through the caul the entrails peered.
> (LFB 617–24)

In Marlowe's Lucanian imagination, bestial blood comes alive, acquires character, performs a part, and enacts its nightmare vision. Here we witness Lucan's extraordinary range of vision, with Marlowe reveling in it: from as far *out* into the black beyond as the annihilating astral bodies to as far *in* as the "gaping liver."

What kind of epic is this? Above all, it is a new kind of epic, a nightmare form depicting what the cosmos looks like when viewed from the black hole of the human heart. What Lucan witnesses during the reign of Nero, Virgil evidently could not anticipate during the reign of Augustus: the madness of empire, the self-destructive desire of the imperial mind, the fatal engine of the gods wheeling a tyrant into a showdown with doom itself.

What possessed Marlowe to make his translation we may never know, but his achievement is to carry the Lucanian nightmare forward into the late Elizabethan era. In the end, his rueful narrative about the end of the Roman Republic and the birth of the Roman Empire challenges the imperial peace of the Tudor crown and finally the Queen's own Cult of the Virgin.

HERO AND LEANDER

Marlowe's late epicist return to the Ovidian amatory mode in *Hero and Leander* produces early modern England's first great poem of *consensually lost virginity*. In his 818-line epyllion, he returns to the heroic couplet developed earlier in *Ovid's Elegies* to narrate a quite different account of Musaeus's and Ovid's stories about tragic deaths through accident, fate, and suicide: "Jewels being lost are found again, this never; / "Tis lost but once, and once lost, lost for ever" (569–70). Marlowe's genius is to use delicious poetry to narrate the traumatic event of lost virginity, and then to present his verse as a new form of literature within the Ovidian poet's oscillating career. *Hero and Leander* is an *erotic* counter-epic of empire. Its story of the tragic relationship between male and female caught in the throes of heterosexual desire forms a diptych with the tragic story of civil war between Caesar and Pompey in *Lucan's First Book*.

In the erotic epyllion, a four-line prologue introduces us to the twin topics of art and desire, the poet's epic venture and the lovers' lost virginity:

> On Hellespont, guilty of true love's blood,
> In view and opposite two cities stood,

> Sea borderers, disjoined by Neptune's might:
> The one Abydos, the other Sestos hight.
>
>   (HL 1–4)

The Hellespont becomes the great landscape of epic, the geographical space where East meets West, Asia joins Europe, and thus the very site separating Greece from Troy in Homeric epic. Hence, in line 153 Marlowe refers to "Love kindling wars, to burn such towns as Troy"—a reference that, however incidental, evokes the generic and political dynamic teeming beneath the surface of Marlowe's smooth verse. If we look carefully at the prologue, we see Marlowe's attention to the epicist dynamic, where "two cities," one named Abydos (home to Leander) and the other Sestos (home to Hero), are as "opposite" in their nationalism as in their topography, "border[ing]" on the sea but "disjoin'd" by it. Chapman, who would continue Marlowe's story in 1598 and go on in 1616 to translate Musaeus's *Hero and Leander* into English, took a special interest in the imperial politics of Marlowe's epic geography: "Abydus and Sestus were two ancient Towns; one in Europe, another in Asia; East and West, opposites." [32]

What is notable is that Marlowe's poem about the tragedy of teen sex should begin in epic territory. By seeing the prologue constructing the very lens for reading the work, we confront a counter-Spenserian idea: that of the separation of the sexes, brought about through the consensual loss of virginity, outside the nascent institution of companionate marriage. [33] In *Hero and Leander,* the poet lodges a complaint against the imperial poetics of companionate marriage championed in Spenser. Rather than being simply a delicious poem about sex, Marlowe's epyllion charts a radical phase of English literary history.

For this reason, "Virginity" (262) turns out to be the topic of the lovers' first conversation (176–340). Naïve about the dangers of Venus' Church, where Hero serves as priestess, Leander mounts a long speech as a rhetorical assault on his beloved's prime value: "Virginity, albeit some highly prize it, / Compared with marriage, had you tried them both, / Differs as much as wine and water doth" (262–64). Although the details of his oratory warrant careful analysis, Leander's inset fantasy about lost virginity inspires awe:

>   this fair gem, sweet in the loss alone,
> When you fleet hence, can be bequeathed to none.
> Or if it could, down from th' enameled sky
> All heaven would come to claim this legacy,

---

[32] Chapman, in *The Works of George Chapman,* ed. Richard Herne Shepherd, 3 vols. (London: Chatto and Windus, 1911–24) 2: 94.

[33] Companionate marriage is a Protestant-based model of marriage emphasizing the mutuality, sympathy, and sometimes equality between man and woman. See, e.g., Russ McDonald, *The Bedford Companion to Shakespeare: An Introduction with Documents,* 2nd ed. (Boston: Bedford-St. Martin's P, 2001) 261–63. Spenser presents this model in The Legend of Chastity, book 3 of *The Faerie Queene,* and elsewhere. See, e.g., Louis Montrose, "Spenser's Domestic Domain: Poetry, Property and the Early Modern Subject," in *Subject and Object in Renaissance Culture,* ed. Margreta de Grazia, Maureen Quilligan, and Peter Stallybrass (Cambridge: Cambridge UP, 1996) 83–122.

And with intestine broils the world destroy,
And quite confound nature's sweet harmony.
                    (HL 247–52)

In this passage, Ovid and Lucan meet and destroy the Virgilian world between them. Here Marlowe penetrates to the eternizing core of the male's fantasy about female virginity. The word "sweet" at the center of the first line evokes feeling, emotion, the inward condition of pleasure, the mind sensing the body's bliss: to experience the high value of sweetness (one of life's greatest goals), "you" have to lose your virginity. Once you lose it, you find yourself trapped inside another paradox, for no longer can you bequeath the value you just surrendered: you lose your "legacy," your inheritance, your right to a future. But "if" you could bottle such sweetness, the gods themselves would come to claim the legacy, making you immortal. This transcendence produces a bang so big it destroys the cosmos, inventing a virtual blackout. Accordingly, consensually lost virginity is also the topic of the "digression" about Mercury and the country maid in lines 377–484.[34]

In the second half of the poem (which Chapman labeled the Second Sestiad), the narrator rehearses the complex details of the lovers' final consummation in Hero's bed: "O who can tell the greeting / These greedy lovers had at their first meeting? / He asked, she gave, and nothing was denied" (507–09). Yet, as Judith Haber shows, Marlowe does not simply stage the consummation; he dilates it, deferring the moment more than once, as if to toy with the reader's desire for an event that can only end in tragedy.[35] Marlowe photographs sexual violence in all its sweet starkness: "So beauty sweetly quickens when 'tis nigh, / But being separated and removed, / Burns where it cherished, murders where it loved" (610–12).

When Marlowe finally fulfills the reader's desire, he breaks down the hymeneal walls of myth and metaphor itself:

Leander now, like Theban Hercules,
Entered the orchard of th' Hesperides,
Whose fruit none rightly can describe but he
That pulls or shakes it from the golden tree.
                    (HL 781–84)

Rather than enjoying the bliss of mutual lovemaking to enter the eternal, Leander assaults the vulnerable body of his beloved, robbing it of its most cherished value. By likening Leander to the mighty athlete Hercules stealing the immortalizing apples from the garden of the Hesperides, Marlowe constructs a rather dubious icon: the male's sexualized quest for transcendence.

This icon reappears powerfully in the double conclusion to the poem: first when Hero instinctively recoils from Leander after losing her virginity, only to become exposed to the mercenary edge of his voyeuristic gaze, and finally when Hesperus, the

---

[34] On the rich philosophical underpinnings of the digression, including Neoplatonism, see Richard Neuse, "Atheism and Some Functions of Myth in Marlowe's Hero and Leander," *Modern Language Quarterly* 31 (1970): 424–39.

[35] Haber, " 'True-loves blood': Narrative and Desire in *Hero and Leander*," *English Literary Renaissance* 28 (1998): 372–86.

morning star, hears the harp of Apollo and gives birth to day by using his "flaring beams" to "mock ugly night" (816): "Till she, o'ercome with anguish, shame, and rage, / Danged down to hell her loathsome carriage"[36] (817–18).

Chapman's Continuation

For many readers today, Chapman's 1598 continuation of *Hero and Leander* has happily fallen out of Marlowe editions. For the most part, scholars have presented Chapman as a stern and serious moralizer, a deep philosophical thinker, and the inventor of a difficult (at time tortuous) verse style. In part, Chapman is responsible for this reception because he opens his Third Sestiad with a clear programmatic statement:

> New light gives new directions, fortunes new,
> [. . .]
> More harsh (at least more hard) more grave and high
> Our subject runs, and our stern muse must fly;
> Love's edge is taken off, and that light flame
> [. . .]
> Must now grow staid, and censure the delights,
> That being enjoyed ask judgement.
>   (*Chapman*, Hero and Leander 3.1–9)

Look at the terms of Chapman's "new direction": *harsh, hard, grave, high, stern, staid, censure, judgment.* After the freedom of Marlowe, who would want to read this?

Chapman does not break his word, but his prologue is happily misleading, for his continuation is a tour de force. While this is not the place for an extended discussion, we might attend briefly to two principal features of his sestiads. The first we have already mentioned in passing: Chapman turns Marlowe's unadorned 818-line "fragment" into a full epic poem in the tradition of Homer and Virgil. Marlovians have complained that Chapman turns Marlowe into something he is not: an epicist in the high and moral tradition of normative poetry. However true, we might also look in on the energy Chapman harnessed to frame Marlowe's text. We may see Chapman's continuation, that is, as an important response to Marlovian art by a contemporary.

The second point follows from what we have emphasized about Marlowe's pioneering role in charting consensually lost virginity. Nothing Chapman says in his programmatic prologue prepares us for his own entry into female space. Indeed, rather than judging the young lovers, he faces head-on the problem he inherits from Marlowe: what to do with Hero, whom Marlowe had left not simply "devirginate" but also ashamed and abandoned. It is her vulnerable interior condition that seems most to

---

[36] On "Hero as Night," see David L. Miller, "The Death of the Modern: Gender and Desire in Marlowe's *Hero and Leander,*" *South Atlantic Quarterly* 88 (1989): 757–87 (781). For other excellent recent commentary, see Georgia Brown, "Breaking the Canon: Marlowe's Challenge to the Literary Status Quo in *Hero and Leander,*" in *Marlowe, History, and Sexuality* 59–75; Joanne Altieri, *"Hero and Leander:* Sensible Myth and Lyric Subjectivity," *John Donne Journal* 8 (1989): 151–66; and Robert A. Logan, "Perspective in Marlowe's *Hero and Leander:* Engaging Our Detachment," in *"A Poet and a filthy Play-maker": New Essays on Christopher Marlowe,* ed. Kenneth Friedenreich, Roma Gill, and Constance B. Kuriyama (New York: AMS P, 1988) 279–91.

have gripped Chapman. Thus, we find ourselves back in Hero's bedroom, discovering her just as Marlowe (and Leander) had left her. Unlike Marlowe, however, Chapman blames Hero's lover: "our Leander [. . .] dissolved her virgin zone" (3.211–13). Chapman's genius is to focus on Hero's mind, to depict her grappling with a traumatic predicament: how may a young girl who has just lost her virginity recover her sacred state? Is there an alternative to despair? To show a way out, Chapman presents Hero undergoing an epiphany, which he unfolds in two major phases. In the first, Hero realizes that she has not been a victim but a willing participant in a holy union with the divine part of herself:

> Had I not yielded, slain myself I had.
> *Hero Leander is, Leander Hero:*
> Such virtue love hath to make one of two.
> If Leander did my maidenhead get,
> Leander being myself I still retain it.
> We break chaste vows when we live loosely ever;
> But bound as we are, we live loosely never.
> Two constant lovers being joined in one.
>   *(Chapman,* Hero and Leander 3.356–64)

Here, the devirginate female probes the philosophical conundrum that had preoccupied thinkers from Plato and Augustine to Spenser and Shakespeare, yet this young woman takes us into territory few if any had gone: she discovers that her spiritual identity with her lover precisely preserves her chastity at the very minute she loses her virginity.

Consequently, she makes a final discovery:

>   O blessed place,
> Image of constancy! Thus my love's grace
> Parts nowhere, but it leaves something behind
> Worth observation: he renowns his kind.
> His motion is like heaven's, orbicular,
> For where he once is, he is ever there.
> This place was mine; Leander, now 'tis thine;
> Thou being myself, then it is double mine,
> Mine, and Leander's mine, Leander's mine.
> O see what wealth it yields me, nay yields him!
>   *(Chapman,* Hero and Leander 3.405–14)

However we might respond to Hero's discovery, Chapman pioneers a model of interiority in which the female turns tragic loss into an epiphany about human reciprocity and sacred meaning.

Petowe's Continuation

If Chapman has been excluded from the Marlowe canon, Henry Petowe has simply been forgotten. We might recall the directive of Stephen Orgel, who first printed this second continuation in an edition of Marlowe's poems:

> [A]s an alternative to Chapman's continuation, Petowe's is worth considering because it deals with those elements of Marlowe's poem that Chapman slights, and that were,

nevertheless, largely responsible for the poem's popularity. Petowe moves *Hero and Leander* toward high chivalry and a happy ending, explicitly avoiding those pressures of judgement that Chapman says are now demanded by the work. Chapman's philosophical moralizing represents one side of the Elizabethan Ovidian tradition; Petowe's cheerful courtly romance embodies, however ineptly, something of the other.

(220)

Perhaps, then, we may view this 628-line poem as another Elizabethan epyllion, important for three primary reasons. First, it constitutes another measurable 1598 response to Marlowe by a contemporary. Second, it enters into dialogue not merely with Marlowe's poem but inadvertently with Chapman's, since the two continuations were written independently and published the same year. And third, as Orgel emphasizes, Petowe turns Marlowe's 818 lines into a second kind of epic: a Spenserian "epic romance" in the chivalric tradition.[37] If Chapman in his continuation is "Edmund Spenser reborn," we have here two different responses to Marlowe along Spenserian lines.[38] Whereas Chapman rewrites Marlowe via Spenser's concern with female consciousness in the central books of *The Faerie Queene* and *Epithalamion,* Petowe rewrites Marlowe via Spenser's representation of knights jousting for ladies' hands in the national epic. If Chapman focuses on the afterlife of lost female virginity, Petowe turns Marlowe's narrative into a tale about "love's firm constancy" (540). Thus, Leander returns to Hero in disguise as a knight and defeats her chief suitor, Duke Euristippus, during a tilting tournament. In Chapman, the lovers commit suicide and become metamorphosed into birds, but in Petowe they reunite happily, turning into two pine trees only after "Their lives' spent date" (621).

THE MANWOOD EPITAPH

The Latin verse epitaph on Sir Roger Manwood complements Marlowe's *Hero and Leander* as a conclusion to his literary career. In 1589, Marlowe and Thomas Watson had confronted Manwood in court when they were called in for the death of William Bradley, after which Manwood evidently dealt leniently with them, since they were freed from Newgate Prison. In his epitaph, Marlowe pays tribute to "The terror of the night-stalker, unhappy lasher of the prodigal, / Jove's Hercules" (1–2). Jove's Hercules had crossed from this world to "Acheron" (6) on December 14, 1592, only six months before Marlowe himself would make the crossing, on May 30, 1593. Thus we know that Marlowe wrote the epitaph during the intervening months, either late in 1592 or early in 1593, perhaps while working on *Hero and Leander* and *Lucan's First Book.*

---

[37] On this form, combining classical epic with medieval romance, see Colin Burrow, *Epic Romance: Homer to Milton* (Oxford: Clarendon P, 1993).

[38] Charlotte Spivak, *George Chapman* (New York: Twayne, 1967) 43. According to Raymond Waddington, "If Chapman can be twinned with any of his contemporaries, a far better case could be made for Edmund Spenser than for John Donne.[. . .] Chapman's true poetic peers are Spenser and Milton, both vatic, public, ceremonious poets as conscious of form and genre as Chapman" (*The Mind's Empire: Myth and Form in George Chapman's Narrative Poems* [Baltimore: Johns Hopkins UP, 1974] 2–3, 13).

Although the epitaph differs in form and length from these two Elizabethan minor epics, they all share a nexus of epic tropes and ideas. We might even think of the Manwood epitaph as a Marlovian epic in miniature.[39]

Most importantly, the epitaph enters the epic terrain of classical mythology, as the references to Hercules, Jove, and Acheron indicate. Marlowe presents Manwood as a divinely appointed hero, a giant among men; the poet's reference to "the barren shores of Acheron" registers his sense of loss for one who has taken "much good [. . .] with him" (6). Marlowe's use of the pagan underworld is neither idle nor ornamental; it is a technically haunting expression for a certain attitude toward death and the afterlife: a non-Christian attitude, most famously articulated by Achilles in the *Odyssey*: "Better I say—to break sod as a farm hand / for some poor country man, on iron rations, / than lord it over all the exhausted dead." [40] As a scholar trained in classical culture, Marlowe views Manwood's passing as a somber event, a sad departure into the grim beyond.

In this epitaph, death visits the heroic individual and leaves behind his "bones"; if properly respected, however, these relics may "lie peacefully." Rather than depicting the Christian soul ascending from its burdensome corpse to heaven, Marlowe imagines the poet's Greco-Roman renown to be more powerful than the monument of the stone mason. Although a slender twelve lines long, the Manwood epitaph leaves for posterity a short and jaunty epic, immortalizing a civic servant for his contribution to the state.

THE DEDICATORY EPISTLE TO MARY SIDNEY HERBERT

Also written late in his career, the Dedicatory Epistle to the countess of Pembroke, Mary Sidney Herbert, shows Marlowe in dialogue with other influential figures of the "court"—yet not the "court of law." As the sister of Sir Philip Sidney, the countess of Pembroke carried on her brother's literary projects, and she became a major patron of poets during the 1590s and an important author in her own right. She wrote devotional poetry, especially a verse translation of the Psalms, and a Continental play, a translation of Robert Garnier's French tragedy, *Antony*. As such, she joins Marlowe as a practicing poet-playwright, perhaps the first English woman to do so.

The Pembroke dedication is unusual in the Marlowe canon because it uses the first-person voice to present a poet with a literary career. Nominally, Marlowe dedicates Watson's *Amintae Gaudia* to the countess and asks for her patronage: "consider it as noble an endeavor to be patroness to this posthumous Amyntas as you would to adopt a son, especially because his father as he lay dying humbly beseeched you and committed to your care the safety of this child." Marlowe can make his request for familial inheritance on Watson's behalf because Herbert is an author who possesses the highest of poetic genealogies: "Delia, born of a race of poets, lawful sister of Sidney

---

[39] For a fine discussion of the Manwood epitaph, see Brown, in *Cambridge Companion* 108–10.
[40] Homer, *Odyssey* 11.542–46, in *Homer: The Odyssey*, trans. Robert Fitzgerald (1961; Garden City, NY: Anchor-Doubleday, 1963).

the Priest of Apollo." Delia, a name for the Roman goddess of chastity and the moon, Diana, is the fictional name Samuel Daniel had given to his own Petrarchan mistress in his sonnet sequence, titled *Delia*. In 1591, twenty-seven of Daniel's sonnets were published in an unauthorized edition of *Astrophil and Stella*. Then, in 1592 Daniel brought out his own edition of fifty sonnets, and he dedicated it to Herbert. Scholars dispute whether Delia represents Herbert (sonnet 53 indicates that Delia lives near Daniel around Beckington, Wiltshire, not at Wilton House, where Herbert lived), but clearly Marlowe felt free to make the identification without offense.

Marlowe sees the sister to Apollo's priest performing an important task in 1590s England: "She was the nurturing mother of letters to whose sinless embrace virtue took refuge, violated by the blows of barbarism and ignorance, just as Philomela once fled the Thracian tyrant." Herbert is both a nurturing patron of learning and a militant combatant against barbaric ignorance. The reference to Philomela might seem indelicate, yet male writers like Spenser had used this Ovidian myth of rape and female silence to complain about English "barbarism and ignorance" (*Teares of the Muses* [1591] 187–89, 235–40). Marlowe follows Spenser in seeing Philomela as a figure for the purity of poetry, but he subtly transposes the nightingale to Mary Herbert, the protector of poetry and its greatest surviving "Muse," able to "inspire the new, young, and gifted poets of our time."

Marlowe includes himself in this company, but he goes on to see Herbert as the celestial inspiration for a generically structured literary career. She is the divine force motivating him to progress from lower to higher forms, along the Virgilian path: "Divine offspring, who inspires my rude reed with high, creative madness which I, by myself, am too wretched a writer to attain without you." The "rude reed" is the *syrinx* or panpipe, the musical instrument of the pastoral poet, while "creative madness" is the high Platonic fury of the divinely inspired poet in Plato's *Phaedrus*, emphasized by Philip Sidney in his *Defence of Poesie*. Marlowe's allusion to Plato's theory of poetic inspiration is learned and philosophical, elevating him above the ignorant barbarians ruining poetry in the early 1590s. Marlowe can be a "rude" pastoral poet producing "high" Platonic fury precisely under Herbert's "inspir[ation]."

Toward the end of the dedication, Marlowe becomes more specific: "Thus I, whose very slim ability is owed to the seashore myrtle of Venus and Daphne's always-greening hair, on the first and every page of these poems will invoke your sponsorship, chosen-lady of the Muses." Here Marlowe recalls his authorial persona as an Ovidian or *myrtilean* poet, familiar to us from *Ovid's Elegies*, "The Passionate Shepherd," and *Hero and Leander*. But he also identifies himself through a new persona: he is a Petrarchan poet pursuing the green laurel of Daphne. In the *Metamorphoses*, Ovid had narrated the myth of Apollo's attempted rape of Daphne, blocked when her prayer secures her metamorphosis into the laurel tree. In his *Rime sparse* (*Scattered Rhymes*), Petrarch had appropriated Apollo's pursuit of Daphne as the central myth of the lyric poet who serves a beautiful mistress in order to become renowned.[41] Marlowe's reference to Venereal poetry makes perfect sense, but his reference to Petrarchan poetry has

---

[41] See Gordon Braden, "Ovid, Petrarch, and Shakespeare's Sonnets," in A. B. Taylor, ed., *Shakespeare's Ovid: The "Metamorphoses" in the Plays and Poems* (Cambridge: Cambridge UP, 2000) 96–112.

created confusion, since we do not know that he wrote sonnets or a sonnet sequence.[42] In the Epilogue to *Doctor Faustus,* however, Marlowe places his tragic hero within the Petrarchan and Ovidian tradition of the laurel poet: "Cut is the branch that might have grown full straight, / And burned is Apollo's laurel bough, / That sometime grew within this learned man" (A text 1–3). Roy T. Eriksen suggests that Marlowe here alludes to song 269 of Petrarch's *Rime sparse:* "Broken are the high column and the Green Laurel" (qtd. in Eriksen 14). Perhaps Marlowe had this authorial signature in mind when claiming Petrarchan status before the sister of the god who made the form famous in England.

Be that as it may, Marlowe promises to serve the countess in a higher form in his subsequent poems. He engages in a specific discourse for a Virgilian career, familiar from Virgil himself (Eclogue 6.1–10), from such continental poets as Sannazaro, and most importantly from England's Virgil, Spenser. About this time, Shakespeare uses the discourse in his dedicatory epistles to the earl of Southampton prefacing *Venus and Adonis* and *The Rape of Lucrece.*[43]

The Herbert dedication sheds light on Marlowe's sense of his role as an Elizabethan poet near the end of his life. He is seeking patronage from the age's most distinguished literary patroness, and he presents himself as an Ovidian and Petrarchan poet on the path to a higher, Virgilian career, in search of fame and glory. The dedication thus casts a glance back at the corpus of Marlowe's poetic career and catches a glimpse of a future career that he would not live to enact. Through this utterance, we may come to view his poetry as a body of verse in its own right and place that verse alongside his plays as the signature of his historic authorship.

---

[42] Earlier in the twentieth century, scholars believed that Marlowe might have been the author of a lost manuscript containing a pastoral eclogue and sixteen sonnets (see Roy T. Eriksen, "Marlowe's Petrarch: *In Morte di Madonna Laura*," *Cahiers Elisabethains* 29 [1986]: 13–25), but in 1986 Sukanta Chaudhuri found the manuscript and determined, persuasively, that its author, one "Ch.M.," was not Christopher Marlowe the poet-playwright but Christopher Morley, a fellow of Trinity College, Cambridge ("Marlowe, Madrigals, and a New Elizabethan Poet," *Review of English Studies* 39 [1988]: 199–216). For more recent detail, see Cheney, *MCP* 331n4.

[43] For details, including on Virgil, Sannazaro, Spenser, and Shakespeare, see Cheney, *Shakespeare,* chapters 3 and 4.

A NOTE ON MARLOWE
AND TRANSLATION

Brian J. Striar

In Christopher Marlowe's ingenious and well-educated hands, the practice of verse translation affected and informed not only his own original writings but also the original writings of other poets, as well as the evolution of English verse itself. First, he is well recognized for developing the heroic couplet from its Chaucerian antiquity into a useful, facile, and felicitous form of rendering Ovidian translations and imitations for the 1590s. Second, he is well known for developing blank verse, earlier adapted by the earl of Surrey for his translations of books 2 and 4 of Virgil's *Aeneid,* to render the rhetorically heroic verse of Lucan, a form that would become the mainstay of Elizabethan and Jacobean drama and of the culminating epic of the English Renaissance, Milton's *Paradise Lost*.

While Lucan and Ovid are notoriously both considered highly rhetorical poets, they are nevertheless totally different from each other both in their methods and in their aims. Some critics have liked to praise Marlowe's evolution beyond the "schoolboy" product of *Ovid's Elegies* to a more "mature" voice in Lucan which culminates the development of the "mighty line" of the plays. Yet such perspectives miss the point about the difference between Lucan and Ovid and about the different demands these two Roman poets make on a translator. Ultimately, Marlowe's voice in *Hero and Leander* is the Ovidian voice that he developed and honed in his *Elegies*. Thus, to compare the *quality* of those translations to, say, *Tamburlaine* is like trying to compare the quality of *Hero and Leander* to *Tamburlaine*—very difficult to do. It is much more appropriate to compare *Lucan's First Book* to any of the plays than it is to compare any of the plays to *Hero and Leander*. In translating Ovid and Lucan, then, Marlowe invents two different voices with different meters to match: that of the elusive, trifling-yet-serious master of love, who plies his tricks within the curious intertwinings of the heroic couplet, and that of the epic poet and dramatist of war, nationhood, and cosmic damnation.

While Marlowe must at times make contortions to translate Ovid's highly stylized elegiac distich into an English heroic couplet, he also at times works miracles. Our purpose here, however, is to eschew as much as possible the judgmental tenor that may have marked the work of earlier annotators in favor of clarifying Marlowe's, Ovid's, and Lucan's meanings and motives. In service of that end we demonstrate moments of both convergence and departure between Marlowe and his classical predecessors when it is relevant and helpful to do so, with regard to both substance and style. Our intention is to offer a commentary that can speak to both undergraduates

and experts, and while it is not necessary to have a copy of Lucan's and Ovid's origi-
nals at hand when reading these translations, ideally one can absorb the most from
our commentary by doing just that.

This intent to be more descriptive than normative notwithstanding, we enter
into a dialogue with earlier editors in somewhat the same spirit Marlowe does with
his contemporaries, as Patrick Cheney explains in his introduction. We are interested
in bringing new ideas and angles to light whenever possible, and so, for instance, we
do not concentrate on Lucan's use of Sulpitius because that has already been compre-
hensively accomplished by Roma Gill. On the other hand, since earlier editors have
taken only modest account of the influence upon Marlowe's *Elegies* of the Latin commentary on the *Amores* by the Venetian Marius Dominicus Niger, we have purposed
to offer a full consideration of that influence wherever we find it relevant and salient
to do so. Likewise, wherever our editorial predecessors have best and most succinctly
explained a particular problem or described a specific mythological backdrop, we are
happy to cite their excellent contribution in place of duplicating that effort. Our basic impulse, then, is like that within the dynamic of Renaissance translation itself: to
maintain the vitality of what has gone before but also, when necessary, to replace it,
update it, or add to it.

The use of commentaries like those of Sulpitius, Beroaldo, and Niger was common among Renaissance poets and translators, all as part of the humanist project of
bringing the learning and writing of Roman antiquity into sixteenth-century ver-
naculars on the Continent and in England. In England, many of the famous names
of the period—among them Sir Philip Sidney and Edmund Spenser—and many of
the less famous also—among them Abraham Fraunce, Abraham Fleming, and
William Webbe—engaged in this humanist project of translating the classics. But
Marlowe's two products—and especially the *Elegies*—are remarkable in ways the
others were not. Marlowe's translation of all three books of Ovid's *Amores* was the first
such translation of that work not only into English but into any modern vernacular.
And as Patrick Cheney has recently shown in *Marlowe's Counterfeit Profession*, Marlowe
clearly engaged upon this path early in his career in just the way that Ovid himself
started first with elegy and then *graduated* to drama and to epic.

At times, Marlowe certainly made mistakes in his translation of Ovid. Yet we
can now see that many such occasions are attributable to textual cruxes or to Niger's
commentary. Similarly, as earlier editors like Roma Gill have demonstrated, in
Lucan's First Book much can be attributable to his use of the commentary by Sulpitius and, to lesser extent, of that by Beroaldo, a commentary that accompanied the
one by Sulpitius in many Renaissance editions of Lucan. While Marlowe develops his
rhetorical skills in the Ovid by having to twist and turn within the demands of
rhymed couplet, he is much less hamstrung in the Lucan, where he is more engaged
in a historical narrative—a mission that the unrhymed blank verse makes infinitely
easier than would the rhymed heroic couplet. In addition to the greater attention
paid to Niger's commentary, the greater length of the Ovid and the distinct natures
of these two texts and their originating poets also mandate that the commentary on
the Ovid is necessarily more involved in literary and rhetorical matters than that on
the Lucan. Again, in the *Elegies* Marlowe was developing the stylistically complex
voice and art of English Ovidianism, while *Lucan's First Book* evokes the sweep and

bombast of historical and tragic drama. We see—in Lucan's early description of the absurd and overblown importance of Nero to maintaining the balance of nature— the hyperbole and the enormity that are animated in the Scourge of God himself, Tamburlaine.

Both texts have timely significance. The Ovid comes along in a cultural moment that finds love poetry abounding in England in the form of the sonnet, and it also augurs the advent of the epyllion, as well as the *Elegies* of John Donne. The Lucan, which tells of the Roman civil war between Pompey and Caesar, summons the civil ferments of sixteenth-century England that will erupt into full civil war in the next century. And it is not at all insignificant that Caesar and Pompey were relatives, just as were so many of the opposing figures within and between the houses of Tudor and Stuart. For these reasons, as well as others, we should come to understand these texts not as pedantic pastimes or schoolboy experiments, but as literary artifacts of their particular historical moment.

READING LIST

For works of scholarship and criticism on individual poems by Marlowe (e.g, *Hero and Leander*), see the notes to Patrick Cheney's introduction.

MARLOWE'S POEMS

Brown, Georgia. "Marlowe's Poems and Classicism." In Cheney, ed., *Cambridge Companion.* 106–26.

Burnett, Mark Thornton. "Introduction." In *Christopher Marlowe: The Complete Poems.* Everyman's Poetry. London: Dent; Rutland, VT: Tuttle, 2000. xiv–xx.

Cheney, Patrick, ed. *Cambridge Companion to Christopher Marlowe.* Cambridge: Cambridge UP, 2004.

———. "Introduction: Marlowe in the Twenty-First Century." In Cheney, ed., *Cambridge Companion.* 1–23.

———. *Marlowe's Counterfeit Profession: Ovid, Spenser, Counter-Nationhood.* Toronto: U of Toronto, 1997.

Eliot, T. S. "Christopher Marlowe." In *Elizabethan Dramatists.* London: Faber, 1963. 58–66.

Gill, Roma. "Christopher Marlowe." In *The Dictionary of Literary Biography: Elizabethan Dramatists.* Ed. Fredson Bowers. Detroit: Gale Research Group, 1987. 62: 212–31.

Hulse, Clarke. "Marlowe, The Primeval Poet." In *Metamorphic Verse: The Elizabethan Minor Epic.* Princeton: Princeton UP, 1981. 93–140.

Leech, Clifford. *Christopher Marlowe: Poet for the Stage.* Ed. Anne Lancashire. New York: AMS, 1986.

Levin, Harry. *The Overreacher: A Study of Christopher Marlowe.* Cambridge, MA: Harvard UP, 1954.

MacLure, Millar. "Introduction." *The Poems: Christopher Marlowe.* The Revels Plays. London: Methuen, 1968. xix–xliv.

Martin, L. C. "Introduction." *Marlowe's Poems.* London: Methuen, 1931. Vol. 4 in *The Works and Life of Christopher Marlowe.* Ed. R. H. Case. 6 vols. London: Methuen, 1930–33. 1–22.

Morris, Harry. "Marlowe's Poetry." *Tulane Drama Review* 8 (1963): 134–54.

Sinfield, Alan. "Marlowe's Erotic Verse." In *Early Modern English Poetry: A Critical Companion.* Ed. Patrick Cheney, Andrew Hadfield, and Garrett Sullivan. New York: Oxford UP, 2006 (forthcoming).

Steane, J. B. *Marlowe: A Critical Study.* Cambridge: Cambridge UP, 1964.

Striar, Brian J. *Theories and Practices of Renaissance Verse Translation.* Diss. Claremont Graduate School, 1984.

MARLOWE'S TRANSLATIONS

Barsby, John, ed. and trans. *Ovid 'Amores' I.* Bristol: Bristol Classical P, 1979.

Booth, Joan., ed. and trans. *Ovid The Second Book of 'Amores.'* Warminster, England: Aris, 1991.

Friedenreich, Kenneth, Roma Gill, and Constance B. Kuriyama, eds. *"A Poet and a filthy Play-maker": New Essays on Christopher Marlowe.* New York: AMS, 1988.

Gill, Roma. "Marlowe and the Art of Translation." In Friedenreich, Gill, and Kuriyama, eds. *"A Poet and a filthy Play-maker."* 327–41.

——. "Marlowe, Lucan, and Sulpitius." *Review of English Studies* 24 (1973): 401–13.

——. "Snakes Leape by Verse." In Morris, ed. *Christopher Marlowe.* 135–50.

Green, Peter, ed. and trans. *Ovid The Erotic Poems.* New York: Penguin, 1982.

Lathrop, Henry Burrowes. *Translations from the Classics into English from Caxton to Chapman 1477–1620.* Madison: U of Wisconsin P, 1933. Rpt. New York: Octagon Books, 1967.

Martindale, Charles, ed. *Ovid Renewed.* Cambridge: Cambridge UP, 1988.

Morris, Brian, ed. *Christopher Marlowe.* New York: Hill, 1968.

Pearcy, Lee T. *The Mediated Muse: English Translations of Ovid 1560–1660.* Hamden, CT: Archon Books, 1984.

Shapiro, James. "'Meter meete to furnish Lucans style': Reconsidering Marlowe's *Lucan.*" In Friedenreich, Gill, and Kuriyama, eds. *"A Poet and a filthy Play-maker."* 315–25.

——. *Rival Playwrights: Marlowe, Jonson, Shakespeare.* New York: Columbia UP, 1991.

NOTE ON THE TEXT

This edition modernizes spelling of all early modern texts.

For all of Marlowe's works, we have modernized the early modern spelling edition of Roma Gill, published by Oxford University Press (1987). For Davies's *Epigrams,* we have modernized the early modern spelling edition of Robert Krueger, *The Poems of Sir John Davies,* also published by Oxford University Press (1975).

For texts by George Chapman, Henry Petowe, and others, we have been guided by the early modern spelling editions of L. C. Martin (1931), Millar MacLure (1968), and Stephen Orgel (1971).

Because this edition is designed primarily for the classroom, we have not done any new collation of early modern copies of Marlowe's poems. Thus we do not record variant spellings or accidental emendations. When textual issues are pertinent to the use of the volume, we discuss them briefly in the commentary. We have kept the commentary to a minimum in the cases of the poems not written by Marlowe, such as Davies's *Epigrams* or the continuations of *Hero and Leander* by Chapman and Petowe.

MARLOWE'S POEMS

OVID'S ELEGIES

P. OVIDII NASONIS AMORUM, LIBER PRIMUS

ELEGIA I

— First programmatic poem; foregrounds the speaker's role of poet

Quemadmodum a Cupidine pro bellis amores scribere coactus sit

We which were Ovid's five books now are three,
For these before the rest preferreth he;
If reading five thou plain'st of tediousness,
Two ta'en away, thy labour will be less.

With Muse prepared I meant to sing of arms,   5
Choosing a subject fit for fierce alarms.
Both verses were alike till Love (men say)
Began to smile and took one foot away.
Rash boy, who gave thee power to change a line?
We are the Muses' prophets, none of thine.   10
What if thy mother take Diana's bow?

Marginal notes:
Rejection of the Virgilian cursus — Love replaces the epic muse!
movement from dactylic hexameter to elegiac distich!

Quemadmodum {. . .} sit: In what way he was forced by Cupid to write about love instead of war.

1–4 *We {. . .} less:* Ovid's first edition of the *Amores* contained five books; he reorganized them into three books for the second edition. The personification of the inanimate objects (i.e., giving them the faculty of speech) is a figure of speech known as "prosopopoeia."

5 *Muse {. . .} arms:* The opening word of the *Amores* (*arma*) is also the opening word of Virgil's *Aeneid.* Thus Ovid shows his intent to write martial epic. Also, Marlowe mentions the muse at the beginning, as is customary, but Ovid does not.

7 *Love:* when capitalized, and often when not capitalized, denotes Cupid (also called Amor or Eros).

7–8 *Both {. . .} away:* The meter of Latin (and Greek) martial epic is dactylic hexameter. Cupid takes a foot away from the second line, leaving what is called an elegiac distich (couplet): a dactylic hexameter followed by what is called a dactylic pentameter. This is the traditional Latin meter for love poetry. Thus, Ovid had no choice but to write love poetry.

11 *thy mother:* Venus, goddess of love and beauty.

Shall Dian fan when love begins to glow? *goddess of agriculture*
In woody groves is't meet that Ceres reign,
And quiver-bearing Dian till the plain? *Rhetorical question, which is making a comparison between Marlowe and Diana → haha! (sexual pun)*
Who'll set the fair-tressed Sun in battle ray,   15
While Mars doth take the Aonian harp to play?
Great are thy kingdoms, over-strong and large,
Ambitious imp, why seek'st thou further charge?
Are all things thine? the Muses' Tempe thine?
Then scarce can Phoebus say, "This harp is mine."   20
When in this work's first verse I trod aloft,
Love slacked my Muse, and made my numbers soft. *haha!*
I have no mistress nor no favourite,
Being fittest matter for a wanton wit.
Thus I complained, but love unlocked his quiver,   25
Took out the shaft, ordained my heart to shiver,
And bent his sinewy bow upon his knee,
Saying, "Poet, here's a work beseeming thee."
O woe is me! he never shoots but hits;
I burn, Love in my idle bosom sits.   30
Let my first verse be six, my last five feet;
Farewell stern war, for blunter poets meet.

11–12 *Diana's bow {. . .} Dian:* Ovid mentions Minerva, not Diana. Diana is the goddess of the
hunt and forest; Minerva is the goddess of wisdom. One possible explanation lies in the fact that
Niger's commentary mentions "Dictynna" at this point. "Dictynna" is an alternative name for
Diana. Marlowe might also have changed it to Diana in order to make a rhyme ("bow") with
"glow": Diana, not Minerva, is known for her bow. Diana is otherwise appropriate to the sense
of these lines, which is to emphasize the virginity of the goddess; since both Diana and Minerva
are virgin goddesses, it is especially inappropriate that they should be taken by passion. So too,
it is most inappropriate that Ovid, trying to write a martial epic, be interfered with by Cupid.
13 *Ceres:* the goddess of agriculture.
15 *fair-tressed Sun:* Apollo, the god of the sun, is known for his blond hair.
16 *Mars:* the god of war. *Aonian:* indicates Mt. Helicon, where the Nine Muses reside. Offspring of
Zeus and Mnemosyne (Memory), the Muses are all female and blond, and they are under the
sponsorship of Apollo, god of poetry and the sun. Each Muse presides over a distinct field of poetry, arts, and sciences, such as Epic, History, Tragedy, Lyric/Pastoral, Comedy, Dance, and Love
Poetry.
19 *Tempe:* a vale in Thessaly. For poets it had come to be a generic term for any valley, and here Ovid
calls it "Heliconian," and thus Marlowe puts "Muses" with "Tempe."
21–22 *aloft {. . .} soft:* The end-rhymes are especially appropriate, since line 21 corresponds to the
brawnier Latin hexameter and line 22 corresponds to the "weaker" Latin pentameter of Ovid's
text.
22 *slacked:* "weakened" (also in a sexual sense). *numbers:* refers to the number of metrical feet.
26 *shiver:* break apart into small fragments.
29–30 *O woe is me {. . .} I burn:* The beginnings of these two lines are direct translations of the beginnings of Ovid's corresponding lines. Ovid's intent was to be mock-epic and mock-heroic, and
also to imply a sexual innuendo.

Erato

Elegian muse, that warblest amorous lays,   see footnote!
Girt my shine brow with sea-bank myrtle sprays.
        adj

ELEGIA II

*A poem of submission; Marlowe's narrator
will not war with love*   — *Also addressed to Cupid*

Quod primo amore correptus, in triumphum duci se a Cupidine patiatur

What makes my bed seem hard seeing it is soft?
Or why slips down the coverlet so oft?
Although the nights be long, I sleep not tho,
My sides are sore with tumbling to and fro.
Were Love the cause, it's like I should descry him,   5
Or lies he close, and shoots where none can spy him?
'Twas so, he struck me with a slender dart,
'Tis cruel Love turmoils my captive heart.
Yielding or struggling do we give him might;
Let's yield, a burden easily borne is light.   10
I saw a brandished fire increase in strength,
Which being not shaked, I saw it die at length.
Young oxen newly yoked are beaten more   } *Pastoral imagery as metaphor*
Than oxen which have drawn the plough before;
And rough jades' mouths with stubborn bits are torn,   15
But managed horses' heads are lightly borne.
Unwilling lovers Love doth more torment
Than such as in their bondage feel content.
Lo, I confess, I am thy captive, I,
And hold my conquered hands for thee to tie.   20
What need'st thou war? I sue to thee for grace;
[With arms to conquer armless men is base.] — *political expression*
Yoke Venus' doves, put myrtle on thy hair,
Vulcan will give thee chariots rich and fair.
The people thee applauding, thou shalt stand,   25

---

33 *Elegian muse:* The muse of Elegy (love poetry) is named Erato.
34 *shine:* shining. *myrtle:* Myrtle is sacred to Venus, and thus is a signifier of love and of love poetry.
    In the Latin it is the Muse's brow, and not the narrator's, which is circled with myrtle. Marlowe's
    narrator thus makes himself his own muse.

i *Quod {. . .} patiatur:* Heartbroken over his first love, he surrenders himself to be drawn in Cupid's
    triumphal procession.
3 *tho:* then.
11 *I saw a brandished fire increase in strength:* In style and substance Marlowe carefully translates
    Ovid's *vidi ego iactatas mota face crescere flammas.* "I saw" renders the positioning of *vidi;* "bran-
    dished" renders the positioning of *iactatas;* "increase" renders both the etymology and the posi-
    tioning of *crescere.*
24 *Vulcan:* husband of Venus and god of fire and the smithy.

Guiding the harmless pigeons with thy hand;
Young men and women shalt thou lead as thrall,
So will thy triumph seem magnifical.
I, lately caught, will have a new-made wound,
And captive-like be manacled and bound.   30
Good meaning, Shame, and such as seek love's wrack
Shall follow thee, their hands tied at their back.
Thee all shall fear, and worship as a king,
"Io," triumphing shall thy people sing.
Smooth Speeches, Fear and Rage shall by thee ride,   35
Which troops have always been on Cupid's side;
Thou with these soldiers conquerest gods and men,
Take these away, where is thine honour then?
Thy mother shall from heaven applaud this show,
And on their faces heaps of roses strow.   40
With beauty of thy wings, thy fair hair gilded,
Ride, golden Love, in chariots richly builded.
Unless I err, full many shalt thou burn,
And give wounds infinite at every turn.
In spite of thee, forth will thine arrows fly,   45
A scorching flame burns all the standers by.
So, having conquered Ind, was Bacchus' hue;
Thee pompous Birds, and him two tigers drew.
Then seeing I grace thy show in following thee,
Forbear to hurt thyself in spoiling me.   50
Behold thy kinsman's Caesar's conquering bands,
Who guards the conquered with his conquering hands.

---

26 *harmless pigeons:* Venus's doves. For Ovid's *"aves,"* Niger comments *imbellibus columbas* ("peaceful, unwarring doves").

31 *Good meaning:* For Ovid's *mens bona* Niger offers, for example, *bonum consilium* ("good counsel"), *animus* ("spirit"), and *ratio* ("reason"), any of which can be construed as "Good meaning," which in turn is perhaps best understood as "good intent" or "goodness."

33 *worship as a king:* For Ovid's *ad te sua bracchia tendens* ("extending their arms to you") Niger comments, for example, *te precibus adorabunt {. . .} imperatorem* ("they will with prayers revere you as king").

34 *Io:* the Roman cry of triumph.

35 *Fear: terrorque;* modern texts, *errorque* ("error").

36 *troops:* derived not merely from *militibus* of the following line, but from Niger's gloss of *milites* for *Blanditiae comites.*

47–48 *So {. . .} Bacchus' hue {. . .} tigers drew:* Bacchus (= Dionysus) was the god of wine (and therefore the grapevine). The large, wild felines were sacred to him, and his chariot was drawn by tigers. He was known for having cultivated the grapevine in India. "hue" means "appearance" or "show."

51 *kinsman's Caesar's:* the Caesars proclaimed themselves to be descended from Aeneas, who was a half-brother to Cupid, because the mother of both was Venus.

ELEGIA III

Ad amicam — To his mistress

I ask but right: let her that caught me late
Either love, or cause that I may never hate.
I ask too much: would she but let me love her;
Love knows with such like prayers I daily move her.
Accept him that will serve thee all his youth,   5
Accept him that will love with spotless truth.
If lofty titles cannot make me thine,
That am descended but of knightly line
(Soon may you plough the little land I have;
I gladly grant my parents given to save),   10
Apollo, Bacchus and the Muses may,
And Cupid, who hath marked me for thy prey,
My spotless life, which but to gods gives place,
Naked simplicity, and modest grace.
I love but one, and her I love change never,   15
If men have faith, I'll live with thee for ever.
The years that fatal destiny shall give
[I'll live with thee,] and die, ere thou shalt grieve. — reference (?) to "The Passionate Shepherd"
Be thou the happy subject of my books,
That I may write things worthy thy fair looks.   20
By verses horned Io got her name,
And she to whom in shape of swan Jove came,

[Handwritten marginal notes: "Image of ploughing once again"; "Fidelity is here an ideal"; "Comparison — like these goddesses, you will be the subject of poetry that will make you immortal"]

---

i *Ad amicam:* To his mistress.

11 *may: hac faciunt* ("are active on my side" or "support me").

13–14 *My spotless life {. . .} / Naked simplicity, and modest grace.* "may" from line 11 (*hac faciunt*) continues to be the verb for "life [. . .] simplicity [. . . and] grace." *which but to gods gives place*: an earlier textual variant, which Niger used, had *non cessuri nisi dis* ("which will not yield except to gods") instead of Ovid's *nulli cessura fides* ("faith which will yield to none").

15 *change never:* Modern texts read *desultor*, which means one who leaps from one horse to another in the circus, and thus metaphorically a promiscuous man. But earlier variants, again which Niger had, read *desertor*, and thus Marlowe's omission of what is otherwise considered to be the principal metaphor of this elegy. Marlowe's claim here to singular fidelity merits comparison with *Elegies* II.iv, which espouses the opposite sentiment of wanting an infinite number of women.

16–18 *I'll live with thee {. . .} live with thee.* The language of "The Passionate Shepherd: "Come live with me, and be my love."

21 *Io:* Jove turned his paramour Io into a cow to hide her, and his assignations with her, from his wife, Juno.

22 *she {. . .} swan:* Jove assumed the form of a swan to have sex with Leda. From that union she produced an egg from which came Castor and Clytemnestra; she also produced another egg, which by some accounts was inseminated by her husband Tyndareos the king of Sparta, which brought forth Pollux and Helen.

And she that on a feigned bull swam to land,
Griping his false horns with her virgin hand.
So likewise we will through the world be rung,   25
And with my name shall thine be always sung.

Because of "my poetry"?

ELEGIA IV

[*Amicam, qua arte, quibusve nutibus in caena, presente viro uti debeat, admonet*] *Haha!*

Thy husband to a banquet goes with me,
Pray God it may his latest supper be.
Shall I sit gazing as a bashful guest,
While others touch the damsel I love best?
Wilt lying under him, his bosom clip?   5
About thy neck shall he at pleasure skip?
Marvel not, though the fair bride did incite
The drunken Centaurs to a sudden fight;
I am no half-horse, nor in woods I dwell, *comparing the beloved to Hippodamia*
Yet scarce my hands from thee contain I well.   10
But how thou shouldst behave thyself now know,
Nor let the winds away my warnings blow.
Before thy husband come, though I not see
What may be done, yet there before him be.
Lie with him gently, when his limbs he spread   15
Upon the bed, but on my foot first tread.
View me, my becks and speaking countenance;
Take and receive each secret amorous glance.
Words without voice shall on my eyebrows sit,
Lines thou shalt read in wine by my hand writ.   20
When our lascivious toys come in thy mind,
Thy rosy cheeks be to thy thumb inclined.
If aught of me thou speak'st in inward thought,

A turn of sorts

---

23 *she {. . .} bull:* Jove assumed the form of a white bull and swam to Crete with Europa on his back. The offspring of their union were Minos, Rhadamanthus, and Sarpedon.

24 *false horns:* Marlowe's text (as did Niger's) reads *cornua falsa;* modern texts read *cornua vara* ("bent horns").

i *Amicam {. . .} admonet:* He admonishes his mistress what signals and body language she should use when they are at a dinner where her husband is also present.

2 *latest:* last.

5 *clip:* embrace, fondle.

7–8 *bride {. . .} fight:* The wedding of Pirithous and Hippodamia, where a battle erupted between the Lapiths and the Centaurs.

9–10 *I am {. . .} I well:* Some of the Centaurs assaulted Hippodamia; yet, even though Marlowe (Ovid) says he is *not* a Centaur, still he cannot keep his hands from his mistress.

Let thy soft finger to thy ear be brought.
When I (my light) do or say aught that please thee,   25
Turn round thy gold ring, as it were to ease thee.
Strike on the board like them that pray for evil,
When thou dost wish thy husband at the devil.
What wine he fills thee, wisely will him drink;
Ask thou the boy what thou enough dost think.   30
When thou hast tasted, I will take the cup,
And where thou drink'st, on that part I will sup.
If he gives thee what first himself did taste,
Even in his face his offered gobbets cast.
Let not thy neck by his vile arms be prest,   35
Nor lean thy soft head on his boist'rous breast.
Thy bosom's roseate buds let him not finger,
Chiefly on thy lips let not his lips linger.
If thou givest kisses, I shall all disclose,
Say they are mine and hands on thee impose.   40
Yet this I'll see, but if thy gown aught cover,
Suspicious fear in all my veins will hover.
Mingle not thighs nor to his leg join thine,
Nor thy soft foot with his hard foot combine.
I have been wanton, therefore am perplexed,   45
And with mistrust of the like measure vexed.
I and my wench oft under clothes did lurk,
When pleasure moved us to our sweetest work.
Do not thou so, but throw thy mantle hence,
Lest I should think thee guilty of offence.   50
Entreat thy husband drink, but do not kiss,
And while he drinks, to add more do not miss;
If he lies down with wine and sleep oppressed,
The thing and place shall counsel us the rest.
When to go homewards we rise all along,   55
Have care to walk in middle of the throng;
There will I find thee, or be found by thee,
There touch whatever thou canst touch of me.
Aye me, I warn what profits some few hours,
But we must part when heav'n with black night lours.   60

---

27 *Strike on the board* [. . .] : MacLure notes "early commentaries refer, for this rite, to Macrobius'
    saturnalia, III.iii."
34 *gobbets:* morsels.
35 *vile: indignis* ("unworthy"); modern texts, *inpositis* ("imposed").
36 *boist'rous:* obsolete, "hard," for *rigido.*

At night thy husband clips thee: I will weep
And to the doors sight of thyself keep.
Then will he kiss thee, and not only kiss,
But force thee give him my stol'n honey bliss.
Constrained against thy will, give it the peasant;   65
Forbear sweet words, and be your sport unpleasant.
To him I pray it no delight may bring,
Or if it do, to thee no joy thence spring;
But though this night thy fortune be to try it,
To me tomorrow constantly deny it.   70

ELEGIA V

Corinnae concubitus

In summer's heat, and mid-time of the day,
To rest my limbs upon a bed I lay;
One window shut, the other open stood,
Which gave such light as twinkles in a wood,
Like twilight glimpse at setting of the sun,   5
Or night being past, and yet not day begun.
Such light to shamefast maidens must be shown,
Where they may sport and seem to be unknown.
Then came Corinna in a long loose gown,
Her white neck hid with tresses hanging down,   10
Resembling fair Semiramis going to bed,
Or Lais of a thousand wooers sped.
I snatched her gown; being thin, the harm was small,
Yet strived she to be covered therewithal,
And striving thus as one that would be cast,   15
Betrayed herself, and yielded at the last.
Stark naked as she stood before mine eye,
Not one wen in her body could I spy.
What arms and shoulders did I touch and see,
How apt her breasts were to be pressed by me!   20
How smooth a belly under her waist saw I,

---

61 *clips:* embraces.
70 *deny it:* Marlowe's last word directly and exactly translates Ovid's last word (*nega*).

i *Corinnae concubitus:* In bed with Corinna.
11 *Semiramis:* mythical queen of Assyria, known for her extraordinary beauty.
12 *Lais:* celebrated Greek courtesan. *wooers:* modern texts read *viris* (= "lovers"); Renaissance texts, including Niger's, read *procis* (= "wooers" or "suitors").
15 *would be cast:* wished to be defeated.

How large a leg, and what a lusty thigh!
[To leave the rest, all liked me passing well;] — haha! Would describe her genitals
I clinged her naked body, down she fell.
Judge you the rest: [being tired she bade me kiss;] Alludes to   25
Jove send me more such afternoons as this.   oral sex?

ELEGIA VI

Ad Janitorem, ut fores sibi aperiat

Unworthy porter, bound in chains full sore,
On moved hooks set ope the churlish door.
Little I ask, a little entrance make;
The gate half-ope my bent side in will take.
Long love my body to such use makes slender,   5
Who is "he"? And to get out doth like apt members render.
[He] shows me how unheard to pass the watch,
And guides my feet lest stumbling falls they catch.
But in times past I feared vain shades, and night,
Wond'ring if any walked without light.   10

---

22 *How large a leg, and what a lusty thigh!:* Ovid's *quantum et quale latus! quam iuvenale femur!* is the
more literally translated "how great (= long) and how beautiful (= of what sort) a side
(= flank), how youthful a thigh." Marlowe's use of "large" is sanctioned by Niger's note on *latus*
as "*magnum*"; his use of "lusty" for "youthful" is in keeping both with Niger's *quam tenellum &*
venustum quale iuvenculae habere solent ("what delicate and sexy [thighs and sides] as very young
women are wont to have") and with the fact that *iuvenalis* is a more erotically charged adjective
in Latin than the more prosaic and technical *iuvenilis.* Finally, the triple "l" alliteration of
Marlowe's line renders the triple "q" alliteration of Ovid's, and this partly accounts for Marlowe's
incorrect translation of *latus* as "leg."

i *Ad {. . .} aperiat:* To her doorkeeper, that he may open the door for him. This poem is a para-
clausithyron, a subgenre of Roman love elegy that means "being locked outside the mistress's
door." The lover thereby is conventionally referred to as the *exclusus amator* ("excluded lover").
2 *hooks:* hinges.
3 *Little {. . .} little:* The repetition not only renders the parallel of *exiguum {. . .} parvo* but also re-
inforces the humor of this line, in that to open the door even a little is to undermine the original purpose of keeping it closed.
6 *And {. . .} render:* In this translation of *apta subducto pondere membra dedit* Marlowe clearly was very
literally translating *subducto,* and without understanding that *subducto* modifies *pondere* (*corpore* in
some Renaissance texts). The literal translation of the entire couplet is: "Having been a lover a
long time has made slender my body for such purposes (= fitting through slightly ajar doors),
and has made my limbs appropriate thereto by virtue of its weight having been diminished."
A possible explanation for Marlowe's rendering might lie in the fact that in the following couplet
(7–8) Ovid, as McKeown points out, is echoing Tibullus 1.2.17ff and 2.1.71ff, which describe
how the *wife* slips by her sleeping husband and the doorkeeper to *exit* her house to meet her lover.
10 *if any:* Some Renaissance texts read *siquis* ("if any") for the modern *quisquis* ("whoever"). *without*
light: in the darkness (of night) (*tenebris*).

Love hearing it laughed with his tender mother,
And smiling said, "Be thou as bold as other."
Forthwith Love came: no dark night-flying sprite,
Nor hands prepared to slaughter, me affright.
Thee fear I too much, only thee I flatter,   15
Thy lightning can my life in pieces batter.
Why enviest me? this hostile den unbar,
See how the gates with my tears watered are.
When thou stood'st naked, ready to be beat,
For thee I did thy mistress fair entreat;   20
But what entreats for thee sometimes took place
(O mischief) now for me obtain small grace.
Gratis thou mayst be free, give like for like,
Night goes away: the door's bar backward strike.
Strike, so again hard chains shall bind thee never,   25
Nor servile water shalt thou drink for ever.
Hard-hearted porter, dost and wilt not hear?
With stiff oak propped the gate doth still appear.
Such rampired gates besieged cities aid,
In midst of peace why art of arms afraid?   30
Exclud'st a lover, how would'st use a foe?
Strike back the bar, night fast away doth go.
Echoes 1.5   With arms or armed men I come not guarded,

---

11 *Love hearing it:* Earlier texts read *audivit* (perfect indicative) for *audirem* (imperfect subjunctive).
   Niger acknowledges that alternative reading but says that *audirem* is the preferred one.
16 *my life:* This rendering of *me* may derive from Niger's comment on the preceding line: *a te uno
   vita mea dependet* ("on you my life completely depends").
17 *enviest:* Renaissance texts read *invideas* ("envy") for *videas* ("see").
21 *entreats:* entreaties.
23 *Gratis thou mayst be free, give like for like:* The Latin itself is vague and problematic (*redde vicem meri-
   tis: grato licet esse quod optas*). Its sense is "Give me back what I have deserved: If you are gracious to
   me, may you have what you wish." Two sections in Niger, though, shed light: (1) *quandoquidem
   potes, mihi gratiam referas* ("since you are able, you may give me thanks"); (2) *ut in correctiori codice
   legimus, loco gratis substitudiendum est grato* ("as we read in the more correct codex, 'gratis' must be
   substituted in the place of 'grato'").
24 *Night goes away: the door's bar backward strike:* In the Latin, this line (*tempora noctis eunt; excute poste
   seram*) is identically repeated in lines 32, 40, 48, and 56. This repetition of a line as a refrain is
   very rare in Latin poetry, though, as Showerman notes, we find it in *Heroides* 9, in Virgil's
   Eclogue 8, in Theocritus 2, and throughout Spenser's *Epithalamion*. Ovid likely intended this refrain to lend an incantatory tone to the lover's importunate lament. Marlowe does not reproduce
   this exact repetition in any of his corresponding lines, thus losing this rare and noteworthy feature of this elegy.
26 *servile water:* literally, the water which a slave drinks, as opposed to the water which slave own-
   ers drink; metonymically, the state of being a slave.
29 *rampired:* fortified.

I am alone, were furious Love discarded.
Although I would, I cannot him cashier   35
Before I be divided from my gear.
See Love with me, wine moderate in my brain,
And on my hairs a crown of flowers remain.
Who fears these arms? who will not go to meet them?
Night runs away; with open entrance greet them.   40
Art careless? or is't sleep forbids thee hear,
Giving the winds my words running in thine ear?
Well I remember when I first did hire thee,
Watching till after midnight did not tire thee;
But now perchance thy wench with thee doth rest—   45
Ah, how thy lot is above my lot blest!
Though it be so, shut me not out therefore;
Night goes away, I pray thee ope the door.
Err we? or do the turned hinges sound,
And opening doors with creaking noise abound?   50
We err: a strong blast seemed the gates to ope;
Aye me, how high that gale did lift my hope!

---

35 *cashier:* dismiss.

36 *my gear:* my very body (= "my very self" [MacLure]).

37–38 *See Love with me, wine moderate in my brain, / And on my hairs a crown of flowers remain:* The Latin
is *ergo Amor et modicum circa mea tempora vinum / mecum est et madidis lapsa corona comis* ("Therefore
Love, and moderate wine around my temples [= in my brain] and a crown fallen from my perfumed hair will be my escort"). Marlowe's departure from the original is significant and closely
related to his departure from the original at the end of I.i where he makes himself his own muse.
Here, Marlowe will *not* relinquish the garland that Ovid has involuntarily lost, and thus
Marlowe maintains the implication of the laurel crown, to wit, that he is a poet laureate, his own
muse, or even Apollo, god of poetry. Moreover, the sense of the original is that even though the
speaker says that he has only moderately imbibed, he is in fact quite drunk because he has lost
the garland from his head; thus, Marlowe undermines and overcomes Ovid by maintaining not
only the crown but also his own self-control, which Ovid has clearly lost, his proclamation to
the contrary notwithstanding.

41 *careless:* uncaring, unconcerned, hard-hearted.

43 *hire:* The Latin, which reads *primo cum te celare volebam,* means "when I first wished to hide myself
from you (= escape your notice)." There seem to be only two possible explanations: (1) Marlowe
incorrectly understood the Latin to mean that the doorkeeper, not the speaker, was hiding, and
Marlowe thus translated "hide" (from *celare*), which somehow became "hire" through editorial
error; (2) He could be referring to line 23 earlier, where he is offering the doorkeeper a bribe by
enticing him with the promise of freedom. The word "hire" at that time could imply such a quid
pro quo.

52 *did lift my hope:* MacLure says, "The sense is reversed. The gust of wind carried away (*tulit*) his
hope." MacLure is ultimately, though not necessarily technically, correct: it should be noted that
tulit can mean to uplift as well as to take away, and perhaps Marlowe took it as such without fully
thinking through the overall sense of the verse.

If, Boreas, bears Orithyia's rape in mind,
Come break these deaf doors with thy boisterous wind.
Silent the city is: night's dewy host   55
March fast away; the bar strike from the post,
Or I more stern than fire or sword will turn
And with my brand these gorgeous houses burn.
Night, love, and wine to all extremes persuade;
Night shameless, wine and love are fearless made.   60
All have I spent: no threats or prayers move thee;
O harder than the doors thou guard'st I prove thee.
No pretty wench's keeper mayst thou be:
The careful prison is more meet for thee.
Now frosty night her flight begins to take,   65
And crowing cocks poor souls to work awake;
But thou my crown, from sad hairs ta'en away,
On this hard threshold till the morning lay,
That when my mistress there beholds thee cast,
She may perceive how we the time did waste.   70
Whate'er thou art, farewell; be like me pained,

---

53 *bears:* you bear. *Boreas {. . .} Orithyia's:* Boreas is the North Wind. He stole the Athenian princess Orithyia away from the games at Ilissus when her father, King Erechtheus, refused to give her to him in marriage.

55–56 *night's dewy host / March fast away:* The enjambment renders Ovid's having made the first hemistich of the pentametric refrain part of the clause begun in the hexameter, and this is important because it shows, as McKeown points out, that the speaker's patience is finally wearing thin to the point that he will propose taking harsh action.

57 *more stern:* Martin comments, "Marlowe translates the reading *potentior* ['more powerful'] not *paratior* ['better armed']." Indeed, Niger suggests *potentior* as a better reading. *stern {. . .} turn:* Marlowe rarely employs internal rhyme throughout the *Elegies.* In this line his doing so emphasizes his attempt to intimidate the doorkeeper—an attempt that, as McKeown points out, is likewise emphasized in the Latin by Ovid's use of strong diction (*ferroque ignique*) ("sword and fire") and by the very extraordinary elision of those words, which thereby displaces the usual hexametric caesura from the third foot into the fourth foot.

58 *gorgeous:* While the sense calls for the basic meaning of "haughty" for *superba,* Niger does say that it is equally acceptable to construe it to mean "*pulchra*" ("beautiful"). Cooper also cites "gorgeous" as a definition.

64 *careful:* full of care: that is, anxious, gloomy (*sollicito*). *meet:* fitting.

67 *crown {. . .} away:* Contrary to lines 37–38 (noted earlier), Marlowe here renders the original sense of the crown fallen from his head. Since the entire couplet, and the entire following couplet, are about that fact, it was infinitely more difficult for him here to depart strategically from the original as he did at 37–38.

71 *be like me pained:* Marlowe's text had *amorem* ("love") for *honorem* ("honor"). Ovid's line (*sentique abeuntis honorem*) means (somewhat sarcastically) "hear [= 'receive the honor of'] my greeting as I leave you."

Careless, farewell, with my fault not distained!
And farewell cruel posts, rough threshold's block,
And doors conjoined with an hard iron lock!

Elegia VII

Ad pacandam amicam, quam verberaverat
Bind fast my hands, they have deserved chains,
While rage is absent, take some friend the pains;
For rage against my wench moved my rash arm,
My mistress weeps whom my mad hand did harm.
I might have then my parents dear misused,   5
Or holy gods with cruel strokes abused.
Why, Ajax, master of the seven-fold shield,
Butchered the flocks he found in spacious field,
And he who on his mother venged his sire
Against the Destinies durst sharp darts require.   10

---

72 *Careless:* as earlier (41), uncaring. *with my fault not distained!:* As McKeown points out in Ovid's
text, so too here the sense is that of a compliment to the doorkeeper, that because he has succeeded in keeping Marlowe out, he cannot be faulted for having failed at his job.

i *Ad {. . .} verberaverat:* To placate his mistress, whom he had beaten.

2 *While {. . .} is:* The Latin *dum* can mean, for example, "while" or "until." Since the accepted text
has *abit* ("goes away"), "until" is in order. However, some Renaissance texts have *abest* ("is away")
for *abit,* and as such, only "while" would make sense. Niger's text had *abest,* though he comments
that *abit* is a better reading; yet, he also comments how to construe it as *abest.* Marlowe seems to
prefer the sense—especially since the succeeding lines talk of the narrator's actions as having
been executed in the past—that his *furor* has subsided, and while he is currently quieted down,
a friend should restrain him in case the *furor* should return, as opposed to the idea that the rage
is still current and that therefore he needs to be restrained until it has finally passed. Marlowe's
construction insinuates much more ambiguity and uncertainty, and perhaps, therefore, excite-
ment into the elegy and its speaker.

7–8 *Ajax {. . .} flocks:* A mock-epic, mock-heroic comparison by the speaker of himself to Ajax,
who went into a rage because the dead Achilles's shield was given to Odysseus instead of him.
While in—and as a result of—this rage, he slaughtered a flock of sheep, mistakenly believing
them to be Agamemnon and Menelaus, the sons of Atreus, who had favored Odysseus in this
matter. On the one hand, the comparison to an epic hero is so preposterous as to reinforce the
clearly humorous tone of this elegy; on the other hand, there is the implication that perhaps the
mistress had similarly favored others (sexually) over the speaker.

9 *he:* A mock-tragic comparison to Orestes, who killed his mother Clytemnestra to avenge her murder of his father (her husband) Agamemnon. Clytemnestra had been carrying on an adulterous
affair with her husband's first cousin Aegisthus, and this background once again insinuates sexual infidelity on the part of the speaker's mistress.

10 *Destinies:* While Ovid's *arcanas deas* is not precise, it seems as though the Furies are intended
(which hounded Orestes, just mentioned). Niger seems also to think this the case. Marlowe's
choice of "Destinies" is sanctioned by a mythographical and lexicographical tradition that confused the Fates and the Furies (see, e.g., Starnes and Talbert 360 fff).

Could I therefore her comely tresses tear?
Yet was she graced with her ruffled hair.
So fair she was, Atalanta she resembled,
Before whose bow th' Arcadian wild beasts trembled;
Such Ariadne was, when she bewails   15
Her perjured Theseus' flying vows and sails;
So, chaste Minerva, did Cassandra fall,
Deflowered except, within thy temple wall.
That I was mad, and barbarous all men cried,
She nothing said, pale fear her tongue had tied;   20
But secretly her looks with checks did trounce me,
Her tears, she silent, guilty did pronounce me.
Would of mine arms my shoulders had been scanted,
Better I could part of myself have wanted.
To mine own self have I had strength so furious,   25
And to myself could I be so injurious?
Slaughter and mischief's instruments, no better,
Deserved chains these cursed hands shall fetter.
Punished I am, if I a Roman beat;
Over my mistress is my right more great?   30
Tydides left worst signs of villainy,
He first a goddess struck; another I.
Yet he harmed less; whom I professed to love
I harmed; a foe did Diomedes' anger move.
Go now, thou Conqueror, glorious triumphs raise,   35
Pay vows to Jove, engirt thy hairs with bays,

---

13 *Atalanta:* a beautiful, mythical huntress. There are two mythological versions of her story, both of which Niger mentions—the Arcadian and the Boeotian. The first is the hunter of the Calydonian boar who shunned men but finally gave in to the suit of Milanion. The second also shunned suitors by challenging them to a race, overtaking them, and then spearing them in the back. She was defeated by Hippomenes (another name for Milanion), who threw golden apples in her way and caused her to lose the race because she stopped to pick them up. Both she and Hippomenes were changed into lions. The comparison especially to the Boeotian Atalanta once again vilifies the mistress while appearing to praise her.

15 *Ariadne:* daughter of King Minos of Crete. She rescued Theseus from the labyrinth built by Daedalus to house the monstrous Minotaur. Theseus repaid her kindness by abandoning her on the island of Naxos.

18 *Deflowred {. . .} wall:* Most editors who annotate this line adjudge Marlowe to have misunderstood the Latin *sic nisi vittatis quod erat Cassandra capillis* ("thus was Cassandra except for the fact that her hair was bound with fillets"). Fillets were tokens of chastity, and the reference is to the final fall of Troy from which Cassandra sought refuge in the temple of Minerva but was raped there by the lesser Ajax. Orgel offers perhaps the most helpful reading: "the fact that the rape took place in Diana's [*sic*] temple was the only sort of chastity left to her."

31 *Tydides:* Diomedes, son of Tydeus: a prominent Greek soldier in the Trojan War.

32 *goddess:* Diomedes struck Venus in battle at Troy.

And let the troops which shall thy chariot follow
"Io, a strong man conquered this wench," hollow.
Let the sad captive foremost with locks spread,
On her white neck but for hurt cheeks be led;   40
Meeter it were her lips were blue with kissing,
And on her neck a wanton's mark not missing.
But though I like a swelling flood was driven,
And as a prey unto blind anger given,
Was 't not enough the fearful wench to chide,   45
Nor thunder in rough threatings' haughty pride,
Nor shamefully her coat pull o'er her crown,
Which to her waist her girdle still kept down?
But cruelly her tresses having rent,
My nails to scratch her lovely cheeks I bent.   50
Sighing she stood, her bloodless white looks showed
Like marble from the Parian mountains hewed;
Her half-dead joints and trembling limbs I saw,
Like poplar leaves blown with a stormy flaw,
Or slender ears, with gentle Zephyr shaken,   55
Or waters' tops with the warm south wind taken.
And down her cheeks the trickling tears did flow
Like water gushing from consuming snow.

---

38 *hollow:* a variant of "hollo," which itself is a variant of "holler."

40 *neck:* The Latin reads *candida tota,* meaning "white from head to foot (except the cheeks)." Some texts had *colla* ("neck") for *tota,* though, as Gill points out, Niger referred to but rejected this meaning, and both MacLure and Martin find the line unclear. It is likely that Marlowe chose *colla* because there was not enough room in the line to translate *tota* and because the use of "spread," necessitated by the rhyme with "led," works much better with "neck." Also, it coheres better with "neck" (*collum*) in line 42. *hurt cheeks:* scratched and reddened by a lovers' (physical) quarrel.

47 *pull o'er her crown:* The Latin (*summa deducere {. . .} ora*) means "tear her dress from its highest hem." Marlowe's construction does not render this meaning and his sense is unclear. It is possible that he derived his construction from a misunderstanding of Niger's comment on this line. Also, Brooke, Bowers, and Gill keep the spelling "ore" for which all others have rendered "o'er": perhaps Marlowe was attempting some kind of translingual wordplay from *ora* to "ore."

52 *Parian:* indicating the isle of Paros in the Aegean Sea, noted for its marble.

54 *flaw:* gust of wind.

55 *ears:* For *harundo* ("reed"), some Renaissance texts (including Niger's) have *aristae* (= awn, beard, or ear of grain), and Niger recommends this construction.

58 *Like {. . .} snow:* The Latin (*qualiter abiecta de nive manat aqua*) implies smooth, even begrudgingly melting snow, as would be keeping with "trickling" (*suspensae*) from the preceding line. "Gushing" and "consuming" therefore are unfitting, but Marlowe likely derives this notion from Niger, who warns that in order not to offend the lady, her tears must be seen as rains cast down to earth by Jove: that is, to construe it "correctly" does not give sufficient deference to the extremity of the lady's situation. Yet the Ovidian version, it must therefore be noted, contains a subtle diminution, perhaps trivialization, of the woman's situation amidst the language's apparent condemnation of it—a typical Ovidian play that is lost in translation. Finally, the Latin *abiecta* itself is textually problematic.

Then first I did perceive I had offended,
My blood the tears were that from her descended.   60
Before her feet thrice prostrate down I fell,
My feared hands thrice back she did repel.
But doubt thou not (revenge doth grief appease)
With thy sharp nails upon my face to seize;
Bescratch mine eyes, spare not my locks to break   65
(Anger will help thy hands though ne'er so weak),
And lest the sad signs of my crime remain,
Put in their place thy kembed hairs again.

ELEGIA VIII

Execratur lenam, quae puellam suam meretricia arte instituebat
There is, whoe'er will know a bawd aright,
Give ear, there is an old trot, Dipsas hight.
Her name comes from the thing: she being wise
Sees not the morn on rosy horses rise,
She magic arts and Thessale charms doth know,   5
And makes large streams back to their fountains flow;
She knows with grass, with threads on wrong wheels spun,
And what with mares' rank humour may be done.
When she will, clouds the darkened heav'n obscure;
When she will, day shines everywhere most pure.   10
(If I have faith) I saw the stars drop blood,
The purple moon with sanguine visage stood.
Her I suspect among night's spirits to fly,
And her old body in birds' plumes to lie.

---

63 *doubt:* hesitate.
65 *to break:* not in the Latin.
68 *kembed:* combed (kempt).

i *Execratur {. . .} instituebat:* He curses the bawd who has been instructing his mistress in the art of
  the courtesan.
2 *trot:* hag. *hight:* named.
3 *Her {. . .} thing:* The name itself means "thirsty." *wise:* The Latin says that she was always drunk
  all night long, and thus she never saw the dawn sober. Cunningham suggested that "wise" was
  "one of the thousand and one euphemisms for 'inebriated,'" but we (and MacLure) can find no
  support for this meaning.
5 *Thessale:* home of Circe (*Aea*) and of witchcraft.
7 *wrong:* The Latin *torto* here demands "crooked." Marlowe uses "wrong" perhaps because Cooper
  offers it as one definition and because the wheels become "wrong" by metonymy, since they are
  perpetuating magic; also, Niger cites one meaning for it as *veneficam* ("poisonous").
8 *humour:* liquid excretion from the genitalia of a mare in heat.
11 *I have faith:* you believe me.

Fame saith as I suspect, and in her eyes   15
Two eyeballs shine and double light thence flies.
Great-grandsires from their ancient graves she chides,
And with long charms the solid earth divides.
She draws chaste women to incontinence,
Nor doth her tongue want harmful eloquence.   20
By chance I heard her talk; these words she said,
While closely hid betwixt two doors I laid:
"Mistress, thou know'st thou hast a blest youth pleased,
He stayed, and on thy looks his gazes seized.
And why shouldst not please? none thy face exceeds;   25
Aye me, thy body hath no worthy weeds.
As thou art fair, would thou wert fortunate!
Wert thou rich, poor should not be my state.
Th' opposed star of Mars hath done thee harm;
Now Mars is gone, Venus thy side doth warm,   30
And brings good fortune: a rich lover plants
His love on thee, and can supply thy wants.
Such is his form as may with thine compare,
Would he not buy thee, thou for him shouldst care."
She blushed. "Red shame becomes white cheeks, but this,   35
If feigned, doth well; if true, it doth amiss.
When on thy lap thine eyes thou dost deject,
Each one according to his gifts respect.
Perhaps the Sabines rude, when Tatius reigned,
To yield their love to more than one disdained;   40
Now Mars doth rage abroad without all pity,
And Venus rules in her Aeneas' city.
Fair women play, she's chaste whom none will have,
Or, but for bashfulness, herself would crave.
Shake off these wrinkles that thy front assault,   45

---

15 *Fame saith:* Rumor has it.

16 *Two eyeballs:* double pupils (meant literally, but also metaphorical for the "evil eye").

23 *blest:* wealthy.

31–32 *plants/His love on thee:* While seemingly far removed from "has desired thee" (*te cupiit*), Marlowe likely used this term not only for the rhyme but also because part of Niger's note is *dignus corpore cultus* ("worthy to be husbanded in [thus 'plants . . . on'] the body").

39–40 *Perhaps {. . .} disdained:* The Sabine women, under their King Tatius, were construed to be people of simple morality.

42 *Aeneas' city:* Rome.

44 *herself would crave:* "herself" is nominative subject of "would crave."

45 *front:* forehead.

45–46 *Shake {. . .} fault:* The Latin—*has quoque, quae frontis rugas in vertice portant / excute de rugis crimina multa cadent*—is properly translated "if you shake those women who carry wrinkles in

Wrinkles in beauty is a grievous fault.

See footnote!

Penelope in bows her youths' strength tried,
Of horn the bow was that approved their side.
Time flying slides hence closely, and deceives us,
And with swift horses the swift year soon leaves us.   50
Brass shines with use; good garments would be worn;
Houses not dwelt in are with filth forlorn.   → *Sexual innuendo*
Beauty not exercised with age is spent,
Nor one or two men are sufficient.   *} Whoa!*
Many to rob is more sure, and less hateful,   55
From dog-kept flocks come preys to wolves most grateful.
Behold, what gives the poet but new verses?] – *haha!*
And thereof many thousand he rehearses.
The poet's god, arrayed in robes of gold,
Of his gilt harp the well-tuned strings doth hold.   60
Let Homer yield to such as presents bring;
(Trust me) to give, it is a witty thing.
Nor, so thou mayst obtain a wealthy prize,
The vain name of inferior slaves despise.
Nor let the arms of ancient lines beguile thee;   65

---

their forehead, then many indiscretions will as a result fall down from those furrows." Dipsas is referring to women who affect, by furrowing their brow, an aura of moral austerity and continence, and she is admonishing the mistress here not to be like them lest no man approach her.

47–48 *Penelope {. . .} side:* a reference to book 21 of Homer's *Odyssey* where Penelope, a legendary model of chastity, tested her suitors with their prowess in stringing and shooting her husband's (Odysseus's) bow, which was made of horn; Odysseus won the contest. "Bow" and "horn" have sexual connotations, and as such, this couplet continues Dipsas's innuendos that even women of unquestioned chastity have promiscuous desires and usually give in to them. *approved their side:* demonstrated their strength.

49 *closely:* imperceptibly (*occulte*).

50 *And {. . .} us:* Modern editions accept *ut celer admissis labitur amnis aquis* ("as a swift stream glides smoothly with its loose [= rapid] currents"); Marlowe's (and Niger's) edition had *et celer admissis labitur annus equis* ("and the swift year glides by with swift horses").

56 *dog-kept:* Here Marlowe has read the adjective *cānis* ("white haired," modifying "wolves") for the noun *cănis* (dog). This is the more remarkable both because Niger clearly indicates the correct definition and because Marlowe could also have understood the difference by metrically scanning Ovid's pentameter.

62 *witty:* smart.

64 *The {. . .} despise:* Some texts had *nomen* ("name") instead of *crimen* ("crime"); Niger's has *crimen* but he discusses the variant and concludes that either is correct—Marlowe chooses *nomen*. "inferior slaves" were those who were imported from outside Rome and whose feet were marked with chalk to evince that distinction.

65 *Nor {. . .} thee:* The accepted Latin reading is *nec te decipiant veteres circum atria cerae* ("do not let the wax masks [of the visages of their ancestors] around the halls [of their houses] deceive you"). Marlowe's text had *nec te decipiant veteris quinquatria cerae* and thus Marlowe's translation: the *quinquatria* was a festival primarily honoring Minerva but secondarily honoring Mars, and thus

Poor lover, with thy grandsires I exile thee.
Who seeks, for being fair, a night to have,
What he will give, with greater instance crave.
Make a small price, while thou thy nets dost lay,
Lest they should fly; being ta'en, the tyrant play.   70
Dissemble so, as loved he may be thought,
And take heed lest he gets that love for nought.
Deny him oft; feign now thy head doth ache.
And Isis now will show what scuse to make.
Receive him soon, lest patient use he gain,   75
Or lest his love oft beaten back should wane.
To beggars shut, to bringers ope thy gate; *And the narrator is a beggar*
Let him within hear barred-out lovers prate.
And as first wronged the wronged sometimes banish, *polyptoton*
Thy fault with his fault so repulsed will vanish.   80
But never give a spacious time to ire,
Anger delayed doth oft to hate retire.
And let thine eyes constrained learn to weep,
That this or that man may thy cheeks moist keep.
Nor, if thou cozen'st one, dread to forswear,   85
Venus to mocked men lends a senseless ear.
Servants fit for thy purpose thou must hire,
To teach thy lover what thy thoughts desire.
Let them ask somewhat; many asking little,
Within a while great heaps grow of a tittle.   90
And sister, nurse, and mother spare him not,
By many hands great wealth is quickly got.
When causes fail thee to require a gift,
By keeping of thy birth make but a shift.

"arms" in Marlowe's construction. Niger's text has the latter reading, though he comments that
he cannot understand it, and while he understands that *atria* might be an independent word, he
seems to have no acquaintance with the textual tradition which substitutes *circum* for *quinqu.*
Finally, the point of the couplet (65–66) is "don't be taken in by a great pedigree if the money
is not there to go with it."

71 *Dissemble so:* Nor is it harmful for you to feign love.

74 *Isis:* a moon goddess, and thus evocative of menstruation.

75 *lest {. . .} gain:* lest he get used to suffering.

79 *And {. . .} banish:* And sometimes injure him with anger as if you are retaliating for having been
injured first by him.

79–80 *wronged {. . .} wronged {. . .} fault {. . .} fault:* Marlowe's use of polyptoton here renders the
same in Ovid's *laesa {. . .} laeso {. . .} culpa culpa.*

86 *mocked men:* Marlowe's text has *illusis,* while modern texts have *in lusis* ("love's deceptions"). The
distinction is largely negligible because the sense is ultimately the same.

94 *but a shift:* The Latin (*natalem libo testificare tuum*) is properly translated "show him it's your birthday by having a cake."

Beware lest he unrivalled loves secure;   95
Take strife away, love doth not well endure.
On all the bed men's tumbling let him view,
And thy neck with lascivious marks made blue;
Chiefly show him the gifts which others send;
If he gives nothing, let him from thee wend.   100
When thou hast so much as he gives no more,
Pray him to lend what thou mayst ne'er restore.
Let thy tongue flatter, while thy mind harm works,
Under sweet honey deadly poison lurks.
If this thou dost, to me by long use known,   105
Nor let my words be with the winds hence blown,
Oft thou wilt say, 'live well'; thou wilt pray oft
That my dead bones may in their grave lie soft."
As thus she spake, my shadow me betrayed,
With much ado my hands I scarcely stayed;   110
But her blear eyes, bald scalp's thin hoary fleeces,
And rivelled cheeks I would have pulled a-pieces.
The gods send thee no house, a poor old age,
Perpetual thirst, and winter's lasting rage.

ELEGIA IX

Ad Atticum, amantem non oportere desidiosum esse, sicuti nec militem

All lovers war, and Cupid hath his tent,
Attic, all lovers are to war far sent.
What age fits Mars, with Venus doth agree,
'Tis shame for eld in war or love to be.
What years in soldiers captains do require,   5
Those in their lovers pretty maids desire.
Both of them watch: each on the hard earth sleeps;
His mistress' doors this, that his captain's keeps.
Soldiers must travel far; the wench forth send,
Her valiant lover follows without end.   10
Mounts, and rain-doubled floods he passeth over,

---

100 *If {. . .} wend:* The sense of the Latin—*si dederit nemo Sacra roganda Via est*—is "If nobody has
given you presents, buy some yourself from the shopping center [to make it appear as if someone has]." Marlowe's text has *si tibi nil dederit,* which accounts for the first half of his line but not
the second half.
112 *rivelled:* wrinkled.

i *Ad {. . .} militem:* To Atticus, that a lover, just like a soldier, may not be lazy.
5 *years:* Marlowe's text has *annos;* modern texts *animos* (courage).

And treads the deserts snowy heaps do cover.
Going to sea, east winds he doth not chide,
Nor to hoist sail attends fit time and tide.
Who but a soldier or a lover is bold   15
To suffer storm-mixed snows with night's sharp cold?
One as a spy doth to his enemies go,
The other eyes his rival as his foe.
He cities great, this thresholds lies before;
This breaks town gates, but he his mistress' door.   20
Oft to invade the sleeping foe 'tis good,
And armed to shed unarmed people's blood.
So the fierce troops of Thracian Rhesus fell,
And captive horses bade their lord farewell.
Sooth, lovers watch till sleep the husband charms,   25
Who slumb'ring, they rise up in swelling arms.
The keeper's hands and corps-du-gard to pass,
The soldier's, and poor lover's work e'er was.
Doubtful is war and love: the vanquished rise,
And who thou never think'st should fall, down lies.   30
Therefore whoe'er love slothfulness doth call,
Let him surcease: love tries wit best of all.
Achilles burned, Briseis being ta'en away;
Trojans, destroy the Greek wealth while you may;
Hector to arms went from his wife's embraces,   35
And on Andromache his helmet laces.
Great Agamemnon was, men say, amazed,
On Priam's loose-tressed daughter when he gazed.
Mars in the deed the blacksmith's net did stable,
In heaven was never more notorious fable.   40

19–20 *He {. . .} this {. . .} This {. . .} he:* "The soldier [. . .] the lover [. . .] the soldier [. . .] the lover." The order of pronouns that Marlowe employs renders the chiastic order of Ovid's *ille {. . .} hic {. . .} hic {. . .} ille.* However, Marlowe's pronouns do not have the same chiastic order of antecedents as Ovid's, wherein Ovid's order, translated, would be "the soldier [. . .] the lover [. . .] the lover [. . .] the soldier."

22 *And armed:* "And to be armed."

23–24 *So {. . .} farewell:* a reference to the actions of Diomedes and Odysseus in *Iliad* 10.435 ff.

32 *love tries wit best of all:* "it takes great ingenuity to be successful at love."

33–34 *Achilles {. . .} may:* Briseis was the slave of Achilles whom Agamemnon forcibly seized from him in *Iliad* 1. *wealth:* Ovid intends *opes* in its sense as "strength," not in its alternative sense of "wealth."

36 *on:* on Hector. The reference is to *Iliad* 6.369 ff.

38 *daughter:* Cassandra.

39–40 *Mars {. . .} fable:* Vulcan, the god of the smithy and husband of Venus, trapped ("did stable") his wife and Mars in bed together by means of an invisible net with which he had lined the bed. He then summoned all of the gods and goddesses of Olympus to behold this adultery.

Myself was dull and faint, to sloth inclined,
Pleasure and ease had mollified my mind;
A fair maid's care expelled this sluggishness,
And to her tents willed me myself address.
Since mayst thou see me watch and night-wars move: 45
He that will not grow slothful, let him love.

ELEGIA X

Ad puellem, ne pro amore praemia poscat

Such as the cause was of two husbands' war,
Whom Trojan ships fetched from Europa far;
Such as was Leda, whom the god deluded
In snow-white plumes of a false swan included;
Such as Amymone through the dry fields strayed,   5
When on her head a water pitcher laid:
Such wert thou, and I feared the bull and eagle,
And whate'er love made Jove should thee inveigle.
Now all fear with my mind's hot love abates,
No more this beauty mine eyes captivates.   10
Ask'st why I change? because thou crav'st reward:
This cause hath thee from pleasing me debarred.
While thou wert plain, I loved thy mind and face,
Now inward faults thy outward form disgrace.
Love is a naked boy, his years sans stain,   15
And hath no clothes, but open doth remain.

The story is from *Odyssey* 8.266 ff, and Ovid reworks it at *Ars Amatoria* 2.561 ff and *Metamorphoses* 4.169 ff.

43 *A fair maid's care:* loving a fair maid.

45 *watch:* Marlowe's text likely had *vigilem;* modern texts have *agilem* ("active").

i *Ad {. . .} poscat:* To his mistress, that she should not request money in return for her love.

1 *cause:* Helen of Troy.

2 *Europa:* Marlowe's text read *Europa,* but modern texts have *Eurota,* indicating the Eurotas River.

3 *Leda:* wife of King Tyndareos of Sparta, who was impregnated by Zeus in the form of a swan. That pregnancy brought forth Pollux and Helen, and a simultaneous impregnation by her husband brought forth Castor and Clytemnestra.

5 *Amymone:* the daughter of Danaus, king of Argos, carried away by Poseidon while fetching water for her father.

7 *bull and eagle:* two of the many animal forms Jove would assume to hide his promiscuous adultery from his wife Hera. As a bull he carried off Europa; as an eagle, Ganymede.

13 *plain:* innocent, unduplicitous.

15 *sans:* without.

16 *but open:* "but" misleads: The sense of both Marlowe and Ovid is "his lack of clothes indicates his innocence."

Will you for gain have Cupid sell himself?
He hath no bosom, where to hide base pelf.
Love and Love's son are with fierce arms to odds;
To serve for pay beseems not wanton gods.   20
The whore stands to be bought for each man's money,
And seeks vile wealth by selling of her coney,
Yet greedy bawd's command she curseth still,
And doth, constrained, what you do of good will.
Take from irrational beasts a precedent;   25
'Tis shame their wits should be more excellent.
The mare asks not the horse, the cow the bull,
Nor the mild ewe gifts from the ram doth pull;
Only a woman gets spoils from a man,
Farms out herself on nights for what she can,   30
And lets what both delight, what both desire,
Making her joy according to her hire.
The sport being such as both alike sweet try it,
Why should one sell it and the other buy it?
Why should I lose, and thou gain by the pleasure   35
Which man and woman reap in equal measure?
Knights of the post of perjuries make sale,
The unjust judge for bribes becomes a stale.
'Tis shame sold tongues the guilty should defend,
Or great wealth from a judgement seat ascend;   40
'Tis shame to grow rich by bed merchandise,
Or prostitute thy beauty for bad prize.
Thanks worthily are due for things unbought,
For beds ill-hired we are indebted nought.
The hirer payeth all, his rent discharged,   45
From further duty he rests then enlarged.
Fair dames forbear rewards for nights to crave,

---

18 *bosom:* from *sinum*, meaning fold or pocket in a garment.

22 *coney:* pudendum (an apt, if vulgarly graphic, synechdochic translation of *corpore*).

24 *good will:* your own will.

31 *lets:* sells.

32 *Making {. . .} hire:* Marlowe reverses the Latin (*et pretium quanti gaudeat ipsa facit*); the proper translation is "calculates her price according to the level of her enjoyment."

37 *Knights of the post:* perjurers.

38 *unjust:* Niger comments that *selecti* (= "chosen") means "corrupt." *becomes a stale:* prostitutes himself.

39 *sold tongues:* Roman law stipulated that lawyers could not charge for their services.

42 *bad prize:* monetary gain.

46 *enlarged:* released.

47 *Fair {. . .} forbear {. . .} for:* The alliteration is noteworthy because Ovid's line also alliterates, albeit with the letter "p."

Ill-gotten goods good end will never have.
The Sabine gauntlets were too dearly won,
That unto death did press the holy nun.   50
The son slew her that forth to meet him went,
And a rich necklace caused that punishment.
Yet think no scorn to ask a wealthy churl;
He wants no gifts into thy lap to hurl.
Take clustered grapes from an o'er-laden vine,   55
May bounteous loam Alcinous' fruit resign.
Let poor men show their service, faith, and care;
All for their mistress, what they have, prepare.
In verse to praise kind wenches 'tis my part,
And whom I like eternize by mine art.   60
Garments do wear, jewels and gold do waste,
The fame that verse gives doth for ever last.
To give I love, but to be asked disdain;
Leave asking, and I'll give what I refrain.

Meta discourse on his own poetry)

ELEGIA XI

Napen alloquitur, ut paratas tabellas ad Corinnam perferat
In skilful gathering ruffled hairs in order,
Nape, free-born, whose cunning hath no border,
Thy service for night's scapes is known commodious,
And to give signs dull wit to thee is odious.

49–50 *The {. . .} nun:* Tarpeia, daughter of a Roman governor, betrayed Rome by opening the city gates to the Sabines in return for their gold bracelets; but as they entered, they threw not only their bracelets but also their shields at her, crushing her to death.

51–52 *The {. . .} punishment:* Eriphyle betrayed her husband Amphiarus in a way that led to his death, in exchange for a gold necklace. Their son Alcmaeon murdered his mother in revenge. The words "that [. . .] went" mistranslate; Ovid says, in effect, "from whom he had been born" (*e quibus exierat {. . .} viscera*).

54 *wants:* lacks.

56 *loam:* field. *Alcinous:* known for the fertility of his orchards, which yielded fruit all year long (*Odyssey* 7.112 ff). *resign:* yield.

61 *wear:* wear out.

63–64 *give {. . .} asked {. . .} asking {. . .} give:* Marlowe renders the chiasmus of *dare {. . .} posci {. . .} poscenti {. . .} dabo.*

i *Napen {. . .} perferat:* He implores Nape to take a love letter to Corinna.

2 *free-born:* a loose translation of *neque ancillas inter habenda* ("not your usual handmaiden"). *whose {. . .} border:* This is not in the Latin.

3 *scapes:* escapades.

4 *And {. . .} odious:* she is skilled in the giving of signals.

Corinna clips me oft by thy persuasion,   5
Never to harm me made thy faith evasion.
Receive these lines, them to thy mistress carry,
Be sedulous, let no stay cause thee tarry.
Nor flint nor iron are in thy soft breast,
But pure simplicity in thee doth rest.   10
And 'tis supposed Love's bow hath wounded thee,
Defend the ensigns of thy war in me.
If what I do, she asks, say "hope for night";
The rest my hand doth in my letters write.
Time passeth while I speak, give her my writ,   15
But see that forthwith she peruseth it.
I charge thee mark her eyes and front in reading,
By speechless looks we guess at things succeeding.
Straight being read, will her to write much back,
I hate fair paper should writ matter lack.   20
Let her make verses, and some blotted letter
On the last edge, to stay mine eyes the better.
What need she tire her hand to hold the quill?
Let this word, "Come," alone the tables fill.
Then with triumphant laurel will I grace them,   25
And in the midst of Venus' temple place them,
Subscribing that to her I consecrate
My faithful tables, being vile maple late.

---

5 *clips:* embraces (sexually).

6 *Never {. . .} evasion:* Marlowe's and Ovid's sense is "often your faithfulness served me well when I needed you."

8 *sedulous:* industrious, zealous. *stay:* delay. *tarry:* to tarry.

10 *But {. . .} rest:* Ovid's sense is that she is not as simple and unsophisticated as an ordinary hand-maiden. Marlowe's rendering is likely attributable to his text having read *sed* ("but") instead of *nec* ("nor").

12 *Defend {. . .} me:* Marlowe's and Ovid's sense is "use your own experience in the war of love to help me in mine."

17 *front:* forehead.

18 *succeeding:* to come.

19 *Straight:* immediately upon the letter. *will:* order.

21–22 *Let {. . .} better:* Ovid's sense is "See to it that her lines are written very close together and even that the margins are filled with her afterthoughts." The point is that he wants to have a lot to read, because he will take that as a sign that she has devoted much time and thought to her response.

24 *tables:* tablets (pages).

25 *laurel:* While laurel crowns marked excellence in poetry, they also marked military success. Given the earlier references to the war of love, the implication here is that if Corinna's letter says what he wishes, then that letter will be a mark of his military success in his war of love with her.

27 *Subscribing:* "writing beneath them." *her:* Venus.

28 *My {. . .} late:* Marlowe's and Ovid's sense is "My faithful tablets (pages), which until now were but modest maple" (maple was used for writing-tablets).

ELEGIA XII

Tabellas quas miserat execratur, quod amica noctem negabat

Bewail my chance: the sad book is returned,
This day denial hath my sport adjourned.
Presages are not vain; when she departed,
Nape by stumbling on the threshold started.
Going out again, pass forth the door more wisely,   5
And somewhat higher bear thy foot precisely.
Hence, luckless tables, funeral wood, be flying,
And thou the wax stuffed full with notes denying,
Which I think gathered from cold hemlock's flower,
Wherein bad honey Corsic bees did pour.   10
Yet as if mixed with red lead thou wert ruddy,
That colour rightly did appear so bloody.
As evil wood thrown in the highways lie,
Be broke with wheels of chariots passing by,
And him that hewed you out for needful uses   15
I'll prove had hands impure with all abuses.
Poor wretches on the tree themselves did strangle;
There sat the hangman for men's necks to angle.
To hoarse screech-owls foul shadows it allows,
Vultures and Furies nestled in the boughs.   20
To these my love I foolishly committed,
And then with sweet words to my mistress fitted;
More fitly had they wrangling bonds contained,
From barbarous lips of some attorney strained.

[handwritten margin note: Ha ha!]

---

i *Tabellas {. . .} negabat:* He curses the tablets he had sent because his mistress would not spend the
   night with him.
1 *chance:* misfortune.
3 *presages:* omens.
4 *started:* stopped still.
7 *tables:* tablets (pages).
8 *wax:* The wood tablets Romans wrote on were covered with wax. *notes denying:* Ovid's and Marlowe's
   sense is "your written words rejecting my expressed desire for us to be together."
11–12 *Yet {. . .} bloody:* Red was a common color for the wax on writing-tablets; the sense here is
   that the red on the tablet is not that wax but his (at least metaphorical) "blood." *red lead:* the
   Latin *minium* is commonly defined as "cinnabar" or "red lead"; Cooper defines it as "red lead."
13 *evil:* useless (*inutile*). *highways:* crossroads (*triviis*).
20 *Furies:* witches or hags. Even though *strix* is defined as a screech-owl, Niger supports this rendering; Cooper also cites *strix* as witch or hag; and there is an obvious relation to *striga,* which
   means witch or hag.
21 *these:* these tablets (pages).
23 *wrangling:* noisy (*garrula*). *bonds:* writs at court, such as bail bonds.
24 *barbarous:* harsh-toned (*duro ore*). Niger employs the phrase *barbare loquendo* ("speaking bar-
   barously") in his comments not on *duro ore* but near them in his comments on *garrula.*

Among day-books and bills they had lain better,   25
In which the merchant wails his bankrupt debtor.
Your name approves you made for such like things,
The number two no good divining brings.
Angry, I pray that rotten age you wracks,
And sluttish white-mould overgrow the wax.   30

ELEGIA XIII

Ad Auroram, ne properet

Now o'er the sea from her old love comes she
That draws the day from heaven's cold axle-tree.
Aurora, whither slidest thou? down again,
And birds for Memnon yearly shall be slain.
Now in her tender arms I sweetly bide,   5
If ever, now well lies she by my side.
The air is cold, and sleep is sweetest now,
And birds send forth shrill notes from every bough:
Whither runn'st thou, that men and women love not?

---

26 *In {. . .} debtor:* The Latin says "And accounts wherein the miser bemoans money he has spent"
(*in quibus absumptas fleret avarus opes*). Niger's comment, though, does open the door for Marlowe
to construe it as he does, and so the requirements of rhyme might not alone explain Marlowe's
departure here from Ovid.

27 *Your {. . .} things:* that is, they are double, folded tablets, and thereby connote duplicity as well
as doubleness, as the next line elaborates. *approves:* proves.

i *Ad {. . .} properet:* To Dawn, that she may not hurry.

1 *old love:* Aurora's husband, Tithonus, who was granted eternal life but not eternal youth to go
with it.

2 *cold axle-tree:* a metaphor for the dawn. "tree" refers to the axle itself, made of wood, around which
the wheel turns, and it is "cold" because it is at the end of the night and before the day. All the
various times of day (morning, day, night, etc.) are often symbolized in classical literature by a
"chariot," the synechdoche for which would be the axle and/or wheels. See Booth at 2.5.38.

3 *slidest:* hurry. *down again:* This is not an answer to the question just posed but an imperative
behest to Dawn to reverse her rising. Moreover, "down again" can be traced to Niger's comment
on *quo properas* ("where are you hurrying?") at line 9 later, which he implies there should apply
here (he makes no comment on this *quo properas* here in his commentary on line 3): [. . .] *ab incepto aliquem desistere volumes* ("from the beginning we want [her] to stop"). *ab incepto* refers to the
beginning of the poem, and *disistere* can be literally translated as "stand down" ("down again").

4 *Memnon:* the son of Aurora and Tithonus. Orgel writes: "He was killed by Achilles at Troy, but
Jupiter granted him immortality. A flock of birds rose from his funeral pyre and fought until
half of them fell into the blaze to appease his spirit. The birds [called the 'Memnonides'] were
said to return annually to the tomb of Memnon and repeat the battle."

7 *sweetest:* from Niger's *molles et suaves.*

8 *shrill:* not indicated by *liquidum,* but again Niger: {. . .} *clamat* {. . .} *horrendum stridens.*

Hold in thy rosy horses that they move not. 10
Ere thou rise, stars teach seamen where to sail,
But when thou comest, they of their courses fail.
Poor travellers, though tired, rise at thy sight,
And soldiers make them ready to the fight.
The painful hind by thee to field is sent, 15
Slow oxen early in the yoke are pent.
Thou cozen'st boys of sleep, and dost betray them
To pedants that with cruel lashes pay them.
Thou mak'st the surety to the lawyer run,
That with one word hath nigh himself undone. 20
The lawyer and the client hate thy view,
Both whom thou raisest up to toil anew.
By thy means women of their rest are barred,
Thou set'st their labouring hands to spin and card.
All could I bear; but that the wench should rise 25
Who can endure, save him with whom none lies?
How oft wished I night would not give thee place,
Nor morning stars shun thy uprising face.
How oft that either wind would break thy coach,
Or steeds might fall, forced with thick clouds' approach. 30
Whither goest thou, hateful nymph? Memnon the elf
Received his coal-black colour from thyself.
Say that thy love with Cephalus were not known,
Then thinkest thou thy loose life is not shown?

14 *them:* themselves.
15 *hind:* archaic for "farmhand."
17 *cozen'st:* defraud, rob.
18 *pedants:* schoolmasters.
19 *lawyer:* Marlowe's text read *consulti* instead of several other alternatives that evince a troubled textual history.
20 *one word:* Green writes: "The court referred to was the praetor's tribunal, which handled civil suits. The 'one-word-pledge' was the verb *spondeo* [hence *sponsum*], 'I guarantee,' and the official formula for going to bail was: 'I guarantee to render a like sum' (*ego idem dare spondeo*)."
26 *none lies:* "no woman sleeps."
29 *oft that:* supply "wished I" (from line 27) between these words.
31–32 *Whither {. . .} thyself:* Memnon was black; "hateful" is for *invida,* which means "envious," and in antiquity and the Renaissance, "black" was often thought to denote envy, as Niger mentions. Ovid is saying that Memnon is literally black because Aurora's heart is metaphorically black (envious, i.e., "hateful"). Aurora is envious of lovers who want to be with each other and therefore do not want the sun to rise because Aurora herself is not so situated; rather, she wants to get away from her aging, undesirable husband Tithonus as soon as possible (see line 37). The phrase "the elf" is used for the rhyme.
33–34 *Say {. . .} shown:* The corresponding Latin lines do not appear in most modern texts: *quid si non Cephali quondam flagrasset amore? / an putat ignotam nequitiam esse suam.* Cephalus, the husband

Would Tithon might but talk of thee awhile, 35
Not one in heaven should be more base and vile.
Thou leav'st his bed because he's faint through age,
And early mount'st thy hateful carriage;
But held'st thou in thine arms some Cephalus,
Then wouldst thou cry, "Stay night, and run not thus." 40
Dost punish me, because years make him wane?
I did not bid thee wed an aged swain.
The moon sleeps with Endymion every day;
Thou art as fair as she, then kiss and play.
Jove, that thou shouldst not haste but wait his leisure, 45
Made two nights one to finish up his pleasure.
I chid no more; she blushed, and therefore heard me, *red sky of the morning*
Yet lingered not the day, but morning scared me.

ELEGIA XIV

Puellam consolatur cui prae nimia cura comae deciderant

"Leave colouring thy tresses," I did cry;
Now hast thou left no hairs at all to dye.
But what had been more fair had they been kept?
Beyond thy robes thy dangling locks had swept.
Fear'dst thou to dress them being fine and thin, 5
Like to the silk the curious Seres spin,
Or threads which spider's slender foot draws out,
Fast'ning her light web some old beam about?
Not black, nor golden were they to our view,

---

of Procris, was loved by Aurora. The clear implication here is that he fathered Memnon, since there is otherwise no explanation for why Memnon is black.

40 *Stay {. . .} thus:* The Latin *lente currite noctis equi* ("Run softly, horses of the night") is spoken by Faustus at the end of *Dr. Faustus,* A Text 5.2.75, as he faces the end of his last night on earth.

43 *moon:* Moon Goddess (Luna).

45 – 46 *Jove {. . .} pleasure:* A reference to Jove who, disguised as Alcmena's husband Amphitryon, stayed in bed with her an extra long time by extending the night. Their union conceived Hercules.

47 – 48 *morning scared me:* Martin, MacLure, and Gill point out that these words are gratuitous. There is, however, another possible explanation: In his commentary on this line Niger quotes from two of Petrarch's odes (22 and 73). Among the lines cited from ode 73 are 71 ff, which contain the word "fiso" ("fixed"). Given the similarity of the Renaissance "s" and "f," and if either Marlowe's text was hard to read or his Italian poor, he might have read it as "fifa," which means "scared."

i *Puellam {. . .} deciderant:* He consoles his mistress whose hair has fallen out because of too much dyeing.

6 *Seres:* Chinese.

Yet although neither, mixed of either's hue,   10
Such as in hilly Ida's wat'ry plains,
The cedar tall spoiled of his bark retains.
And they were apt to curl an hundred ways,
And did to thee no cause of dolour raise.
Nor hath the needle, or the comb's teeth reft them,   15
The maid that kembed them ever safely left them.
Oft was she dressed before mine eyes, yet never,
Snatching the comb to beat the wench, out drave her.
Oft in the morn, her hairs not yet digested,
Half-sleeping on a purple bed she rested;   20
Yet seemly, like a Thracian bacchanal,
That tired doth rashly on the green grass fall.
When they were slender, and like downy moss,
Thy troubled hairs, alas, endured great loss.
How patiently hot irons they did take,   25
In crooked trammels crispy curls to make.
I cried, "'Tis sin, 'tis sin, these hairs to burn,
They well become thee, then to spare them turn.
Far off be force, no fire to them may reach,
Thy very hairs will the hot bodkin teach."   30
Lost are the goodly locks, which from their crown
Phoebus and Bacchus wished were hanging down.
Such were they as Diana painted stands
All naked holding in her wave-moist hands.
Why dost thy ill-kembed tresses' loss lament?   35

---

10 *Yet {. . .} hue:* the correspondence of dictional etymology and placement of English-to-Latin is
remarkable: *sed quamvis neuter mixtus uterque color.*

12 *spoiled:* stripped.

15 *needle:* hairpin.

16 *kembed:* combed.

17 *she:* her hair (the mistress's).

18 *drave:* drove.

19 *digested:* arranged.

21 *Thracian bacchanal:* Thrace was an indefinite stretch of land at the southeastern extremity of
Europe, to the north of Greece. Bacchanals were people who engaged in frenzied, sometimes or-
giastic festivals celebrating the god Bacchus (Dionysus).

26 *trammels:* braids.

30 *bodkin:* curling iron.

33 *Diana:* Dione is an alternative name for Venus, or sometimes the mother of Venus, and Ovid
clearly was referring to the painting by Apelles—the most celebrated painter of ancient Greece
who lived in the fourth century BCE—of Venus coming out of the ocean. Niger also talks at
length about this reference. Gill observes: "I cannot believe that Marlowe would have mistaken
Ovid's *Dione* for Diana, although it is an error that might be expected of a compositor replacing
the unknown by the known."

Why in thy glass dost look being discontent?
Be not to see with wonted eyes inclined;
To please thyself, thyself put out of mind.
No charmed herbs of any harlot scathed thee,
No faithless witch in Thessale waters bathed thee.   40
No sickness harmed thee (far be that away!),
No envious tongue wrought thy thick locks decay.
By thine own hand and fault thy hurt doth grow,
Thou mad'st thy head with compound poison flow.
Now Germany shall captive hair-tires send thee,   45
And vanquished people curious dressings lend thee,
Which some admiring, O thou oft wilt blush,
And say, "He likes me for my borrowed bush,
Praising for me some unknown Guelder dame,
But I remember when it was my fame."   50
Alas she almost weeps, and her white cheeks,
Dyed red with shame, to hide from shame she seeks.
She holds, and views her old locks in her lap;
Aye me, rare gifts unworthy such a hap.
Cheer up thyself, thy loss thou mayst repair,
And be hereafter seen with native hair.

ELEGIA XV

Ad invidos, quod fama poetarum sit perennis

Envy, why carp'st thou my time is spent so ill,
And term'st my works fruits of an idle quill?
Or that unlike the line from whence I come,
War's dusty honours are refused, being young?

---

39 *harlot:* rival.
45 *captive hair-tires:* "wigs from the hair of captives" (Orgel).
46 *curious dressings:* intricately woven wigs.
49 *Guelder:* German.
50 *my fame:* my own glory.
54 *rare {. . .} hap:* Marlowe's and Ovid's sense is "Rare gifts are unworthy of such ill fate (= placement in her lap)."
56 *native:* your own.

i *Ad {. . .} perennis:* To those who are envious that the fame of poets is eternal.
1 *carp'st:* renders *obicis* ("to object") and not *edax;* however, in Latin the verb *carpo* can mean the same as in English, as in "criticize' or "slander," and in his note on *edax* Niger quotes *Metamorphoses* 2.780–81: *sed videt ingratos intabescitque videndo / successus hominum carpitque et carpitur una* ("she is displeased—and it eats away at her—to see the successes of others, and her humiliation is that at once she reviles and is reviled").
4 *being young:* modifies "I" of line 3.

Nor that I study not the brawling laws, 5
Nor set my voice to sale in every cause?
Thy scope is mortal, mine eternal fame,
That all the world may ever chant my name.
Homer shall live while Tenedos stands and Ide,
Or into sea swift Simois doth slide. 10
Ascraeus lives while grapes with new wine swell,
Or men with crooked sickles corn down fell.
The world shall of Callimachus ever speak;
His art excelled, although his wit was weak.
For ever lasts high Sophocles' proud vein, 15
With sun and moon Aratus shall remain.
While bondmen cheat, fathers be hard, bawds whorish,
And strumpets flatter, shall Menander flourish.
Rude Ennius, and Plautus full of wit,
Are both in fame's eternal legend writ. 20
What age of Varro's name shall not be told,
And Jason's Argos and the fleece of gold?
Lofty Lucretius shall live that hour
That nature shall dissolve this earthly bower.
Aeneas' war, and Tityrus shall be read, 25
While Rome of all the conquered world is head.

---

5 *brawling:* for *verbosas* ("wordy"). According to dictionaries of the time, "to brawl" meant, for example, "to disagree in words," and in current usage it still carries a connotation of "noise."

9–10 *Tenedos:* island opposite Troy where Greeks hid to make the Trojans think they were going home. *Ide:* Mt. Ida, site of the Judgment of Paris, which set the stage for the Trojan War. *Simois:* river flowing from Mt. Ida.

11 *Ascraeus:* the Greek poet Hesiod who wrote, for example, *Works and Days,* which gives instructions on wine and corn.

13 *Callimachus:* a third-century BCE Alexandrian (Greek) poet.

14 *wit:* creative genius.

15 *Sophocles' {. . .} vein:* Sophocles was the fifth-century BCE Greek tragedian.

16 *With {. . .} remain:* Marlowe means, as does Ovid's Latin, "The poetry of Aratus will live as long as the sun and moon." Aratus was a third-century BCE Greek poet known best for his *Phaenomena,* a poem about astronomy.

18 *Menander:* Greek comedic dramatist of the fourth century BCE.

19 *Ennius:* second-century BCE Latin poet and first Latin epic poet. He is "rude" because while he is strong on creative genius, he lacks artistry and style (the opposite of Callimachus—earlier, line 13). *Plautus:* Marlowe mistakes Ovid's *Accius* for Marcus Accius Plautus, a Latin comedic playwright of the third century BCE; Ovid meant Lucius Accius, a Latin tragedian of the second century BCE.

21 *age:* generation. *Varro:* first-century BCE Latin epic poet who apparently wrote about Jason's Argo and the Golden Fleece.

23 *Lucretius:* first-century BCE writer of the great philosophical poem *De Rerum Natura.*

25 *Aeneas' war:* Virgil's *Aeneid. Tityrus:* Virgil's *Eclogues.* See later note on Ben Jonson's translation of this elegy.

Till Cupid's bow and fiery shafts be broken,
Thy verses, sweet Tibullus, shall be spoken.
And Gallus shall be known from east to west;
So shall Lycoris whom he loved best.   30
Therefore when flint and iron wear away,
Verse is immortal, and shall ne'er decay.
To verse let kings give place, and kingly shows, } *Reference to the Ren. stage?*
And banks o'er which gold-bearing Tagus flows.)
Let base-conceited wits admire vile things,   35
Fair Phoebus lead me to the Muses' springs.
About my head be quivering myrtle wound,
And in sad lovers' heads let me be found.
The living, not the dead, can envy bite,
For after death all men receive their right.   40
Then though death rakes my bones in funeral fire,
I'll live, and as he pulls me down mount higher.

The name by B J

Envy, why twitt'st thou me, my time's spent ill?
And call'st my verse fruits of an idle quill?
Or that (unlike the line from whence I sprung)
War's dusty honours I pursue not young?
Or that I study not the tedious laws,   5
And prostitute my voice in every cause?
Thy scope is mortal; mine eternal fame,
Which through the world shall ever chant my name.
Homer will live, whilst Tenedos stands, and Ide,
Or to the sea fleet Simois doth slide: 10
And so shall Hesiod too, while vines do bear,

---

28 *Tibullus:* Albius Tibullus, a first-century BCE Roman elegiac poet and precursor of Ovid, who
   was known especially for the smoothness and mellifluousness of his verse; in that regard, the Renaissance English poet Edmund Waller is often referred to as "the English Tibullus."
29 *Gallus:* early-first-century BCE writer of a Latin love elegy about a woman named Lycoris.
34 *Tagus:* a Spanish river believed to have gold in its riverbed.
37 *myrtle:* sacred to Venus.

Ben Jonson's translation of Elegy 1.15 is printed after Marlowe's translation in the third or complete edition of *All Ovid's Elegies.* Jonson prints his translation in his play *Poetaster* (1601) at
   1.1.43–84. Perhaps the most important emendation occurs at line 25: whereas Marlowe erases
   Virgil's genre of georgic poetry and scrambles the sacred Virgilian progression of genres from
   pastoral-georgic-epic to simply epic-pastoral, Jonson restores the sacred order (noted by
   MacLure). Jonson also importantly changes the meaning of Marlowe's concluding two lines
   about poetic fame. But what might be surprising is that Jonson accepts and repeats a large per-
   centage of Marlowe's poem and later prints it as his own, a form of poetic translation that looks ✓
   to modern eyes (but not to early modern ones) to be plagiarism.

Or crooked sickles corn the ripened ear;
Callimachus, though in invention low,
Shall still be sung, since he in art doth flow.
No loss shall come to Sophocles' proud vein;   15
With sun and moon Aratus shall remain.
Whilst slaves be false, fathers hard, and bawds be whorish,
Whilst harlots flatter, shall Menander flourish.
Ennius, though rude, and Accius' high-rear'd strain,
A fresh applause in every age shall gain.   20
Of Varro's name, what ear shall not be told?
Of Jason's Argos, and the fleece of gold?
Then shall Lucretius' lofty numbers die,
When earth and seas in fire and flames shall fry.
Tityrus, Tillage, Aeney shall be read,   25
Whilst Rome of all the conquered world is head.
Till Cupid's fires be out, and his bow broken,
Thy verses (neat Tibullus) shall be spoken.
Our Gallus shall be known from east to west;
So shall Lycoris, whom he now loves best.   30
The suffering ploughshare or the flint may wear,
But heavenly poesy no death can fear.
Kings shall give place to it, and kingly shows,
The banks o'er which gold-bearing Tagus flows.
Kneel hinds to trash: me let bright Phoebus swell,   35
With cups full flowing from the Muses' well.
The frost-drad myrtle shall impale my head,
And of sad lovers I'll be often read.
Envy the living, not the dead, doth bite,
For after death all men receive their right.   40
Then when this body falls in funeral fire,
My name shall live, and my best part aspire.

P. OVIDII NASONIS AMORUM, LIBER SECUNDUS

ELEGIA I

Quod pro gigantomachia amores scribere sit coactus
I, Ovid, poet of my wantonness,
Born at Peligny, to write more address.

---

i *Quod {. . .} coactus:* Why he is forced to write about love instead of about the wars in heaven.
2 *Peligny:* Ovid was born in Sulmo, which was inhabited by the Paeligny people. *to {. . .} address:*
   Marlowe means "set out to write more."

So Cupid wills; far hence be the severe:
You are unapt my looser lines to hear.
Let maids whom hot desire to husbands lead,   5
And rude boys touched with unknown love, me read,
That some youth hurt as I am with Love's bow
His own flame's best acquainted signs may know,
And long admiring say, "By what means learned
Hath this same poet my sad chance discerned?"   10
I durst the great celestial battles tell,
Hundred-hand Gyges, and had done it well,
With earth's revenge, and how Olympus' top
High Ossa bore, Mount Pelion up to prop.
Jove and Jove's thunderbolts I had in hand,   15
Which for his heaven fell on the giants' band.
My wench her door shut, Jove's affairs I left,
Even Jove himself out of my wit was reft.
Pardon me, Jove, thy weapons aid me nought,
Her shut gates greater lightning than thine brought.   20
Toys and light elegies, my darts, I took,
Quickly soft words hard doors wide open strook.
Verses reduce the horned bloody moon,
And call the sun's white horses back at noon.
Snakes leap by verse from caves of broken mountains,   25
And turned streams run backward to their fountains.
Verses ope doors; and locks put in the post,
Although of oak, to yield to verses boast.

---

3 *severe:* prudish.

5 *desire {. . .} lead:* subject and subjunctive verb after a relative (Martin).

9 *admiring:* amazed.

11–12 *celestial battles {. . .} Gyges:* The reference here is the *Gigantomachia,* or the battle of the race of Giants—who were half-human, half-divine; lived either on or in the Earth; and one of whom is Gyges [actually "Gyen" or "Gyas"]—against the Olympian deities.

13–14 *Olympus' top {. . .} prop:* In their attempt to scale to heaven to do battle with and to overthrow the gods, the Giants piled Mt. Pelion on Mt. Ossa, and Mt. Ossa on Mt. Olympus. Jove defeated them by throwing thunderbolts at the mountains, which caused the Giants to be thrown off and down (see lines 15–16).

15 *I {. . .} hand:* that is, he was about to write about this.

22 *strook:* struck.

23 *reduce:* bring down.

25 *Snakes {. . .} mountains:* The Latin is *carmine dissiliunt abruptis faucibus angues,* the literal translation of which is "poetry bursts snakes apart and pulls out their fangs." The consensus of editors is that this demonstrates Marlowe's complete failure, at least in this instance, to understand Latin. It is also quite possible, though, that Marlowe is here completing Jove's expulsion of the Giants from Olympus, which Ovid abruptly had to interrupt in line 17: many Renaissance mythographies speak of the Giants either as being snakes or as having the feet of snakes.

What helps it me of fierce Achill to sing?
What good to me will either Ajax bring?   30
Or he who warred and wandered twenty year?
Or woeful Hector, whom wild jades did tear?
But when I praise a pretty wench's face,
She in requital doth me oft embrace.
A great reward: heroes, O famous names,   35
Farewell; your favour nought my mind inflames.
Wenches, apply your fair looks to my verse,
Which golden Love doth unto me rehearse.

ELEGIA II

Ad Bagoum, ut custodiam puellae sibi commissae laxiorem habeat

Bagous, whose care doth thy mistress bridle,
While I speak some few but fit words, be idle.
I saw the damsel walking yesterday
There where the porch doth Danaus' fact display.
She pleased me soon, I sent, and her did woo,   5
Her trembling hand writ back she might not do.
And asking why, this answer she redoubled,
Because thy care too much thy mistress troubled.
Keeper, if thou be wise, cease hate to cherish;

---

29 *fierce:* with regard to *velox* ("swift"), Niger offers, for example, *iracundus* ("wrathful") among other adjectives used to modify Achilles. Achilles was the great and indispensable Greek warrior whose anger is the principal focus of the *Iliad.*

30 *either Ajax:* Marlowe's text read *Aiaces,* thus meaning the greater and lesser Ajaxes (Telemonian and Oileus) instead of the modern reading *Atrides,* which would mean Agamemnon and Menelaus, the sons of Atreus. All four are major Greek figures in the *Iliad.*

31 *he:* Odysseus.

32 *Hector {. . .} tear:* Hector was the greatest warrior for the Trojans. Achilles killed him and dragged his body around the walls of Troy on the back of his chariot. *jades:* horses.

i *Ad Bagoum {. . .} habeat:* To Bagous, that he be a more lax watchman over his (Ovid's) mistress who has been entrusted to his (Bagous's own) safekeeping.

1 *Bagous:* a frequently used name for eunuchs (McKeown), who are assigned, usually by their husbands, to chaperone women.

4 *Danaeus fact:* Green observes: "The cloister (or portico) described here was in the temple of Apollo on the Palatine. [. . .] It contained [. . .] statues of the fifty daughters of Danaus [, a king of Argos], and opposite them their fifty cousins and suitors, the sons of Aegyptos [, the brother of Danaus]. When forced into marriage, all the brides (with the single exception of Hypermnestra) killed their husbands on their wedding-night—an interesting association of ideas for this erotic elegy on the pursuit-and-rejection theme."

5–6 *She {. . .} do:* Marlowe's and Ovid's sense is "I fell in love with her at first sight, and sent a letter asking her to be with me (sexually), and she wrote back saying 'no.'"

Believe me, whom we fear, we wish to perish.   10
Nor is her husband wise; what needs defence,
When unprotected there is no expense?
But furiously he follow his love's fire,
And think her chaste whom many do desire.
Stol'n liberty she may by thee obtain,   15
Which giving her, she may give thee again.
Wilt thou her fault learn, she may make thee tremble;
Fear to be guilty, then thou mayst dissemble.
Think when she reads, her mother letters sent her;
Let him go forth known, that unknown did enter;   20
Let him go see her though she do not languish,
And then report her sick and full of anguish.
If long she stays, to think the time more short,
Lay down thy forehead in thy lap to snort.
Enquire not what with Isis may be done,   25
Nor fear lest she to the theatres run.
Knowing her scapes, thine honour shall increase,
And what less labour than to hold thy peace?
Let him please, haunt the house, be kindly used,
Enjoy the wench, let all else be refused.   30
Vain causes feign of him, the true to hide,
And what she likes let both hold ratified.
When most her husband bends the brows and frowns,
His fawning wench with her desire he crowns.

---

12 *When {. . .} expense:* MacLure notes: "The sense of the original is: 'Even if you didn't guard her,
nothing would be lost.'"

17–18 *Wilt {. . .} dissemble:* Marlowe's and Ovid's sense is: "A slave/guardian who is willing to conspire with his charge will gain her favor; if he is unwilling, at least he should pretend as if he
were willing and thereby still gain her favor."

21–22 *him:* her. The sense of the Latin is "Let her say that she has gone to see a sick female friend who
in fact is neither female nor sick, and even if you know the truth, you report it as she tells it to you."

24 *snort:* snore (i.e., take a nap).

25–26 *with Isis {. . .} theatres:* at the temple of Isis. Temples and theaters were notorious locations
for trysts.

27 *scapes:* escapades.

29–30 *Let {. . .} refused:* a difficult translation, partly because of Latin textual issues. The currently
accepted Latin is *ille placet versatque domum neque verbera sentit/ille potens alii sordida turba iacent,*
which translates as "the accomplice is favored, has the run of the house, is not punished for any-
thing; he is 'on top,' while all the others lie [at his feet] (= do his bidding)." Marlowe's Latin
line 30, however, likely read *ille placet dominae caetera turba iacet,* which is translated as "he pleases
(= does the bidding of) his mistress, while the rest of the crowd lie [at his feet] (= serve him)."

31 *of him:* for him (her husband).

32 *both:* husband and wife.

34 *he crowns:* He does what his wife wants.

But yet sometimes to chide thee let her fall 35
Counterfeit tears, and thee lewd hangman call.
Object thou then what she may well excuse,
To stain all faith in truth, by false crimes' use.
Of wealth and honour so shall grow thy heap;
Do this and soon thou shalt thy freedom reap. 40
On tell-tales' necks thou seest the link-knit chains,
The filthy prison faithless breasts restrains.
Water in waters, and fruit flying touch
Tantalus seeks, his long tongue's gain is such;
While Juno's watchman Io too much eyed, 45
Him timeless death took, she was deified.
I saw one's legs with fetters black and blue,
By whom the husband his wife's incest knew.
More he deserved; to both great harm he framed;
The man did grieve, the woman was defamed. 50
Trust me, all husbands for such faults are sad,
Nor make they any man that hear them glad.
If he loves not, deaf ears thou dost importune;
Or if he loves, thy tale breeds his misfortune.
Nor is it easily proved, though manifest, 55

37–38 *Object {. . .} use:* Marlowe's and Ovid's sense is "In return, you should call into question activities of hers which she can easily explain away; in so concocting a false charge and its easy explanation, you can divest true accusations of any credibility." This elegy, both here and elsewhere, is remarkably reminiscent of the basic theme of Shakespeare's sonnet 138.

43–44 *Water {. . .} such:* Tantalus angered the gods by failing to keep their secrets (by one account) or by stealing their food (by another account). He was sentenced for eternity to stand in a pool of fresh water that always receded when he stooped to drink, and near a tree with delicious fruit, which likewise always receded just beyond his reach when he would try to pluck and eat it. From this comes the verb "to tantalize," in that the water and tree constituted an endless teasing of Tantalus. Noteworthy is that Marlowe renders, exactly, Ovid's "Tantalizing" suspension, and enjambment, of Tantalus's name at the beginning of the second line of the couplet (*quaerit aquas in aquis et poma fugacia captat / Tantalus: hoc illi garrula lingua dedit*).

45–46 *While {. . .} deified:* Io was a priestess of Hera (= Juno) whom Hera turned into a heifer because Zeus loved her. Hera assigned hundred-eyed Argus to be her watchman over Io. Zeus commissioned Hermes to kill Argus, but Hera set Io to flight by sending a gadfly after her to pursue and bother her perpetually. Io's flight finally ended in Egypt, which is why she is often thought to have been an *alter ego* of the goddess Isis.

46 *Him {. . .} took:* Death took him too young.

47 *one's:* a watchman's.

48 *incest:* adultery. Marlowe apparently translated the Latin *incestum* very literally, though in antiquity and in the Renaissance the Latin word extended to all kinds of illicit sexual relations, and there is some indication that the same was true of the English word itself in the Renaissance.

53 *If {. . .} not:* If the husband does not love his wife . . .

55 *it:* a wife's transgression.

She safe by favour of her judge doth rest.
Though himself see, he'll credit her denial,
Condemn his eyes, and say there is no trial.
Spying his mistress' tears, he will lament
And say, "This blab shall suffer punishment." 60
Why fight'st 'gainst odds? to thee, being cast, do hap
Sharp stripes; she sitteth in the judge's lap.
To meet for poison or vile facts we crave not,
My hands an unsheathed shining weapon have not.
We seek that, through thee, safely love we may; 65
What can be easier than the thing we pray?

Elegia III

Ad Eunuchum servantem dominam

Aye me, an eunuch keeps my mistress chaste,
That cannot Venus' mutual pleasure taste.
Who first deprived young boys of their best part,
With selfsame wounds he gave he ought to smart.
To kind requests thou wouldst more gentle prove, 5
If ever wench had made lukewarm thy love:
Thou wert not born to ride, or arms to bear,
Thy hands agree not with the warlike spear.
Men handle those; all manly hopes resign,
Thy mistress' ensigns must be likewise thine. 10
Please her, her hate makes others thee abhor;
If she discards thee, what use serv'st thou for?
Good form there is, years apt to play together,
Unmeet is beauty without use to wither.

---

56 *judge:* husband.
58 *trial:* transgression.
60 *blab:* storyteller (liar).
61 *cast:* undone, defeated.
62 *stripes:* lashes (floggings with a whip).
63 *vile facts:* evil deeds.

i *Ad {. . .} dominam:* To the eunuch guarding his mistress.
2 *That:* who (the eunuch).
3 *Who:* He who.
6 *made lukewarm:* understand "even" between these two words.
11 *her hate {. . .} abhor:* Ovid's sense is "Her good will is to your favor" (*huius tibi gratia prosit*).
13 *Good {. . .} together:* The Latin *est etiam facies sunt apti lusibus anni* means "her beauty and youth make her ripe for the games of love."
14 *Unmeet {. . .} wither:* Marlowe's and Ovid's sense is "It is unfitting for such beauty to be wasted by not being enjoyed" (*indigna est pigro forma perire situ*).

She may deceive thee, though thou her protect,   15
What two determine never wants effect.
Our prayers move thee to assist our drift,
While thou hast time yet to bestow that gift.

ELEGIA IV

Quod amet mulieres, cuiuscunque formae sint
I mean not to defend the scapes of any,
Or justify my vices being many.
For I confess, if that might merit favour,
Here I display my lewd and loose behaviour.
I loathe, yet after that I loathe I run;   5
O how the burden irks, that we should shun.
I cannot rule myself, but where love please
Am driven like a ship upon rough seas.
No one face likes me best, all faces move,
A hundred reasons make me ever love.   10
If any eye me with a modest look,
I burn, and by that blushful glance am took.
And she that's coy I like, for being no clown,
Methinks she would be nimble when she's down.
Though her sour looks a Sabine's brow resemble,   15
I think she'll do, but deeply can dissemble.
If she be learned, then for her skill I crave her;
If not, because she's simple I would have her.
Before Callimachus one prefers me far;
Seeing she likes my books, why should we jar?   20

---

18 *While {. . .} yet:* While you are still in a position . . .

i *Quod {. . .} sint:* He loves every kind of woman. This poem is a possible inspiration for Donne's
"The Indifferent."
1 *scapes of any:* my own cheating ways (*mendosos mores*).
5 *that:* that which.
6 *irks:* Ovid's words literally convey the idea that this burden is serious and heavy (*grave*); however,
that particular claim, as well as the whole tone of this elegy, is tongue-in-cheek. While "irks"
connotes something much lighter and less serious than Ovid's words literally convey, and while
it therefore might seem to be an inappropriate translation, in fact it is completely in keeping
with the bemused and sarcastic sensibility pervading this elegy and in this particular line.
9 *likes:* attracts.
13 *clown:* rustic, unsophisticated girl.
15 *sour:* sober. Sabine women were known for their quiet and continent morality.
16 *do:* be willing (sexually). *but {. . .} dissemble:* she misrepresents how she truly feels.
19–20 *Before {. . .} jar:* A clearer sense of the Latin is "If a girl tells me that Callimachus's poems
are unsophisticated compared to mine, then of course I will immediately be attracted to such a

Another rails at me, and that I write;
Yet would I lie with her if that I might.
Trips she, it likes me well; plods she, what then?
She would be nimbler, lying with a man.
And when one sweetly sings, then straight I long   25
To quaver on her lips even in her song.
Or if one touch the lute with art and cunning,
Who would not love those hands for their swift running?
And her I like that with a majesty
Folds up her arms and makes low courtesy.   30
To leave myself, that am in love with all,
Some one of these might make the chastest fall.
If she be tall, she's like an Amazon,
And therefore fills the bed she lies upon;
If short, she lies the rounder; to say troth,   35
Both short and long please me, for I love both.
I think what one undecked would be, being dressed;
Is she attired? then show her graces best.
A white wench thralls me, so doth golden yellow,

---

person who praises me so highly" (*est quae Callimachi prae nostris rustica dicat/carmina cui placeo protinus ipsa placet*). Callimachus (see 1.15.13) was a third-century BCE Greek poet whom Ovid highly respected especially for the sophisticated artistry of his poetry. The scansion of Marlowe's couplet also merits attention. Both the rhythm of line 19 and its metrical complementarity with line 20 demand that the last two syllables of "Callimachus" be unaccented and count as the single unaccented syllable of the third iamb. Both lines, then, become iambic pentameter without an eleventh unaccented syllable at the end, and this is remarkable because of the feminine rhyme of this couplet: usually, feminine rhymes employ the eleventh unaccented syllable.

21 *that:* that which.

23 *Trips {. . .} plods:* treads lightly [. . .] treads hard.

29–30 *And {. . .} courtesy:* The sense of the Latin (*illa placet gestu numerosaque bracchia ducit/et tenerum molli torquet ab arte latus*) is "Another girl pleases me with her dancing, moving her arms rhythmically and turning her slender side with smooth skill."

31–32 *To {. . .} fall:* The sense of the Latin (*ut taceam de me qui causa tangor ab omni/illic Hippolytum pone Priapus erit*) is "Put Hippolytus in front of her—not to mention me, who is attracted to every woman—and he will be Priapus!" Hippolytus, the asexual son of Theseus and stepson of Phaedra, was a symbol of sexual disinterest; Priapus, son of Aphrodite and Dionysus, was the god of fertility and was signified by a permanently erect phallus.

33 *Amazon:* heroines of old (*veteres heroidas*).

37–38 *I {. . .} best:* The sense of the Latin (*non est culta subit quid cultae accedere possit / ornata est dotes exhibet ipsa suas*) is difficult and somewhat ambiguous, but is perhaps best understood as "a woman who is not well dressed and coiffed—though I might wonder what she would look like if she were—is sufficiently well adorned nevertheless: she herself is her own dowry and is attractive as she is." The more common constructions of the Latin interpret this couplet to refer to two different women—one who is well dressed, one who is not; in that case, the Latin pentameter would be translated "a well adorned woman exhibits her beauty through her rich attire." However, the sense, diction, and grammar seem more indicative of one woman.

39 *thralls:* enthralls, subdues.

And nut-brown girls in doing have no fellow.   40
If her white neck be shadowed with black hair,
Why, so was Leda's, yet was Leda fair.
Amber-tressed is she? then on the morn think I;
My love alludes to every history.
A young wench pleaseth, and an old is good: 45
This for her looks, that for her womanhood.
Nay what is she that any Roman loves
But my ambitious ranging mind approves?

ELEGIA V

Ad amicam corruptam

No love is so dear (quivered Cupid, fly!)
That my chief wish should be so oft to die.
Minding thy fault, with death I wish to revel;
Alas, a wench is a perpetual evil.
No intercepted lines thy deeds display,   5
No gifts given secretly thy crime bewray:
O would my proofs as vain might be withstood,
Aye me, poor soul, why is my cause so good?
He's happy, that his love dares boldly credit,

---

40 *in doing {. . .} fellow:* in making love have no equal. The "have no equal" does not properly render the Latin, which simply places dark women on the same level with fair ones (*est etiam in fusco grata colore venus*). And, while most translators simply say that a dark woman is also attractive, without bringing sex into the translation, Marlowe is on firm ground, indeed is the more correct, to do so ("doing") because "Venus" means not only the goddess of love and sex but also those very attributes that she signifies.

42 *Leda's:* See 1.10.3n.

43 *morn:* Aurora, goddess of the dawn.

44 *My {. . .} history:* Marlowe's and Ovid's sense is "My love life evokes all the women and love stories of mythology."

47–48 *Nay {. . .} approves?:* Marlowe's and Ovid's sense is "Whatever kinds of women are found in Rome, I am ready to love all of them."

i *Ad {. . .} corruptam:* To his unfaithful mistress.

3 *Minding {. . .} revel:* Ovid's Latin (*vota mori mea sunt cum te pecasse recordor*) is more clearly translated as "Ever mindful of your sexual betrayals to me, I am always praying for (my own) death."

5 *intercepted:* Some earlier texts had *deprensae* ("detected") instead of *deceptae* ("camouflaged"). Niger does not have it or mention it, but his one-word annotation for *deceptae* is *"interceptae."* *lines:* (love) letters.

7–8 *O {. . .} good:* Marlowe's and Ovid's sense is "I wish that the evidence of infidelity I have were wrong and thus so too would be my accusation" (*O utinam arguerem sic ut non vincere possem / me miserum quare tam bona causa mea est*).

9 *that:* who.

To whom his wench can say, "I never did it." 10
He's cruel, and too much his grief doth favour,
That seeks the conquest by her loose behaviour.
Poor wench, I saw when thou didst think I slumbered;
Not drunk, your faults on the spilt wine I numbered.
I saw your nodding eyebrows much to speak, 15
Even from your cheeks part of a voice did break.
Not silent were thine eyes, the board with wine
Was scribbled, and thy fingers writ a line.
I knew your speech (what do not lovers see?)
And words that seemed for certain marks to be. 20
Now many guests were gone, the feast being done,
The youthful sort to divers pastimes run.
I saw you then unlawful kisses join
(Such with my tongue it likes me to purloin).
None such the sister gives her brother grave, 25
But such kind wenches let their lovers have.
Phoebus gave not Diana such, 'tis thought,
But Venus often to her Mars such brought.
"What dost?" I cried, "transport'st thou my delight?
My lordly hands I'll throw upon my right. 30
Such bliss is only common to us two,
In this sweet good, why hath a third to do?"
This, and what grief enforced me say, I said;
A scarlet blush her guilty face arrayed,
Even such as by Aurora hath the sky, 35

13–14 *Poor {. . .} numbered:* more clearly and correctly, "I, wretched but rather sober, saw your (sexual) transgressions when you thought I had fallen asleep from drinking the wine you had given me" (*ipse miser vidi cum me dormire putares / sobrius apposito crimina vestra mero*).

15–16 *your {. . .} your:* These two possessive pronouns refer to both the mistress and her lover.

19 *I {. . .} (what {. . .} see?):* Marlowe's text (and Niger's) read, indeed, *sermonem agnovi (quid non videatur amanti?)*. Modern texts read *sermonem agnovi quod non videatur agentem* ("I recognized your speech to be saying things not readily apparent in the words themselves").

24 *it likes me to purloin:* I like to steal.

27 *Phoebus {. . .} Diana:* Phoebus (god of the sun, of healing, and of poetry) and Diana (goddess of the moon, of virgins, and of the hunt) were brother and sister.

28 *Venus {. . .} Mars:* Venus (goddess of love) and Mars (god of war) carried on an infamous love affair.

29 *dost:* are you doing. *transport'st thou my delight?:* Ovid's sense is "Where are you spreading joys (kisses) that should be reserved only for me?" (*quo nunc mea gaudia defers*).

30 *my right:* those things that are rightfully mine alone.

32 *third:* third person (interloper).

34 *arrayed:* permeated.

35 *Aurora:* the dawn.

Or maids that their betrothed husbands spy;
Such as a rose mixed with a lily breeds,
Or when the moon travails with charmed steeds,
Or such as, lest long years should turn the dye,
Arachne stains Assyrian ivory.   40
To these, or some of these, like was her colour,
By chance her beauty never shined fuller.
She viewed the earth: the earth to view beseemed her.
She looked sad: sad, comely I esteemed her.
Even kembed as they were, her locks to rend,   45
And scratch her fair soft cheeks I did intend.
Seeing her face, mine upreared arms descended,
With her own armour was my wench defended.
I that erewhile was fierce, now humbly sue,
Lest with worse kisses she should me endue.   50
She laughed, and kissed so sweetly as might make
Wrath-kindled Jove away his thunder shake.
I grieve lest others should such good perceive,
And wish hereby them all unknown to leave.
Also much better were they than I tell,   55
And ever seemed as some new sweet befell.

---

36 *betrothed husbands:* "The *sponsus novus* may be either a newly affianced suitor or a new bridegroom" (McKeown). *spy:* look upon. According to the Latin, "husbands" is the subject of "spy," though in the English the subject could also be "maids."

37 *breeds:* a likely alternative spelling of the archaic "bredes" for "braids," thus "intertwines." While Marlowe omits the Latin *fulgent,* he may have picked up on Niger's citation of several classical authors who write of intertwining roses and lilies, especially Pliny, *Nat.* xxi. 22: *lilium {. . .} impositum* [*sic* Niger, but actually *interpositum*] *maxime rosas decet* ("a lily is most attractive when intertwined with roses").

38 *travails {. . .} steeds:* struggles to drive her chariot.

40 *Arachne:* Martin observes: "There is no reference to Arachne here [in Ovid], but in Ovid's *Metamorphoses* 6, Arachne has the epithet 'Maeonia' and her father dyes his wool." Arachne was turned into a spider by Minerva after losing a needlework contest with the goddess and hanging herself. There is no reference to her in Niger's commentary.

43 *viewed the earth {. . .} earth to view:* Marlowe's chiasmus precisely renders Ovid's *spectabat terram terram spectare.*

44 *sad, comely {. . .} her:* Marlowe's and Ovid's sense is "Her sadness befitted her and made her comely" (*maesta erat in vultu maesta decenter erat*).

45 *kembed:* literally, "combed," and here meaning "well arranged."

50 *worse:* that is, worse than those described earlier in 23 ff.

53 *good perceive:* good kisses have.

54 *And {. . .} leave:* The sense of the Latin is "And I do not want another to have this particular special kiss of yours" (*et volo non ex hac illa fuisse nota*).

55–56 *Also {. . .} befell:* The sense of the Latin is "And those kisses are much better than the ones I taught you; you seem to have added some new (kissing) tricks to your repertoire" (*haec quoque quam docui multo meliora fuerunt / et quiddam visa est addidicisse novi*).

'Tis ill they pleased so much, for in my lips
Lay her whole tongue hid, mine in hers she dips.
This grieves me not; no joined kisses spent
Bewail I only, though I them lament.   60
Nowhere can they be taught but in the bed;
I know no master of so great hire sped.

ELEGIA VI

In mortem psittaci

The parrot, from east India to me sent,
Is dead; all fowls her exequies frequent!
Go, godly birds, striking your breasts bewail,
And with rough claws your tender cheeks assail.
For woeful hairs let piece-torn plumes abound,   5
For long shrilled trumpets let your notes resound.
Why, Philomel, dost Tereus' lewdness mourn?
All-wasting years have that complaint outworn.
Thy tunes let this rare bird's sad funeral borrow,
Itys is great, but ancient cause of sorrow.   10
All you whose pinions in the clear air soar,
But most, thou friendly turtle dove, deplore;
Full concord all your lives was you betwixt,
And to the end your constant faith stood fixed.
What Pylades did to Orestes prove,   15
Such to the parrot was the turtle dove.
But what availed this faith? her rarest hue?
Or voice that how to change the wild notes knew?

---

59 *This {. . .} not:* This is not the only thing I grieve (*nec tamen hoc unum doleo*).
62 *I [. . .] sped:* Marlowe's and Ovid's sense is "I do not know the teacher who has received this great
reward."

i *In mortem psittaci:* On the death of his parrot.
7 *dost:* do you. Philomel was raped by her brother-in-law Tereus, who cut out her tongue so that
she could not report who violated her. She instead wove a tapestry that indicated her assailant.
She then with her sister took revenge by feeding Tereus his son Itys. Philomel was later turned
into a nightingale. See Ovid, *Metamorphoses* 6.426–674.
12 *deplore:* "grieve" ("you" [line 11] and "turtle dove" are both subjects of this verb).
15 *Pylades {. . .} Orestes:* first cousins known for their mutual friendship and loyalty. Pylades helped
his cousin Orestes murder Orestes's mother Clytemnestra in order to avenge her murder of her
husband (Orestes's father) Agamemnon.
18 *Or {. . .} knew?:* The sense of the Latin (*quid vox mutandis ingeniosa sonis*) is "a voice skilled in
mimicking sounds." There is no apparent warrant or explanation for Marlowe's "wild"; however,
his use of "notes" for "sounds," while certainly a valid translation on its own, might be explained
by Niger's citation of an earlier textual variant—which Niger himself rejects—of *notis* for *sonis*.
Modern textual *apparati critici* make no note of such a variant.

What helps it thou wert given to please my wench?
Birds' hapless glory, death thy life doth quench.   20
Thou with thy quills mightst make green emeralds dark,
And pass our scarlet of red saffron's mark;
No such voice-feigning bird was on the ground,
Thou spokest thy words so well with stammering sound.
Envy hath rapt thee, no fierce wars thou movedst,   25
Vain babbling speech and pleasant peace thou lovedst.
Behold how quails among their battles live,
Which do perchance old age unto them give.
A little filled thee, and for love of talk,
Thy mouth to taste of many meats did balk.   30
Nuts were thy food, and poppy caused thee sleep,
Pure water's moisture thirst away did keep.
The ravenous vulture lives, the puttock hovers
Around the air, the cadess rain discovers,
And crow survives arms-bearing Pallas' hate,   35
Whose life nine ages scarce bring out of date.
Dead is that speaking image of man's voice,
The parrot given me, the far world's best choice.
The greedy spirits take the best things first,
Supplying their void places with the worst.   40
Thersites did Protesilaus survive,

---

20 *Birds' {. . .} glory:* appositive to an understood "you."
21 *quills: pinnis* implies the feathers of wings, and it needs to be remembered that the feather consists of soft down attached to a central spine or "quill." Moreover, the second definition in Cooper is "quills." *green:* Marlowe's text had *viridis* instead of *fragiles.*
22 *And {. . .} mark:* The sense of the Latin (*tincta gerens rubro Punica rostra croco*) is "Your beak was red tinged with yellow." Marlowe very likely read *rostra* as *nostra*. Still, his line is difficult, and "pass" means "surpass."
23 *on the ground:* in all the world.
25 *rapt thee:* taken your life. *fierce {. . .} movedst:* "thou" is the subject, "wars" the object.
29–30 *A {. . .} balk:* The sense is that the parrot is so busy talking all the time that his mouth is always filled with words, and therefore he has very little time, and very little space in his mouth, for food.
33 *puttock:* kite (a kind of hawk).
34 *cadess:* jackdaw (a kind of crow).
35–36 *And {. . .} date:* Gill observes: "In Ovid's *Metamorphoses,* ii. 552 ff, the Crow tells why she is hated by Pallas Athene (Minerva). An attempt to ravish Athene by Vulcan resulted in the birth of Erichthonius, whom Pallas tried to smuggle away. The Crow saw what happened, and talked about it." And Mckeown: "The crow is perhaps cited at the culmination of the catalogue [of birds in this elegy] not only because it was so particularly well known for longevity, but also because a contrast is implied between its loss of its mistress' favour and the parrot's retention of Corinna's."
41–42 *Thersites {. . .} alive:* Protesilaus was the first Greek hero killed at Troy, and Hector, greatest warrior of the Trojans, died before the sack of Troy where most or all of his remaining brothers died. Thersites was a base character in the Greek camp.

And Hector died, his brothers yet alive.
My wench's vows for thee what should I show,
Which stormy south winds into sea did blow?
The seventh day came, none following mightst thou see,　　45
And the Fate's distaff empty stood to thee;
Yet words in thy benumbed palate rung:
"Farewell, Corinna," cried thy dying tongue.
Elysium hath a wood of holm-trees black,
Whose earth doth not perpetual green grass lack;　　50
There good birds rest (if we believe things hidden)
Whence unclean fowls are said to be forbidden;
There harmless swans feed all abroad the river,
There lives the Phoenix one alone bird ever,
There Juno's bird displays his gorgeous feather,　　55
And loving doves kiss eagerly together.
The parrot into wood received with these,
Turns all the goodly birds to what she please.
A grave her bones hides; on her corpse' great grave
The little stones these little verses have:　　60
"This tomb approves I pleased my mistress well,
My mouth in speaking did all birds excel."

ELEGIA VII

Amicae se purgat quod ancillam non amet
Dost me of new crimes always guilty frame?
To overcome, so oft to fight I shame.
If on the marble theatre I look,
One among many is to grieve thee took.
If some faire wench me secretly behold,　　5
Thou arguest she doth secret marks unfold.
If I praise any, thy poor hairs thou tearest;
If blame, dissembling of my fault thou fearest.

---

45 *seventh day:* "the seventh [. . .] day of an illness was regarded as critical" (McKeown).
46 *Fate's distaff:* a reference to the prominent motif of the personification of Fate as a goddess, or three goddesses, who weave, spin, and ultimately cut the thread of life.
49 *holm-tree:* ilex.
55 *Juno's bird:* the peacock.
i *Amicae {. . .} amet:* He acquits himself to his mistress of the charge that he loves her maidservant Cypassis.
4 *One {. . .} took:* Ovid's and Marlowe's sense is "You will think that I am looking at one (out of many) particularly attractive woman" (*elegis e multis unde dolere velis*).

If I look well, thou think'st thou dost not move;
If ill, thou say'st I die for others' love.   10
Would I were culpable of some offence,
They that deserve pain, bear't with patience.
Now rash accusing, and thy vain belief,
Forbid thine anger to procure my grief.
Lo, how the miserable great-eared ass,   15
Dulled with much beating, slowly forth doth pass.
Behold Cypassis, wont to dress thy head,
Is charged to violate her mistress' bed.
The gods from this sin rid me of suspicion,
To like a base wench of despised condition.   20
With Venus' game who will a servant grace?
Or any back made rough with stripes embrace?
Add she was diligent thy locks to braid,
And for her skill to thee a grateful maid,
Should I solicit her that is so just,   25
To take repulse, and cause her show my lust?
I swear by Venus, and the winged boy's bow,
Myself unguilty of this crime I know.

ELEGIA VIII

Ad Cypassim ancillam Corinnae

Cypassis, that a thousand ways trim'st hair,
Worthy to kemb none but a goddess fair,
Our pleasant scapes show thee no clown to be,
Apt to thy mistress, but more apt to me.
Who that our bodies were compressed bewrayed?   5

---

9 *If {. . .} move:* Marlowe's and Ovid's sense is "If I look well, you think it is because you are not having an effect on me [because someone else is giving me her love]" (*sive bonus color est in te quoque frigidus esse*).
18 *to violate:* of violating.
19–20 *The {. . .} condition:* understand "May" to begin this couplet.
24 *grateful:* pleasing (*grata*).
25–26 *Should {. . .} lust?:* Marlowe's and Ovid's sense is "Why should I chase after her who, because she is your servant, would reject me and then tell you of my interest in her?" (*scilicet ancillam quod erat tibi fida rogarem? / quid nisi ut indicio iuncta repulsa foret*).

i *Ad {. . .} Corinnae:* To Cypassis, Corinna's maidservant.
2 *kemb none but:* comb only.
3 *scapes:* escapades. *clown:* a naive or unsophisticated rustic (a "country bumpkin").
4 *Apt {. . .} apt:* suited [. . .] suited.
5 *Who {. . .} bewrayed?:* Ovid's sense is "Who has insinuated that we are having an affair?" (*quis fuit inter nos sociati corporis index?*).

Whence knows Corinna that with thee I played?
Yet blushed I not, nor used I any saying,
That might be urged to witness our false playing.
What if a man with bondwomen offend,
To prove him foolish did I e'er contend?   10
Achilles burned with face of captive Briseis,
Great Agamemnon loved his servant Chryseis.
Greater than these myself I not esteem;
What graced kings, in me no shame I deem.
But when on thee her angry eyes did rush,   15
In both thy cheeks she did perceive thee blush.
But being present, might that work the best,
By Venus' deity how did I protest!
Thou, goddess, dost command a warm south blast
My false oaths in Carpathian seas to cast.   20
For which good turn my sweet reward repay,
Let me lie with thee, brown Cypass, today.
Ungrate, why feignest new fears, and dost refuse?
Well mayst thou one thing for thy mistress use.
If thou deniest, fool, I'll our deeds express,   25
And as a traitor mine own fault confess,
Telling thy mistress where I was with thee,
How oft, and by what means we did agree.

---

8 *That {. . .} playing:* Ovid's sense is "That might have exposed our affair" (*furtivae Veneris conscia signa dedi?*).

9–10 *What {. . .} contend?:* Ovid's sense is "Should I actually maintain that a man would be crazy to fall in love with a slave?" (*quid quod in ancilla si quis delinquere possit/illum ego contendi mente carere bona?*). This is a rhetorical question, as is evinced by the following examples of mythological heroes who had affairs with slavegirls.

11–12 *Achilles {. . .} Chryseis:* Achilles was the great warrior, and Agamemnon the commander-in-chief, of the Greek host at Troy. As Orgel succinctly notes: "Chryseis was Agamemnon's prisoner; when forced to return her to Troy to avert a plague, he took Achilles' prisoner Briseis instead, thus prompting Achilles' wrath and retirement from the war."

16 *she did perceive:* Marlowe's text had *vidit;* modern ones have *vidi* ("I did perceive").

17–18 *But {. . .} protest!:* MacLure writes: "a far from clear translation of 'but how much more self-possessed I was, if you remember, when I swore my fidelity by the mighty name of Venus.'"

20 *My false oaths:* Modern Latin editions have the oxymoronic *animi periuria puri* ("the false oaths of a pure heart"), but Marlowe's text had *nostri* for *puri. Carpathian:* the Aegean Sea between Crete and Rhodes, so called from the island Carpathus (Orgel and MacLure).

23 *Ungrate:* Ingrate (vocative address).

24 *Well {. . .} use.:* The Latin (*unum est e dominis emeruisse satis*) says "It is enough to have merited the approval of one of your masters." There is no apparent explanation for Marlowe's translation.

28 *and {. . .} agree:* and in what ways (positions) we had sex.

ELEGIA IX

Ad Cupidinem

O Cupid, that dost never cease my smart,
O boy, that liest so slothful in my heart,
Why me that always was thy soldier found,
Dost harm, and in thy tents why dost me wound?
Why burns thy brand, why strikes thy bow thy friends?   5
More glory by thy vanquished foes ascends.
Did not Pelides whom his spear did grieve,
Being required, with speedy help relieve?
Hunters leave taken beasts, pursue the chase,
And than things found do ever further pace.   10
We people wholly given thee feel thine arms,
Thy dull hand stays thy striving enemies' harms.
Dost joy to have thy hooked arrows shaked
In naked bones? love hath my bones left naked.
So many men and maidens without love!   15
Hence with great laud thou mayst a triumph move.
Rome, if her strength the huge world had not filled,
With strawy cabins now her courts should build.
The weary soldier hath the conquered fields,
His sword laid by, safe, though rude places yields.   20
The dock inharbours ships drawn from the floods,
Horse freed from service range abroad the woods.

---

i *Ad Cupidinem:* To Cupid.

4 *thy:* Marlowe's text had *tuis;* modern ones have *meis.*

7 *Pelides:* Achilles. *whom:* him whom—the object of both "grieve" and "relieve" (8)—= Telephus. Achilles wounded him and subsequently cured him by scraping rust onto his wound from the very sword that wounded him.

8 *Being required:* Marlowe's text had *cum petiit;* modern texts have *confossum* ("pierced thoroughly" or, literally, "dug in").

10 *And {. . .} pace:* Ovid's sense is "And pursue prey yet to be sighted more so than that which has already been found" (*semper et inventis ulteriora petit*). (We are grateful to James McKeown for help with this line.)

11–12 *arms:* weapons. Ovid's sense is "Those of us who readily acknowledge your sovereignty cannot resist your overwhelming power, and we feel the pain and weight of your weapons; yet, you are slow to move against those who do try to resist you" (*nos tua sentimus populus tibi deditus arma / pigra reluctanti cessat in hoste manus*).

13–14 *Dost {. . .} bones?:* Marlowe's and Ovid's sense is "Does it give you pleasure to mash your hooked arrows on naked bones?" (*quid iuvat in nudis hamata retundere tela / ossibus? ossa mihi nuda reliquit Amor*). The intent is similar to that of "pouring salt on an open wound."

17 *Rome {. . .} filled:* "strength" is the subject and "world" is the object of "filled."

19–22 *The {. . .} woods:* The problem is that Marlowe's lines 20 and line 22 are, in modern texts, reversed. The sense of the two couplets then is "The weary soldier retires to the fields he earned

And time it was for me to live in quiet,
That have so oft served pretty wenches' diet.
Yet should I curse a god, if he but said,   25
"Live without love," so sweet ill is a maid.
For when my loathing it of heat deprives me,
I know not whither my mind's whirlwind drives me.
Even as a headstrong courser bears away
His rider vainly striving him to stay,   30
Or as a sudden gale thrusts into sea
The haven-touching bark now near the lea,
So wavering Cupid brings me back amain,
And purple Love resumes his darts again.
Strike, boy, I offer thee my naked breast,   35
Here thou hast strength, here thy right hand doth rest.
Here of themselves thy shafts come, as if shot;
Better than I their quiver knows them not.
Hapless is he that all the night lies quiet,
And slumb'ring, thinks himself much blessed by it.   40
Fool, what is sleep but image of cold death?
Long shalt thou rest when Fates expire thy breath.
But me let crafty damsel's words deceive,
Great joys by hope I inly shall conceive.
Now let her flatter me, now chide me hard,   45

---

for his service; the race-horse to the pasture; ships to dry-dock; and the pointed sword is laid aside for the blunted sword."

27–28 *For {. . .} me:* a confused translation of *cum bene pertaesum est animoque relanguit ardor/nescioquo miserae turbine mentis agor* ("When I have wearied of love and my passion for love has cooled, I am driven, I know not why, by a despairing storm in my heart"). That Marlowe's text had *animi* for *animo* and *revanuit* ("vanished") for *relanguit* ("cooled") does not account for the difficulty of the translation.

30 *striving him to stay:* striving to stay (= restrain) him.

32 *haven:* implying land as safe haven from a stormy sea.

33 *wavering Cupid:* unpredictable love. The Latin here continues and complements the metaphor of rough seas by referring specifically to, and implying, the "inconstant winds [on the sea] of love" (*incerta Cupidinis aura*). Marlowe's rendering lacks this essential feature of the original.

34 *purple:* blushing.

35 *my naked breast:* myself unarmed.

36 *rest:* have power ("strike" from line 35).

37 *as if shot:* as if summoned (*tamquam iussae*). Unfortunately, the use of "shot" confounds the sense of "of themselves" for *sponte* ("of their own accord," or, perhaps better, "on their own power").

44 *Great {. . .} conceive:* I shall make great joys for myself merely by hoping (*sperando certe gaudia magna feram*). *joys:* Marlowe's text read *gaudia,* modern texts *praemia. inly:* inwardly ("inside myself").

Let her enjoy me oft, oft be debarred.
Cupid, by thee Mars in great doubt doth trample,
And thy stepfather fights by thy example.
Light art thou, and more windy than thy wings;
Joys with uncertain faith thou takest and brings.   50
Yet, Love, if thou with thy fair mother hear,
Within my breast no desert empire bear;
Subdue the wand'ring wenches to thy reign,
So of both people shalt thou homage gain.

ELEGIA X

Ad Graecinum quod eodem tempore duas amet

Graecinus (well I wot) thou told'st me once
I could not be in love with two at once.
By thee deceived, by thee surprised am I,
For now I love two women equally.
Both are well favoured, both rich in array,   5
Which is the loveliest it is hard to say.
This seems the fairest, so doth that to me,
And this doth please me most, and so doth she.
Even as a boat tossed by contrary wind,
So with this love and that, wavers my mind.   10

---

46 *Let {. . .} debarred:* In the Latin it is the speaker who enjoys her and who is "debarred."

47 *Cupid {. . .} trample:* Ovid's sense is "Cupid, it is because of you that your stepfather Mars (= war and warfare) is unpredictable" (*quod dubius Mars est per te privigne Cupido est*). McKeown writes: "Dr. Debra Hershkowitz points out to me that, instead of love being likened to war by the conventional metaphor of *militia amoris,* developed particularly in 1.9, here, by a neat reversal, the nature of war is attributed to love."

52 *no {. . .} bear:* keep your realm eternally (literally, "unforsaken"—*indeserta*) (*indeserta meo pectore regna gere*). In Marlowe's time the adjectival use of "desert" was acceptable.

54 *people:* sexes.

i *Ad {. . .} amet:* To Graecinus, that he can love two women at the same time.

1 *wot:* understand.

4 *For {. . .} equally:* It is important to note that Marlowe's (and Niger's) text read *solus* for *turpis.* In the Latin line 4, *solus* is basically insignificant, and thus Marlowe's translation is not diminished by its omission. However, the modern *turpis,* which means "foul person that I am," is typical Ovidian tongue-in-cheek sarcasm, and an English translation failing to render that sense and tone is significantly diminished. Again, though, it is not Marlowe's responsibility because his text read *solus.*

5 *favoured:* literally, "formed," that is, well formed and, therefore, beautiful.

7–8 *This {. . .} that {. . .} this:* understand "one" after each word.

Venus, why doublest thou my endless smart?
Was not one wench enough to grieve my heart?
Why add'st thou stars to heaven, leaves to green woods,
And to the vast deep sea fresh water floods?
Yet this is better far than lie alone;   15
Let such as be mine enemies have none.
Yea, let my foes sleep in an empty bed,
And in the midst their bodies largely spread.
But may soft love rouse up my drowsy eyes,
And from my mistress' bosom let me rise.   20
Let one wench cloy me with sweet love's delight,
If one can do 't, if not, two every night.
Though I am slender, I have store of pith,
Nor want I strength, but weight, to press her with.
Pleasure adds fuel to my lustful fire,   25
I pay them home with that they most desire.
Oft have I spent the night in wantonness,
And in the morn been lively ne'er the less.
He's happy who love's mutual skirmish slays,
And to the gods for that death Ovid prays.   30
Let soldiers chase their enemies amain,
And with their blood eternal honour gain;
Let merchants seek wealth with perjured lips,
Being wracked, carouse the sea tired by their ships;
But when I die, would I might droop with doing,   35
And in the midst thereof, set my soul going,
That at my funerals some may weeping cry,
"Even as he led his life, so did he die."

---

16 *none:* no lover.

18 *largely:* Marlowe's text read *late* ("widely"); modern texts, *laxe* ("loosely").

19 *soft:* Dyce's suggestion that Marlowe may have read *suavis* ("smooth") for *saevus* ("fierce") deserves consideration.

20 *And {. . .} rise: simque mei lecti non ego solus onus* ("May I not be the only body weighting down my bed").

26 *that:* that which (sexual vigor).

29 *who:* whom.

31 *Let {. . .} amain:* Let the soldier give his chest to be covered with the enemy's spears (*induat adversis contraria pectora telis*).

33–34 *Let {. . .} ships:* Let the greedy merchant seek wealth, and shipwrecked, let him drink with his lying mouth the waters that his ship's back-and-forth movements have ploughed into weariness (*quaerat avarus opes et quae lassarit arando/aequora periuro naufragus ore bibat*).

35 *doing:* sexual activity.

36 *set my soul going:* to die (both orgasmically and literally—i.e., to die "in the act"). Niger offers *deficiam* ("may I die") for *solvar* ("may I be dissolved").

ELEGIA XI

Ad amicam navigantem

The lofty pine, from high Mount Pelion raught,
Ill ways by rough seas wond'ring waves first taught,
Which rashly-twixt the sharp rocks in the deep
Carried the famous golden-fleeced sheep.
O would that no oars might in seas have sunk,   5
The Argos wracked had deadly waters drunk.
Lo, country gods and known bed to forsake
Corinna means, and dangerous ways to take.
For thee the east and west winds make me pale,
With icy Boreas, and the southern gale.   10
Thou shalt admire no woods or cities there,
The unjust seas all bluish do appear.
The ocean hath no painted stones or shells,
The sucking shore with their abundance swells.

---

i *Ad {. . .} navigantem:* To his mistress sailing. In Roman elegy this kind of poem is known as a
propemptikon, an address to the mistress by the poet as she is about to take a sea voyage, often im-
ploring her not to go.

1–6 *The {. . .} drunk:* The mythological background evoked here is that of the story of Jason and
the Argonauts, who took to the high seas to retrieve the Golden Fleece. Their ship, the Argo,
was made of pine trees from Mt. Pelion.

1–2 *The lofty pine {. . .} taught:* The translation here, especially line 2, is difficult. Literally, it is "It
was the pine [= metonymy for ship] cut down from the very top of Mt. Pelion that first taught
[men] the evil pathways of the seas, with the waves looking on in awe" (*prima malas docuit mi-
rantibus aequoris undis / Peliaco pinus vertice caesa vias*). Noteworthy is that the great, vertical, topo-
graphical distance between the top of the mountain and sea level is embodied, in Ovid's couplet,
by the early placement of *malas* and late, indeed couplet-ending placement of its noun *vias,* and
this phenomenon is rendered, even more precisely with regard to the pertinent diction, with the
beginning-to-end distance between "The lofty pine" and its verb "taught."

5–6 *O {. . .} drunk:* Marlowe confuses and cross-allocates certain words and ideas so that his
rendering is not correct. The sense is expressed best in Booth's translation: "Would that, to
deter anyone from disturbing the expanse of the deep with an oar, the Argo had been crushed and
drunk in the deadly waters!" (*o utinam ne quis remo freta longa moveret / Argo funestas pressa bibisset
aquas*).

7 *country gods:* Marlowe's text read *patriosque penates;* modern texts read *sociosque penates* ("our shared
household gods").

10 *Boreas:* the North Wind.

12 *The {. . .} appear:* Ovid's point is not conveyed by Marlowe's rendering. The point is not that the
seas are blue, but that the vast, blue sea is the only thing, or "all," she will see: it will therefore
be an unscenic and boring trip. Thus, Marlowe's "all" used adverbially to modify "bluish" fails
properly to render Ovid's *una.*

13–14 *The {. . .} swells:* Mckeown writes: "Professor Diggle observes to me that '13–14 are the
most musical lines in Ovid, with the soft lapping of the waves on the shore conveyed by the

Maids, on the shore with marble-white feet tread,   15
So far 'tis safe; but to go farther dread.
Let others tell how winds fierce battles wage,
How Scylla's and Charybdis' waters rage,
And with what rocks the feared Cerannia threat,
In what gulf either Syrtes have their seat.   20
Let others tell this, and what each one speaks
Believe; no tempest the believer wreaks.
Too late you look back, when with anchors weighed,
The crooked bark hath her swift sails displayed.
The careful shipman now fears angry gusts,   25
And with the waters sees death near him thrusts.
But if that Triton toss the troubled flood,
In all thy face will be no crimson blood.
Then wilt thou Leda's noble twin-stars pray,
And "he is happy whom the earth holds" say.   30
It is more safe to sleep, to read a book,
The Thracian harp with cunning to have strook;

---

liquid *l* and the sound clusters p*ictosque lapillos* / p*ontus habet bibuli litoris illa mora est.*'" Marlowe
has rendered this to some extent thus: "The ocean hath not painted stones or shells, / The sucking shore with their abundance swells."

14 *sucking:* Niger mentions, for example, *sorbet,* which means "to suck," but the ultimately intended
meaning of *bibuli* is "arid."

15–16 *Maids {. . .} dread:* Marlowe's and Ovid's sense is that it is safe for girls to walk along the
shore but not to walk into the ocean.

18 *Scylla's {. . .} waters:* "The rocks and whirlpools of the sea between Italy and Sicily" (Gill).

19 *Cerannia:* "The Ceraunia, mountains of Epirus which extend far into the sea, forming a promontory that divides the Ionian from the Adriatic" (Gill).

20 *either Syrtes:* "Two large sandbanks in the Mediterranean on the coast of Africa [one called the
Greater, the other the Lesser]. They were never stable, being sometimes very high, sometimes
very low under water, and therefore most dangerous to navigation" (Gill).

22 *wreaks:* "harms," contextually and etymologically evocative of "shipwrecks."

24 *crooked:* curved.

25 *now:* then (i.e., once the ship has already set sail).

26 *thrusts:* not in the Latin.

27 *Triton:* a sea-god who is the son of the preeminent sea-god Neptune, although Neptune is probably meant.

28 *will {. . .} blood:* The sense is "You will turn white with fear."

29 *Then {. . .} pray:* understand "to" before "Leda's." The stars refer to Castor and Pollux, the sons
of Leda and Zeus (and therefore sometimes referred to as the *Dioscuri*). They were changed into
stars, by some accounts the *Gemini,* and they became tutelary deities of men in war and at sea.

30 *holds:* holds back from the ocean.

32 *Thracian harp:* Orphean lyre. Orpheus was a mythological, early poet, born in Thrace, who
played his lyre, given him by Apollo, to enchant both animals and inanimate objects. *cunning:*
skill (not in the Latin).

But if my words with winged storms hence slip,
Yet, Galatea, favour thou her ship.
The loss of such a wench much blame will gather,   35
Both to the sea-nymphs and the sea-nymphs' father.
Go, minding to return with prosperous wind,
Whose blast may hither strongly be inclined,
Let Nereus bend the waves unto this shore,
Hither the winds blow, here the spring-tide roar.   40
Request mild Zephyr's help for thy avail,
And with thy hand assist the swelling sail.
I from the shore thy known ship first will see,
And say it brings her that preserveth me.
I'll clip and kiss thee with all contentation,   45
For thy return shall fall the vowed oblation,
And in the form of beds we'll strew soft sand,
Each little hill shall for a table stand:
There wine being filled, thou many things shalt tell,
How almost wracked thy ship in main seas fell,   50
And hasting to me, neither darksome night,
Nor violent south winds did thee aught affright.
I'll think all true, though it be feigned matter;
Mine own desires why should myself not flatter?
Let the bright day-star cause in heaven this day be,   55
To bring that happy time so soon as may be.

---

33 *slip:* are carried away.

34 *Galatea:* a sea-nymph.

36 *father:* Nereus (father of many sea-nymphs).

37 *minding:* Marlowe here departs from Ovid, where *memor nostri* means "mindful of me."

41 *Zephyr:* the West Wind.

44 *that:* who. Marlowe's construction of *nostros deos* as, in effect, *nostram deam* ("my goddess"), is an ambiguity intended by Ovid and affirmed by Niger, who offers *meam felicitatem*—"my happiness," or "salvation."

45 *clip:* embrace. *contentation:* pleasure. Marlowe's line departs from the original in major ways. The precise translation, and ultimate sense, are "I will [run out to meet you and] take you onto my shoulders [and bring you back to shore myself in that way] and snatch kisses from you all over" (*excipiamque umeris et multa sine ordine carpam loscula*). Moreover, Marlowe's line lacks the bathos effected by Ovid in the evocation of Aeneas's rescue of Anchises from Troy on his shoulders— Niger also notes this aspect to the Ovidian text.

46 *For {. . .} oblation:* Marlowe's and Ovid's sense is "The victim appointed to be sacrificed in return for your safe homecoming will fall" (*pro reditu victima vota cadet*).

55–56 *Let {. . .} be:* Both lines, especially 55, do not conform to the meter or the rhythms of iambic pentameter. The Latin line 55 (*haec mihi quam primum caelo nitidissimus alto*) has five consecutive, long, midline syllables (*quam primum caelo*), the first four of which forming two spondaic feet, and this is rendered by Marlowe's four consecutive, strong, midline syllables forming two feet: "bright day-star cause."

ELEGIA XII

Exultat, quod amica potitus sit

About my temples go, triumphant bays!
Conquered Corinna in my bosom lays,
She whom her husband, guard, and gate, as foes,
Lest art should win her, firmly did enclose.
That victory doth chiefly triumph merit,   5
Which without bloodshed doth the prey inherit.
No little ditched towns, no lowly walls,
But to my share a captive damsel falls.
When Troy by ten years' battle tumbled down,
With the Atrides many gained renown: 10
But I no partner of my glory brook,
Nor can another say his help I took.
I, guide and soldier, won the field and wear her,
I was both horseman, footman, standard-bearer.
Nor in my act hath fortune mingled chance;   15
O care-got triumph, hitherwards advance!
Nor is my war's cause new; but for a queen
Europe and Asia in firm peace had been.
The Lapiths, and the Centaurs, for a woman,
To cruel arms their drunken selves did summon.   20

---

i *Exultat {. . .} sit:* He exults in the conquest of his mistress.
1 *bays:* Laurel bays were traditionally placed around the temples of Roman military commanders
   having returned triumphant from campaigns of conquest.
2 *lays:* lies.
3 *as foes:* as foes to the narrator who was trying to get to her.
4 *art:* any trick or stratagem of the narrator.
7 *ditched:* moated (surrounded by moats).
8 *to my share:* as my prize of victory.
10 *With {. . .} many:* understand "along" before "with" and "others also" after "many." *Atrides:* the
   sons of Atreus, Agamemnon and Menelaus.
11–12 *But {. . .} took:* More precisely, "But my glory is separate and distinct from all other soldiers',
   and no other can lay claim to my rightful reward" (*at mea seposita est et ab omni milite dissors / gloria
   nec titulum muneris alter habet*). Marlowe does not render the structural embodiment of the sense
   of this couplet in Ovid's suspension of *gloria.*
13 *wear her:* That is, he wears "her" by virtue of his wearing the triumphant laurel bays, or, alter-
   natively, he enjoys her as a man enjoys a woman whom he has battled for and won. This sexual
   allusion is not in the Latin, but it is in keeping with Ovid's sensibility.
17 *queen:* Helen.
19 *woman:* Hippodamia (see 1.4.7–8n).

A woman forced the Trojans new to enter
Wars, just Latinus, in thy kingdom's centre;
A woman against late-built Rome did send
The Sabine fathers, who sharp wars intend.
I saw how bulls for a white heifer strive,   25
She looking on them did more courage give.
And me with many, but yet me without murther,
Cupid commands to move his ensigns further.

ELEGIA XIII

Ad Isidem, ut parientem Corinnam iuvet

While rashly her womb's burden she casts out,
Weary Corinna hath her life in doubt.
She secretly with me such harm attempted,
Angry I was, but fear my wrath exempted.
But she conceived of me; or I am sure   5
I oft have done what might as much procure.
Thou that frequents Canopus' pleasant fields,
Memphis, and Pharos that sweet date trees yields,
And where swift Nile in his large channel skipping,
By seven huge mouths into the sea is slipping,   10
By feared Anubis' visage I thee pray,
So in thy temples shall Osiris stay,

21–22 *A {. . .} centre:* The reference is to the battle between Turnus, king of the Rutulians, and
Aeneas over Lavinia, the daughter of Latinus, king of Latium. The story is told in the second half
of the *Aeneid. new:* anew, that is, a second time.

23 *woman:* The reference is to the rape of the Sabine women by the Romans when Rome was still a
young city.

26 *courage:* encouragement.

27 *murther:* murder.

i *Ad {. . .} iuvet:* To Isis, that she should help Corinna give birth.

3 *secretly with me:* keeping it a secret from me (*clam me*).

4 *exempted:* vacated.

5–6 *But {. . .} procure:* Marlowe's sense is "She conceived by me, or at least I know I have often done
what it would take to impregnate her"; Ovid's sense is "Yet it was I by whom she conceived—
or so I believe; often I accept as fact what really is only possibility" (*sed tamen aut ex me conceperat
aut ego credo/est mihi pro facto saepe quod esse potest*).

7–14 *Thou {. . .} keep:* Gill writes: "The poet addresses Isis. This Egyptian goddess, with her brother
(and husband) Osiris, comprehended all nature and all heathen deities. By the time Ovid was
writing, the cult of Isis had spread over the whole empire: '*Canopus*', '*Memphis*', '*Pharos*', and
'swift *Nile*' allude to its Egyptian source, and to certain elements of its ritual. Anubis is the
Egyptian Mercury, a man with the head of a dog, who accompanies Osiris on his expedition
against India. Osiris was murdered and his body cut in pieces by his brother, Set. Isis collected
and buried the mangled remains, while Osiris' soul entered the ox, the beast most useful in the

And the dull snake about thy off'rings creep,
And in thy pomp horned Apis with thee keep:
Turn thy looks hither, and in one spare twain: 15
Thou givest my mistress life, she mine again.
She oft hath served thee upon certain days,
Where the French rout engirt themselves with bays.
On labouring women thou dost pity take,
Whose bodies with their heavy burdens ache.   20
My wench, Lucina, I entreat thee favour;
Worthy she is, thou shouldst in mercy save her.
In white, with incense I'll thine altars greet,
Myself will bring vowed gifts before thy feet,
Subscribing, "Naso with Corinna saved."   25
Do but deserve gifts with this title graved.
But if in so great fear I may advise thee,
To have this skirmish fought, let it suffice thee.

ELEGIA XIV

In amicam, quod abortivum ipsa fecerit

What helps it woman to be free from war,
Nor, being armed, fierce troops to follow far,
If without battle self-wrought wounds annoy them,
And their own privy-weaponed hands destroy them?

---

cultivation of the earth, and became the god Apis. It was a good omen that the snake should
glide around the temple offerings."

13 *dull:* slow, sluggish (*pigra*).

15–16 *Turn {. . .} again:* perhaps a contributory inspiration for Donne's "The Flea."

18 *Where {. . .} bays:* MacLure notes: "The original has: 'Where the Gallic squadron rides near
(*tangit*) thy laurel trees.' There was a temple of Isis in the campus Martius [= an open plain near
Rome consecrated to the god Mars where horse races took place and where soldiers returning triumphant from battle would decamp because no returning triumphant soldiers were allowed to
enter Rome proper]. But Marlowe's text reads *cingit* ('engirt') for *tangit* and *turba* ('rout') for *turma*
('squadron')."

21 *Lucina:* goddess of childbirth. Modern texts have *Ilithya*, the Greek equivalent of *Lucina.*

27 *thee:* Corinna.

28 *To {. . .} thee:* that is, "do not put yourself in this situation again." The "t" alliteration of Marlowe's
line renders the same in Ovid's, and this is possibly significant because "the alliteration of 't' may
suggest Ovid's fear for Corinna's life" (McKeown).

i *In {. . .} fecerit:* To his mistress, who has attempted her own abortion.

2 *Nor {. . .} far:* Marlowe's and Ovid's sense is "and to avoid armed warfare."

3 *annoy:* injure.

Who unborn infants first to slay invented,   5
Deserved thereby with death to be tormented.
Because thy belly should rough wrinkles lack,
Wilt thou thy womb-inclosed offspring wrack?
Had ancient mothers this vile custom cherished,
All human kind by their default had perished;   10
Or stones, our stock's original, should be hurled
Again by some in this unpeopled world.
Who should have Priam's wealthy substance won,
If wat'ry Thetis had her child fordone?
In swelling womb her twins had Ilia killed,   15
He had not been that conquering Rome did build.
Had Venus spoiled her belly's Trojan fruit,
The earth of Caesars had been destitute.
Thou also, that wert born fair, hadst decayed,
If such a work thy mother had assayed.   20
Myself, that better die with loving may,
Had seen, my mother killing me, no day.
Why takest increasing grapes from vine-trees full?
With cruel hand why dost green apples pull?
Fruits ripe will fall, let springing things increase,   25
Life is no light price of a small surcease.
Why with hid irons are your bowels torn?
And why dire poison give you babes unborn?
At Colchis stained with children's blood men rail,

---

5 *Who:* She who.

8 *Wilt {. . .} wrack?:* The Latin (*sternetur pugnae tristis harena tuae*), which translates "you would scatter the tragic sands of deadly combat?" (Showerman), refers to the gladiatorial arena where sand would be scattered to absorb the blood of combat. Marlowe bypasses this reference, even though Niger clearly explains it.

11–12 *Or {. . .} world:* Deucalion and Pyrrha repopulated the world after the flood brought by Jupiter by throwing stones behind them; the stones became men and women. See *Metamorphoses* 1.398ff.

14 *wat'ry Thetis {. . .} child:* Thetis was a sea-nymph (thus "wat'ry") and the mother of Achilles, the great hero without whom the Greeks could not have triumphed over the Trojans (Priam was king of Troy).

15 *Ilia:* Rhea Silvia, the mother of Romulus and Remus, the mythical founders of Rome; understand "If" before "in."

16 *He:* Romulus, the more prominent of the two, would not have existed (and thus neither would Rome).

17–18 *Had {. . .} destitute:* Venus was the mother of Aeneas, who survived the fall of Troy and founded Rome and its race of Caesars.

23 *increasing:* not yet fully ripe.

26 *of:* for. *surcease:* delay.

27 *hid:* deeply inserted.

29 *Colchis:* home of Medea, who murdered her two children.

And mother-murdered Itys they bewail;   30
Both unkind parents, but for causes sad,
Their wedlock's pledges venged their husbands bad.
What Tereus, what Jason you provokes
To plague your bodies with such harmful strokes?
Armenian tigers never did so ill,   35
Nor dares the lioness her young whelps kill.
But tender damsels do it, though with pain;
Oft dies she that her paunch-wrapt child hath slain;
She dies, and with loose hairs to grave is sent,
And whoe'er see her, worthily lament.   40
But in the air let these words come to nought,
And my presages of no weight be thought.
Forgive her, gracious gods, this one delict,
And on the next fault punishment inflict.

ELEGIA XV

Ad annulum, quem dono amicae dedit
Thou ring that shalt my fair girl's finger bind,
Wherein is seen the giver's loving mind,
Be welcome to her, gladly let her take thee,
And her small joint's encircling round hoop make thee.
Fit her so well, as she is fit for me,   5
And of just compass for her knuckles be.
Blest ring, thou in my mistress' hand shalt lie;
Myself, poor wretch, mine own gifts now envy.
O would that suddenly into my gift
I could myself by secret magic shift!   10

---

30 *Itys:* murdered by his mother Procne (see 2.6.7n.).

40 *worthily lament:* that is, those who attend the funeral cry out that she has gotten what she deserved.

43 *delict:* transgression (from "dereliction").

i *Ad {. . .} dedit:* To the ring that he has given to his mistress.

3 *welcome:* pleasing.

4 *And {. . .} thee:* The Latin (*protinus articulis induat illa suis*) is translated "Let her place you immediately on her finger."

5 *Fit her {. . .} she {. . .} fit:* These words form a chiasmus, which reflects an almost exactly corresponding chiasmus in the original (*convenias quam mecum convenit*). A chiasmus especially befits this line and couplet, which explicate the perfect circular fit of the ring and the perfect matching (intertwining) of the lovers.

10 *by secret magic shift:* These words incorporate the characterizations, but omit the specific references, of Circe and Proteus (*Aeaeae Carpathiive*).

Then would I wish thee touch my mistress' pap,
And hide thy left hand underneath her lap;
I would get off though strait, and sticking fast,
And in her bosom strangely fall at last.
Then I, that I may seal her privy leaves,   15
Lest to the wax the hold-fast dry gem cleaves,
Would first my beauteous wench's moist lips touch,
Only I'll sign nought that may grieve me much.
I would not out, might I in one place hit,
But in less compass her small fingers knit.   20
My life, that I will shame thee, never fear,
Or be a load thou shouldst refuse to bear.
Wear me, when warmest showers thy members wash,
And through the gem let thy lost waters pash.
But seeing thee, I think my thing will swell,   25
And even the ring perform a man's part well.
Vain things why wish I? go, small gift from hand,
Let her my faith with thee given understand.

ELEGIA XVI

Ad amicam, ut ad rura sua veniat

Sulmo, Peligny's third part, me contains,
A small, but wholesome soil with wat'ry veins.

---

11 *pap:* breast.

13 *strait:* tight.

14 *strangely:* with wondrous skill (*mira {. . .} ab arte*).

15 *privy leaves:* private letters.

16 *hold-fast:* tenacious.

17–18 *Would {. . .} much:* The Latin (*umida formosae tangam prius ora puellae/tantum ne signem scripta dolenda mihi*) is the more clearly translated "I would first touch the moist lips of my beautiful mistress, but not, I pray, for the purpose of sealing letters that will bring me grief" (= e.g., a "Dear John" letter).

19–20 *I {. . .} knit: si dabor ut condar loculis, exire negabo/astringens digitos orbe minore tuos:* If I am to be given over to and left in your jewelry box, then I will refuse to leave your finger, holding myself even closer and tighter to your finger.

21 *My life:* vocative address to Corinna.

24 *pash:* splash. .

25 *thing:* phallus.

26 *even {. . .} perform:* Marlowe's and Ovid's sense is "even though I am a ring I will perform (as your male lover)."

28 *Let {. . .} understand:* Marlowe's and Ovid's sense is "Let her understand that through contact with you she has my fidelity."

i *Ad {. . .} veniat:* To his mistress, that she should come to see him in the country.

1 *Sulmo, Peligny's:* see 2.1.2n.

Although the sun to rive the earth incline,
And the Icarian froward dog-star shine,
Pelignian fields with liquid rivers flow,   5
And on the soft ground fertile green grass grow.
With corn the earth abounds, with vines much more,
And some few pastures Pallas' olives bore.
And by the rising herbs, where clear springs slide,
A grassy turf the moistened earth doth hide.   10
But absent is my fire: lies I'll tell none,
My heat is here, what moves my heat is gone.
Pollux and Castor might I stand betwixt,
In heaven without thee would I not be fixed.
Upon the cold earth pensive let them lay   15
That mean to travel some long irksome way,
Or else will maidens, young men's mates, to go
If they determine to persever so.
Then on the rough Alps should I tread aloft,
My hard way with my mistress would seem soft.   20

---

3 *Although {. . .} incline:* Marlowe's and Ovid's sense is "Although the heat of the sun when it angles close to the earth may crack the earth."

4 *Icarian {. . .} dog-star:* MacLure writes: "Icarius, an Athenian, was given the gift of the vine by Dionysus, and was killed by those who thought its effects were poison. The discovery of his body by his dog was commemorated in the festival of Aiora, and the dog stellified as Canicula (Procyon)."

7 *vines:* grapevines.

8 *Pallas' olives:* Pallas Athena created the olive tree.

13–14 *Pollux {. . .} fixed:* Booth writes: "Castor and Pollux were identified with the constellation Gemini. After Castor, who was born mortal [. . .], had been killed while fighting alongside his divine twin Pollux to retain possession of the daughters of Leucippus whom they had abducted, he was allowed to share his brother's immortality on condition that they lived by turns in heaven and Hades [. . .] [in some versions of the story Pollux asked to share heaven with his brother Castor (and this bears special relevance here where Ovid does not wish to be in heaven without his mistress) and in other versions they exchanged places with each other daily] (McKeown). Thus, their celestial existence was only part-time and also inevitably separated them from their beloveds. No wonder Ovid did not want to join them! [. . .] Castor and Pollux were believed to be the special protectors of seafarers, and so the reference to them here obliquely prepares for the shipwreck theme which emerges in vv. 22–32 (establishing at the same time one of the poem's many links with poem [2.] 11)."

15 *Upon {. . .} lay:* Marlowe's and Ovid's sense is "May they lie weighted down beneath the heavy earth" (*solliciti iaceant terraque premantur iniqua*). "Pensive" is used here in its etymological sense (and thus proto-Miltonically) of "weighty" (from both *premantur* and *iniqua*), and this is meant as a curse because it is "an inversion of the usual prayer that the earth lie lightly on the dead person" (McKeown).

17–18 *Or {. . .} so:* Booth's translation is helpful: "Or they should have bidden girls to accompany young men on their travels, if the earth *had* to be opened up for long journeys" (*aut iuvenum comites iussissent ire puellas / si fuit in longas terra secanda vias*).

With her I durst the Lybian Syrtes break through,
And raging seas in boist'rous south winds plough.
No barking dogs that Scylla's entrails bear,
Nor thy gulfs, crooked Malea, would I fear;
No flowing waves with drowned ships forth-poured   25
By cloyed Charybdis, and again devoured.
But if stern Neptune's windy power prevail,
And waters' force, force helping gods to fail,
With thy white arms upon my shoulders seize,
So sweet a burden I will bear with ease.   30
The youth oft swimming to his Hero kind,
Had then swum over, but the way was blind.
But without thee, although vine-planted ground
Contains me, though the streams in fields surround,
Though hinds in brooks the running waters bring,   35
And cool gales shake the tall trees' leafy spring,
Healthful Peligny I esteem nought worth,
Nor do I like the country of my birth.
Scythia, Cilicia, Britain are as good,
And rocks dyed crimson with Prometheus' blood.   40
Elms love the vines, the vines with elms abide,
Why doth my mistress from me oft divide?
Thou swarest division should not 'twixt us rise,
By me, and by my stars, thy radiant eyes.
Maids' words more vain and light than falling leaves,   45

21–24 *With {. . .} fear:* Gill explains: "Ovid lists navigational hazards which he would willingly endure in his mistress's company. The *'Lybian Syrtes'* are the sandbanks off the coast of Africa [see 2.11.20n.]; Scylla and Charybdis the rocks and whirlpools between Italy and Sicily [see 2.11.18n.]; the former is portrayed as a girl as far as the waist, but below that as a pack of snarling, dog-like monsters. Malea is a promontory to the south-east of Laconia, where the sea is always rough."

28 *helping gods:* images of tutelary deities on the stern.

31 *youth:* Leander.

32 *Had then:* Marlowe's sense is "Would have at that last fateful time again." *blind:* dark (because Hero's torch had extinguished).

35 *hinds:* farmhands.

36 *spring:* that is, leaves that have *sprung* from the trees.

39 *Scythia:* a vast area extending throughout the eastern half of northern Europe and western and central Asia. *Cilicia:* a Roman province of Asia Minor.

40 *Prometheus:* As punishment for stealing fire from the gods and giving it to mankind, Prometheus was chained to a rock, where vultures would come to feed on his liver.

41 *Elms {. . .} vines {. . .} vines {. . .} elms:* Marlowe reproduces Ovid's chiasmus *ulmus {. . .} vitem vitis ulmum.*

43 *swarest:* sworest.

Which, as it seems, hence wind and sea bereaves.
If any godly care of me thou hast,
Add deeds unto thy promises at last,
And with swift nags drawing thy little coach,
(Their reins let loose), right soon my house approach.   50
But when she comes, you swelling mounts sink down,
And falling valleys be the smooth ways' crown.

ELEGIA XVII

Quod Corinnae soli sit serviturus

To serve a wench if any think it shame,
He being judge, I am convinced of blame.
Let me be slandered, while my fire she hides,
That Paphos, and the flood-beat Cythera guides.
Would I had been my mistress' gentle prey,   5
Since some fair one I should of force obey.
Beauty gives heart; Corinna's looks excel;
Aye me, why is it known to her so well?
But by her glass disdainful pride she learns,
Nor she herself, but first trimmed up, discerns.   10
Not though thy face in all things make thee reign
(O face, most cunning mine eyes to detain!),

---

46 *Which {. . .} bereaves:* a troubled line. Marlowe's text had *ut visum est* ("as it seems") instead of *qua visum est* ("in what place, it seems"—this phrase makes little sense even within its own Latin line [*inrita qua visum est ventus et unda ferunt*—"useless, where, it seems, the wind and the wave drive them"]). Moreover, "wind and sea" are supposed to be the subjects of "bereaves," and the antecedent of "Which" is supposed to be "leaves"—but the line simply does not work. Perhaps Marlowe makes "bereaves" singular instead of plural because of the rhyme.

i *Quod {. . .} serviturus:* That he will serve only Corinna.
1 *any:* any person.
2 *convinced:* convicted.
3 *while {. . .} hides:* Marlowe's and Ovid's sense is "if only Venus would burn me with more moderate fires" (*dum me moderatius urat*).
4 *Paphos, Cythera:* places sacred to Venus.
5 *Would {. . .} prey:* Ovid's sense is "Would I had fallen prey to a merciful mistress" (*utinam dominae miti {. . .} praeda fuissem*).
7 *heart:* Several editors and translators render *animos* as "arrogance," which is correct, because while *animus* in the singular means "heart," "spirit," and so on, in the plural it means, for example, "pride," whence "arrogance" can rightfully derive. Also understand "to the one that has it" after "heart" (= arrogance).
8 *it:* the fact that Corinna's "looks excel" (from the previous line).
9 *glass:* mirror.
10 *Nor {. . .} discerns:* Marlowe's and Ovid's sense is "She never looks at herself in the mirror until she has her make-up on."

Thou oughtst therefore to scorn me for thy mate:
Small things with greater may be copulate.
Love-snared Calypso is supposed to pray,   15
A mortal nymph's refusing lord to stay.
Who doubts with Peleus Thetis did consort,
Egeria with just Numa had good sport,
Venus with Vulcan, though, smith's tools laid by,
With his stump foot he halts ill-favouredly.   20
This kind of verse is not alike, yet fit,
With shorter numbers the heroic sit.
And thou, my light, accept me howsoever,
Lay in the mid-bed, there be my lawgiver.
My stay no crime, my flight no joy shall breed,   25
Nor of our love to be ashamed we need.
For great revenues, I good verses have,
And many by me to get glory crave.
I know a wench reports herself Corinne:

---

13 *Thou {. . .} mate:* The sense of this line is that of a question being asked that expects, or demands, the answer "no."

14 *copulate:* suited. For Ovid's *aptari* Niger offers, only, *componi,* the first definition for which in Cooper is "to put or join together." When the requirements of rhyme are taken into account, Marlowe's arrival at "copulate" appears predictable. And, at that time, the adjectival use of "copulate" (as opposed to the modern "copulative") was fully accepted.

15–16 *Love-snared {. . .} stay:* Here is a case where Niger clearly explained the Latin but Marlowe either did not read it or did not pay attention to it. The Latin (*traditur* [Niger's text has *creditur*— the difference is negligible] *et nymphe mortalis amore Calypso/capta recusantem detinuisse virum*) is translated "It is told that the [immortal] sea-nymph Calypso was enthralled by the love of a mortal, and that she held him captive against his will." The reference is to the seven-year detention of Odysseus (*Odyssey* 5). Martin and Gill both suggest that Marlowe read the Greek nominative *nymphe* as the Latin genitive *nymphae* (and this is a distinct possibility especially because in earlier texts the two vowels composing diphthongs were often crushed into each other). However, as just noted, Niger clearly explains the grammar and syntax of this line as well as the fact that it is Odysseus who is mortal. That Marlowe should err in this particular couplet is of interest because of its reference: as McKeown writes, "*mortalis,* pointedly juxtaposed to *nymphe,* is emphatic: Calypso tempted Odysseus to stay with her by promising him immortality."

17 *Pelius Thetis:* Pelius, a mortal man, and Thetis, an immortal sea-nymph, were the parents of Achilles.

18 *Egeria {. . .} Numa:* Gill notes: "Numa Pompilius, the second king of Rome, famed as a lawgiver and religious reformer [. . .] encouraged a rumour that he paid frequent visits to the nymph Egeria, so that he could use this immortal's name to give sanction to the laws and institutions which he introduced."

21–22 *This {. . .} sit:* This refers to the peculiar nature of the Latin elegiac couplet, which consists of a longer hexameter and a shorter pentameter (see 1.1).

24 *mid-bed:* Marlowe must have construed *foro* as *toro.*

27 *For:* Instead of.

28 *And {. . .} crave:* Marlowe's and Ovid's sense is "Many women hope to acquire eternal fame through my verses" (see 1.3).

What would not she give that fair name to win?   30
But sundry floods in one bank never go,
Eurotas cold, and poplar-bearing Po.
Nor in my books shall one but thou be writ,
Thou dost alone give matter to my wit.

ELEGIA XVIII

Ad Macrum, quod de amoribus scribat

To tragic verse while thou Achilles train'st,
And new-sworn soldiers' maiden arms retain'st,
We, Macer, sit in Venus' slothful shade,
And tender love hath great things hateful made.
Often at length, my wench depart I bid,   5
She in my lap sits still as erst she did.
I said, "It irks me"; half to weeping framed,
"Aye me," she cries, "to love why art ashamed?"
Then wreathes about my neck her winding arms,
And thousand kisses gives, that work my harms.   10
I yield, and back my wit from battles bring,
Domestic acts, and mine own wars to sing.
Yet tragedies and sceptres filled my lines,
But though I apt were for such high designs,
Love laughed at my cloak, and buskins painted,   15
And rule so soon with private hands acquainted.

---

32 *Eurotas, Po:* The Po is a major river in northern Italy, and the Eurotas (also called Laconia) is a major river of Greece.

34 *Thou {. . .} wit:* again, see 1.3.

i *Ad {. . .} scribat:* To Macer, about his love poetry.

1–2 *To {. . .} retain'st:* Marlowe's and Ovid's sense is "While you now turn your poem to wrathful Achilles and dress the chieftains who have sworn to stay until the job is done in their armor not yet broken in by battle."

3 *We:* I. *Macer:* A poet and friend of Ovid who, according to Ovid in this poem, is writing an epic poem about the events leading up to the Trojan War.

4 *And {. . .} made:* Like 1.1 and 2.1, the reference here and in the following lines is to Ovid's attempts to write epic, which are always aborted by Love, or love, or the mistress. *great things:* subject matter suited to epic poetry.

7 *half {. . .} framed:* Marlowe's and Ovid's sense is "scarcely holding back her tears."

13 *tragedies {. . .} sceptres {. . .} lines:* Ovid is known to have written a tragedy, the *Medea*, extant in two lines, and the scepter is one sign of Tragedy personified. Niger notes a textual alternative for *cura* in *versu*, and thus Marlowe's "lines."

15 *buskins:* thick boots that signified tragedy. See also 3.1.13–14, 31.

16 *rule:* the scepter. *private hands:* "my own commoner's hands."

My mistress' deity also drew me fro it,
And Love triumpheth o'er his buskined poet.
What lawful is, or we profess love's art,
(Alas, my precepts turn myself to smart!)   20
We write, or what Penelope sends Ulysses,
Or Phyllis' tears that her Demophoon misses,
What thankless Jason, Macareus, and Paris,
Phaedra, and Hippolyte may read, my care is,
And what poor Dido with her drawn sword sharp   25
Doth say, with her that loved the Aonian harp.
As soon as from strange lands Sabinus came,
And writings did from diverse places frame,
White-cheeked Penelope knew Ulysses' sign,
The stepdame read Hippolytus' lustless line,   30
Aeneas to Elisa answer gives,
And Phyllis hath to read, if now she lives.
Jason's sad letter doth Hypsipyle greet,
Sappho her vowed harp lays at Phoebus' feet.
Nor of thee, Macer, that resound'st forth arms,   35
Is golden love hid in Mars' mid-alarms:
There Paris is, and Helen's crime's record,
With Laodamia, mate to her dead lord.

---

17 *mistress' deity:* divine power of my mistress. *fro:* away from.

19 *What {. . .} art:* Ovid's sense is "What can I do? either I profess the art of tender love" (*quod licet aut artes teneri profitemur Amoris*). This is very likely a reference to Ovid's *Ars Amatoria.*

21–37 *We {. . .} or:* "Or I write." The characters referred to in these lines are from Ovid's *Heroides,* which were complaint-epistles by women deserted by their lovers (a few of the epistles were by men).

25 *drawn sword:* Dido commits suicide (*Aeneid* 4.641 ff).

26 *her:* Sappho. *Aonian:* see 1.1.16n.

27 *Sabinus:* a poet and friend of Ovid who wrote replies to several letters from Ovid's *Heroides* and who might also have penned an epic poem.

28 *from:* about.

29 *White-cheeked:* for *candida,* which here is meant figuratively as "chaste" (Niger agrees). *sign:* seal from his signet ring.

30 *lustless:* Hippolytus was known for his asexuality, especially in response to his stepmother's advances.

31 *Elisa:* Dido.

34 *Sappho {. . .} feet:* Sappho dedicates her lyre to Apollo in return for Phaon's requital of Sappho's love.

38 *Laodamia:* The wife of Protesilaus, the first Greek to be killed at Troy. Upon hearing of her husband's demise, she had an image of him made and slept with it. Laodamia finally killed herself to join her husband in death. McKeown's observation is salient: "A fine contrast: whereas adulterous passion led Helen to accompany Paris at Troy, thus causing the Trojan War, marital fidelity led Laodamia to accompany her husband in death, when Protesilaus was the first Greek to be killed at Troy."

Unless I err, to these thou more incline
Than wars, and from thy tents wilt come to mine.   40

Elegia XIX

Ad rivalem, cui uxor curae non erat
Fool, if to keep thy wife thou hast no need,
Keep her for me, my more desire to breed.
We scorn things lawful, stol'n sweets we affect,
Cruel is he that loves whom none protect.
Let us both lovers hope and fear alike,   5
And may repulse place for our wishes strike.
What should I do with fortune that ne'er fails me?
Nothing I love that at all times avails me.
Wily Corinna saw this blemish in me,
And craftily knows by what means to win me.   10
Ah often, that her hale head ached, she lying,
Willed me, whose slow feet sought delay, be flying;
Ah oft, how much she might, she feigned offence,
And, doing wrong, made show of innocence.
So having vexed she nourished my warm fire,   15
And was again most apt to my desire.
To please me, what fair terms and sweet words has she!
Great gods, what kisses, and how many gave she!
Thou also, that late took'st mine eyes away,
Oft cozen me, oft being wooed, say nay;   20
And on thy threshold let me lie dispread,
Suff'ring much cold by hoary night's frost bred.

---

39 *these:* literally, these characters, but ultimately stories and meters of love.

i *Ad {. . .} erat:* To his rival, her husband, who does not guard his wife.
1 *keep:* guard (from paramours).
3 *affect:* desire.
6 *And {. . .} strike:* Ovid's sense is "And let the sometime refusal spur our desire even more" (*et faciat voto rara repulsa locum*).
9 *blemish:* weakness.
13–14 *Ah {. . .} innocence:* The sense of the Latin (*a quotiens finxit culpam quantumque licebat/insonti speciem praebuit esse nocens*) is "Oh, how often she feigned the commission of a transgression and put forth a show of guilt as well as anyone ever could who was in fact innocent." Marlowe's pentameter (14) is explained by the fact that his text read *insontis* for *insonti* and *ipsa* for *esse*, as well as the fact that modern texts place a comma after *insonti* but earlier texts placed it after *licebat* at the end of the hexameter.
20 *cozen:* deceive. Marlowe's text had *fac insidias*, whereas modern texts have *time insidias* (fear deceptions).
21 *dispread:* stretched out.

So shall my love continue many years;
This doth delight me, this my courage cheers.
Fat love, and too much fulsome, me annoys,   25
Even as sweet meat a glutted stomach cloys.
In brazen tower had not Danae dwelt,
A mother's joy by Jove she had not felt;
While Juno Io keeps, when horns she wore,
Jove liked her better than he did before.   30
Who covets lawful things takes leaves from woods,
And drinks stol'n waters in surrounding floods.
Her lover let her mock that long will reign;
Aye me, let not my warnings cause my pain!
Whatever haps, by suff'rance harm is done;   35
What flies I follow, what follows me I shun.
But thou, of thy fair damsel too secure,
Begin to shut thy house at evening sure.
Search at the door who knocks oft in the dark,
In night's deep silence why the ban-dogs bark.   40
Whether the subtle maid lines brings and carries,

23–24 *So {. . .} cheers:* The Latin (*sic mihi durat amor longosque adolescit in annos/hoc iuvat haec animi sunt alimenta mei*) is translated "Thus my love endures and continues to grow over the long years; this gratifies me, and all of this is food for my passion." Marlowe's omission of the digestive metaphor is significant because that metaphor lays the groundwork for its continuation in the following couplet (25–26). Marlowe's use of "courage" for *animi* appears, on its face, to be in error, since "courage" and "pride" are definitions for *animus* in the plural but not in the singular. It is possible, though, that Marlowe intended "courage" in its etymological sense of "heart" and thus figuratively "passion."

27 *Danae:* Danae was locked in a tower by her father because of a prophecy that she would bear a son who would kill her father. Jupiter came to her through a window as a shower of gold and impregnated her. She subsequently gave birth to Perseus, who grew up and fulfilled the prophecy.

29 *Io:* One of Jove's paramours, whom he turned into a heifer.

30 *her:* Io.

31 *Who:* He who.

33–34 *Her {. . .} pain:* Marlowe's and Ovid's sense is "Let her who wants to maintain the upper hand in the relationship speak down to her lover; Oh me, Let me not be undone by my own advice!" (*si qua volet regnare diu deludat amantem. / ei mihi ne monitis torquear ipse meis*).

35 *by {. . .} done:* Marlowe's and Ovid's sense is "It is harmful if love comes too easily."

36 *What {. . .} shun:* The chiastic construction is important here because it embodies the content of the line and renders the chiasmus in Ovid's line (*quod sequitur fugio quod fugit ipse sequor*). Perhaps this may be a contributory inspiration for Ben Jonson's "Song: That Women Are but Men's Shadows."

37 *thou:* The husband is now being addressed again. *secure:* careless, that is, not taking care to keep her away from potential paramours.

40 *ban-dogs:* watchdogs.

41 *lines:* secret letters.

Why she alone in empty bed oft tarries.
Let this care sometimes bite thee to the quick,
That to deceits it may me forward prick.
To steal sands from the shore he loves a-life,   45
That can affect a foolish wittol's wife.
Now I forewarn, unless to keep her stronger
Thou dost begin, she shall be mine no longer.
Long have I borne much, hoping time would beat thee
To guard her well, that well I might entreat thee.   50
Thou suffer'st what no husband can endure,
But of my love it will an end procure.
Shall I, poor soul, be never interdicted,
Nor never with night's sharp revenge afflicted?
In sleeping shall I fearless draw my breath?   55
Wilt nothing do, why I should wish thy death?
Can I but loathe a husband grown a bawd?
By thy default thou dost our joys defraud.
Some other seek that may in patience strive with thee;
To pleasure me, forbid me to corrive with thee.   60

P. OVIDII NASONIS AMORUM, LIBER TERTIUS

ELEGIA I

Deliberatio poetae, utrum elegos pergat scribere an potius tragedias
An old wood stands uncut, of long years' space,
'Tis credible some godhead haunts the place.

---

42 *she:* his wife (not the maid).

44 *deceits:* schemes (to be with his wife).

45–46 *To {. . .} wife:* difficult to understand. The Latin (*ille potest vacuo furari litore harenas/uxorem stulti si quis amare potest*) is translated "Whoever would have an affair with the wife of a fool might just as well steal the sands from a deserted shore." The point is that the sands are not worth stealing (and therefore neither is the wife); otherwise, the shore would not be deserted.

47 *keep:* guard. *stronger:* understood adverbially as "more closely and carefully."

49 *Long {. . .} much:* These exact words also begin 3.11.1, just as Ovid also uses the same words there and here (*multa diuque tuli*).

50 *entreat:* trick, cheat.

52 *it:* your complacence.

53 *interdicted:* kept from seeing her.

56 *Wilt {. . .} should:* Will you do nothing to cause me to.

59 *other:* other rival.

60 *corrive:* be a rival. These final two lines are both hexameters.

i *Deliberatio {. . .} tragedias:* The poet's deliberation over whether to continue writing elegy or to turn to tragedy.

In midst thereof a stone-paved sacred spring,
Where round about small birds most sweetly sing.
Here while I walk, hid close in shady grove,   5
To find what work my muse might move, I strove.
Elegia came with hairs perfumed sweet,
And one, I think, was longer of her feet;
A decent form, thin robe, a lover's look,
By her foot's blemish greater grace she took.   10
Then with huge steps came violent Tragedy:
Stern was her front, her cloak on ground did lie;
Her left hand held abroad a regal sceptre,
The Lydian buskin in fit paces kept her.
And first she said, "When will thy love be spent,   15
O poet careless of thy argument?
Wine-bibbing banquets tell thy naughtiness,
Each cross-way's corner doth as much express.
Oft some points at the prophet passing by,
And, 'This is he whom fierce love burns,' they cry.   20
A laughing-stock thou art to all the city,
While without shame thou sing'st thy lewdness' ditty.
'Tis time to move grave things in lofty style,
Long hast thou loitered; greater works compile.
The subject hides thy wit; men's acts resound;   25
This thou wilt say to be a worthy ground.
Thy muse hath played what may mild girls content,
And by those numbers is thy first youth spent.
Now give the Roman Tragedy a name,
To fill my laws thy wanton spirit frame."   30
This said, she moved her buskins gaily varnished,
And seven times shook her head with thick locks garnished.
The other smiled (I wot) with wanton eyes;

---

3 *stone-paved:* cave with hanging rock (*speluncaque pumice pendens*).
8 *longer {. . .} feet:* a reference to the fact that the elegiac couplet in Latin consisted of a dactylic hexameter followed by what is called a dactylic pentameter—see 1.1 and 2.1.
9 *decent* (*decens*): becoming.
12 *front:* forehead. *did lie:* trailed.
13–14 *sceptre {. . .} buskin:* see 2.18.15–16n. *fit:* Marlowe's text had *apta*, modern texts *alta* ("high").
16 *careless:* slow to let go (*lente*).
19 *some:* someone. *prophet:* The Latin word *vates* meant both "prophet" and "poet," which speaks to the sense of poets having a somewhat superhuman capacity of perception and perspicacity.
29 *a name:* renown.
30 *fill:* fulfill.

Err I? or myrtle in her right hand lies.
"With lofty words, stout Tragedy," she said,					35
"Why tread'st me down? art thou aye gravely played?
Thou deign'st unequal lines should thee rehearse;
Thou fight'st against me using mine own verse,
Thy lofty style with mine I not compare,
Small doors unfitting for large houses are.					40
Light am I, and with me, my care, light Love,
Not stronger am I than the thing I move.
Venus without me should be rustical;
This goddess' company doth to me befall.
What gate thy stately words cannot unlock,					45
My flatt'ring speeches soon wide open knock.
And I deserve more than thou canst in verity,
By suff'ring much not borne by thy severity.
By me Corinna learns, cozening her guard,
To get the door with little noise unbarred;					50
And slipped from bed, clothed in a loose nightgown,
To move her feet unheard in setting down.
Ah, how oft on hard doors hung I engraved,
From no man's reading fearing to be saved!
But till the keeper went forth, I forget not,					55
The maid to hide me in her bosom let not.
What gift with me was on her birthday sent,
But cruelly by her was drowned and rent.
First of thy mind the happy seeds I knew,
Thou hast my gift, which she would from thee sue."					60

---

34 *myrtle:* sacred to Venus, and thus symbolic of both love and love poetry.

35 *stout:* Cooper cites this definition, for example, for *animosa.*

37–38 *Thou {. . .} verse:* that is, Elegy wittily undercuts Tragedy's criticism by pointing out that Tragedy is conveying that very criticism in elegiac couplet.

40 *large:* Niger points out that earlier texts read *vasta* for *vestra* and that the former is preferred.

42 *move:* write.

43 *should:* would. *rustical:* "inelegant."

47 *canst:* do (i.e., do deserve).

48 *By {. . .} severity:* that is, even though my meter is lighter (less "severe") than yours, I actually suffer more (e.g., unrequited love) than you do even though your "severe" (heavier) meter would indicate otherwise. Both lines (47–48) of Marlowe's couplet are arguably hexameters, which therefore ironically gives the (metrical) lie to what Elegy is claiming here.

53 *engraved:* Marlowe's text read *incisa;* modern ones read *infixa* ("fastened").

54 *From {. . .} saved:* "Not ashamed to be seen by others."

56 *let:* failed.

57–60 *What {. . .} sue:* In these four lines Elegy now seems to be addressing Ovid rather than Tragedy.

57 *What {. . .} sent:* What you sent me [= elegiac love poem] as a birthday gift.

She left; I said, "You both I must beseech,
To empty air may go my fearful speech.
With sceptres and high buskins th' one would dress me,
So through the world should bright renown express me.
The other gives my love a conquering name;   65
Come therefore, and to long verse shorter frame.
Grant, Tragedy, thy poet time's least tittle,
Thy labour ever lasts, she asks but little."
She gave me leave, soft loves in time make haste,
Some greater work will urge me on at last.   70

Elegia II

Ad amicam cursum equorum spectantem

I sit not here the noble horse to see,
Yet whom thou favour'st, pray may conqueror be.
To sit and talk with thee I hither came,
That thou mayst know with love thou mak'st me flame.
Thou view'st the course, I thee: let either heed   5
What please them, and their eyes let either feed.
What horse-driver thou favour'st most is best,
Because on him thy care doth hap to rest.
Such chance let me have: I would bravely run,
On swift steeds mounted till the race were done.   10
Now would I slack the reins, now lash their hide,
With wheels bent inward now the ring-turn ride;
In running if I see thee, I shall stay,
And from my hands the reins will slip away.
Ah, Pelops from his coach was almost felled,   15

---

61 *left:* that is, left off, stopped.
62 *empty air:* Modern texts read *vacuas aures,* which means "open ears"; Marlowe's text read *vacuas aures.*
64 *So {. . .} me:* Marlowe's text read *iam nunc contracto magnus in orbe sonor;* modern texts read *iam nunc contracto magnus in ore sonus* ("already your grand style is imbedded in my mouth").
67 *Grant {. . .} tittle:* Marlowe's and Ovid's sense is "Give a little more time, O Tragedy, to your poet [to indulge himself with elegy]."
68 *she:* Elegy.
69 *She:* Tragedy.

i *Ad {. . .} spectantem:* To his mistress watching the chariot races.
12 *With {. . .} ride:* With the inner wheel now grazing the turning-post.
13 *In running:* As I race by. *stay:* slow down.
15–17 *Pelops {. . .} her:* Hippodamia's father promised her to the man who could beat him in a chariot race. Hippodamia rode next to the suitor to distract him so that her father could win; however, she became attracted to Pelops, whom she helped win the race.
15 *from his coach:* Marlowe's text had *axe;* modern texts have *hasta* (spear).

Hippodamia's looks while he beheld,
Yet he attained by her support to have her:
Let us all conquer by our mistress' favour.
In vain, why fly'st back? force conjoins us now:
The place's laws this benefit allow.   20
But spare my wench, thou at her right hand seated,
By thy side's touching ill she is entreated.
And sit thou rounder, that behind us see;
For shame press not her back with thy hard knee.
But on the ground thy clothes too loosely lie;   25
Gather them up, or lift them, lo, will I.
Envious garments so good legs to hide!
The more thou look'st, the more the gown envied.
Swift Atalanta's flying legs, like these,
Wish in his hands grasped did Hippomenes.   30
Coat-tucked Diana's legs are painted like them,
When strong wild beasts she stronger hunts to strike them.
Ere these were seen, I burned; what will these do?
Flames into flame, floods thou pour'st seas into.
By these I judge delight me may the rest,   35
Which lie hid under her thin veil suppressed.
Yet in the meantime wilt small winds bestow,
That from thy fan, moved by my hand, may blow?
Or is my heat of mind, not of the sky?
Is 't women's love my captive breast doth fry?   40
While thus I speak, black dust her white robes ray;
Foul dust, from her fair body go away.

---

19 *force {. . .} us:* grooves (*linea*) were carved into the marble to enforce the limits of each seat.

22 *entreated:* treated.

23 *rounder:* with knees drawn in (*tua contrahe crura*).

27–28 *Envious {. . .} envied:* This sentiment is like that of the narrator toward the ring (*annulus*) in 2.15.

29–30 *Atalanta's {. . .} Hippomenes:* see 1.7.13n.

31 *are painted:* appear in paintings.

32 *When {. . .} them:* The "s" alliteration renders the "f" alliteration of the Latin, and the two alliterations largely correspond between the same words in the two languages.

33 *Ere {. . .} do?:* Ovid's sense, alluding to lines 26 earlier and 35–36 later, is "I burned with passion while I had not yet seen your legs covered by your cloak; what will become of me when I see your legs and other things covered by it after having lifted it up?" (*his ego non visis arsi quid fiet ab ipsis?*).

38 *That {. . .} blow:* The "a" assonance of this line renders the "a" assonance of Ovid's line.

39 *mind:* heart (passion). *sky:* air (i.e., climatic).

40 *women's love:* "love for a woman."

41 *ray:* bewray, make dirty.

Now comes the pomp; themselves let all men cheer:
The shout is nigh, the golden pomp comes here.
First, Victory is brought with large spread wing: 45
Goddess, come here, make my love conquering.
Applaud you Neptune, that dare trust his wave,
The sea I use not: me my earth must have.
Soldier, applaud thy Mars: no wars we move,
Peace pleaseth me, and in mid-peace is love.   50
With augurs Phoebus, Phoebe with hunters stands,
To thee, Minerva, turn the craftsmen's hands;
Ceres and Bacchus countrymen adore,
Champions please Pollux, Castor loves horsemen more;
Thee, gentle Venus, and the boy that flies   55
We praise; great goddess, aid my enterprise.
Let my new mistress grant to be beloved;
She becked, and prosperous signs gave as she moved.
What Venus promised, promise thou we pray;
Greater than her, by her leave, th' art, I'll say.   60
The gods and their rich pomp witness with me,

43–44 *Now {. . .} here:* Green writes: "The races were preceded by a procession (*pompa*) of ivory images of the gods, borne on wagons or floats, and escorted by officials. The *pompa*, setting out from the Capitol, made its way through the Forum and the Forum Boarium, and so to the Circus by way of the Via Sacra. Once there, it paraded the entire length of the race-track, with the spectators applauding their patron deities."

43 *themselves {. . .} cheer:* The Latin (*linguis animisque favete*) means "attend to your tongues and thoughts," which means "keep quiet." Gill notes that "Marlowe makes an identical error at 3.12.29." An inspection of Niger's commentary here and there is helpful. Here, Niger says that indeed the sense of these words is to "keep quiet" when the context is a sacred one, but when the context is the public games, it is incumbent upon people to show their favor: *Hoc autem verbo in sacris taciturnitas: in ludis necessarius favor indicitur* ("Applause is the more necessary at the games; however, silence is to be observed in sacred places"). In his commentary on 3.12.29, he mentions only that the sense is, indeed, to keep silent, and that agrees with what he has said here because that context is a sacred one. At 3.12.29, however, Marlowe does not follow Niger and so makes the "mistake" only there.

48 *me {. . .} have:* While the primary intent is literal, within the context of this poem the "earth" alludes figuratively to the body of the woman he desires. This reference, therefore, perhaps anticipates the comparisons of women's bodies to land masses, which appear in the coming years in English poetry—Donne's elegy "Going to Bed" and possibly his lyric "The Sunne Rising" come to mind.

51 *augurs {. . .} hunters:* Marlowe renders the (effectual) chiasmus of *auguribus Phoebus Phoebe venantibus.*

53 *Bacchus:* god of wine.

54 *Champions:* boxers. *Pollux, Castor:* see 2.16.13–14n. Also, we know from *Iliad* 3 that Pollux was known for his horsemanship and Castor for his boxing ability.

55 *boy:* Cupid. The modern accepted Latin is *puerisque,* but Niger's text has *puerique;* more significantly, Niger in his commentary says that the word denotes Cupid only.

58 *She becked:* Venus nodded. *prosperous:* favorable. Niger notes *prospera* for Ovid's *secunda.*

For evermore thou shalt my mistress be.
Thy legs hang down, thou mayst, if that be best,
Awhile thy tiptoes on the footstool rest.
Now greatest spectacles the praetor sends,   65
Four-chariot horses from the lists' even ends.
I see whom thou affectest: he shall subdue;
The horses seem as thy desire they knew.
Alas, he runs too far about the ring;
What dost? thy wagon in less compass bring.   70
What dost, unhappy? her good wishes fade,
Let with strong hand the rein to bend be made.
One slow we favour; Romans, him revoke,
And each give signs by casting up his cloak.
They call him back; lest their gowns toss thy hair,   75
To hide thee in my bosom straight repair.
But now again the barriers open lie,
And forth the gay troops on swift horses fly.
At least now conquer, and outrun the rest;
My mistress' wish confirm with my request   80
My mistress hath her wish; my wish remain:
He holds the palm, my palm is yet to gain.
She smiled, and with quick eyes behight some grace:
Pay it not here, but in another place.

---

64 *tiptoes:* toes.

65 *praetor sends:* The praetor signaled the start of the race by dropping a cloth.

66 *Four-chariot horses:* four-horse chariots. *lists' even ends:* the starting-chambers, which were all equidistant from the starting point.

67 *affectest:* care for.

68 *as:* as if.

69 *far:* wide.

70 *thy {. . .} bring:* The modern Latin has *subit* ("to approach, to follow after") and thus is talking about the charioteer just behind the one Ovid is addressing ("he is gaining on you"); however, Marlowe's (and Niger's) text reads *subi,* which is a second-person imperative command, and thus Marlowe's "bring."

71 *What {. . .} unhappy?:* What are you doing, O Wretched One?

73 *One {. . .} favor:* Marlowe's and Ovid's sense is "We're 'putting our money' on a loser!" *revoke:* "call all the drivers back."

74 *And {. . .} cloak:* In this way the audience could demand a rematch. *each:* each of the spectators. *give:* gives. *his:* his own.

77 *barriers {. . .} lie:* the doors closing off the starting chambers are opened.

78 *gay:* brightly colored.

81 *remain:* remains.

82 *palm:* winner's prize. *gain:* be gained.

83 *quick: argutis* is best translated as "piercing" or "bright." Niger offers, for example, both "*mobilibus*" ("rapid") and "*veloces ingenio*" (denoting those who are swift in mind). *behight:* promised.

Elegia III

De amica, quae periuraverat

What, are there gods? herself she hath forswore,
And yet remains the face she had before.
How long her locks were, ere her oath she took,
So long they be since she her faith forsook.
Fair white with rose red was before commixed;   5
Now shine her looks pure white and red betwixt.
Her foot was small: her foot's form is most fit;
Comely tall was she: comely tall she's yet.
Sharp eyes she had: radiant like stars they be,
By which she perjured oft hath lied to me.   10
In sooth th' eternal powers grant maids' society
Falsely to swear, their beauty hath some deity.
By her eyes, I remember, late she swore,
And by mine eyes, and mine were pained sore.
Say, gods: if she unpunished you deceive,   15
For other's faults why do I loss receive?
But did you not so envy Cepheus' daughter,
For her ill-beauteous mother judged to slaughter?
'Tis not enough she shakes your record off,
And, unrevenged, mocked gods with me doth scoff.   20
But by my pain to purge her perjuries,
Cozened, I am the cozener's sacrifice.
God is a name, no substance, feared in vain,
And doth the world in fond belief detain,
Or if there be a God, he loves fine wenches,   25
And all things too much in their sole power drenches.
Mars girts his deadly sword on for my harm;

---

i *De {. . .} periuraverat:* About his mistress, who had lied to him.

7 *most fit:* Marlowe (and Niger) reads *aptissima*, while modern texts have *artissima* ("most dainty").

17–18 *But {. . .} slaughter:* The reference is to Andromeda, daughter of Cepheus and Cassiopeia. Cassiopeia had boasted herself to be more beautiful than Juno and the Nereids. To punish her the gods bound her daughter Andromeda to a rock to be ravaged by a sea-monster; Perseus saved her.

19–20 *'Tis {. . .} scoff:* MacLure observes: "a very imperfect version of 'Isn't it enough that I've found your witness worthless, and that she goes unpunished, mocking the gods as well as me?'"

21–22 *But {. . .} sacrifice:* MacLure writes: "Ovid says: 'Am I to suffer so that she may redeem her false oaths, and I, deceived, be the victim of my deceiver?'"

23 *God is:* Either God is.

24 *fond:* foolish, futile.

26 *And {. . .} drenches:* Marlowe's and Ovid's sense is "And he gives too much power to women over all things."

27 *my harm:* that is, to the detriment of all men.

Pallas' lance strikes me with unconquered arm;
At me Apollo bends his pliant bow;
At me Jove's right hand lightning hath to throw.   30
The wronged gods dread fair ones to offend,
And fear those, that to fear them least intend.
Who now will care the altars to perfume?
Tut, men should not their courage so consume.
Jove throws down woods and castles with his fire,   35
But bids his darts from perjured girls retire.
Poor Semele, among so many burned,
Her own request to her own torment turned;
But when her lover came, had she drawn back,
The father's thigh should unborn Bacchus lack.   40
Why grieve I? and of heaven reproaches pen?
The gods have eyes, and breasts as well as men.
Were I a god, I should give women leave
With lying lips my godhead to deceive.
Myself would swear the wenches true did swear,   45
And I would be none of the girls severe,
But yet their gift more moderately use,
Or in mine eyes, good wench, no pain transfuse.

ELEGIA IV

Ad virum servantem coniugem

Rude man, 'tis vain thy damsel to commend
To keeper's trust: their wits should them defend.

---

28 *me:* us (all men). This applies also to "me" in the next two lines.
34 *Tut {. . .} consume:* Ovid's sense is "Surely there must be more courage within men" (*certe plus animi debet inesse viris*).
35 *throws down:* destroys.
37–40 *Poor {. . .} lack:* Green writes: "Zeus seduced Semele, daughter of Cadmus: Hera discovered the liaison, and persuaded Semele to ask [Zeus] to appear to her in all his glory. [. . .] Since Zeus had promised Semele to do whatever she asked, he could not refuse: he 'came to her bridal chamber in a chariot, with lightnings and thunderings, and launched a thunderbolt.' Semele, not surprisingly, was either burnt to a crisp or else died of fright (accounts differ), but in any case aborted her [. . .] child, Dionysus. Zeus, ever resourceful, proceeded to sew the baby into his thigh, whence it was born at the proper term."
42 *breasts:* hearts (*pectus*).
48 *in:* into.

i *Ad {. . .} coniugem:* To a man who guards his wife.
1 *Rude:* harsh.

Who, without fear, is chaste, is chaste in sooth:
Who, because means want, doeth not, she doth.
Though thou her body guard, her mind is stained: 5
Nor, lest she will, can any be restrained.
Nor canst by watching keep her mind from sin;
All being shut out, th' adulterer is within.
Who may offend, sins least; power to do ill
The fainting seeds of naughtiness doth kill.   10
Forbear to kindle vice by prohibition,
Sooner shall kindness gain thy will's fruition.
I saw a horse against the bit stiff-necked
Like lightning go, his struggling mouth being checked;
When he perceived the reins let slack, he stayed,   15
And on his loose mane the loose bridle laid.
How to attain what is denied we think,
Even as the sick desire forbidden drink.
Argus had either way an hundred eyes,
Yet by deceit love did them all surprise;   20
In stone and iron walls Danae shut,
Came forth a mother, though a maid there put.
Penelope, though no watch looked unto her,
Was not defiled by any gallant wooer.
What's kept, we covet more: the care makes theft;   25
Few love what others have unguarded left.
Nor doth her face please, but her husband's love;
I know not what men think should thee so move.
She is not chaste that's kept, but a dear whore;
Thy fear is than her body valued more.   30
Although thou chafe, stol'n pleasure is sweet play;

3–4 *Who {. . .} doth:* Marlowe's and Ovid's sense is "She who is not afraid of being caught because she has nothing to hide is chaste in her inner nature; however, she who does not sexually cheat because she fears being caught—that one will do it if she can get away with it and therefore is not chaste in her inner nature" (*si qua metu dempto casta est ea denique casta est/quae quia non liceat non facit illa facit*).

6 *she will:* a woman wishes it. *any:* any woman.

19 *Argus:* the watchman sent by Juno to guard Io. He had one hundred eyes; here, Ovid doubles it to one hundred behind and one hundred in front.

21 *Danae:* see 2.19.27n.

23 *Penelope:* faithful wife of Odysseus.

25 *care makes:* safeguarding itself invites.

27 *face please:* beauty make her desirable.

28 *I {. . .} move:* Marlowe's and Ovid's sense is "There is something [about her], I know not what, which has made her irresistible to you."

30 *is than:* makes.

She pleaseth best, "I fear" if any say.
A free-born wench no right 'tis up to lock,
So use we women of strange nations' stock.
Because the keeper may come say, "I did it,"   35
She must be honest to thy servant's credit.
He is too clownish whom a lewd wife grieves,
And this town's well-known custom not believes,
Where Mars his sons not without fault did breed,
Remus and Romulus, Ilia's twin-born seed.   40
Cannot a fair one, if not chaste, please thee?
Never can these by any means agree.
Kindly thy mistress use, if thou be wise;
Look gently, and rough husbands' laws despise.
Honour what friends thy wife gives, she'll give many;   45
Least labour so shall win great grace of any;
So shalt thou go with youths to feast together,
And see at home much that thou ne'er brought'st thither.

ELEGIA V

Ad amnem, dum iter faceret ad amicam
Flood with reed-grown slime banks, till I be past
Thy waters stay; I to my mistress haste.
Thou hast no bridge, nor boat with ropes to throw,
That may transport me without oars to row.
Thee I have passed, and knew thy stream none such,   5
When thy wave's brim did scarce my ankles touch.
With snow thawed from the next hill now thou rushest,

---

34 *strange:* foreign.

36 *honest:* chaste.

37 *clownish:* rustic, unsophisticated. *grieves:* aggrieves, that is, cheats on.

39 *Mars:* Gill explains: "Mars violated the chastity of Rhea Silvia (Ilia), a vestal virgin, who then became the mother of Romulus and Remus, the founders of Rome."

41 *Cannot {. . .} thee?:* Why did you marry a beauty if you also want your wife to be chaste? (*quo tibi formosam si non nisi casta placebat?*).

42 *these:* beauty and chastity.

45 *gives, give:* brings, bring.

46 *Least:* This small.

48 *much:* many gifts.

i *Ad {. . .} amicam:* To a river, as he makes his way to his mistress. (In modern editions of Ovid there is another poem in place of this one, while this one is printed as number six.)

2 *waters stay:* "waters" is the direct object of the imperative "stay."

5 *none such:* "not as it is now" (i.e., high and swift).

And in thy foul deep waters thick thou gushest.
What helps my haste? what to have ta'en small rest?
What day and night to travel in her quest,   10
If standing here I can by no means get
My foot upon the further bank to set?
Now wish I those wings noble Perseus had,
Bearing the head with dreadful adders clad;
Now wish the chariot, whence corn seeds were found   15
First to be thrown upon the untilled ground.
I speak old poets' wonderful inventions,
Never was, nor shall be, what my verse mentions.
Rather, thou large bank-overflowing river,
Slide in thy bounds, so shalt thou run for ever.   20
Trust me, land-stream, thou shalt no envy lack,
If I a lover be by thee held back.
Great floods ought to assist young men in love,

---

10 *What {. . .} quest:* Add "good has it done me" after "What."

13–14 *Now {. . .} clad:* Perseus, son of Danae, was given winged sandals by Mercury when he went to kill the gorgon Medusa who had snakes for hair, and he carried her head on his shield.

15–16 *Now {. . .} ground:* The reference is to Ceres's chariot, which was drawn by snakes to scatter seeds to cultivate the earth (see *Metamorphoses* 5.643ff).

23–54 *Great floods {. . .} Laomedon:* Gill writes: "The poem addressed to the small stream gives Ovid the opportunity to write on the subject of the loves between men and rivers. Inachus (25) was a river-god, the son of Oceanus, who gave his name and protection to a river in Argolis; he married a daughter of Oceanus, the nymph Melia. [. . .] Scamander (28), or Xanthus [. . .] took part in the Trojan War [. . .]; the river's association with Neara [. . .] cannot be traced, however. Alpheus (29) was a river of Elis which fell in love with Arethusa when she was bathing in his stream; in human shape he pursued her until she appealed to Diana for help. Diana answered her prayer by turning Arethusa into water and, when Alpheus promptly changed back into a river, carried her underground to the island of Ortygia at Syracuse, where the spring of Arethusa was a noted feature. A scribal error in the transmission of Ovid's text is to be blamed for the confusion in line 31. Xantho here seems to have been caught up from Xanthe (Marlowe's 'Scamander') three lines earlier. Modern additions accept the conjecture Xutho. Xuthus, the son of Hellen (and grandson of Deucalion) married Creusa, daughter of Erechtheus, King of Athens, but she was stolen from him by Peneus (32), a river-god of Thessaly, and was carried away to Phthiotis, a district [. . .] of that country. Marlowe's 'Aesope' (33) is Asopus, a river in Boeotia; he is said to have been the father, not the husband, of Thebe (34), from whom the Boeotian town of Thebes took its name. Achelous (35), the most celebrated of rivers and the largest watercourse in Greece, fought against Hercules ('Alcides', 36) for the hand of Deianira (38), daughter of Oeneus, King of Calydon (37). Achelous turned himself into a wild bull, but Hercules broke off one of his horns (which was made into the Horn of Plenty). Nothing is known of an Evadne (41) in connection with the Nile (39); in the Latin she is said to have been the daughter of Asopus. The god Poseidon loved Tyro [also called Salmonis] (43), daughter of Salmoneus, and visited her disguised as the Thessalian river Enipeus (43). Ovid explains that it was in order to dry himself for Tyro's embraces that the god commanded the river waters to retire. When Ilia (Rhea Silva, 47) violated her vow of chastity as a vestal virgin, becoming by Mars (49) the mother of Romulus and Remus, she was thrown into the river Anio, a tributary of the Tiber, by the order of her uncle Amulius, and became the wife of the river-god."

Great floods the force of it do often prove.
In mid-Bithynia, 'tis said, Inachus   25
Grew pale, and in cold fords hot lecherous.
Troy had not yet been ten years' siege outstander,
When nymph Neaera rapt thy looks, Scamander.
What, not Alpheus in strange lands to run
Th' Arcadian virgin's constant love hath won?   30
And Creusa unto Xanthus first affied,
They say Peneus near Phthia's town did hide.
What should I name Aesope, that Thebe loved,
Thebe who mother of five daughters proved.
If, Achelous, I ask where thy horns stand,   35
Thou say'st, broke with Alcides' angry hand.
Not Calydon, nor Aetolia did please;
One Deianira was more worth than these.
Rich Nile by seven mouths to the vast sea flowing,
Who so well keeps his water's head from knowing,   40
Is by Evadne thought to take such flame
As his deep whirlpools could not quench the same,
Dry Enipeus, Tyro to embrace,
Fly back his stream charged; the stream charged, gave place.
Nor pass I thee, who hollow rocks down tumbling,   45
In Tibur's field with wat'ry foam art rumbling,
Whom Ilia pleased, though in her looks grief revelled;
Her cheeks were scratched, her goodly hairs dishevelled.
She, wailing Mars' sin and her uncle's crime,
Strayed barefoot through sole places on a time.   50
Her from his swift waves the bold flood perceived,
And from the mid-ford his hoarse voice upheaved,
Saying, "Why sadly tread'st my banks upon,
Ilia, sprung from Idaean Laomedon?
Where's thy attire? why wand'rest here alone?   55
To stay thy tresses white veil hast thou none?
Why weep'st, and spoil'st with tears thy wat'ry eyes,
And fiercely knock'st thy breast that open lies?
His heart consists of flint and hardest steel,
That seeing thy tears can any joy then feel.   60

---

24 *it:* love.
44 *Fly {. . .} charged:* Ovid's sense is "ordered his stream to run backwards" (*cedere iussit aquam*).
46 *wat'ry foam:* In his commentary Niger notes the textual alternative of *spumifer* for *pomifer* ("fruit-bearing").
50 *sole places:* lonely places. *on a time:* not in the Latin.
51 *flood:* Anio.

Fear not: to thee our court stands open wide,
There shalt be loved: Ilia, lay fear aside.
Thou o'er a hundred nymphs or more shalt reign,
For five score nymphs or more our floods contain.
Nor, Roman stock, scorn me so much (I crave)   65
Gifts than my promise greater thou shalt have."
This said he: she her modest eyes held down,
Her woeful bosom a warm shower did drown.
Thrice she prepared to fly, thrice she did stay,
By fear deprived of strength to run away.   70
Yet rending with enraged thumb her tresses,
Her trembling mouth these unmeet sounds expresses:
"O would in my forefathers' tomb deep laid
My bones had been, while yet I was a maid.
Why being a vestal am I wooed to wed,   75
Deflowered and stained in unlawful bed?
Why stay I? men point at me for a whore,
Shame, that should make me blush, I have no more."
This said, her coat hoodwinked her fearful eyes,
And into water desperately she flies.   80
'Tis said the slippery stream held up her breast,
And kindly gave her what she liked best.
And I believe some wench thou hast affected,
But woods and groves keep your faults undetected.
While thus I speak the waters more abounded,   85
And from the channel all abroad surrounded.
Mad stream, why dost our mutual joys defer?
Clown, from my journey why dost me deter?
How wouldst thou flow wert thou a noble flood,
If thy great fame in every region stood?   90
Thou hast no name, but com'st from snowy mountains;
No certain house thou hast, nor any fountains.
Thy springs are nought but rain and melted snow,
Which wealth cold winter doth on thee bestow.
Either th' art muddy in mid-winter tide,   95
Or full of dust dost on the dry earth slide.
What thirsty traveller ever drunk of thee?
Who said with grateful voice, "Perpetual be"?
Harmful to beasts and to the fields thou proves;

---

72 *unmeet:* indignant (*indignos*).
79 *hoodwinked:* covered.
82 *kindly {. . .} best:* gave her the rights of the marriage bed (*socii iura dedisse tori*).
88 *Clown:* O one unskilled [in the art of love] (*rustice*).

Perchance these others, me mine own loss moves.   100
To this I fondly loves of floods told plainly,
I shame so great names to have used so vainly.
I know not what expecting, I erewhile
Named Achelaus, Inachus, and Nile.
But for thy merits I wish thee, white stream,   105
Dry winters aye, and suns in heat extreme.

ELEGIA VI

Quod ab amica receptus cum ea coire non potuit, conqueritur
Either she was foul, or her attire was bad,
Or she was not the wench I wished t' have had.
Idly I lay with her, as if I loved not,
And like a burden grieved the bed that moved not.
Though both of us performed our true intent,   5
Yet could I not cast anchor where I meant.
She on my neck her ivory arms did throw,
Her arms far whiter than the Scythian snow,
And eagerly she kissed me with her tongue,
And under mine her wanton thigh she flung.   10
Yea, and she soothed me up, and called me "Sir,"
And used all speech that might provoke and stir.
Yet like as if cold hemlock I had drunk,
It mocked me, hung down the head, and sunk.
Like a dull cipher or rude block I lay,   15
Or shade or body was I, who can say?

---

101 *this:* this river. *fondly:* foolishly.

105 *white:* Ovid's *non candide* should be translated as "unclear," "muddy," or "agitated" (*sic* Niger, who says "*turbide*"). Martin and MacLure both suggest that Marlowe's earlier text may have read *nunc* for *non*.

i *Quod {. . .} conqueritur:* He is overwhelmed by the fact that when his mistress wanted him sexually, he was unable to perform. This anticipates a whole subgenre of English lyric poetry to appear contemporaneously and over the next century in the poetry of, for example, Nashe, Behn, and Rochester, called "the imperfect enjoyment poem" ("imperfect" meaning, in its etymological sense, "incomplete").

1–2 *Either {. . .} or {. . .} Or:* Martin and MacLure both say that Marlowe's text read *Aut {. . .} aut {. . .} aut* instead of *At {. . .} at {. . .} at.* Niger's text has *at,* though in his commentary he engages in a long discussion about earlier texts having *aut* and then Niger advises that *at* is preferable because it preserves the irony intended by Ovid, given that later in the poem the mistress is described as beautiful. Marlowe ignored that sense voiced by Niger.

3 *Idly:* limply. The line's languid "l" alliteration renders Ovid's "l" alliteration of *nullos {. . .} male languidus.*

16 *Or:* Whether.

What will my age do, age I cannot shun,
When in my prime my force is spent and done?
I blush, that being youthful, hot, and lusty,
I prove neither youth nor man, but old and rusty.   20
Pure rose she, like a nun to sacrifice,
Or one that with her tender brother lies.
Yet boarded I the golden Chie twice,
And Libas, and the white cheeked Pitho thrice.
Corinna craved it in a summer's night,   25
And nine sweet bouts we had before daylight.
What, waste my limbs through some Thessalian charms?
May spells and drugs do silly souls such harms?
With virgin wax hath some imbased my joints,
And pierced my liver with sharp needles' points?   30
Charms change corn to grass and make it die;
By charms are running springs and fountains dry.
By charms mast drops from oaks, from vines grapes fall,
And fruit from trees when there's no wind at all.
Why might not then my sinews be enchanted,   35
And I grow faint as with some spirit haunted?
To this add shame: shame to perform it quailed me,
And was the second cause why vigour failed me.
My idle thoughts delighted her no more
Than did the robe or garment which she wore.   40
Yet might her touch make youthful Pylius fire,
And Tithon livelier than his years require.
Even her I had and she had me in vain,

---

21 *rose:* arose.

22 *Or {. . .} lies:* Ovid's sense is "Or as a sister leaves behind her dear brother who respects her" (*surgit et a caro fratre verenda soror*).

23–24: *golden:* blond. *Chie {. . .} Libas {. . .} Pitho:* the names of three other (fictional) women he has successfully "boarded."

27 *What {. . .} charms:* Marlowe's and Ovid's sense is "Does my body languish because it has been undone by some Thessalian drug?"

29 *With {. . .} joints:* Has some witch defiled my name by covering my image in red wax? *sagave poenicea defixit nomina cera*). See Martin for a possible explanation.

30 *liver:* In antiquity, the liver was often considered to be the seat of love and passion within the human body.

33 *mast:* acorns.

37 *quailed:* withered.

39–40 *My {. . .} wore:* The correct translation is "What a girl I just saw and touched—I touched her just as closely as her clothes do" (*at qualem vidi tantum tetigique puellam /sic etiam tunica tangitur illa sua*).

41 *Pylius:* Nestor, extremely elderly and respected member of the Greek host at Troy.

42 *Tithon:* Tithonus, husband of Aurora, who has eternal life but not youth.

What might I crave more, if I ask again?
I think the great gods grieved they had bestowed   45
The benefit which lewdly I forslowed.
I wished to be received in, in I get me;
To kiss, I kiss; to lie with her she let me.
Why was I blest? why made king to refuse it?
Chuff-like had I not gold and could not use it?   50
So in a spring thrives he that told so much,
And looks upon the fruits he cannot touch.
Hath any rose so from a fresh young maid,
As she might straight have gone to church and prayed?
Well, I believe she kissed not as she should,   55
Nor used the sleight and cunning which she could.
Huge oaks, hard adamants might she have moved,
And with sweet words cause deaf rocks to have loved.
Worthy she was to move both gods and men,
But neither was I man nor lived then.   60
Can deaf ear take delight when Phaemius sings,
Or Thamyras in curious painted things?
What sweet thought is there but I had the same?
And one gave place still as another came.
Yet notwithstanding, like one dead it lay,   65
Drooping more than a rose pulled yesterday.
Now, when he should not jet, he bolts upright,
And craves his task, and seeks to be at fight.
Lie down with shame, and see thou stir no more,

---

44 *What {. . .} again?:* Ovid's sense is "How can I ever again ask for sexual favors if now, when they
are mine for the taking, I do not avail myself of them?"

46 *which {. . .} forslowed:* Marlowe's and Ovid's sense is "which I, by (my member) being slack, dis-
gracefully made use of."

47 *get:* got.

48 *To kiss:* Understand "I wished," from line 47, to precede these words.

49 *why {. . .} it:* Marlowe's and Ovid's sense is "Why be made a king if I refuse to take the scepter?"

50 *Chuff:* Miser.

51 *he:* Tantalus. As MacLure and Orgel point out, the use of "thrives" is ironic.

53 *any rose:* "any man risen in the morning" (*quisquam {. . .} surgit mane*).

59 *gods and men:* Marlowe's text read *divosque virosque* instead of the modern accepted *vivosque virosque*
("people who are men and alive").

61 *Phemius:* the minstrel who sang to Penelope's suitors in the *Odyssey*.

62 *Thamyras:* a musician who lost a challenge to the Muses who robbed him of his eyesight. *curious:* intricately.

65 *it:* my member.

67 *Now:* (neither the proper time nor place). *jet:* thrash about.

69–70 *shame {. . .} see {. . .} stir {. . .} / Seeing {. . .} wouldst deceive me as:* This "s" alliteration and "ee"
assonance effect an appropriately inculpatory and sneering tone, which is likewise effected in

Seeing thou wouldst deceive me as before.   70
Thou cozenest me: by thee surprised am I,
And bide sore loss with endless infamy.
Nay more, the wench did not disdain a whit
To take it in her hand and play with it,
But when she saw it would by no means stand,   75
But still drooped down, regarding not her hand,
"Why mock'st thou me," she cried, "or being ill,
Who bade thee lie down here against thy will?
Either th' art witched with blood of frogs new dead,
Or jaded cam'st thou from some other's bed."   80
With that, her loose gown on, from me she cast her;
In skipping out her naked feet much graced her.
And lest her maid should know of this disgrace,
To cover it, spilt water on the place.

ELEGIA VII

Quod ab amica non recipiatur, dolet
What man will now take liberal arts in hand,
Or think soft verse in any stead to stand?
Wit was sometimes more precious than gold,
Now poverty great barbarism we hold.
When our books did my mistress fair content,   5
I might not go whither my papers went.
She praised me, yet the gate shut fast upon her,
I here and there go, witty with dishonour.
See a rich chuff, whose wounds great wealth inferred,
For bloodshed knighted, before me preferred!   10

Ovid's corresponding couplet by the "s" and the "p" alliteration of *istic pudibunda iaces pars pes-*
sima nostri / sic sum pollicitis captus {. . .} tuis.
71 *cozenest:* deceive.
79 *th' art witch'd:* "you're bewitched." *blood {. . .} dead:* "Either a Circean witch has cursed you by
piercing a wool-woven figure of you" (*aut te traiectus Aeaea venefica lanis/devovet*). The suggestion
from Niger's commentary (*ut de rubetis intelligatur, quarum maximus in magicus usus*) is supported
by Gill, MacLure, and Martin, who observe that sixteenth-century texts noted a variant of *ranis*
("frogs") for *lanis* ("wool" [from Circe's spinning]), and that bloody frogs or toads were considered the best form of poison.

i *Quod {. . .} dolet:* He grieves because his mistress will not see him.
1 *liberal:* Niger's interpretation (*liberales*) of *ingenuas* (noble, natural).
2 *in {. . .} stand?:* has any value.
5 *our:* my.
9–10 *See {. . .} preferred:* Ovid is indignant because he himself came from a long line of equestrian
soldiers and now he is being displaced by a newly arrived, nouveau riche knight who boasts no

Fool, canst thou him in thy white arms embrace?
Fool, canst thou lie in his enfolding space?
Knowest not this head a helm was wont to bear?
This side that serves thee, a sharp sword did wear.
His left hand, whereon gold doth ill alight,   15
A target bore; blood-sprinkled was his right.
Canst touch that hand wherewith someone lie dead?
Ah whither is thy breast's soft nature fled?
Behold the signs of ancient fight, his scars,
Whate'er he hath his body gained in wars.   20
Perhaps he'll tell how oft he slew a man,
Confessing this, why dost thou touch him then?
I, the pure priest of Phoebus and the Muses,
At thy deaf doors in verse sing my abuses.
Not what we slothful knew, let wise men learn,   25
But follow trembling camps and battles stern,
And for a good verse draw the first dart forth:
Homer without this shall be nothing worth.
Jove, being admonished gold had sovereign power,
To win the maid came in a golden shower.   30
Till then, rough was her father, she severe,
The posts of brass, the walls of iron were;
But when in gifts the wise adulterer came,
She held her lap ope to receive the same.
Yet when old Saturn heaven's rule possessed,   35
All gain in darkness the deep earth suppressed.
Gold, silver, iron's heavy weight, and brass,
In hell were harboured; here was found no mass.

---

such lineage. This horse-soldier has gained renown and reward by shedding the blood of his enemies on the battlefield.

11–12 *Fool, Fool:* Marlowe's text reads *stulta;* modern texts read *vita* ("my life").

13 *helm:* helmet.

15 *gold {. . .} alight:* horse-soldiers wore a gold ring on their left hand.

16 *target:* shield.

17 *Canst:* Can you.

27 *for:* instead of.

28 *Homer {. . .} worth:* The sense of the Latin (*nox tibi si belles possit Homere dari*) is "Even you, Homer, would be able to get a woman if you also went to war [not if you stayed at home and wrote poetry]."

30 *maid:* Danae.

35 *Yet {. . .} possessed:* a reference to the Golden Age, which was renowned for its cultivation of the earth and of a simple, selfless, and civilized way of life. Saturn was an ancient king of Italy who became confused and conflated with Cronos, the father of Jove.

36 *gain:* riches, for example, gold, silver, and so on.

But better things it gave, corn without ploughs,
Apples, and honey in oaks' hollow boughs.   40
With strong ploughshares no man the earth did cleave,
The ditcher no marks on the ground did leave,
Nor hanging oars the troubled seas did sweep;
Men kept the shore, and sailed not into deep.
Against thyself, man's nature, thou wert cunning,   45
And to thine own loss was thy wit swift running.
Why gird'st thy cities with a towered wall?
Why let'st discordant hands to armour fall?
What dost with seas? with th' earth thou wert content;
Why seek'st not heaven, the third realm, to frequent?   50
Heaven thou affects; with Romulus, temples brave
Bacchus, Alcides, and now Caesar have.
Gold from the earth instead of fruits we pluck;
Soldiers by blood to be enriched have luck.
Courts shut the poor out; wealth gives estimation,   55
Thence grows the judge, and knight of reputation.
All they possess: they govern fields and laws,
They manage peace, and raw war's bloody jaws.
Only our loves let not such rich churls gain;
'Tis well if some wench for the poor remain.   60
Now, Sabine-like, though chaste she seems to live,
One her commands, who many things can give.
For me, she doth keeper and husband fear;
If I should give, both would the house forbear.
If of scorned lovers god be venger just,   65
O let him change goods so ill got to dust.

---

42 *ditcher:* digger (*fossor*). Later editions read *mensor,* translated as "surveyor."
44 *kept:* kept to. *deep:* the deep.
48 *discordant:* warring (*discordes*).
49 *What dost:* Why bother with. *wert:* should have been.
50 *the:* for a.
51 *affects:* reaches for.
52 *Alcides:* Hercules.
54 *blood:* their bloody conquests.
55 *estimation:* (etymologue of "esteem") influence.
55–59 *Courts {. . .} gain:* The sentiment of these lines perhaps anticipates the opening stanza of Donne's "The Canonization."
61 *Sabine-like:* virtuous.
64 *If {. . .} forbear:* Ovid's and Marlowe's sense is "They would both leave the house to her and me alone if I would only pay them!"
65 *If {. . .} just:* Ovid's and Marlowe's sense is "If only there were a god to avenge neglected lovers."
66 *change:* transform. *got:* gotten.

ELEGIA VIII

Tibulli mortem deflet

If Thetis and the Morn their sons did wail,
And envious Fates great goddesses assail,
Sad Elegia, thy woeful hairs unbind:
Ah now a name too true thou hast, I find.
Tibullus, thy work's poet, and thy fame,   5
Burns his dead body in the funeral flame.
Lo Cupid brings his quiver spoiled quite,
His broken bow, his firebrand without light.
How piteously with drooping wings he stands,
And knocks his bare breast with self-angry hands.   10
The locks spread on his neck receive his tears,
And shaking sobs his mouth for speeches bears.
So at Aeneas' burial, men report,
Fair-faced Iulus, he went forth thy court.
And Venus grieves, Tibullus' life being spent,   15
As when the wild boar Adon's groin had rent.
The gods' care we are called, and men of piety,
And some there be that think we have a deity.
Outrageous death profanes all holy things,
And on all creatures obscure darkness brings.   20
To Thracian Orpheus what did parents good,
Or songs amazing wild beasts of the wood?
Where Linus by his father Phoebus laid
To sing with his unequalled harp is said.

---

i *Tibulli mortem deflet:* He bewails the death of Tibullus (one of Ovid's poetic predecessors in the writing of Latin love elegy).

1 *Thetis:* mother of Achilles. *Morn:* Aurora, the Dawn, mother of Memnon. Achilles killed Memnon, and Paris killed Achilles. *wail:* bewail, mourn.

2 *envious Fates:* grievous death.

4 *name too true:* Ovid considers elegy here to be a eulogy or lament.

14 *Iulus:* Ascanius, son of Aeneas. *court:* escort.

16 *Adon:* Adonis.

17 *we:* we poets. *men of piety:* sacred.

18 *we:* we poets. *have a deity:* have godhead within ourselves.

19 *Outrageous:* grievous.

21 *Thracian Orpheus:* The son of Calliope and Apollo or Oeagrus, the king of Thrace. The sound of his lyre could tame wild beasts and soothe trees and mountains. *what did parents good:* Marlowe's and Ovid's sense is "What good did it do him to have parents?"

23 *Linus:* another son of Apollo known for his poetic skill.

23–24 *Where {. . .} said:* The Ovidian text is notoriously corrupt and variegated, and this partly accounts for the difficulty of Marlowe's couplet. The reference is to Apollo's lament over the death

See Homer from whose fountain ever filled   25
Pierian dew to poets is distilled:
Him the last day in black Averne hath drowned;
Verses alone are with continuance crowned.
The work of poets lasts Troy's labour's fame,
And that slow web night's falsehood did unframe.   30
So Nemesis, so Delia famous are:
The one his first love, th' other his new care.
What profit to us hath our pure life bred?
What to have lain alone in empty bed?
When bad fates take good men, I am forbod   35
By secret thoughts to think there is a god.
Live godly, thou shalt die; though honour heaven,
Yet shall thy life be forcibly bereaven.
Trust in good verse: Tibullus feels death's pains,
Scarce rests of all what a small urn contains.   40
Thee, sacred poet, could sad flames destroy?
Nor feared they thy body to annoy?
The holy gods' gilt temples they might fire,
That durst to so great wickedness aspire.
Eryx' bright empress turned her looks aside,   45
And some, that she refrained tears, have denied.
Yet better is 't, than if Corcyra's isle
Had thee unknown interred in ground most vile.
Thy dying eyes here did thy mother close,
Nor did thy ashes her last off'rings lose.   50

---

of his son Linus. The sense is best apprehended by rearranging and adding to Marlowe's words
thus: "Where Phoebus is said to sing with his unequalled harp [of] Linus, laid by his father." It
might also be helpful to construe "laid" as "layed" (= "having been sung") as Gill suggests.
26 *Pierian:* from the spring sacred to the Muses.
27 *the last day:* the day he died. *Averne:* Avernus—a lake consecrated to Pluto, god of the Underworld, and thus a metonym for hell.
28 *Verses {. . .} crowned:* Marlowe's and Ovid's sense is "Poetry alone lives eternally."
29 *lasts:* outlasts.
30 *And {. . .} unframe:* a reference to Penelope's nightly unraveling of the cloth she wove every day.
Understand "which" between "web" and "night's."
31 *Nemesis, Delia:* the names of Tibullus's mistresses in his elegies.
33 *What {. . .} bred?* Marlowe omits *quid nunc Aegyptia prosunt / sistra?* which means "of what profit
was the Egyptian sistrum (rattle)?" This refers to the rites of Isis, whom Delia worshipped.
35 *forbod:* forbidden.
40 *rests of all:* remains of him.
41 *sad flames:* the funeral pyre.
43 *fire:* burn.
45 *Eryx {. . .} empress:* Venus, also called Erycine, because of her temple on Mt. Eryx in Sicily.
47 *Corcyra:* Corfu, where Tibullus once had fallen seriously ill.

Part of her sorrow here thy sister bearing
Comes forth her unkembed locks asunder tearing.
Nemesis and thy first wench join their kisses
With thine, nor this last fire their presence misses.
Delia departing, "Happier loved," she saith,   55
"Was I: thou livedst, while thou esteemedst my faith."
Nemesis answers, "What's my loss to thee?
His fainting hand in death engrasped me."
If aught remains of us but name and spirit,
Tibullus doth Elysium's joy inherit.   60
Your youthful brows with ivy girt to meet him,
With Calvus, learned Catullus come, and greet him,
And thou, if falsely charged to wrong thy friend,
Gallus, that car'st not blood and life to spend.
With these thy soul walks: souls if death release,   65
The godly, sweet Tibullus doth increase.
Thy bones I pray may in the urn safe rest,
And may th' earth's weight thy ashes nought molest.

ELEGIA IX

Ad Cererem, conquerens quod eius sacris cum amica concumbere non permittatur
Come were the times of Ceres' sacrifice:
In empty bed alone my mistress lies.
Golden-haired Ceres, crowned with ears of corn,

---

52 *unkembed:* uncombed, disheveled.

53–54 *kisses/with thine:* This critical enjambment, which embodies the content, renders the same
   in the Latin (*cumque tuis sua iunxerunt Nemesisque priorque/oscula*); moreover, the enjambment in
   the Latin is even more enforced by the possibility to elide, vocally, the "e" of *priorque* into the "o"
   of *oscula.*

56 *Was I:* This enjambment renders the same in the Latin (*sum tibi*). Marlowe omits the metalepsis
   on the idea, and diction, of "fire," from that of the preceding lines alluding to Tibullus's funeral
   pyre up to this line 56 where Ovid writes (in Delia's words) *vixisti, dum tuus ignis eram* ("you lived
   as long as I was your fire [= passion]").

62 *Calvus, Catullus:* Latin poets prior to and influential upon Tibullus.

63–64 *And {. . .} spend:* Gallus was another early Latin poet who killed himself after being accused
   of betraying the trust of his patron Augustus Caesar.

68 *molest:* a Miltonic (etymological) use of the word that arguably derives from the Latin *moles*
   ("weight"). The Latin *molestus* ("annoying") could also be in play because the corresponding word
   in Ovid is *onerosa* (whence "onus"), which connotes primarily literal weight but also metaphorical weight ("burdensome").

i *Ad {. . .} permittatur:* He complains to Ceres that because of the observation of her scared rites he
   may not sleep with his mistress.

1 *Ceres:* goddess of agriculture.

Why are our pleasures by thy means forborne?
Thee, goddess, bountiful all nations judge,   5
Nor less at man's prosperity any grudge.
Rude husbandmen baked not their corn before,
Nor on the earth was known the name of floor;
On mast of oaks, first oracles, men fed,
This was their meat, the soft grass was their bed.   10
First Ceres taught the seed in fields to swell,
And ripe-eared corn with sharp-edged scythes to fell;
She first constrained bulls' necks to bear the yoke,
And untilled ground with crooked ploughshares broke.
Who thinks her to be glad at lovers' smart,   15
And worshipped by their pain and lying apart?
Nor is she, though she loves the fertile fields,
A clown, nor no love from her warm breast yields.
Be witness Crete (nor Crete doth all things feign),
Crete proud that Jove her nursery maintain.   20
There he who rules the world's star-spangled towers,
A little boy, drunk teat-distilling showers.
Faith to the witness Jove's praise doth apply;
Ceres, I think, no known fault will deny.
The goddess saw Iasion on Candian Ide,   25
With strong hand striking wild beasts' bristled hide;
She saw, and as her marrow took the flame,
Was divers ways distract with love and shame.

---

4 *forborne:* forbidden.

6 *Nor {. . .} grudge:* Marlowe's and Ovid's sense is "Nor is there any goddess who less envies human prosperity."

8 *floor:* threshing-floor for grain.

9 *mast:* acorns. The oak was sacred to, and thus a signifier of, Jove; this reference is to the oak, at the shrine of Jove at Dodona, which was said to be oracular of the gods.

10 *This {. . .} bed:* Marlowe translates *haec cibus et teneri cespitis herba torus,* while later texts have *haec erat et teneri caespitis herba cibus* ("[acorns] and the herbs growing from the tender grass were man's food").

12 *And {. . .} fell:* "with" is included for the meter; thus, "scythes" is the accusative subject of the infinitive "to fell," and "corn" is the direct object of that infinitive.

18 *clown:* rustic.

19 *Crete:* Crete was considered the home of Jove, and Cretans were considered liars.

20 *Crete {. . .} maintain:* Marlowe's and Ovid's sense is "Crete was proud to be the place which cultivated (i.e., maintained a cult of worship to) Jove."

22 *A:* As a. *drunk:* drank.

23 *Faith {. . .} apply:* Marlowe's and Ovid's sense is "The Cretans' praise of Jove testifies to their veracity."

24 *known:* Marlowe's text had *nota,* while modern texts have *nostra* ("my").

25 *Iasion:* A Cretan lover of Ceres. *Candian Ide:* Mt. Ida on Crete.

27 *marrow:* heart.

Love conquered shame, the furrows dry were burned,
And corn with least part of itself returned.   30
When well-tossed mattocks did the ground prepare,
Being fit broken with the crooked share,
And seeds were equally in large fields cast,
The ploughman's hopes were frustrate at the last.
The grain-rich goddess in high woods did stray,   35
Her long hair's ear-wrought garland fell away.
Only was Crete fruitful that plenteous year;
Where Ceres went, each place was harvest there.
Ida, the seat of groves, did sing with corn,
Which by the wild boar in the woods was shorn.   40
Law-giving Minos did such years desire,
And wished the goddess long might feel love's fire.
Ceres, what sports to thee so grievous were,
As in thy sacrifice we them forbear?
Why am I sad, when Proserpine is found,   45
And Juno-like with Dis reigns underground?
Festival days ask Venus, songs and wine,
These gifts are meet to please the powers divine.

ELEGIA X

Ad amicam, a cuius amore discedere non potest
Long have I borne much, mad thy faults me make:
Dishonest love, my wearied breast forsake!

---

30 *corn {. . .} returned:* Marlowe's and Ovid's sense is "the sown seed yielded back only the scarcest
part of itself."
32 *Being {. . .} broken:* that is, the ground. *share:* ploughshare.
36 *ear-wrought:* made of ears of corn.
39 *Ida {. . .} corn:* Gill notes: "Marlowe mistakes *cānebat* ('was white' [with corn]) for *cănebat* ('sang').
However, he has some precedent for the singing conceit in Coverdale's translation of Psalm 65:
14, used in the *Book of Common Prayer:* 'the valleys also shall stand so thick with corn that they
shall laugh and sing.'"
41 *Minos:* king and law-giver of Crete and supreme judge of the Underworld. *years:* fertile seasons.
43–44 *Ceres {. . .} forbear?:* Marlowe's and Ovid's sense is "Ceres, just because you had the sadness
of sleeping alone, why should I have to endure the same when observing your sacred rites?"
45–46: *Proserpine, Dis:* Proserpine, the daughter of Ceres, spends half the year ruling the Underworld with her husband Dis, the king of the Underworld.
47 *ask:* "call for."
48 *meet:* appropriate, fitting.

i *Ad {. . .} potest:* To his mistress from whose love he cannot pull himself away.
1 *thy faults:* Most translations infer *"my faults"* (though the Latin is technically ambiguous since
there is no possessive adjective modifying *vitiis*), and as such, the sense is that Ovid is berating

Now have I freed myself, and fled the chain,
And what I have borne, shame to bear again.
We vanquish, and tread tamed Love under feet,   5
Victorious wreaths at length my temples greet.
Suffer, and harden: good grows by this grief,
Oft bitter juice brings to the sick relief.
I have sustained so oft thrust from the door,
To lay my body on the hard moist floor.   10
I know not whom thou lewdly didst embrace,
When I to watch supplied a servant's place;
I saw when forth a tired lover went,
His side past service, and his courage spent.
Yet this is less than if he had seen me;   15
May that shame fall mine enemies' chance to be.
When have not I, fixed to thy side, close laid?
I have thy husband, guard, and fellow played.
The people by my company she pleased;
My love was cause that more men's love she seized.   20
What should I tell her vain tongue's filthy lies,
And, to my loss, god-wronging perjuries?
What secret becks in banquets with her youths,
With privy signs, and talk dissembling truths?
Hearing her to be sick, I thither ran,   25
But with my rival sick she was not then.
These hardened me, with what I keep obscure;
Some other seek, who will these things endure.
Now my ship in the wished haven crowned,
With joy hears Neptune's swelling waters sound.   30
Leave thy once powerful words, and flatteries;
I am not as I was before, unwise.

---

himself for his own "weakness" to be enslaved by his feelings. Marlowe's use of "thy" is reinforced
by Niger's comment on *vitiis: "criminibus puellae"* ("the faults of the girl").
4 *what {. . .} again:* Marlowe's and Ovid's sense is "I am ashamed to endure now what in the past
I was not ashamed to endure."
9 *sustained:* endured.
10 *hard moist floor:* the ground (earth).
14 *side:* groin.
15 *Yet {. . .} me:* Marlowe's and Ovid's sense is "Yet this is less painful than the shame that I felt by
his espying me spying on him."
18 *fellow:* lover.
21 *What:* why.
27 *These {. . .} obscure:* Marlowe's and Ovid's sense is "These things I have mentioned, and others
which I have not [= 'keep obscure'], have hardened me."
30 *With joy:* Marlowe read *laeta,* not the *lenta* ("unagitated") of modern texts.

Now love and hate my light breast each way move,
But victory, I think, will hap to love.
I'll hate, if I can; if not, love 'gainst my will: 35
Bulls hate the yoke, yet what they hate have still.
I fly her lust, but follow beauty's creature;
I loathe her manners, love her body's feature.
Nor with thee, nor without thee can I live,
And doubt to which desire the palm to give.   40
Or less fair, or less lewd would thou mightst be;
Beauty with lewdness doth right ill agree.
Her deeds gain hate, her face entreateth love;
Ah, she doth more worth than her vices prove.
Spare me, O by our fellow-bed, by all   45
The gods who by thee to be perjured fall,
And by thy face to me a power divine,
And by thine eyes whose radiance burns out mine.
Whate'er thou art, mine art thou: choose this course,
Wilt have me willing, or to love by force?   50
Rather I'll hoist up sail, and use the wind,
That I may love yet, though against my mind.

Elegia XI

Dolet amicam suam ita suis carminibus innotuisse ut rivales multos sibi pararit

What day was that which, all sad haps to bring,
White birds to lovers did not always sing?
Or is I think my wish against the stars?
Or shall I plain some god against me wars?
Who mine was called, whom I loved more than any,   5

---

33 *light breast:* fickle heart.
41 *Or:* Either.
44 *she:* her face.
45 *our fellow-bed:* by the bed of lovemaking we share.
46 *perjured:* deceived.
52 *mind:* will.

i *Dolet {. . .} pararit:* He grieves that his mistress has been made so famous by his poems that she
    has made herself available to many rival lovers.
1–2 *What {. . .} sing?:* Ovid's sense is "What day was it when you birds not white sang sad omens
    to the constant lover?" (*quis fuit ille dies quo tristia semper amanti /omina non albae concinuistis aves?*).
3 *Or {. . .} stars?:* Or am I to think that I live under an unlucky star?
4 *plain:* complain.

I fear with me is common now to many.
Err I? or by my books is she so known?
'Tis so: by my wit her abuse is grown.
And justly: for her praise why did I tell?
The wench by my fault is set forth to sell.   10
The bawd I play, lovers to her I guide:
Her gate by my hands is set open wide.
'Tis doubtful whether verse avail or harm,
Against my good they were an envious charm.
When Thebes, when Troy, when Caesar should be writ,   15
Alone Corinna moves my wanton wit.
With Muse opposed, would I my lines had done,
And Phoebus had forsook my work begun.
Nor, as use will not poets' record hear,
Would I my words would any credit bear.   20
Scylla by us her father's rich hair steals,
And Scylla's womb mad raging dogs conceals.
We cause feet fly, we mingle hairs with snakes,
Victorious Perseus a winged steed's back takes.
Our verse great Tityus a huge space outspreads,   25
And gives the viper-curled dog three heads.
We make Enceladus use a thousand arms,

---

8 *wit:* creative genius.

14 *good:* welfare. *they:* the "verse"(s) of the preceding line.

15–16 *When {. . .} wit: cf.* 1.1 and 2.1.

19–20 *Nor {. . .} bear:* Marlowe's and Ovid's sense is "As it is not usual that the words of poets be heeded, I preferred that mine would carry no weight."

21ff These lines catalogue a number of horrendous stories and characters that have been the subject of poetry.

21 *Scylla:* daughter of Nisus, king of Megara, who stole a lock of her father's hair on which his life depended.

22 *And {. . .} conceals:* This refers to another Scylla, a woman whom Circe changed into a monster with barking dogs' heads about her waist.

23 *we:* poets. *feet fly:* a reference to Mercury. *hairs {. . .} snakes:* a reference to Medusa, one of the Gorgons.

24 *Victorious {. . .} takes:* Perseus killed Medusa and rode off on the horse Pegasus, which sprang from Medusa's blood.

25 *Tityus:* one of the race of Giants whom Jove consigned to hell with vultures constantly pecking at his liver.

26 *And {. . .} heads:* a reference to the three-headed dog Cerberus, a gatekeeper of the Underworld.

27 *Enceladus:* one of the race of Giants whom Jove imprisoned under Mt. Aetna. He was fabled, here by Ovid, to have had one thousand arms with which he hurled one thousand spears against the gods in the Giants' attempt to overthrow Olympus.

And men enthralled by mermaids' singing charms.
The east winds in Ulysses' bags we shut,
And blabbing Tantalus in mid-waters put.   30
Niobe flint, Callist we make a bear,
Bird-changed Progne doth her Itys tear;
Jove turns himself into a swan, or gold,
Or his bull's horns Europa's hand doth hold.
Proteus what should I name? teeth, Thebes' first seed?   35
Oxen in whose mouths burning flames did breed?
Heav'n star Electra, that bewailed her sisters?
The ships whose godhead in the sea now glisters?
The sun turned back from Atreus' cursed table?
And sweet touched harp that to move stones was able?   40
Poets' large power is boundless and immense,
Nor have their words true history's pretence.
And my wench ought to have seemed falsely praised.
Now your credulity harm to me hath raised.

---

28 *mermaids:* the Sirens. Gill and Bullen assert that Ovid was here referring to the Sphinx (*ambiguae {. . .} virginis ore*); others think the Sirens. Niger attributes this characterization to the Sirens.

30 *Tantalus:* see 2.2.43–44n.

31 *Niobe:* turned into a stream-giving stone because of her hubris. *Callist:* Callisto, a lover of Jove whom Juno turned into a bear, and whom Jove in turn transformed into a constellation (Ursa Major).

32 *Progne* [= Procne] [. . .] *Itys:* see 2.6.7n.

33 *swan:* reference to Leda (see 1.10.3n). *gold:* reference to Danae (see 2.19.27n).

34 *bull's {. . .} Europa's:* Jove came to her as a bull and carried her on his back to Crete.

35 *Proteus:* constantly changes his shape. *teeth {. . .} seed:* a reference to Cadmus, who sowed the teeth of a dragon he had slain from which an army sprang to build the city of Thebes.

36 *Oxen {. . .} breed:* Jason, who also sowed land at Colchis with dragons' teeth, first ploughed the land with oxen who breathed fire.

37 *Heav'n {. . .} sisters:* The Latin's textual history is difficult, as is Marlowe's translation. Ovid is referring to the sisters of Phaethon, who bewailed his death when Jove had to blast him out of the sky because he could not control the carriage of the sun. Marlowe, despite Niger's extensive commentary to the same, understands rather a reference to the Pleiades.

38 *The {. . .} glisters:* a reference to Aeneas's ships (*Aeneid* 9.77–102), which were metamorphosed into nymphs to protect them from Turnus.

39 *The {. . .} table:* Green writes: "The myth of the sun turning back in the heavens seems originally to have formed part of a competition between Atreus and Thyestes for the kingship over Mycenae: each produced a portent, but that of Atreus (the sun setting in the east) was adjudged clearly superior. However, Ovid prefers a tradition more popular among Roman poets, that the sun turned back *in horror at Atreus,* who first murdered Thyestes' children, then served them up to their unsuspecting father for dinner."

40 *And {. . .} able:* Gill writes: "Finally, Ovid refers to the magical power of poetry, exemplified in the harp and music of Amphion; those who do not give Cadmus the credit for founding Thebes give it to this musician, and say that the very stones moved at the sound of his harp and formed the city walls of their own accord."

ELEGIA XII

De Iunonis festo

When fruit-filled Tuscia should a wife give me,
We touched the walls, Camillus, won by thee.
The priests to Juno did prepare chaste feasts,
With famous pageants, and their home-bred beasts.
To know their rites well recompensed my stay,   5
Though thither leads a rough steep hilly way.
There stands an old wood with thick trees dark clouded:
Who sees it grants some deity there is shrouded.
An altar takes men's incense and oblation,
An altar made after the ancient fashion.   10
Here, when the pipe with solemn tunes doth sound,
The annual pomp goes on the covered ground.
White heifers by glad people forth are led,
Which with the grass of Tuscan fields are fed,
And calves from whose feared front no threat'ning flies,   15
And little pigs, base hogsties' sacrifice,
And rams with horns their hard heads wreathed back;
Only the goddess-hated goat did lack,
By whom disclosed, she in the high woods took,
Is said to have attempted flight forsook.   20
Now is the goat brought through the boys with darts,
And given to him that the first wound imparts.
Where Juno comes, each youth and pretty maid
Show large ways, with their garments there displayed.
Jewels and gold their virgin tresses crown,   25
And stately robes to their gilt feet hang down.
As is the use, the nuns in white veils clad,
Upon their heads the holy mysteries had.

---

i *De Iunonis festo:* On the feast of Juno.
1 *Tuscia:* the town Falerii (*Faliscis*) in Tuscany.
2 *Camillus:* M. Furius Camillus captured Falerii in the fourth century BCE.
18 *Only {. . .} lack:* only the goat was missing because it is unpleasing to Juno.
19 *whom:* the goat. *she:* Juno.
21–22 *Now {. . .} imparts:* Marlowe's and Ovid's sense is that it has now become a custom for children to throw darts at the goat, and the goat is then given to the child who wounds it.
24 *Show {. . .} displayed:* Ovid's sense is that they precede and sweep (*praeverrunt*) with their trailing garments the path of the following goddess. Marlowe's text has *praebuerant* ("to show") for *praeverrunt.*
28 *mysteries:* vessels, offerings.

When the chief pomp comes, loud the people hollow,
And she her vestal virgin priests doth follow.   30
Such was the Greek pomp, Agamemnon dead,
Which fact, and country wealth Halesus fled,
And having wandered now through sea and land,
Built walls high towered with a prosperous hand.
He to th' Hetrurians Juno's feast commended;   35
Let me, and them by it be aye befriended.

ELEGIA XIII

Ad amicam, si peccatura est, ut occulte peccet
Seeing thou art fair, I bar not thy false playing,
But let not me, poor soul, know of thy straying.
Nor do I give thee counsel to live chaste,
But that thou wouldst dissemble, when 'tis past.
She hath not trod awry, that doth deny it.   5
Such as confess have lost their good names by it.
What madness is 't to tell night's pranks by day,
And hidden secrets openly to bewray?
The strumpet with the stranger will not do
Before the room be clear, and door put to.   10
Will you make shipwrack of your honest name,
And let the world be witness of the same?
Be more advised, walk as a puritan,
And I shall think you chaste, do what you can.
Slip still, only deny it when 'tis done,   15
And before folk immodest speeches shun.
The bed is for lascivious toyings meet;
There use all tricks, and tread shame under feet.
When you are up and dressed, be sage and grave,

---

29 *hollow:* shout. See 3.2.43n.
32 *Halesus:* son of Agamemnon who founded Falerii.
35 *Hetrurians:* Etrurians, Tuscans.

i *Ad {. . .} peccet:* To his mistress, that if she is to cheat on him, she should do it discreetly. The entire elegy is like a long extension of the final couplet of I.iv.
2 *poor soul:* appositive to "me," not a vocative address to her.
6 *Such as:* Only those who.
9 *do:* engage in sexual relations.
10 *clear:* cleared. *put to:* locked.
13 *advised:* wise. *walk {. . .} puritan:* Marlowe's and Ovid's sense is "at least *act* as if you are chaste."
14 *do {. . .} can:* even though you are not.
17 *meet:* appropriate.

And in the bed hide all the faults you have.   20
Be not ashamed to strip you, being there,
And mingle thighs, yours ever mine to bear.
There in your rosy lips my tongue entomb,
Practise a thousand sports when there you come.
Forbear no wanton words you there would speak,   25
And with your pastime let the bedstead creak.
But with your robes put on an honest face,
And blush, and seem as you were full of grace.
Deceive all; let me err, and think I am right,
And like a wittol think thee void of sleight.   30
Why see I lines so oft received and given?
This bed and that by tumbling made uneven?
Like one start up, your hair tossed and displaced,
And with a wanton's tooth your neck new-raced?
Grant this, that what you do I may not see;   35
If you weigh not ill speeches, yet weigh me.
My soul fleets when I think what you have done,
And thorough every vein doth cold blood run.
Then thee whom I must love, I hate in vain,
And would be dead, but dead with thee remain.   40
I'll not sift much, but hold thee soon excused,
Say but thou wert injuriously accused.
Though while the deed be doing you be took,
And I see when you ope the two-leaved book,
Swear I was blind, deny, if you be wise,   45
And I will trust your words more than mine eyes.
From him that yields, the palm is quickly got,
Teach but your tongue to say, "I did it not,"

---

30 *wittol:* foolish cuckold. *sleight:* deception.

31 *lines:* messages.

32 *and that:* For the sense, omit these words.

33 *Like {. . .} displaced:* Marlowe's and Ovid's sense is "Why is your hair all disheveled like one who has just risen from a bed of hot and heavy sex?"

34 *new-raced:* newly marked.

36 *speeches:* gossip about your own reputation.

37 *fleets:* fails, dies.

41 *sift:* inquire.

42 *Say {. . .} accused:* Marlowe's text read *falsi criminis* for *falli muneris;* the modern version is translated "How great a gift it will be to be deceived."

44 *ope {. . .} book:* spread your legs. Here Marlowe is (metaphorically) much more graphic than Ovid, who says "and your shameful act will have been seen by my eyes" (*et fuerint oculis probra videnda meis*).

And being justified by two words, think
The cause acquits you not, but I that wink.   50

ELEGIA XIV

Ad Venerem, quod elegis finem imponat
Tender Love's mother, a new poet get;
This last end to my Elegies is set,
Which I, Peligny's foster-child, have framed
(Nor am I by such wanton toys defamed),
Heir of an ancient house, if help that can,   5
Not only by war's rage made gentleman.
In Virgil Mantua joys, in Catull Verone,
Of me Peligny's nation boasts alone,
Whom liberty to honest arms compelled,
When careful Rome in doubt their prowess held.   10

---

49 *two words:* In Ovid's Latin "I did it not" (line 48) is the two words *non feci*.

50 *The {. . .} wink:* The Latin (*etsi non causa iudice vince tuo*) is translated "if not by means of your cause, then by means of your judge, (you) conquer." "I wink" has several possible senses here. Most literally, as MacLure notes, it means "I shut my eyes." "Wink" is also etymologically related to, and indeed in earlier English is often interchangeable with, "wince," which indicates "to feel pain." The use of wink, therefore, and even more so because it ends the poem, underscores the ambivalence (whether real or rhetorical) of the Ovidian narrator who may always have serious pain beneath the seemingly satirical exterior. Finally, Marlowe's choice of "wink" not only in its meaning but also in its visual similarity renders and evokes Ovid's *vince*, and translating in this way—with the other dimensions just noted—is what Ezra Pound called "logopoeia."

i *Ad Venerem quod elegis finem imponat:* To Venus as he puts an end to his elegies.

3 *Peligny's:* See 2.1.2n.

6 *Not {. . .} gentleman:* Most translators take *non modo* as "not only," "not just," or "not merely," and the sense of the soldier is that of one who has newly gained his place in high society by deeds rather than by birth, contrary to the image Ovid seemingly wants to claim for himself as coming from a long line of highborn ancestors. This sense is certainly obvious and primary; however, the ambiguity of the Latin provides for another ironic possibility, one very much consonant with the ethos of Roman love elegy. Whereas the Latin (*non modo militiae turbine factus eques*) is most readily translated "I am not merely a soldier [newly] minted [into the upper classes] by the engine of warfare," it can also be translated "I am a [high-class] soldier not merely by reason of the engine of warfare." This construction implies the underlying stock elegiac motif of the "soldier of sex" who plies his trade on the "battlefield of the bed" and who suffers extreme emotional "battles" as well (as is extenuated in 1.9). In English, Marlowe renders this sense by translating *non modo* as "not only" and by constructing the line as he does. In that case, "war" means that of the "battlefield" of love.

7 *Catull:* Catullus.

9–10 *Whom {. . .} held:* a reference to the war in 90 BCE between Rome and other Italian communities in which the Paeligni distinguished themselves.

10 *careful:* anxious ("full of care [worry]"). *their:* their own (Rome's).

And some guest, viewing wat'ry Sulmo's walls,
Where little ground to be enclosed befalls,
"How such a poet could you bring forth?" says;
"How small soe'er, I'll you for greatest praise."
Both loves to whom my heart long time did yield,   15
Your golden ensigns pluck out of my field.
Horned Bacchus greater fury doth distil,
A greater ground with great horse is to till.
Weak Elegies, delightful Muse, farewell;
A work that after my death here shall dwell.   20
        FINIS

Sir John Davies, *Epigrams*

Ad Musam. 1

Fly, merry Muse, unto that merry town,
Where thou mayst plays, revels, and triumphs see,
The House of Fame, and Theatre of Renown,
Where all good wits and spirits love to be.

Fall in between their hands, that praise and love thee,   5
And be to them a laughter and a jest.
But as for them which scorning shall reprove thee,
Disdain their wits, and think thine own the best.

But if thou find any so gross and dull,
That think I do to private taxing lean,   10

---

11 *Sulmo:* Ovid's birthplace.

14 *greatest:* Ovid says only "great" (*magna*).

15 *Both loves:* Venus and Cupid. *to {. . .} yield:* Marlowe's text read *mihi tempore longo* instead of the modern reading *Amathusia culti* ("Venus, mother of the worshipped child").

17 *Bacchus:* indicative of drama and thus of Ovid's intention to write his tragedy *Medea* (extant in two lines). *fury:* For *thyrso,* Niger notes *furore.*

Most of the titles to Davies's *Epigrams* are in Latin and address a person ("Rufus" or "Titus") or a type of figure ("muse" or "gull"). The Latin word "Ad" means "To," while "In" means "On."

1 *merry town:* London, imagined here as a famous theatrical city, but also in line 12 as a site for "an epigram" itself.

7 *reprove:* express disapproval of.

10–13 *taxing {. . .} taxeth:* accuse, blame, reprove, censure.

Bid him go hang, for he is but a gull,
And knows not what an epigram doth mean,

> Which taxeth under a particular name,
> A general vice that merits public blame.

Of a Gull. 2

Oft in my laughing rhymes, I name a gull,
But this new term will many questions breed;
Therefore at first I will express at full,
Who is a true and perfect gull indeed.

A gull is he, who fears a velvet gown,   5
And when a wench is brave, dares not speak to her;
A gull is he which traverseth the town,
And is for marriage known a common wooer.

A gull is he, which while he proudly wears
A silver hilted rapier by his side,   10
Endures the lies, and knocks about the ears,
Whilst in his sheath, his sleeping sword doth bide.

A gull is he which wears good handsome clothes,
And stands in presence stroking up his hair,
And fills up his unperfect speech with oaths,   15
But speaks not one wise word throughout the year.

> But to define a gull in terms precise,
> A gull is he which seems, and is not wise.

In Rufum. 3

Rufus the Courtier, at the theater,
Leaving the best and most conspicuous place,

---

11 *gull:* not merely a gullible person, but a fool, dupe, simpleton. Defined at 2.5–18.

3 *express:* describe, disclose.
5 *velvet:* an expensive cloth of silk, suggesting wealth and position.
6 *brave:* finely dressed.
11 *Endures the lies:* permits being called a liar. To be *given the lie* was so serious an insult it required an Elizabethan gentleman to issue a challenge.
14 *in presence:* in ceremonial attendance on a person of higher social rank.

2 *the best and most conspicuous place:* in an Elizabethan playhouse, the Lord's room, the elevated seating gallery located at the rear of the inner stage.

Doth either to the stage himself transfer,
Or through a grate, doth show his doubtful face,

For that the clamorous fry of Inns of Court,   5
Fills up the private rooms of greater price;
And such a place where all may have resort,
He in his singularity doth despise.

Yet doth not his particular humour shun
The common stews and brothels of the town,   10
Though all the world in troops do thither run,
Clean and unclean, the gentle and the clown.

Then why should Rufus in his pride abhor,
A common seat that loves a common whore.

In Quintum. 4

Quintus the Dancer useth evermore,
His feet in measure and in rule to move,
Yet on a time he called his mistress whore,
And thought with that sweet word to win her love.
Oh, had his tongue like to his feet been taught,   5
It never would have uttered such a thought.

In Plurimos. 5

Faustinus, Sextus, Cinna, Ponticus,
With Gella, Lesbia, Thais, Rhodope,
Rode all to Staines for no cause serious,
But for their mirth, and for their lechery.

Scarce were they settled in their lodging, when   5
Wenches with wenches, men with men fell out.

---

4 *grate:* in the Lord's room, a casement of metal bars through which Rufus looks.
5 *Inns of Court:* the buildings in London known as the Inner Temple, the Middle Temple, Lincoln's
    Inn, and Gray's Inn, belonging to the legal societies having the right to admit persons to prac-
    tice at the bar.
6 *private rooms:* the boxes, for upper-class seating.
9 *humour:* "In ancient and mediæval physiology, one of the four chief fluids (cardinal humours) of
    the body (blood, phlegm, choler, and melancholy or black choler), by the relative proportions of
    which a person's physical and mental qualities and disposition were held to be determined"
    (*OED*). Thus a humour is a disposition of character.
10 *stews:* brothels.

2 *Gella {. . .} Rhodope:* courtesans famed in antiquity.
3 *Staines:* a town near London popular for outings.

Men with their wenches, wenches with their men,
Which straight dissolved this ill assembled route.

But since the Devil brought them thus together,
To my discoursing thoughts it is a wonder,   10
Why presently as soon as they came thither,
The self same Devil did them part asunder.

    Doubtless it seems it was a foolish Devil,
    That thus would part them, ere they did some evil.

In Titum. 6

Titus the brave and valorous young gallant,
Three years together in this town hath been,
Yet my lord Chancellor's tomb he hath not seen,
Nor the new water-work, nor the elephant.
    I cannot tell the cause without a smile,   5
    He hath been in the Counter all this while.

In Faustum. 7

Faustus not lord, nor knight, nor wise, nor old,
To every place about the town doth ride.
He rides into the fields, plays to behold,
He rides to take boat at the waterside.
He rides to Paul's, he rides to th'ordinary,   5
He rides unto the house of bawdery too.
Thither his horse so often doth him carry,
That shortly he will quite forget to go.

In Katam. 8

Kate being pleased, wished that her pleasure could,
Endure as long as a buff jerkin would.

---

12 *did them part:* parted them.

3 *lord Chancellor's tomb:* the elaborate tomb of Sir Christopher Hatton in St. Paul's Cathedral, London, completed in 1591.
4 *new water-work:* Krueger cites John Stow, *Survey of London,* on the building of a new water-work that conveyed water from the Thames into houses near St. Paul's Cathedral. *elephant:* A popular elephant was performing at this time in London.
6 *Counter:* a London debtor's prison.

3 *fields:* both the Theatre and Curtain playhouses were situated in fields just north of London.
5 *Paul's:* St. Paul's Cathedral, a popular meeting place for gallants and lawyers, and the center of the book world. *ordinary:* a tavern or eating-house at which public meals were provided for a fixed price.
6 *house of bawdery:* brothel.

2 *buff jerkin:* a short military coat made of leather. See Shakespeare, *1 Henry IV* 1.2.46.

Content thee, Kate, although thy pleasure wasteth,
Thy pleasures place like a buff jerkin lasteth:
    For no buff jerkin hath been oftner worn,   5
    Nor hath more scrapings or more dressings born.

In Librum. 9

Liber doth vaunt how chastely he hath lived
Since he hath been in town, seven years and more,
For that he swears he hath four only swived,
A maid, a wife, a widow and a whore.
    Then Liber thou hast swived all women kind,   5
    For a fifth sort I know thou canst not find.

In Medontem. 10

Great Captain Medon wears a chain of gold,
Which at five hundred crowns is valued,
For that it was his grandsire's chain of old,
When great king Henry, Boulogne conquered.
    And wear it, Medon, for it may ensue,   5
    That thou by virtue of this massy chain,
    A stronger town than Boulogne mayst subdue,
    If wise men's saws be not reputed vain.
For what said Phillip, King of Macedon?
There is no castle so well fortified,   10
But if an ass laden with gold come on,
The guard will stoop, and gates fly open wide.

In Gellam. 11

Gella, if thou dost love thy self, take heed,
Lest thou my rhymes unto thy lover read,
For straight thou grinst, and then thy lover seeth,
Thy canker-eaten gums, and rotten teeth.

---

3 *swived:* had sexual intercourse with.

1 *Medon:* perhaps a contemporary; Krueger cites "'Captain Medon's grandfather'" from John Harington's *Metamorphosis of Ajax* (1591).

3 *grandsire:* grandfather.

4 *Henry, Boulogne:* in 1544, Henry VIII captured Boulogne, a port city on the northern coast of France.

8 *reputed:* reported, accounted.

9–12 *For {. . .} wide:* a proverbial statement that Plutarch attributed to King Philip of Macedon (Krueger).

In Quintum. 12

Quintus his wit infused into his brain,
Misliked the place, and fled into his feet,
And there it wanders up and down the street,
Dabbled in the dirt, and soaked in the rain.
    Doubtless his wit intends not to aspire,   5
    Which leaves his head to travel in the mire.

In Severum. 13

The Puritan Severus oft doth read,
This text that doth pronounce vain speech a sin,
That thing defiles a man that doth proceed
From out the mouth, not that which enters in.
Hence is it, that we seldom hear him swear,   5
And thereof like a Pharisee he vaunts,
But he devours more capons in a year,
Than would suffice a hundredth Protestants.
And sooth, those sectaries are gluttons all,
As well the threadbare cobbler as the knight,   10
For those poor slaves which have not wherewithal
Feed on the rich, till they devour them quite.
    And so like Pharaoh's kine, they eat up clean,
    Those that be fat, yet still themselves be lean.

In Leucam. 14

Leuca in presence once a fart did let,
Some laughed a little, she forsook the place;
And mazed with shame, did eke her glove forget,
Which she returned to fetch with bashful grace.
    And when she would have said, this is my glove,   5
    My fart (quoth she) which did more laughter move.

In Macrum. 15

Thou canst not speak yet, Macer, for to speak,
Is to distinguish sounds significant.

---

2 *Misliked:* displeased.

1 *Severus:* in Latin, meaning *severe;* an appropriate name for a Puritan.
6 *Pharisee:* a self-righteous person. See Luke 18:10–14.
7 *capons:* castrated cocks.
9 *sectaries:* the aforementioned Protestants.
13 *Pharaoh's kine:* cattle of the Pharaoh in Genesis 41:2–4.

3 *mazed:* delirious or bewildered. *eke:* also.

Thou with harsh noise the air dost rudely break,
But what thou utterest common sense doth want:
    Half English words, with fustian terms among,   5
    Much like the burthen of a Northern song.

In Faustum. 16

That youth, sayth Faustus, hath a lion seen,
Who from a dicing house comes money-less,
But when he lost his hair, where had he been?
I doubt me he had seen a lioness.

In Cosmum. 17

Cosmus hath more discoursing in his head,
Than Jove, when Pallas issued from his brain,
And still he strives to be delivered,
Of all his thoughts at once, but all in vain.
For as we see at all the playhouse doors,   5
When ended is the play, the dance, and song,
A thousand townsmen, gentlemen, and whores,
Porters and serving-men together throng.
So thoughts of drinking, thriving, wenching, war,
And borrowing money, raging in his mind,   10
To issue all at once so forward are,
As none at all can perfect passage find.

In Flaccum. 18

The false knave Flaccus once a bribe I gave,
The more fool I to bribe so false a knave;
But he gave back my bribe, the more fool he,
That for my folly, did not cozen me.

---

5 *fustian:* bombastic.
6 *burthen:* refrain or chorus in a song.

1 *hath {. . .} seen:* the custom of going to see the lions kept at the Tower of London, meaning "to have had a real experience."
2 *dicing house:* gambling-house, where dice are played.
3 *lost his hair:* from venereal disease.
4 *lioness:* a prostitute.

1 *discoursing:* moving rapidly as thought.
2 *Jove {. . .} brain:* Pallas Athena, Greek goddess of wisdom, was sprung full-born from the brain of her father, Jove.
8 *Porters:* people who guard entrances, doorkeepers.
9 *thriving:* prospering.

4 *cozen:* cheat, deceive.

In Cineam. 19

Thou dogged Cineas, hated like a dog,
For still thou grumblest like a masty dog,
Comparst thy self to nothing but a dog.
Thou sayst thou art as weary as a dog,
As angry, sick, and hungry as a dog,   5
As dull and melancholy as a dog,
As lazy, sleepy, idle as a dog.
But why dost thou compare thee to a dog?
In that, for which all men despise a dog,
I will compare thee better to a dog.   10
Thou art as fair and comely as a dog,
Thou art as true and honest as a dog,
Thou art as kind and liberal as a dog,
Thou art as wise and valiant as a dog.
　　But Cineas, I have often heard thee tell,   15
　　Thou art as like thy father as may be.
　　'Tis like enough, and faith I like it well,
　　But I am glad thou art not like to me.

In Gerontem. 20

Geron, whose moldy memory corrects
Old Holinshed, our famous chronicler,
Which moral rules, and policy collects
Out of all actions done these fourscore year,
　　Accounts the time of every odd event,   5
　　Not from Christ's birth, nor from the Prince's reign,
　　But from some other famous accident,
　　Which in men's general notice doth remain.
The siege of Boulougne, and the plaguey sweat,
The going to Saint-Quentin's and New Haven,   10

---

1 *Cineas:* the name suggests *cynic.* Originally, the Cynics were Greek philosophers who met at a building called the Cynogurgus, which had the figure of a dog on it, and their behavior was considered brutish.
2 *Masty:* mastiff, a large dog known for its strength and courage, often used as a watchdog.
13 *liberal:* bountiful, generous.

1 *Geron:* the name suggests *old man.*
2 *Old Holinshed:* Raphael Holinshed (d. c. 1582), editor of the *Chronicles* (1577), a history of England important to such authors as Spenser, Marlowe, and Shakespeare.
3 *policy:* government administration.
9 *Boulogne:* see 11.4.
10 *Saint-Quentin's:* a cathedral city in Picardie, northern France.

The rising in the North, the frost so great,
That cartwheel prints on Thames' face were graven,
    The fall of money, and burning of Paul's steeple,
    The blazing star and Spaniards' overthrow:
    By these events, notorious to the people,   15
    He measures times, and things forpast doth shew.
But most of all, he chiefly reckons by
A private chance, the death of his curst wife.
This is to him the dearest memory,
And th' happiest accident of all his life.   20

In Marcum. 21

When Marcus comes from Mins, he still doth swear
By, come on seven, that all is lost and gone,
But that's not true, for he hath lost his hair;
Only for that, he came too much on one.

In Ciprium. 22

The fine youth Ciprius is more terse and neat,
Than the new garden of the old Temple is,
And still the newest fashion he doth get,
And with the time doth change from that to this.
He wears a hat now of the flat crown-block,   5
The treble ruffs, long cloak and doublet French.
He takes tobacco, and doth wear a lock,
And wastes more time in dressing than a wench.

---

11 *rising {. . .} North:* In 1569, the northern earls rebelled against Queen Elizabeth I, in support of
  the Catholic Mary, Queen of Scots.
13 *Paul's steeple:* steeple of St. Paul's Cathedral.
14 *Spaniards' overthrown:* the English defeat of the Spanish Armada in 1588.

1 *Mins:* Unknown, but possibly the name of a dicing-house.
2 *come on seven:* said when throwing dice.
3 *lost his hair:* one effect of venereal disease.

1 *terse:* spruce.
2 *old Temple:* at the Inns of Court (see 3.5).
5 *hat {. . .} crown-block:* sign of a modish, overdressed young man, often the butt of satire.
6 *treble ruff:* a new and fashionable garment of the 1590s. "The treble consisted of three layers, fastened to a band under the chin, and raised at the back so that the ruff rested on the doublet in
  front (in contrast to the earlier style, which was worn lower, but at right angles to the throat)"
  (Krueger). *doublet French:* French doublet, which had slashes in the sleeve revealing the shirt
  underneath.
7 *lock:* "The love-lock, or Bourbon lock, was a tress of hair grown long, curled, often beribboned,
  and pulled forward from the nape of the neck to lie over the chest" (Krueger).

Yet this new-fangled youth, made for these times,
Doth above all, praise old George Gascoine's rhymes. 10

In Cineam. 23

When Cineas comes amongst his friends in morning,
He slyly looks who first his cap doth move:
Him he salutes, the rest so grimly scorning,
As if forever they had lost his love.
    I, knowing how it doth the humor fit, 5
    Of this fond gull to be saluted first,
    Catch at my cap, but move it not a whit,
    Which he perceiving seems for spite to burst.
But Cineas, why expect you more of me,
Than I of you? I am as good a man, 10
And better too by many'a quality,
For vault, and dance, and fence, and rhyme I can.
    You keep a whore at your own charge men tell me,
    Indeed, friend (Cineas), therein you excel me.

In Gullum. 24

Gallus hath been this summer in Friesland,
And now returned he speaks such warlike words
As if I could their English understand,
I fear me they would cut my throat like swords.
    He talks of counters-carves and casomates, 5
    Of parapets, curtains and palisados,
    Of flankers, ravelins, gabions, he prates,
    And of false brays, and sallies and scalados.
But to requite such gulling terms as these,
With words of my profession I reply. 10

---

10 *George Gascoine's:* Elizabethan England's major poet before Edmund Spenser; died in 1577. Krueger suggests that Davies cites Gascoigne because this older poet's "satiric writing seems cumbersome if compared with Davies's epigrams."

2 *move:* remove.

5 *humor:* see note to 3.9.

11 *quality:* "A mental or moral attribute, trait, or characteristic; a feature of one's character"; "An accomplishment or attainment" (*OED*).

1 *Friesland:* a province in the Netherlands where a war for independence was fought against Spain with English aid. Religious issues were also at stake between English Protestants and Spanish Catholics.

5–8 *He {. . .} scalados:* military terms.

I tell of fourching, vouchers, counterpleas,
Of withernams, essoigns, and champarty.
   So neither of us understanding either,
   We part as wise as when we came together.

In Decium. 25

Audacious painters have Nine Worthies made,
But poet Decius more audacious far,
Making his mistress march with men of war,
With title of tenth worthy doth her lade.
   Me thinks that gull did use his terms as fit,   5
   Which termed his love a giant for her wit.

In Gellam. 26

If Gella's beauty be examined,
She hath a dull dead eye, a saddle nose,
An ill shaped face, with morphew overspread,
And rotten teeth, which she in laughing shows.
   Briefly, she is the filthiest wench in town,   5
   Of all that do the art of whoring use;
   But when she hath put on her satin gown,
   Her cut lawn apron, and her velvet shoes,
Her green silk stockings, and her petticoat,
Of taffeta, with golden fringed around;   10
And is withal perfumed with civet hot,
Which doth her valiant stinking breath confound.
   Yet she with these addictions is no more,
   Than a sweet, filthy, fine, ill favored whore.

In Sillam. 27

Silla is often challenged to the field,
To answer like a gentleman his foes,

11–12 *I {. . .} champarty:* legal terms.

Ben Jonson told Drummond of Hawthornden that in this epigram Davies satirized poet and playwright Michael Drayton (Krueger).
1 *Nine Worthies:* Joshua, David, Judas Maccabeus, Hector, Alexander, Julius Caesar, Arthur, Charlemagne, and Godfrey of Boulogne.
4 *lade:* load abundantly.

3 *morphew:* "Any of various skin diseases characterized by localized or generalized discoloration of the skin; (also) a discoloured lesion of the skin" (*OED*).
10 *taffeta:* "A name applied at different times to different fabrics. In early times apparently a plain-wove glossy silk (of any colour). [. . .] In the 16th c. mention is also made of 'linen taffety'" (*OED*).
11 *civet:* a catlike mammal that secretes a musky scent.

But then doth he this only answer yield,
That he hath livings and fair lands to lose.
   Silla, if none but beggars valiant were,   5
   The King of Spain would put us all in fear.

In Sillam. 28

Who dares affirm that Silla dares not fight?
When I dare swear he dares adventure more,
Than the most brave, and most all-daring knight,
That ever arms with resolution bore.
   He that dares touch the most unwholesome whore,   5
   That ever was retired into the spittle;
   And dares court wenches standing at a door,
   The portion of his wit being passing little.
He that dares give his dearest friend offences,
Which other valiant fools do fear to do;   10
And when a fever doth confound his senses,
Dares eat raw beef, and drink strong wine thereto.
   He that dares take tobacco on the stage,
   Dares man a whore at noon-day through the street,
   Dares dance in Paul's, and in this formal age,   15
   Dares say and do what ever is unmeet.
Whom fear of shame could never yet affright,
Who dares affirm that Silla dares not fight?

In Haywodum. 29

Heywood which did in epigrams excel,
Is now put down since my light muse arose:
As buckets are put down into a well,
Or as a schoolboy putteth down his hose.

---

6 *King of Spain:* Phillip II, a Catholic, married to the Catholic queen of England, Mary Tudor
(1553–58).

6 *spittle:* hospital, where a prostitute could be treated for venereal disease.
12 *raw {. . .} wine:* raw beef and strong wine were believed to increase bodily heat.
14 *man:* escort, but with a bawdy pun.
15 *Paul's:* St. Paul's Cathedral, London. *formal:* committed to exact form but also perhaps to outward appearance.
16 *unmeet:* unfitting, inappropriate.

1 *Heywood:* John Heywood (?1497–1580), the leading epigram writer before Davies who published
six hundred epigrams in 1562.
2 *light:* of slender weight, but also wanton.
4 *hose:* breeches.

In Dacum. 30

Amongst the poets Dacus numbered is,
Yet could he never make an English rhyme,
But some prose speeches I have heard of his,
Which have been spoken many'a hundreth time.
    The man that keeps the elephant hath one,   5
    Wherein he tells the wonders of the beast.
    Another Banks pronounced long agone,
    When he his curtails qualities expressed.
He first taught him that keeps the monuments
At Westminster his formal tale to say,   10
And also him which puppets represents,
And also him which with the ape doth play.
    Though all his poetry be like to this,
    Amongst the poets Dacus numbered is.

In Priscum. 31

When Priscus raised from low to high estate,
Rode through the streets in pompous jollity,
Caius his poor familiar friend of late,
Be-spake him thus, "Sir, now you know not me";
    "'Tis likely, friend" (quoth Priscus) "to be so,   5
    For at this time myself I do not know."

In Brunum. 32

Brunus, which thinks himself a fair sweet youth,
Is nine and thirty years of age at least.
Yet was he never, to confess the truth,
But a dry starveling when he was at best.
    This gull was sick to show his night cap fine,   5
    And his wrought pillow overspread with lawn.
    But hath been well since his grief's cause hath line,
    At Trollops by Saint Clement's church in pawn.

---

1 *Dacus:* Perhaps an allusion to poet and playwright Samuel Daniel (see epigram 45 and Krueger's note).
5 *elephant:* See 6.4.
7 *Banks:* the horse Morocco of one Banks was famous for its performances. See also 48.5.
8 *curtails:* a horse with a short tail.
10 *Westminster:* Westminster Abbey, London. *formal:* see 28.15.

2 *pompous:* with pomp or stately show, splendid. *jollity:* festivity.

6 *wrought:* embroidered.
7 *line:* lain.
8 *Trollops:* perhaps the name of a pawnshop.

In Francum. 33

When Francus comes to solace with his whore
He sends for rods and strips himself stark naked:
For his lust sleeps, and will not rise before,
By whipping of the wench it be awaked.

    I envy him not, but wish I had the power,   5
    To make myself his wench but one half hour.

In Castorem. 34

Of speaking well, why do we learn the skill,
Hoping thereby honour and wealth to gain.
Sith railing Castor doth by speaking ill,
Opinion of much wit, and gold obtain.

In Septimum. 35

Septimus lives, and is like garlic seen,
For though his head be white, his blade is green.
This old mad colt deserves a martyr's praise,
For he was burned in Queen Mary's days.

Of Tobacco. 36

Homer of moly, and nepenthe sings,
Moly, the Gods' most sovereign herb divine.
Nepenthe, Helen's drink which gladness brings,
Heart's grief expels, and doth the wits refine.

    But this our age another world hath found,   5
    From whence an herb of heavenly power is brought,
    Moly is not so sovereign for a wound,
    Nor hath nepenthe so great wonders wrought.

It is tobacco, whose sweet subtle fume,
The hellish torment of the teeth doth ease   10
By drawing down, and drying up the room,
The mother and the nurse of each disease.

---

2 *blade:* body, perhaps with sexual innuendo. A *blade* was also a gallant.
4 *burned:* infected with a venereal disease. *Queen Mary's:* Queen Mary I, reigned 1553–58; older sister to Davies's sovereign, Elizabeth I.

1 *moly:* In Homer's *Odyssey* (book 10), the god of reason, Hermes, gives the plant moly to Odysseus to protect him from the enchantress Circe. *nepenthe:* Also in the *Odyssey* (book 4), Helen of Troy, back home in Sparta with her husband Menelaus, gives the drink nepenthe to Odysseus's son Telemachus. Nepenthe makes people forget their troubles, and, as Davies says in line 3, "gladness brings."
5 *this {. . .} found:* a reference to Elizabethan discovery of the Americas.
6 *herb:* tobacco.

It is tobacco which doth cold expel,
And clears the obstructions of the arteries,
And surfeits threatening death, digesteth well,   15
Decocting all the stomach's crudities.
It is tobacco which hath power to clarify,
The cloudy mists before dim eyes appearing.
It is tobacco which hath power to rarefy,
The thick gross humour which doth stop the hearing.   20
   The wasting hectic and the quartan fever,
   Which doth of physic make a mockery,
   The gout it cures, and helps ill breaths for ever,
   Whether the cause in tooth or stomach be.
And though ill breaths were by it but confounded,   25
Yet that vile medicine it doth far excel,
Which by Sir Thomas More hath been propounded,
For this is thought a gentleman-like smell.
   O that I were one of these mountebanks,
   Which praise their oils, and powders which they sell,   30
   My customers would give me coin with thanks,
   I for this ware, so smooth a tale would tell.
Yet would I use none of those terms before,
I would but say, that it the pox will cure.
This were enough, without discoursing more,   35
All our brave gallants in the town t'allure.

In Crassum. 37

Crassus his lies are not pernicious lies,
But pleasant fictions, hurtful unto none,
But to himself, for no man counts him wise,
To tell for truth, that which for false is known.

---

16 *Decocting:* digesting.

19 *rarefy:* purify, refine.

21 *wasting {. . .} fever:* Hectic fever is a debilitating, exhausting disease like consumption. The *quartan* is an illness characterized by fits of chills and shivering.

22 *physic:* medicine.

27 *Thomas More:* Sir Thomas More. "In Epigram 238, Sir Thomas More recommends eating onions to take away the smell of leeks, garlic for the smell of onions: 'But if your breath remains offensive even after the garlic, then either it is incurable or nothing but excrement will remove it'" (Krueger). *propounded:* proposed, put forward.

29 *mountebanks:* cheats, scoundrels. "An itinerant charlatan who sold supposed medicines and remedies, freq. using various entertainments to attract a crowd of potential customers" (*OED*).

32 *ware:* an article of commerce, merchandise.

He swears that Ghent is threescore miles about,   5
And that the bridge at Paris on the Seine,
Is of such thickness, length and breadth, throughout
That six-score arches can it scarce sustain.
He swears he saw so great a dead man's skull,
At Canterbury digged out of the ground,   10
That would contain of wheat, three bushels full,
And that in Kent, are twenty yeomen found,
  Of which the poorest every year dispends
Five thousand pound. These and five thousand more
So oft he hath recited to his friends,   15
  That now himself persuades himself 'tis so:
But why doth Crassus tell his lies so rife,
Of bridges, towns, and things that have no life?
  He is a lawyer, and doth well espy,
  That for such lies an action will not lie.   20

In Philonem. 38

Philo the gentleman, the fortune teller,
The schoolmaster, the midwife and the bawd,
The conjurer, the buyer and the seller,
Of painting which with breathing will be thawed,
  Doth practice physic, and his credit grows,   5
  As doth the ballad-singer's auditory,
  Which hath at Temple Bar his standing chose,
  And to the vulgar sings an alehouse story.
First stands a porter, then an oyster-wife
Doth stint her cry and stay her steps to hear him;   10
Then comes a cutpurse ready with his knife,
And then a country client presseth near him.
  There stands the constable, there stands the whore,
  And harkning to the song mark not each other.

---

5 *Ghent:* a city in present-day Belgium.

6 *Seine:* the river running through Paris, France.

12 *yeomen:* "A man holding a small landed estate; a freeholder under the rank of a gentleman; hence vaguely, a commoner or countryman of respectable standing, esp. one who cultivates his own land" (*OED*).

13 *dispends:* spends.

20 *action {. . .} lie:* "he will not be sued for libel or slander of inanimate things" (Krueger).

2 *bawd:* prostitute.

5 *physic:* medicine.

6 *auditory:* audience.

9 *oyster-wife:* woman who sells oysters.

11 *cutpurse:* pickpocket.

There by the sergeant stands the debtor poor,   15
    And doth no more mistrust him than his brother:
Thus Orpheus to such hearers giveth music,
And Philo to such patients giveth physic.

In Fuscum. 39

Fuscus is free, and hath the world at will,
Yet in the course of life that he doth lead.
He's like a horse, which turning round a mill,
Doth always in the selfsame circle tread.
    First he doth rise at ten, and at eleven   5
    He goes to Giles, where he doth eat till one,
    Then sees a play till six, and sups at seven,
    And after supper, straight to bed is gone.
And there till ten next day he doth remain,
And then he dines, then sees a comedy.   10
And then he sups, and goes to bed again,
Thus round he runs without variety.
    Save that sometimes he comes not to the play,
    But falls into a whore house by the way.

In Afrum. 40

The smell feast Afer travails to the Burse
Twice every day the flying news to hear,
Which when he hath no money in his purse,
To rich men's tables he doth often bear.
    He tells how Gronigen is taken in,   5
    By the brave conduct of illustrious Vere;
    And how the Spanish forces Brest would win,
    But that they do victorious Norris fear.
No sooner is a ship at sea surprised,
But straight he learns the news and doth disclose it,   10
No sooner hath the Turk a plot devised
To conquer Christendom, but straight he knows it.

---

15 *sergeant:* a sheriff's deputy, a steward of an estate.

17 *Orpheus:* legendary founder of poetry, who used his music to control nature and calm wild beasts, and eventually to rescue his wife from the underworld.

6 *Giles:* St. Giles, a section of London around St. Giles Church.

1 *Burse:* the Royal Exchange, the commercial center of London that also served as a meeting place.

5–6 *Groningen {. . .} Vere:* Sir Francis Vere (1560–1609) was the general of English troops in the Netherlands. Vere's forces captured the northeastern city of Groningen in July 1594.

7–8 *Brest {. . .} Norris:* Sir John Norris (?1547–97) successfully attacked a Spanish fort in November 1594, cutting the city of Brest off from the sea.

Fair written in a scroll he hath the names,
Of all the widows which the plague hath made,
And persons, times and places, still he frames,   15
To every tale, the better to persuade.
We call him Fame, for that the wide-mouth slave
Will eat as fast as he will utter lies:
For Fame is said an hundreth mouths to have,
And he eats more than would five-score suffice.   20

In Paulum. 41

By lawful mart, and by unlawful stealth,
Paulus, in spite of envy, fortunate,
Derives out of the ocean so much wealth,
As he may well maintain a lord's estate.
  But on the land a little gulf there is,   5
  Wherein he drowneth all that wealth of his.

In Licum. 42

Lycus which lately is to Venice gone,
Shall if he do return, gain three for one.
But ten to one, his knowledge and his wit,
Will not be bettered nor increased a whit.

In Publium. 43

Publius, student at the common law,
Oft leaves his books, and for his recreation
To Paris Garden doth himself withdraw,
Where he is ravished with such delectation
As down amongst the dogs and bears he goes,   5

---

1 *mart:* commerce, bartering.

2 *Paulus:* perhaps Sir Walter Raleigh (see Krueger), who was envied for his power and wealth. For his secret marriage to Elizabeth Throckmorton he was imprisoned in the Tower in 1592. He was released to supervise the distribution of spoils from the Spanish treasure ship *Madre de Dios,* captured by his ships in September. After his capture, he paid the queen her rightful share of the riches, as well as a significant portion of his own. The queen released him in December, and therefore, his wife is considered the gulf "wherein he drowneth all that wealth of his."

3 *ocean:* perhaps an allusion to Raleigh's name in his epyllion about his troubled relationship with Queen Elizabeth after his secret marriage, *Ocean to Cynthia.* Raleigh called himself "Ocean" because Cynthia (his nickname for Queen Elizabeth) called him Water (Walter).

2 *gain:* the practice of travelers wagering on their safe return, instituted because travel at this time was so dangerous.

3 *Paris Garden:* a bear garden in Southwark, across the Thames from London, and near the Rose Theatre (and, after 1599, the Globe).

4 *delectation:* delight

Where whilst he skipping cries "To head, To head,"
His satin doublet and his velvet hose
Are all with spittle from above be-spread.
Then is he like his father's country hall,
Stinking with dogs, and muted all with hawks.   10
And rightly too on him this filth doth fall,
Which for such filthy sports his books forsakes,
Leaving old Ployden, Dyer and Broke alone,
To see old Harry Hunks and Sacarson.

In Sillam. 44

When I this proposition have defended,
A coward cannot be an honest man.
Thou, Silla, seemest forthwith to be offended,
And holds the contrary and swears he can.
But when I tell thee that he will forsake   5
His dearest friend, in peril of his life,
Thou then art changed and sayst thou didst mistake,
And so we end our argument and strife.
    Yet I think on, and think I think aright,
    Thy argument argues thou wilt not fight.   10

In Dacum. 45

Dacus, with some good colour and pretence,
Terms his love's beauty silent eloquence:
For she doth lay more colours on her face,
Than ever Tully used his speech to grace.

In Marcum. 46

Why dost thou, Marcus, in thy misery,
Rail and blaspheme, and call the heavens un-kind.
The heavens do owe no kindness unto thee,
Thou hast the heavens so little in thy mind:
For in thy life thou never usest prayer,   5
But at primero, to encounter fair.

---

13 *Ployden {. . .} Broke:* Edward Plowden, Sir James Dyer, and Sir Robert Broke were well-known
   Elizabethan lawyers whose case reports were used as textbooks.
14 *Harry {. . .} Sacarson:* famous bears who performed at Paris Garden.

1 *Dacus:* once more, perhaps Samuel Daniel (see epigram 30). *colour:* show.
3 *colours:* makeup.
4 *Tully:* Marcus Tullius Cicero (106–43 BC), famed Roman orator and statesman, often called
   Tully by the Elizabethans.

6 *primero:* a card game similar to poker.

Meditations of a Gull. 47

See yonder melancholy gentleman,
Which hoodwinked with his hat, alone doth sit.
Think what he thinks and tell me if you can,
What great affairs troubles his little wit.
    He thinks not of the war 'twixt France and Spain,   5
    Whether it be for Europe's good or ill,
    Nor whether the Empire can itself maintain
    Against the Turkish power encroaching still.
Nor what great town in all the Netherlands,
The states determine to besiege this spring,   10
Nor how the Scottish policy now stands,
Nor what becomes of th'Irish mutining.
    But he doth seriously bethink him whether
    Of the gull people he be more esteemed,
    For his long cloak, or for his great black feather,   15
    By which each gull is now a gallant deemed.
Or of a journey he deliberates,
To Paris Garden cock-pit or the play:
Or how to steal a dog he meditates,
Or what he shall unto his mistress say.   20
    Yet with these thoughts he thinks himself most fit
    To be of counsel with a king for wit.

Ad Musam. 48

Peace, idle Muse, have done, for it is time,
Since lousy Ponticus envies my fame,
And swears the better sort are much to blame
To make me so well known for so ill rhyme.
    Yet Banks his horse is better known than he,   5
    So are the camels and the western hog,

---

5 *war {. . .} Spain:* the war between France and Spain began in January 1595.

7 *Empire:* the German or Holy Roman Empire under the Hapsburg dynasty.

10 *states:* the legislative body of the Netherlands.

11 *Scottish policy:* the English policy toward Scotland.

12 *Irish mutining:* in Ireland, the mutiny of the Irish rebels against the English.

15 *black feather:* a new fashion signaling melancholy in which men wore an ostrich feather dyed black in their hats, in response to the old fashion of wearing hats with brightly colored feathers.

18 *Paris Garden cock-pit:* site of cockfights in Southwark, across the Thames from London.

2 *lousy:* infested with lice.

5 *Banks his horse:* see 30.7.

6 *camels {. . .} hog:* camels were performing in London at this time, but the western hog is unknown (Krueger).

And so is Lepidus his printed dog.
Why doth not Ponticus their fames envy?
Besides, this muse of mine, and the black feather,
Grew both together fresh in estimation,   10
And both grown stale, were cast away together:
What fame is this that scarce lasts out a fashion?
    Only this last in credit doth remain,
    That from henceforth, each bastard cast forth rhyme
    Which doth but savor of a libel vain,   15
    Shall call me father, and be thought my crime.
So dull and with so little sense endued,
Is my gross headed judge, the multitude.
    FINIS

---

7 *Lepidus:* "A picture of his dog, Bungey, appears on the title-page of Sir John Harington's translation of *Orlando Furioso*" (Krueger).

"The Passionate Shepherd to His Love"

From *England's Helicon* (1600)

Come live with me, and be my love,
And we will all the pleasures prove
That valleys, groves, hills and fields,
Woods, or steepy mountain yields.

And we will sit upon the rocks,   5
Seeing the shepherds feed their flocks
By shallow rivers, to whose falls
Melodious birds sing madrigals.

This version of the poem, in six stanzas, is the version printed most widely today and is identified as Marlowe's for the first time in this popular collection of verse.

2 *prove:* experience, try.

4 *steepy:* steep. *yields:* continues the quasi-scientific language from *prove* in line 2.

5–6 Introduces a dramatic setting of theater or performance, in which the shepherd and his beloved serve as audience to the actor-shepherds.

5–8 Conventional pastoral locale and action (*locus amoenus*) and the site of poetry (*locus poeticus*), familiar from Theocritus (*Idylls* 1.1–8), Virgil (*Eclogues* 1.52–59), and their Renaissance heirs, including Marot (*Lamentation for Madame Louise of Savoy* 1–4, 17–20) and especially Spenser in *The Shepheardes Calender* (e.g., *Aprill* 33–36, *June* 7–8, *August* 153–56, *December* 1–4). See also Ovid, *Amores* 3.1.1–4, translated by Marlowe in *OE* 3.1.1–4.

7 *shallow rivers:* in *The Merry Wives of Windsor,* Shakespeare presents Sir Hugh Evans singing a garbled version of this stanza and part of the next, and brooding over this particular phrase, even using it as a stage cue to Justice Shallow (2.3.17–35). The river is a figure for poetic inspiration, and its shallowness introduces a wry humor into the pastoral representation. For Elizabethans, the waterfall was a trope specifically associated with Spenser (e.g., *Return from Parnassus* 7: 279–80).

8 *Melodious birds:* in "The Nymph's Reply," Raleigh identifies the species as the nightingale, the most melodious of birds for pastoral poets. *madrigals:* a precise, artistic term during the period,

And I will make thee beds of roses,
And a thousand fragrant posies,   10
A cap of flowers, and a kirtle,
Embroidered all with leaves of myrtle.

A gown made of the finest wool
Which from our pretty lambs we pull,
Fair lined slippers for the cold,   15
With buckles of the purest gold.

A belt of straw and ivy buds,
With coral clasps and amber studs,
And if these pleasures may thee move,
Come live with me, and be my love.   20

The shepherd swains shall dance and sing,
For thy delight each May-morning.
If these delights thy mind may move,
Then live with me, and be my love.
          FINIS   *Chr. Marlow.*

---

obscure in origin but perhaps tracing to the Italian word for "herd," *mandria,* as well as to the Greek word for "fold," thus suggesting "pastoral song" (*OED*). According to the *OED,* the word has three separate meanings: (1) "A short lyrical poem of amatory character"; (2) in music, "a kind of part song for three or more voices (usually, five or six) characterized by adherence to an ecclesiastical mode, elaborate contrapuntal imitation, and the absence of instrumental accompaniment"; and (3) the second definition used figuratively as a "song, ditty." Spenser uses the word in his *Dedicatory Sonnet* to Raleigh in the 1590 *Faerie Queene* (15.3), linked with the nightingale (15.1).

9 *beds of roses:* see Spenser, *Faerie Queene* 2.12.77, locale of the enchantress Acrasia.

10 *posies:* a collection of flowers, but also a familiar Elizabethan trope for poetry, spelled "poesies" in the original text of *England's Helicon.*

11 *kirtle:* a smock, coat, or gown, worn by a shepherdess. Cf. Hero's "kirtle blue" in *HL* 15.

12 *myrtle:* sacred to Venus, Roman goddess of beauty. See Ovid, *Amores* 1.1.34, translated by Marlowe in *OE* 1.1.34.

15 *cold:* a subtle and paradoxical reminder of winter and time.

21–22 The speaking shepherd promises that the shepherds who performed in lines 5–6 will now perform for his beloved's "delight."

23 *mind:* a climactic signal of the intellectual or subjective (as opposed to the purely erotic) drift of the shepherd's song.

From *The Passionate Pilgrim* (1599)

Live with me and be my love,
And we will all the pleasures prove
That hills and valleys, dales and fields,
And all the craggy mountains yield.

There will we sit upon the rocks,   5
And see the shepherds feed their flocks,
By shallow rivers, by whose falls
Melodious birds sing madrigals.

There will I make thee a bed of roses,
With a thousand fragrant posies,   10
A cap of flowers, and a kirtle,
Embroidered all with leaves of myrtle.

A belt of straw and ivy buds,
With coral clasps and amber studs.
And if these pleasures may thee move,   15
Then live with me, and be my love.

Sir Walter Raleigh, "The Nymph's Reply"

If all the world and love were young,
And truth in every shepherd's tongue,
These pretty pleasures might me move
To live with thee and be thy love.

But Time drives flocks from field to fold,   5
When rivers rage and rocks grow cold,

This version of the poem, in four stanzas, is the first known printed version, and does not appear
   with Marlowe's name attached. It is poem 19 in a twenty-poem anthology of poems that the title
   page attributes (erroneously of course) to William Shakespeare.
1 *Live with me:* alters the more famous opening, "Come live with me."

This poem follows Marlowe's in *England's Helicon* (1600).

And Philomel becometh dumb;
The rest complains of cares to come.

The flowers do fade, and wanton fields
To wayward winter reckoning yields;   10
A honey tongue, a heart of gall
Is fancy's spring, but sorrow's fall.

Thy gowns, thy shoes, thy beds of roses,
Thy cap, thy kirtle, and thy posies,
Soon break, soon wither, soon forgotten,   15
In folly ripe, in reason rotten.

Thy belt of straw and ivy buds,
Thy coral clasps and amber studs,
All these in me no means can move
To come to thee and be thy love.   20

But could youth last and love still breed,
Had joys no date, nor age no need,
Then these delights my mind might move
To live with thee and be thy love.

Anonymous, "Another of the Same Nature, Made Since"

Come live with me and be my dear,
And we will revel all the year,
In plains and groves, on hills and dales,
Where fragrant air breeds sweetest gales.

---

7 *Philomel {. . .} dumb:* Philomela, a princess of Athens, was raped by her brother-in-law, Tereus, who cut out her tongue so she could not reveal the crime. While imprisoned in a hut in the forest, she wove a tapestry depicting the crime and sent it to her sister, Procne, who freed her. Together, the sisters plotted revenge against Tereus: they killed his son, Itys, and served him in a pie to his father. When Tereus chased them, they metamorphosed into birds, Philomela becoming the nightingale.

12 *fancy's:* imagination's.

16 *folly {. . .} reason:* Raleigh responds to the *intellectual* drive of Marlowe's soft pastoral.

22 *date:* "The limit, term, or end of a period of time, or of the duration of something" (*OED*).

This poem follow's Raleigh's in *England's Helicon* (1600).

There shall you have the beauteous pine,   5
The cedar and the spreading vine,
And all the woods to be a screen,
Lest Phoebus kiss my summer's queen.

The seat for your disport shall be
Over some river, in a tree,   10
Where silver sands and pebbles sing
Eternal ditties with the spring.

There shall you see the nymphs at play,
And how the satyrs spend the day,
The fishes gliding on the sands,   15
Offering their bellies to your hands.

The birds with heavenly tuned throats
Possess woods-echoes with sweet notes,
Which to your senses will impart
A music to inflame the heart.   20

Upon the bare and leafless oak
The ring-doves' wooings will provoke
A colder blood than you possess
To play with me and do no less.

In bowers of laurel trimly dight   25
We will outwear the silent night,
While Flora busy is to spread
Her richest treasure on our bed.

Ten thousand glow-worms shall attend,
And all their sparkling fights shall spend,   30
All to adorn and beautify
Your lodging with most majesty.

Then in mine arms will I enclose
Lilies' fair mixture with the rose,

---

8 *Phoebus:* Apollo, the sun. *queen:* the first formal political term in the sequence of three poems from *England's Helicon.*
9 *disport:* recreation, pastime, merriment, sport.
25 *trimly dight:* nicely adorned.
27 *Flora:* goddess of flowers.

Whose nice perfections in love's play   35
Shall tune me to the highest key.

Thus as we pass the welcome night
In sportful pleasures and delight,
The nimble fairies on the grounds
Shall dance and sing melodious sounds.   40

If these may serve for to entice
Your presence to love's paradise,
Then come with me and be my dear,
And we will straight begin the year.

John Donne, "The Bait"

Come live with me and be my love,
And we will some new pleasures prove,
Of golden sands and crystal brooks,
With silken lines and silver hooks.

There will the river whispering run,   5
Warmed by thine eyes more than the sun;
And there th' enamoured fish will stay,
Begging themselves they may betray.

When thou wilt swim in that live bath,
Each fish, which every channel hath,   10
Will amorously to thee swim,
Gladder to catch thee than thou him.

If thou to be so seen beest loth
By sun or moon, thou dark'nest both;
And if myself have leave to see,   15
I need not their light, having thee.

Let others freeze with angling reeds,
And cut their legs with shells and weeds,

First published 1633 in Donne's *Songs and Sonets,* but written around 1600.

Or treacherously poor fish beset
With strangling snare, or windowy net: 20

Let coarse bold hands from slimy nest
The bedded fish in banks out-wrest,
Or curious traitors, sleave-silk flies
Bewitch poor fishes' wand'ring eyes.

For thee, thou need'st no such deceit,   25
For thou thyself art thine own bait;
That fish that is not catched thereby,
Alas, is wiser far than I.

From Marlowe, *The Jew of Malta* (4.2.99–109)

ITHAMORE. Content, but we will leave this paltry land,
    And sail from hence to Greece, to lovely Greece.   100
    I'll be thy Jason, thou my Golden Fleece;
    Where painted carpets o'er the meads are hurled,
    And Bacchus' vineyards overspread the world;
    Where woods and forests go in goodly green,
    I'll be Adonis, thou shalt be Love's Queen;   105
    The meads, the orchards, and the primrose-lanes,
    Instead of sedge and reed, bear sugar-canes:
    Thou in those groves, by Dis above,
    Shalt live with me and be my love.

---

23 *curious:* elaborate. *sleave-silk:* silk divided into fine strands.

99 *Ithamore:* In act 4, scene 3, Barabas, Ithamore's owner, discovers that Ithamore has betrayed him. Here Ithamore woos the courtesan Bellamira with a parody of "The Passionate Shepherd."

101 *Jason { . . .} golden fleece:* in classical mythology, Helle joined her brother Phryxus in trying to escape persecution from their stepmother Ino by fleeing on a golden ram. Helle became faint and drowned, while Phryxus carried the ram; arriving in Colchis, he sacrificed the animal but retained its fleece, thereby creating the Golden Fleece. Jason organized the Argonauts and set sail on the ship *Argo* to search for the Golden Fleece.

103 *Bacchus:* god of wine.

105 *Adonis:* in classical mythology, Adonis was loved and pursued by Venus.

108 *Dis:* Pluto, god of wealth and the classical underworld.

From William Shakespeare, *The Merry Wives of Windsor* (3.1.8–35)

Evans: I most fehemently desire you you will
also look that way.

Simple: I will, sir.   *{Exit.}*   10

Evans: Jeshu pless my soul! how full of chollors
I am and trempling of mind! I shall be glad if he
have deceived me. How melancholies I am! I will
knog his urinals about his knave's costard when I
have good opportunities for the ork. 'Pless my   15
soul!   *{Sings.}*

> "To shallow rivers, to whose falls
> Melodious birds sings madrigals;
> There will we make our peds of roses,
> And a thousand fragrant posies.   20
> To shallow—"

Mercy on me! I have a great dispositions to cry.
                              {Sings.}

> "Melodious birds sing madrigals—
> When as I sat in Pabylon—
> And a thousand vagram posies.   25
> To shallow, etc."

        {Enter Simple.}

Simple: Yonder he is coming, this way, Sir Hugh.

Evans: He's welcome.   *{Sings.}*

> "To shallow rivers, to whose falls—"

Heaven prosper the right! What weapons is he?   30

In Shakespeare's comedy, Sir Hugh Evans, the Welsh parson, tries humorously to control his fear
  before dueling Doctor Caius by garbling "The Passionate Shepherd." Sir Hugh is accompanied
  by John Simple, a servant to Abraham Slender, a cousin to Robert Shallow, a country justice.
8 *fehemently:* vehemently.
11 *pless:* bless. *chollors:* choler, anger.
12 *trempling:* trembling.
14 *knog:* knock. *costard:* apple but meaning a human head.
15 *ork:* work.
18 *peds:* beds.
23 *Pabylon:* Babylon. This is the first line of a metrical version of Psalm 137.
24 *vagram:* vagrant, but Evans confuses it with *fragrant*.

Simple: No weapons, sir. There comes my master, Master Shallow, and another gentleman—from Frogmore, over the stile, this way.

Evans: Pray you give me my gown, or else keep it in your arms.   *{Reads a book.}*

   {Enter} PAGE, SHALLOW, SLENDER.

J. Paulin, "Love's Contentment"

Come, my Clarinda, we'll consume
Our joys no more at this low rate;
More glorious titles let's assume
And love according to our state.

For if Contentment wears a crown   5
Which never tyrant could assail,
How many monarchs put we down
In our Utopian commonweal?

As princes rain down golden showers
On those in whom they take delight,   10
So in this happier court of ours,
Each is the other's favourite.

Our privacies no eye dwells near,
But unobserved we embrace,
And no sleek courtier's pen is there   15
To set down either time or place.

No midnight fears disturb our bliss,
Unless a golden dream awake us,
For care we know not what it is,
Unless to please doth careful make us.   20

---

33 *stile:* steps for crossing a fence or wall.

This poem appears only in an undated manuscript of a miscellaneous collection of poems, but probably dates from the 1640s (MS Harley 6918, folio 92) (see Orgel 260).
5 *crown:* signals the overtly political afterlife of Marlowe's lyric, which the rest of Paulin's poem ex-
   tends.
8 *Utopian commonweal:* an imaginary kingdom.

We fear no enemy's invasion,
Our counsel's wise and politic;
With timely force, if not persuasion,
We cool the homebred schismatic.

All discontent thus to remove   25
What monarch boasts but thou and I?
In this content we live and love,
And in this love resolve to die:

That when, our souls together fled,
One urn shall our mixed dust enshrine,   30
In golden letters may be read,
Here lie Content's late King and Queen.

Robert Herrick, "To Phillis to love, and live with him"

Live, live with me, and thou shalt see
The pleasures I'll prepare for thee:
What sweets the Country can afford
Shall bless thy bed, and bless thy board.
The soft sweet moss shall be thy bed,   5
With crawling woodbine overspread:
By which the silver-shedding streams
Shall gently melt thee into dreams.
Thy clothing next shall be a gown
Made of the fleeces purest down.   10
The tongues of kids shall be thy meat;
Their milk thy drink; and thou shalt eat
The paste of filberts for thy bread

---

24 *homebred schismatic:* "In Caroline England on the verge of civil war, this had a variety of applica-
tions, ranging from political schismatics who refused Charles his ship money to Scottish Pres-
byterians who resisted the imposition of the new prayer book. Since Charles' 'timely force' was,
on the whole, singularly ineffective, the following two lines have an ironic force that it is difficult
to believe was unintentional" (Orgel).

Published in Herrick's *Hesperides* (1648).
6 *woodbine:* a climbing vine, especially the honeysuckle.
13 *filberts:* also called hazelnuts.

With cream of cowslips buttered.
Thy feasting-tables shall be hills   15
With daisies spread, and daffodils;
Where thou shalt sit, and red-breast by,
For meat, shall give thee melody.
I'll give thee chains and carcanets
Of primroses and violets.   20
A bag and bottle thou shalt have;
That richly wrought, and this as brave;
So that as either shall express
The wearer's no mean shepherdess.
At sheering-times, and yearly wakes,   25
When Themilis his pastime makes,
There thou shalt be; and be the wit,
Nay more, the feast, and grace of it.
On holy-days, when virgins meet
To dance the heys with nimble feet;   30
Thou shalt come forth, and then appear
The Queen of Roses for that year.
And having danc't ('bove all the best)
Carry the garland from the rest.
In wicker-baskets maids shall bring   35
To thee (my dearest shephardling)
The blushing apple, bashful pear,
And shame-fac't plum (all simp'ring there).
Walk in the Groves, and thou shalt find
The name of Phillis in the rind   40
Of every straight, and smooth-skin tree;
Where kissing that, I'll twice kiss thee.
To thee a sheep-hook I will send,
Be-pranckt with ribbands, to this end,
This, this alluring hook might be   45
Less for to catch a sheep, than me.
Thou shalt have possets, wassails fine,
Not made of ale, but spiced wine;

---

14 *cowslips:* Eurasian primroses with fragrant yellow flowers.

19 *carcanets:* jeweled necklaces, collars, or headbands.

30 *heys:* "A country dance having a winding or serpentine movement, or being of the nature of a reel" (*OED*).

44 *ribbands:* ribbons.

47 *possets:* hot sweetened milk curdled with wine or ale. *wassails:* the drinks used in toasting, usually wine or ale spiced with apples and sugar.

To make thy maids and self free mirth,
All sitting near the glitt'ring hearth.   50
Thou sha't have ribbands, roses, rings,
Gloves, garters, stockings, shoes, and strings
Of winning colours, that shall move
Others to lust, but me to love.
These (nay) and more, thine own shall be,   55
If thou wilt love, and live with me.

Lucan's First Book

THE FIRST BOOK OF LUCAN
TRANSLATED INTO ENGLISH

To His Kind and True Friend,
Edward Blount.

Blount: I purpose to be blunt with you, and out of my dullness to encounter you with a dedication in the memory of that pure elemental wit Chr. Marlowe, whose ghost or genius is to be seen walk the churchyard in (at the least) three or four sheets. Methinks you should presently look wild now, and grow humourously frantic upon the taste of it. Well, lest you should, let me tell you. 5
This spirit was sometime a familiar of your own, *Lucan's first book translated*, which (in regard of your old right in it) I have raised in the circle of your patronage. But stay now, Edward: if I mistake not, you are to accommodate yourself with some few instructions touching the property of a patron, that you are not yet possessed of, and to study them for your better grace as our gallants do 10
fashions. First, you must be proud, and think you have merit enough in you, though you are ne'er so empty; then, when I bring you the book, take physic, and keep state, assign me a time by your man to come again, and afore the day be sure to have changed your lodging; in the meantime sleep little, and sweat with the invention of some pitiful dry jest or two which you may happen to ut- 15
ter, with some little (or not at all) marking of your friends, when you have found a place for them to come in at; or if by chance something has dropped from you worthy the taking up, weary all that come to you with the often repetition of it; censure scornfully enough, and somewhat like a traveler; commend nothing lest you discredit your (that which you would seem to have) 20
judgement. These things if you can mould yourself to them, Ned, I make no question but they will not become you. One special virtue in our patrons of these days I have promised myself you shall fit excellently, which is to give

---

Edward Blount: (?–1631); printer and bookseller.
3 *churchyard:* St. Paul's Churchyard, in the printing district.
4 *sheets:* with a pun on printers' sheets. *humorously:* with excess of humor (emotion).
9 *property:* qualities.

nothing; yes, thy love I will challenge as my peculiar object, both in this, and (I hope) many more succeeding offices. Farewell: I affect not the world should measure my thoughts to thee by a scale of this nature: leave to think good of me when I fall from thee.

> Thine in all rites of perfect friendship,
> THOM. THORPE

Wars worse than civil on Thessalian plains,
And outrage strangling law, and people strong
We sing, whose conquering swords their own breasts launched,
Armies allied, the kingdom's league uprooted,
Th' affrighted world's force bent on public spoil,   5
Trumpets and drums like deadly threat'ning other,
Eagles alike displayed, darts answering darts.

Romans, what madness, what huge lust of war,
Hath made barbarians drunk with Latin blood?
Now Babylon (proud through our spoil) should stoop,   10
While slaughtered Crassus' ghost walks unrevenged,
Will ye wage war, for which you shall not triumph?
Aye me, O what a world of land and sea
Might they have won whom civil broils have slain!
As far as Titan springs, where night dims heaven,   15
Aye, to the torrid zone where mid-day burns,
And where stiff winter, whom no spring resolves,
Fetters the Euxine Sea with chains of ice;

Thom. Thorpe: Thomas Thorpe (fl. 1584–1625); bookseller; most famous for his edition of Shakespeare's Sonnets (1609), with its enigmatic dedication to "Mr W.H."

1 *worse than civil:* "worse" because Pompey and Caesar were related through marriage. *Thessalian:* Lucan's word is *Emathios* for Emathian, a part of Macedonia often ascribed to nearby Thessaly (a vast plain in Greece). Pharsalis was a town in Thessaly. These terms were conventionally interchangeable, along with Philippi, which was technically a city in Macedonia.

2 *outrage {. . .} law:* crime made legal.

3 *launched:* wounded.

4 *Armies allied:* relatives fighting each other. *league:* the First Triumvirate (Pompey, Caesar, and Crassus).

6 *like:* alike.

7 *Eagles:* The Roman legion's standard of battle had an eagle at its top.

10 *Now {. . .} stoop:* Lucan's sense is "Then proud Babylon should have been stripped of its spoils and made to bow" (*cumque superba foret Babylon spolianda tropaeis*).

15 *Titan:* the sun.

17 *resolves:* melts (the winter's snow and ice).

18 *Euxine Sea:* the Black Sea.

Scythia and wild Armenia had been yoked,
And they of Nilus' mouth (if there live any).   20
Rome, if thou take delight in impious war,
First conquer all the earth, then turn thy force
Against thyself: as yet thou wants not foes.
That now the walls of houses half-reared totter,
That rampires fallen down, huge heaps of stone   25
Lie in our towns, that houses are abandoned,
And few live that behold their ancient seats,
Italy many years hath lien untilled
And choked with thorns, that greedy earth wants hinds,
Fierce Pyrrhus, neither thou nor Hannibal   30
Art cause; no foreign foe could so afflict us;
These plagues arise from wreak of civil power.
But if for Nero (then unborn) the Fates
Would find no other means (and gods not slightly
Purchase immortal thrones, nor Jove joyed heaven   35
Until the cruel Giants' war was done)
We plain not heavens, but gladly bear these evils
For Nero's sake: Pharsalia groan with slaughter,

---

19 *Scythia:* By the time of Republican and Augustan Rome, this term described any part or all of
   northern Asia.

20 *Nilus' mouth:* the source of the Nile.

21 *impious: nefandi* ("unspeakable," because it was both interfamilial and intrafamilial).

23 *wants:* "lacks."

24 *half-reared:* half-destroyed.

25 *rampires:* ramparts.

28 *lien:* lain.

29 *wants hinds:* lacks farmhands (to cultivate the soil).

30 *Pyrrhus, Hannibal:* historically, two of Rome's greatest enemies. Pyrrhus was the king of Epirus
   who defeated the Romans in the third century BCE; Hannibal of Carthage invaded Italy in the
   Second Punic War later in that same century.

31 *Art cause:* the enjambment and dictional placement render the same of *Poenus erit.*

32 *These {. . .} power:* Lucan's sense is "deep-seated are the wounds of civil warfare" (*alta sedent civilis
   volnera dextrae*).

34–36 *gods {. . .} done:* a reference to the Gigantomachia. See *OE* 2.1.

35 *joy'd:* enjoyed.

37 *plain {. . .} heavens:* do not complain against the gods.

38 *groan:* a possible transcribal mistake from an original manuscript or a possible pun by Marlowe.
   Gill cites an original spelling of "grone," which *OED* cites as an obsolete spelling of "groan." The
   Latin, however (*inpleat*), would indicate "grown." If "groan" is intended, serious puns may obtain: (1) "groan" is an obsolete spelling of (the noun) "ground" (*OED*), which would also fit the
   context; (2) "groan" is etymologically related to "green" (*OED*)—green plants grow out of
   the ground—and the ironic point would be that this ground is not green but red with blood
   (the following line).

And Carthage souls be glutted with our bloods;
At Munda let the dreadful battles join;   40
Add, Caesar, to these ills, Perusian famine,
The Mutin toils, the fleet at Leuca sunk,
And cruel field near burning Aetna fought.
Yet Rome is much bound to these civil arms,
Which made thee emperor, thee (seeing thou, being old,   45
Must shine a star) shall heaven (whom thou lovest)
Receive with shouts, where thou wilt reign as king,
Or mount the sun's flame-bearing chariot,
And with bright restless fire compass the earth,
Undaunted though her former guide be changed;   50
Nature and every power shall give thee place,
What god it please thee be, or where to sway.
But neither choose the north t' erect thy seat,
Nor yet the adverse reeking southern pole,
Whence thou shouldst view thy Rome with squinting beams.   55
If any one part of vast heaven thou swayest,
The burdened axis with thy force will bend;
The midst is best; that place is pure and bright.
There, Caesar, mayst thou shine and no cloud dim thee,
Then men from war shall bide in league and ease,   60
Peace through the world from Janus' fane shall fly,
And bolt the brazen gates with bars of iron.
Thou, Caesar, at this instant art my god:
Thee if I invoke, I shall not need
To crave Apollo's aid or Bacchus' help,   65

---

39 *glutted {. . .} bloods:* the heightened effect of these words through assonance renders the same for
   the alliteration of the corresponding Latin words *saturentur sanguine.*
40 *Munda:* in Spain, where Caesar defeated Pompey's sons in 45 BCE.
41 *Perusian famine:* a reference to Octavian's blockade of Perugia in 41–40 BCE.
42 *Mutin toils:* the fighting at Mutina (now Modena), where Octavian triumphed over Antony in
   43 BCE. *Leuca:* a reference to the battle of Actium, where Octavian defeated Antony and Cleopatra in 31 BCE.
43 *And {. . .} fought:* "The reference is to the war in Sicily, which was fought by Agrippa (on behalf
   of Octavius Caesar) against Sextus Pompeius during 36 BC" (Gill).
53–58 As Gill notes, "At this point the panegyric almost overbalances into the ludicrous, with the
   notion that the deified Nero must be careful to maintain the balance of the universe by settling
   in the center: if he were to choose either pole, his weight would cause it to sink down (like a see-
   saw)"–see 70–73n. later.
52 *sway:* rule.
54 *reeking:* hot.
55 *squinting:* oblique, aslant.
61 *Janus' fane:* "The doors of the temple of Janus were always open in time of war, and closed in
   peacetime" (Gill).

Thy power inspires the Muse that sings this war.
The causes first I purpose to unfold
Of these garboils, whence springs a long discourse,
And what made madding people shake off peace.
The Fates are envious, high seats quickly perish,   70
Under great burdens falls are ever grievous;
Rome was so great it could not bear itself.
So when this world's compounded union breaks,
Time ends, and to old Chaos all things turn,
Confused stars shall meet, celestial fire   75
Fleet on the floods, the earth shoulder the sea,
Affording it no shore, and Phoebe's wain
Chase Phoebus, and enraged affect his place,
And strive to shine by day, and full of strife
Dissolve the engines of the broken world.   80
All great things crush themselves; such end the gods
Allot the height of honour, men so strong
By land and sea no foreign force could ruin.
O Rome, thyself art cause of all these evils,
Thyself thus shivered out to three men's shares: 85
Dire league of partners in a kingdom last not.
O faintly-joined friends, with ambition blind,
Why join you force to share the world betwixt you?
While th' earth the sea, and air the earth sustains,
While Titan strives against the world's swift course,   90

---

68 *garboils:* commotions.

69 *madding:* frenzied.

70–73 *The {. . .} breaks:* These lines can be seen to effect lines 53–58 as noted earlier by Gill, where
here "Rome" would be "Nero."

77 *Phoebe's wain:* the moon (Diana, Cynthia, etc.—twin sister of Phoebus Apollo).

78 *Phoebus:* the sun. *affect:* covet.

80 *Dissolve {. . .} world:* MacLure and Martin both note that Marlowe seems to have taken "Phoebe's
wain" as the subject of the transitive verb "Dissolve," whereas the Latin makes "engines" the subject of what would then be the intransitive verb "Dissolve" (*machina divolsi turbabit foedera mundi*).
If, however, we recall the image of Nero balancing the world in 53–58 and then breaking of the
world in 70–73, the construction of "engines" as the subject (as per Lucan's text) would make
more sense. That is to say, this passage, along with 70–73, implies a criticism of Nero that is lu-
dicrously exploited in 53–58 and that culminates in 81 with "all great things crush themselves."

85 *shivered {. . .} to:* "split among." Lucan's sense is "having been made the common property of
three masters" (*facta tribus dominis communis Roma*); therefore, Marlowe's use of "shivered" continues the idea of the "breaking apart" of the empire implied in 53–58, 70–73, and 80–81.
three men's: the First Triumvirate.

87 *faintly:* for evil purposes. *blind:* modifies "friends," not "ambition" (so too in the Latin).

90 *Titan:* the sun.

Or Cynthia, night's queen, waits upon the day,
Shall never faith be found in fellow kings.
Dominion cannot suffer partnership;
This need no foreign proof nor far-fet story:
Rome's infant walls were steeped in brother's blood;   95
Nor then was land, or sea, to breed such hate,
A town with one poor church set them at odds.

Caesar's and Pompey's jarring love soon ended,
'Twas peace against their wills; betwixt them both
Stepped Crassus in, even as the slender Isthmus   100
Betwixt the Aegean and the Ionian sea
Keeps each from other, but being worn away,
They both burst out, and each encounter other:
So whenas Crassus' wretched death, who stayed them
Had filled Assyrian Carra's walls with blood,   105
His loss made way for Roman outrages.
Parthians, y' afflict us more than ye suppose:
Being conquered, we are plagued with civil war.
Swords share our empire; Fortune, that made Rome
Govern the earth, the sea, the world itself,   110
Would not admit two lords; for Julia,
Snatched hence by cruel fates with ominous howls,
Bare down to hell her son, the pledge of peace,
And all bands of that death-presaging alliance.

---

91 *Cynthia:* the moon.

93 *suffer:* allow, endure.

95 *Rome's {. . .} blood:* a reference to the founders of Rome, Romulus and Remus, of whom the former killed the latter.

97 *church:* Lucan has *asylum.* Romulus established an asylum for criminals. Cooper translates the Latin word as "sanctuarie." By (and long before, and since) Marlowe's time, churches have been considered places of sanctuary for criminals.

100 *Isthmus:* the Isthmus of Corinth, joining the north of Greece to the Peloponnesus (southern part of Greece).

104 *stayed them:* kept them apart.

105 *Assyrian Carra:* Carrhae, in Syria, where Crassus fell to the Parthians.

109 *share:* divide.

111 *Julia:* the daughter of Julius Caesar who married Pompey. She died in childbirth and the baby boy died a few days afterward.

112 *with ominous howls:* Both Martin and MacLure note that this is Marlowe's addition and that it may be related to Lucan's *omine.* Beroaldo comments *Omen dicitur osme{n}, ex ore manans* ("[language of birds] is considered an omen, emanating from the mouth"). There is no Latin word *osmen,* but this might have been a misprint for *oscen,* which indicates augural language of birds. Whatever that word is in Beroaldo, the rest of the comment also indicates something coming out of the mouth. Because it certainly befits the context, Marlowe's addition here, therefore, likely derives from this comment.

Julia, had heaven given thee longer life,   115
Thou hadst restrained thy headstrong husband's rage,
Yea, and thy father too, and, swords thrown down,
Made all shake hands as once the Sabines did;
Thy death broke amity, and trained to war
These captains emulous of each other's glory.   120
Thou fearedst, great Pompey, that late deeds would dim
Old triumphs, and that Caesar's conquering France
Would dash the wreath thou wear'st for pirates' wrack.
Thee war's use stirred, and thoughts that always scorned
A second place; Pompey could bide no equal,   125
Nor Caesar no superior: which of both
Had justest cause unlawful 'tis to judge.
Each side had great partakers: Caesar's cause
The gods abetted, Cato liked the other.
Both differed much: Pompey was strook in years,   130
And by long rest forgot to manage arms,
And being popular sought by liberal gifts
To gain the light unstable commons' love,
And joyed to hear his theatre's applause;
He lived secure, boasting his former deeds,   135
And thought his name sufficient to uphold him,
Like to a tall oak in a fruitful field,
Bearing old spoils and conquerors' monuments,
Who though his root be weak, and his own weight
Keep him within the ground, his arms all bare,   140
His body (not his boughs) send forth a shade;
Though every blast it nod, and seem to fall,
When all the woods about stand bolt upright,
Yet he alone is held in reverence.
Caesar's renown for war was less, he restless,   145

---

118 *Sabines:* once enemies of Rome who became allies.

120 *emulous of:* rivaling.

123 *pirates' wrack:* In 67 BCE Pompey routed the pirates from the Mediterranean.

124 *Thee:* Caesar.

126 *which of both:* which one of the two.

129 *Cato {. . .} other:* Cato helped Pompey. Cato was an enemy of Caesar who killed himself in 46 BCE.

134 *And {. . .} applause:* Pompey had built a theatre in Rome.

139–44 *his {. . .} his {. . .} him {. . .} his {. . .} His {. . .} his {. . .} he:* these pronouns all refer to the oak.

142 *Though every:* supply "at" between these two words.

145 *Caesar's {. . .} less:* As MacLure and Martin both note, Lucan says that Caesar was not the only one renowned for military leadership (*sed non in Caesare tantum / Nomen erat nec fama ducis*)—so too was Pompey.

Shaming to strive but where he did subdue;
When ire or hope provoked, heady and bold,
At all times charging home, and making havoc;
Urging his fortune, trusting in the gods,
Destroying what withstood his proud desires,   150
And glad when blood and ruin made him way:
So thunder which the wind tears from the clouds,
With crack of riven air and hideous sound
Filling the world, leaps out and throws forth fire,
Affrights poor fearful men, and blasts their eyes   155
With overthwarting flames, and raging shoots
Alongst the air, and, nought resisting it,
Falls, and returns, and shivers where it lights.
Such humours stirred them up; but this war's seed
Was even the same that wracks all great dominions.   160
When Fortune made us lords of all, wealth flowed,
And then we grew licentious and rude;
The soldiers' prey and rapine brought in riot;
Men took delight in jewels, houses, plate,
And scorned old sparing diet, and ware robes   165
Too light for women; Poverty (who hatched
Rome's greatest wits) was loathed, and all the world
Ransacked for gold, which breeds the world decay;
And then large limits had their butting lands,
The ground which Curius and Camillus tilled   170
Was stretched unto the fields of hinds unknown.
Again, this people could not brook calm peace,
Them freedom without war might not suffice;
Quarrels were rife, greedy desire, still poor,
Did vile deeds; then 'twas worth the price of blood,   175

---

146 *Shaming {. . .} subdue:* "his one disgrace was to conquer without war" (Duff) (*solusque pudor non vincere bello*).

151 *made him way:* cleared the path (for him to attain his ambitions).

156 *overthwarting:* crossing, oblique.

158 *shivers {. . .} lights:* "spreads destruction far and wide, and then recomposes its dispersed flames" (MacLure).

161 *us:* Rome.

165 *ware:* wore.

166 *light:* skimpy.

169 *And {. . .} lands:* people's properties became larger and larger.

170 *Curius, Camillus:* two very early Roman leaders instrumental in setting Rome on the path to world dominance (third and fourth century BCE, respectfully).

171 *hinds:* farmhands.

173 *Them:* For them.

And deemed renown to spoil their native town;
Force mastered right, the strongest governed all.
Hence came it that th' edicts were overruled,
That laws were broke, tribunes with consuls strove,
Sale made of offices, and people's voices   180
Bought by themselves and sold, and every year
Frauds and corruption in the field of Mars;
Hence interest and devouring usury sprang,
Faith's breach, and hence came war, to most men welcome.

Now Caesar overpassed the snowy Alps;   185
His mind was troubled, and he aimed at war,
And coming to the ford of Rubicon,
At night in dreadful vision fearful Rome
Mourning appeared, whose hoary hairs were torn,
And on her turret-bearing head dispersed,   190
And arms all naked, who with broken sighs,
And staring, thus bespoke: "What mean'st thou, Caesar?
Whither goes my standard? Romans if ye be,
And bear true hearts, stay here!" This spectacle
Strook Caesar's heart with fear, his hair stood up,   195
And faintness numbed his steps there on the brink.
He thus cried out: "Thou thunderer that guard'st
Rome's mighty walls built on Tarpeian rock,
Ye gods of Phrygia and Iulus' line,
Quirinus' rites and Latian Jove advanced   200
On Alba hill, O vestal flames, O Rome,
My thought's sole goddess, aid mine enterprise!
I hate thee not, to thee my conquests stoop;
Caesar is thine, so please it thee, thy soldier;
He, he afflicts Rome that made me Rome's foe."   205
This said, he laying aside all lets of war,

---

182 *field of Mars:* the Campus Martius, where elections took place.
187 *Rubicon:* a small river just north of Ariminum, forming the northern border of Italy, separating Caesar's own province of Cisalpine Gaul (see line 218) from Italy proper. Crossing it was tan-
tamount to a declaration of war against Italy (Rome and Pompey).
196 *brink:* river-bank.
197 *thunderer:* Jove.
198 *Tarpeian rock:* the Capitol, site of the temple of Jove.
199 *Phrygia:* Troy. *Iulus:* Ascanius, son of Aeneas.
200 *Quirinus:* Romulus. *advanced:* raised high.
201 *Alba hill:* a town built by Ascanius.
206 *lets of:* impediments to.

Approached the swelling stream with drum and ensign;
Like to a lion of scorched desert Afric,
Who, seeing hunters, pauseth till fell wrath
And kingly rage increase, then having whisked   210
His tail athwart his back, and crest heaved up,
With jaws wide open ghastly roaring out
(Albeit the Moor's light javelin or his spear
Sticks in his side), yet runs upon the hunter.

In summer time the purple Rubicon,   215
Which issues from a small spring, is but shallow,
And creeps along the vales dividing just
The bounds of Italy from Cisalpine France;
But now the winter's wrath, and wat'ry moon
Being three days old, enforced the flood to swell,   220
And frozen Alps thawed with resolving winds.
The thunder-hoofed horse, in a crooked line,
To scape the violence of the stream, first waded,
Which being broke the foot had easy passage.
As soon as Caesar got unto the bank   225
And bounds of Italy, "Here, here," saith he,
"An end of peace; here end polluted laws;
Hence, leagues and covenants; Fortune, thee I follow,
War and the Destinies shall try my cause."
This said, the restless general through the dark   230
(Swifter than bullets thrown from Spanish slings,
Or darts which Parthians backward shoot) marched on,
And then (when Lucifer did shine alone,
And some dim stars) he Ariminum entered.
Day rose, and viewed these tumults of the war;   235
Whether the gods or blust'ring south were cause

219–220 *wat'ry {. . .} old:* it had rained for three days.
221 *resolving winds:* winds that thaw, reduce to liquid.
222 *crooked:* slantwise (*obliquum*).
223 *scape:* negotiate (successfully).
224 *Which:* the stream of the previous line—more specifically, the current.
228 *Hence:* Away with.
229 *Destinies:* Marlowe's text read *fatis* ("fates") for *satis* ("enough")
232 *Parthians {. . .} shoot:* Parthians were infamous for feigning retreat and shooting back arrows in their pretended flight.
233 *Lucifer:* the morning star (Venus).
234 *Ariminum:* a settlement of military and cultural significance near the Alps at the outermost northern borders of Rome (Italy)—see 187n.
236 *south:* South Wind.

I know not, but the cloudy air did frown.
The soldiers having won the market-place,
There spread the colours, with confused noise
Of trumpet's clange, shrill cornets, whistling fifes.   240
The people started; young men left their beds,
And snatched arms near their household-gods hung up,
Such as peace yields: worm-eaten leathern targets
Through which the wood peered, headless darts, old swords
With ugly teeth of black rust foully scarred.   245
But seeing white eagles, and Rome's flags well known,
And lofty Caesar in the thickest throng,
They shook for fear, and cold benumbed their limbs,
And muttering much, thus to themselves complained:
"O walls unfortunate, too near to France,   250
Predestinate to ruin! all lands else
Have stable peace, here war's rage first begins,
We bide the first brunt. Safer might we dwell
Under the frosty Bear, or parching East,
Wagons or tents, than in this frontier town   255
We first sustained the uproars of the Gauls
And furious Cimbrians, and of Carthage Moors;
As oft as Rome was sacked, here 'gan the spoil."
Thus sighing whispered they, and none durst speak
And show their fear or grief; but as the fields,   260
When birds are silent thorough winter's rage,
Or sea far from the land, so all were whist.
Now light had quite dissolved the misty night,
And Caesar's mind unsettled musing stood;
But gods and fortune pricked him to this war,   265
Infringing all excuse of modest shame,
And labouring to approve his quarrel good.
The angry Senate, urging Gracchus' deeds,
From doubtful Rome wrongly expelled the tribunes

---

243 *targets:* shields.
254 *Under {. . .} Bear:* in the north.
255 *Wagons {. . .} town:* "and made us guard the tents of nomads rather than the gates of Italy"
    (Duff).
257 *Cimbrians:* German invaders. *Carthage Moors:* Hannibal's troops.
262 *whist:* silent.
268 *urging {. . .} deeds:* "The tribunes Tiberius and Caius Gracchus were popular reformers who in-
    curred the hostility of the senate and were murdered in [. . .] 133 and 121 BC. The Senate is now
    using this as a precedent [. . .] for the expulsion of the tribunes Antony and Q. Cassius" (Gill).
269 *doubtful:* confused.

That crossed them; both which now approached the camp,   270
And with them Curio, sometime tribune too,
One that was fee'd for Caesar, and whose tongue
Could tune the people to the nobles' mind.
"Caesar," said he, "while eloquence prevailed,
And I might plead, and draw the commons' minds   275
To favour thee, against the Senate's will,
Five years I lengthened thy command in France;
But law being put to silence by the wars,
We, from our houses driven, most willingly
Suffered exile: let thy sword bring us home.   280
Now, while their part is weak and fears, march hence:
Where men are ready, lingering ever hurts.
In ten years won'st thou France; Rome may be won
With far less toil, and yet the honour's more;
Few battles fought with prosperous success   285
May bring her down, and with her all the world.
Nor shalt thou triumph when thou com'st to Rome,
Nor Capitol be adorned with sacred bays.
Envy denies all; with thy blood must thou
Aby thy conquest past: the son decrees   290
To expel the father; share the world thou canst not;
Enjoy it all thou mayst." Thus Curio spake,
And therewith Caesar, prone enough to war,
Was so incensed as are Eleius steeds
With clamours, who, though locked and chained in stalls,   295
Souse down the walls, and make a passage forth.
Straight summoned he his several companies
Unto the standard; his grave look appeased
The wrestling tumult, and right hand made silence,
And thus he spake: "You that with me have borne   300
A thousand brunts, and tried me full ten years,
See how they quit our blood shed in the north,
Our friends' death, and our wounds, our wintering
Under the Alps! Rome rageth now in arms
As if the Carthage Hannibal were near.   305
Cornets of horse are mustered for the field,
Woods turned to ships; both land and sea against us.

---

272 *fee'd for:* bought and paid for by.
290 *Aby:* atone for. *son:* Pompey, Caesar's son-in-law.
294 *Eleius steeds:* the racehorses at Elis, site of the Olympic games.
296 *Souse {. . .} walls:* Try to break down the walls of their holding-stalls.
302 *quit:* requite.
306 *Cornets of horse:* cavalry.

Had foreign wars ill-thrived, or wrathful France
Pursued us hither, how were we bested,
When, coming conqueror, Rome afflicts me thus?   310
Let come their leaders whom long peace hath quailed,
Raw soldiers lately pressed, and troops of gowns;
Brabbling Marcellus; Cato whom fools reverence;
Must Pompey's followers, with strangers' aid
(Whom from his youth he bribed), needs make him king? 315
And shall he triumph long before his time,
And having once got head still shall he reign?
What should I talk of men's corn reaped by force,
And by him kept of purpose for a dearth?
Who sees not war sit by the quivering judge,   320
And sentence given in rings of naked swords,
And laws assailed, and armed men in the Senate?
'Twas his troop hemmed in Milo being accused;
And now, lest age might wane his state, he casts
For civil war, wherein through use he's known   325
To exceed his master, that arch-traitor Sulla.
A brood of barbarous tigers, having lapped
The blood of many a herd, whilst with their dams
They kenneled in Hircania, evermore
Will rage and prey: so Pompey, thou having licked   330
Warm gore from Sulla's sword, art yet athirst;
Jaws fleshed with blood continue murderous.
Speak, when shall this thy long-usurped power end?
What end of mischief? Sulla teaching thee,
At last learn, wretch, to leave thy monarchy.   335
What, now Sicilian pirates are suppressed,
And jaded king of Pontus poisoned slain,

---

311 *quailed:* made soft.

312 *of gowns:* dressed in togas (and therefore not fit for fighting).

313 *Marcellus:* three consuls bearing this name opposed Caesar.

320–323 *Milo {. . .} accused:* "The reference is to the trial of Milo in 52 BC, when he was accused of the murder of Clodius. Pompey's soldiers occupied the Forum, to maintain order; but the orator, Cicero, was so intimidated by the soldiers that he forgot most of his argument, and Milo was condemned" (Gill).

324 *wane:* diminish.

326 *Sulla:* vicious dictator of Rome, 82–79 BCE.

329 *Hircania:* a province of Asia bordered on the north by the Caspian Sea.

331 *warm gore {. . .} sword:* the assonance renders the same (indeed, the very same "or" sound of the precisely corresponding words) of *caesorum {. . .} cruor armentorum.*

336–337 *What {. . .} slain:* "The Cilicians stand for the Mediterranean pirates generally. The King of Pontus was Mithradates; when reduced to despair [after a long struggle against Pompey], he took poison, but it failed to kill him" (Duff).

Must Pompey as his last foe plume on me,
Because at his command I wound not up
My conquering eagles? say I merit nought,   340
Yet, for long service done, reward these men,
And so they triumph, be 't with whom ye will.
Whither now shall these old bloodless souls repair?
What seats for their deserts? what store of ground
For servitors to till? what colonies   345
To rest their bones? say, Pompey, are these worse
Than pirates of Sicilia? they had houses.
Spread, spread these flags that ten years' space have conquered!
Let's use our tried force; they that now thwart right,
In wars will yield to wrong: the gods are with us.   350
Neither spoil nor kingdom seek we by these arms,
But Rome at thraldom's feet to rid from tyrants."
This spoke, none answered; but a murmuring buzz
Th' unstable people made: their household gods
And love to Rome (though slaughter steeled their hearts,   355
And minds were prone) restrained them; but war's love
And Caesar's awe dashed all. Then Laelius,
The chief centurion, crowned with oaken leaves
For saving of a Roman citizen,
Stepped forth, and cried: "Chief leader of Rome's force,   360
So be I may be bold to speak a truth,
We grieve at this thy patience and delay.
What doubt'st thou us? even now when youthful blood
Pricks forth our lively bodies, and strong arms
Can mainly throw the dart, wilt thou endure   365
These purple grooms, that Senate's tyranny?
Is conquest got by civil war so heinous?
Well, lead us then to Syrtes' desert shore,
Or Scythia, or hot Libya's thirsty sands.
This band, that all behind us might be quailed,   370

---

338 *Must {. . .} me:* "Must I be the last feather in Pompey's cap?" (Orgel).

345 *servitors:* retired soldiers.

347 *they had houses:* Martin and MacLure both note that this is Marlowe's addition; Gill and
    Burnett note that Pompey made the pirates Calabrian colonists after he defeated them.

349–350 *they {. . .} wrong:* "he who denies the armed man his rights puts everything into his
    hands" (Martin).

365 *mainly:* forcefully.

366 *purple grooms:* low-class men attired in the togas of the aristocracy.

368 *Syrtes:* from the Arabic *sert* for "desert," the two gulfs in the Libyan Sea on the north coast of
    Africa. Their shallow rocks were dangerous to navigation.

Hath with thee passed the swelling ocean,
And swept the foaming breast of Arctic's Rhene.
Love overrules my will, I must obey thee,
Caesar; he whom I hear thy trumpets charge
I hold no Roman; by these ten blest ensigns   375
And all thy several triumphs, shouldst thou bid me
Entomb my sword within my brother's bowels,
Or father's throat, or women's groaning womb,
This hand (albeit unwilling) should perform it;
Or rob the gods, or sacred temples fire.   380
These troops should soon pull down the church of Jove.
If to encamp on Tuscan Tiber's streams,
I'll boldly quarter out the fields of Rome;
What walls thou wilt be levelled with the ground,
These hands shall thrust the ram, and make them fly,   385
Albeit the city thou wouldst have so razed
Be Rome itself." Here every band applauded,
And with their hands held up all jointly cried
They'll follow where he please. The shouts rent heaven,
As when against pine-bearing Ossa's rocks   390
Beats Thracian Boreas, or when trees bowed down
And rustling swing up as the wind fets breath.

When Caesar saw his army prone to war,
And Fates so bent, lest sloth and long delay
Might cross him, he withdrew his troops from France,   395
And in all quarters musters men for Rome.
They by Lemannus' nook forsook their tents;
They whom the Lingones foiled with painted spears,
Under the rocks by crooked Vogesus;
And many came from shallow Isara,   400
Who, running long, falls in a greater flood,
And ere he sees the sea loseth his name;

---

372 *Arctic's Rhene:* the north Rhine.
391 *Thracian Boreas:* the North Wind.
392 *fets breath:* fetches (tries to catch its) breath.
393 *prone to:* ready for.
397 *Lemannus' nook:* Lake Geneva.
398 *Lingones:* a Gallic tribe.
399 *Vogesus:* the Vosges mountains.
400 *Isara:* the Isere River.
401 *Who:* Which.
402 *he, his:* the Isere.

The yellow Ruthens left their garrisons;
Mild Atax glad it bears not Roman boats,
And frontier Varus that the camp is far,   405
Sent aid; so did Alcides' port, whose seas
Eat hollow rocks, and where the north-west wind
Nor Zephyr rules not, but the north alone
Turmoils the coast, and enterance forbids;
And others came from that uncertain shore   410
Which is nor sea, nor land, but ofttimes both,
And changeth as the ocean ebbs and flows;
Whether the sea rolled always from that point
Whence the wind blows, still forced to and fro,
Or that the wandering main follow the moon,   415
Or flaming Titan (feeding on the deep)
Pulls them aloft, and makes the surge kiss heaven,
Philosophers, look you, for unto me,
Thou cause, whate'er thou be whom God assigns
This great effect, art hid. They came that dwell   420
By Nemes' fields, and banks of Satirus,
Where Tarbel's winding shores embrace the sea;
The Santons that rejoice in Caesar's love,
Those of Bituriges and light Axon pikes;
And they of Rhene and Leuca, cunning darters,   425
And Sequana that well could manage steeds;
The Belgians apt to govern British cars;

---

403 *Ruthens:* a Gallic tribe.

404–406 *Atax, Varus, Alcides' port:* "*Atax* {. . .} and *Varus* {. . .} are the rivers Aude and Var; in Lucan's day the latter formed the boundary between Italy and the *provincia.* Monaco is the name now given to '*Alcides* port', deriving from *portus Herculis Monoeci*—the harbour sacred to Hercules the solitary dweller" (Gill).

408 *Zephyr:* the West Wind.

410 *uncertain shore:* either the Netherlands or Belgium.

416 *Titan:* the sun.

418 *Philosophers:* Today we would not tend to think of philosophy as the study of natural and physical phenomena, but in antiquity it encompassed those topics (e.g., Lucretius, Aristotle) as well as the more traditionally "philosophical" ones.

418–420 *Philosophers* {. . .} *hid:* The syntax and sense are difficult to discern. The point is that the cause of these ocean upheavals is kept hidden from us by the gods.

420ff *They came* {. . .}: Orgel points out that this is "a brief account of the geography and population of Roman Gaul, though Marlowe has a number of the names wrong," and MacLure advises that "the geography of these peoples may be studied in R.J. Getty, ed., *M.A. Lucani De Bello Civili Liber I* (Cambridge, 1940)." Also, Gill points out the dwellers are not "the natives of '*Nemes fields*', but [. . .] the Roman forces who occupied this and the other named regions."

423 *love:* leaving (Marlowe likely mistakes *amato* for *amoto*).

427 *cars:* chariots.

Th' Averni too, which boldly feign themselves
The Romans' brethren, sprung of Ilian race;
The stubborn Nervians stained with Cotta's blood,   430
And Vangions who, like those of Sarmata,
Wear open slops; and fierce Batavians,
Whom trumpets' clange incites, and those that dwell
By Cinga's stream, and where swift Rhodanus
Drives Araris to sea; they near the hills   435
Under whose hoary rocks Gebenna hangs;
And Trevier, thou being glad that wars are past thee;
And you, late-shorn Ligurians, who were wont
In large-spread hair to exceed the rest of France;
And where to Hesus and fell Mercury   440
They offer human flesh, and where Jove seems
Bloody like Dian, whom the Scythians serve.
And you, French Bardi, whose immortal pens
Renown the valiant souls slain in your wars,
Sit safe at home and chant sweet poesy.   445
And, Druides, you now in peace renew
Your barbarous customs and sinister rites;
In unfelled woods and sacred groves you dwell,
And only gods and heavenly powers you know,
Or only know you nothing. For you hold   450
That souls pass not to silent Erebus
Or Pluto's bloodless kingdom, but elsewhere
Resume a body: so (if truth you sing)
Death brings long life. Doubtless these northern men,
Whom death, the greatest of all fears, affright not,   455
Are blest by such sweet error; this makes them
Run on the sword's point and desire to die,
And shame to spare life which being lost is won.
You likewise that repulsed the Cayc foe,
March towards Rome; and you, fierce men of Rhene,   460
Leaving your country open to the spoil.
These being come, their huge power made him bold
To manage greater deeds; the bordering towns
He garrisoned, and Italy he filled with soldiers.

---

430 *Cotta:* a Roman Proconsul of Gaul murdered by Belgian tribes ("Nervians") in 73 BCE.
432 *open slops:* loose fitting pants.
443 *French:* As Gill notes, Sulpitius supplies the national identity for the Bards (*"Gallica"*).
444 *renown:* a now obsolete use of this word as a transitive verb.
451–52 *Erebus, Pluto:* the Underworld (Hades) of which Pluto is king.

Vain Fame increased true fear, and did invade 465
The people's minds, and laid before their eyes
Slaughter to come, and swiftly bringing news
Of present war, made many lies and tales.
One swears his troops of daring horsemen fought
Upon Mevania's plain, where bulls are grazed; 470
Other that Caesar's barbarous bands were spread
Along Nar flood that into Tiber falls,
And that his own ten ensigns and the rest
Marched not entirely, and yet hide the ground;
And that he's much changed, looking wild and big, 475
And far more barbarous than the French (his vassals)
And that he lags behind with them of purpose
Born 'twixt the Alps and Rhene, which he hath brought
From out their northern parts, and that Rome,
He looking on, by these men should be sacked. 480
Thus in his fright did each man strengthen Fame,
And, without ground, feared what themselves had feigned.
Nor were the commons only strook to heart
With this vain terror, but the Court, the Senate:
The fathers' selves leaped from their seats, and, flying, 485
Left hateful war decreed to both the consuls.
Then, with their fear and danger all distract,
Their sway of flight carries the heady rout
That in chained troops break forth at every port;
You would have thought their houses had been fired, 490
Or, dropping-ripe, ready to fall with ruin;
So rushed the inconsiderate multitude
Thorough the city, hurried headlong on,
As if the only hope that did remain
To their afflictions were t' abandon Rome. 495
Look how when stormy Auster from the breach
Of Libyan Syrtes rolls a monstrous wave,
Which makes the mainsail fall with hideous sound,
The pilot from the helm leaps in the sea,

---

465 *Fame:* rumor (also 481).
470 *Mevania:* in Umbria.
474 *not entirely:* As several editors have noted, this means not as a whole, or not in a single column.
482 *feigned:* imagined.
485 *fathers' selves:* senators themselves.
489 *chained troops:* "long continuous columns" (Martin).
492 *inconsiderate:* "unthinking" (Orgel).
496 *Auster:* the South Wind.

And mariners, albeit the keel be sound,   500
Shipwrack themselves: even so, the city left,
All rise in arms, nor could the bedrid parents
Keep back their sons, or women's tears their husbands;
They stayed not either to pray or sacrifice,
Their household gods restrain them not, none lingered   505
As loth to leave Rome whom they held so dear;
Th' irrevocable people fly in troops.
O gods, that easy grant men great estates,
But hardly grace to keep them: Rome, that flows
With citizens and captives, and would hold   510
The world (were it together) is by cowards
Left as a prey, now Caesar doth approach.
When Romans are besieged by foreign foes,
With slender trench they escape night stratagems,
And sudden rampire raised of turf snatched up   515
Would make them sleep securely in their tents.
Thou, Rome, at name of war runn'st from thyself,
And wilt not trust thy city walls one night:
Well might these fear, when Pompey feared and fled.
Now evermore, lest some one hope might ease   520
The commons' jangling minds, apparent signs arose,
Strange sights appeared, the angry threat'ning gods
Filled both the earth and seas with prodigies;
Great store of strange and unknown stars were seen
Wandering about the north, and rings of fire   525
Fly in the air, and dreadful bearded stars,
And comets that presage the fall of kingdoms;
The flattering sky glittered in often flames,
And sundry fiery meteors blazed in heaven,
Now spear-like, long, now like a spreading torch;   530
Lightning in silence stole forth without clouds,
And from the northern climate snatching fire
Blasted the Capitol; the lesser stars,
Which wont to run their course through empty night,
At noonday mustered; Phoebe, having filled   535
Her meeting horns to match her brother's light,
Strook with th' earth's sudden shadow, waxed pale;

---

507 *irrevocable:* determined.
508 *easy:* easily.
535 *Phoebe:* the moon. The next two lines describe an eclipse (Burnett).
536 *brother's:* Phoebus's (the sun).

Titan himself throned in the midst of heaven
His burning chariot plunged in sable clouds,
And whelmed the world in darkness, making men   540
Despair of day, as did Thyestes' town,
Mycenae, Phoebus flying through the east.
Fierce Mulciber unbarred Aetna's gate,
Which flamed not on high, but headlong pitched
Her burning head on bending Hespery.   545
Coal-black Charybdis whirled a sea of blood;
Fierce mastiffs howled; the vestal fires went out;
The flame in Alba, consecrate to Jove,
Parted in twain, and with a double point
Rose like the Theban brothers' funeral fire;   550
The earth went off her hinges, and the Alps
Shook the old snow from off their trembling laps.
The ocean swelled as high as Spanish Calpe,
Or Atlas' head. Their saints and household gods
Sweat tears to show the travails of their city.   555
Crowns fell from holy statues, ominous birds
Defiled the day, and wild beasts were seen,
Leaving the woods, lodge in the streets of Rome.
Cattle were seen that muttered human speech;
Prodigious births with more and ugly joints   560
Than nature gives, whose sight appals the mother;
And dismal prophecies were spread abroad;
And they whom fierce Bellona's fury moves
To wound their arms, sing vengeance; Sibyl's priests,
Curling their bloody locks, howl dreadful things;   565
Souls quiet and appeased sighed from their graves;
Clashing of arms was heard; in untrod woods
Shrill voices shright, and ghosts encounter men.

---

538 *Titan:* the sun.
541–42 *as {. . .} east:* "Mycenae was plunged into darkness when the sun fled back to its place of
    rising [. . .] in horror at the sight of Thyestes, who banqueted on his own sons" (Gill).
543 *Mulciber {. . .} gate:* Vulcan, god of fire and the smithy, kept his workshop under Mt. Aetna.
545 *Hespery:* always indicative of the West—here, the west coast of Italy.
547 *Fierce mastiffs:* Scylla.
550 *Theban brothers:* Polynices and Eteocles, warring sons of Oedipus.
553 *Calpe:* Gibraltar.
554 *Atlas' head:* "high mountain range" (Burnett).
560 *joints:* limbs.
563 *Bellona:* goddess of war.
564 *Sibyl:* Cybele, goddess of nature and the underworld.
568 *shright:* shrieked.

Those that inhabited the suburb fields
Fled; foul Erinnys stalked about the walls,   570
Shaking her snaky hair and crooked pine
With flaming top, much like that hellish fiend
Which made the stern Lycurgus wound his thigh,
Or fierce Agave mad; or like Megaera
That scared Alcides, when by Juno's task   575
He had before looked Pluto in the face.
Trumpets were heard to sound; and with what noise
An armed battle joins, such and more strange
Black night brought forth in secret: Sulla's ghost
Was seen to walk, singing sad oracles;   580
And Marius' head above cold Tav'ron peering
(His grave broke open) did affright the boors.
To these ostents (as their old custom was)
They call th' Etrurian augurs, amongst whom
The gravest, Arruns, dwelt in forsaken Luca,   585
Well skilled in pyromancy, one that knew
The hearts of beasts, and flight of wand'ring fowls.
First he commands such monsters Nature hatched
Against her kind (the barren mule's loathed issue)
To be cut forth and cast in dismal fires;   590
Then, that the trembling citizens should walk
About the city; then the sacred priests
That with divine lustration purged the walls,
And went the round, in and without the town.
Next, an inferior troop, in tucked-up vestures,   595
After the Gabine manner; then the nuns
And their veiled matron, who alone might view
Minerva's statue; then, they that keep and read
Sibylla's secret works, and washed their saint

---

570 *Erinnys:* one of the Furies.
573 *Lycurgus:* king of Thrace who broke his own legs while trying to destroy the vineyards of
    Bacchus.
574 *Agave:* queen of Thebes who killed her own son. *Megaera:* a Fury.
575 *Alcides:* Hercules.
576 *Pluto:* king of the Underworld and, by metonymy, death.
581 *Marius {. . .} Tav'ron:* Marius was a general whom Sulla defeated and whose body Sulla ordered
    thrown into the the Anio (Teverone).
583 *ostents:* omens.
586 *pyromancy:* the ability to interpret lightning.
593 *lustration:* religious purification.
596 *Gabine manner:* a style of wearing the toga.
599 *Sibylla:* Editors disagree whether this refers to the Cumaean Sibyl or to Cybele.

In Almo's flood; next, learned augurs follow,   600
Apollo's soothsayers, and Jove's feasting priests,
The skipping Salii with shields like wedges,
And flamens last, with network woollen veils.
While these thus in and out had circled Rome,
Look what the lightning blasted, Arruns takes,   605
And it inters with murmurs dolorous,
And calls the place bidental; on the altar
He lays a ne'er-yoked bull, and pours down wine,
Then crams salt leaven on his crooked knife;
The beast long struggled, as being like to prove   610
An awkward sacrifice, but by the horns
The quick priest pulled him on his knees and slew him.
No vein sprung out, but from the yawning gash,
Instead of red blood, wallowed venomous gore.
These direful signs made Arruns stand amazed,   615
And searching farther for the gods' displeasure,
The very colour scared him; a dead blackness
Ran through the blood, that turned it all to jelly,
And stained the bowels with dark loathsome spots;
The liver swelled with filth, and every vein   620
Did threaten horror from the host of Caesar:
A small thin skin contained the vital parts;
The heart stirred not, and from the gaping liver
Squeezed matter; through the caul the entrails peered,
And which (aye me) ever pretendeth ill,   625
At that bunch where the liver is, appeared
A knob of flesh, whereof one half did look
Dead and discoloured, th' other lean and thin.
By these he seeing what mischiefs must ensue
Cried out, "O gods! I tremble to unfold   630
What you intend: great Jove is now displeased,
And in the breast of this slain bull are crept
Th' infernal powers. My fear transcends my words,
Yet more will happen than I can unfold.
Turn all to good, be augury vain, and Tages,   635

---

602 *skipping Salii:* dancing priests of Mars.
603 *flamens:* priests. *network* (adj.): finely and intricately woven.
605 *Look:* "Behold."
607 *Bidental:* refers to *bidens,* meaning an ox or other animal, which would be sacrificed for religious purposes—here because places struck by lightning were considered sacred.
624 *caul:* outer membranes of the bowel.
625 *pretendeth:* portends.
635 *Tages:* grandson of Jove known for powers of prophecy.

Th' art's master, false!" Thus, in ambiguous terms
Involving all, did Arruns darkly sing.
But Figulus, more seen in heavenly mysteries,
Whose like Egyptian Memphis never had
For skill in stars and tuneful planeting,   640
In this sort spake: "The world's swift course is lawless
And casual; all the stars at random rage;
Or if Fate rule them, Rome, thy citizens
Are near some plague. What mischief shall ensue?
Shall towns be swallowed? shall the thickened air   645
Become intemperate? shall the earth be barren?
Shall water be congealed and turned to ice?
O gods, what death prepare ye? with what plague
Mean ye to rage? the death of many men
Meets in one period. If cold noisome Saturn   650
Were now exalted, and with blue beams shined,
Then Ganymede would renew Deucalion's flood,
And in the fleeting sea the earth be drenched.
O Phoebus, shouldst thou with thy rays now singe
The fell Nemean beast, th' earth would be fired,   655
And heaven tormented with thy chafing heat;
But thy fires hurt not. Mars, 'tis thou inflam'st
The threatening Scorpion with the burning tail,
And fir'st his cleyes. Why art thou thus enraged?
Kind Jupiter hath low declined himself;   660
Venus is faint; swift Hermes retrograde;
Mars only rules the heaven. Why do the planets
Alter their course, and vainly dim their virtue?
Sword-girt Orion's side glisters too bright:

---

638 *Figulus:* a sage.

639 *like:* equal.

640 *tuneful planeting:* a reference to the harmony of heavenly bodies (see 638 —"heavenly mysteries").

649–50 *death {. . .} Meets {. . .} period:* "The deaths of many will all occur at the same time" (*extremi multorum tempus in unum / convenere dies*).

650 *noisome:* Lucan has *nocens,* whence the English "noxious," for which "noisome" is an obsolete spelling.

651 *blue:* Lucan has *nigros* ("black"). Orgel suggests Marlowe chose "blue" for the context since, as the *OED* notes, blue at that time was "the color of plagues and things hurtful."

652 *Ganymede:* Lucan has *Aquarius* (the ocean). Gill notes that Marlowe chooses Ganymede based on Sulpitius's note.

655 *Nemaean beast:* a reference to the constellation Leo created by Hercules's killing of a lion.

659 *cleyes:* claws.

660 – 62 *Jupiter {. . .} Venus {. . .} Hermes* [Mercury] *{. . .} Mars:* The planets, not the mythological gods, are being referred to here.

661 *Hermes:* Mercury.

664 *Orion:* the constellation Orion.

War's rage draws near, and to the sword's strong hand   665
Let all laws yield, sin bear the name of virtue.
Many a year these furious broils let last;
Why should we wish the gods should ever end them?
War only gives us peace. O Rome, continue
The course of mischief, and stretch out the date   670
Of slaughter; only civil broils make peace."
These sad presages were enough to scare
The quivering Romans, but worse things affright them.
As Maenas full of wine on Pindus raves,
So runs a matron through th' amazed streets,   675
Disclosing Phoebus' fury in this sort:
"Paean, whither am I haled? where shall I fall,
Thus borne aloft? I see Pangaeus' hill
With hoary top, and under Haemus' mount
Philippi plains. Phoebus, what rage is this?   680
Why grapples Rome, and makes war, having no foes?
Whither turn I now? thou lead'st me toward th' east,
Where Nile augmenteth the Pelusian sea;
This headless trunk that lies on Nilus' sand
I know. Now throughout the air I fly   685
To doubtful Syrtes and dry Afric, where
A fury leads the Emathian bands; from thence
To the pine-bearing hills, hence to the mounts
Pyrene, and so back to Rome again.
See impious war defiles the Senate-house,   690
New factions rise; now through the world again
I go; O Phoebus, show me Neptune's shore,
And other regions, I have seen Philippi."
This said, being tired with fury she sunk down.
     FINIS

669–71 *War {. . .} peace {. . .} civil broils {. . .} peace:* Lucan's seer says that as long as there is civil war, freedom will survive; only when war ends will freedom die, because war will culminate only in the ascendancy of a dictator (*duc Roma malorum / continuam seriem clademque in tempora multa / extrahe civili tantum iam libera bello*).

674 *Maenas:* a priestess of Dionysus. *Pindus:* a mountain in Thessaly.

675 *amazed:* stunned.

677 *Paean:* alternative name for Apollo. *Haled:* taken.

680 *Philippi:* site of the decisive civil war of 42 BCE, conventionally referred to also as "Pharsalus."

684 *trunk:* Pompey.

686 *doubtful:* treacherous.

687 *Emathian:* Macedonian.

690 *impious {. . .} house:* a foreshadowing of Caesar's murder.

693 *And {. . .} Philippi:* As Gill points out, she has already seen one battle of Philippi (Pharsalia) and does not want to see a "new Philippi" (the battle that will come in 42 BCE).

HERO AND LEANDER

To the Right Worshipful,
Sir Thomas Walsingham, Knight

Sir, we think not ourselves discharged of the duty we owe to our friend, when
we have brought the breathless body to the earth: for albeit the eye there taketh
his ever farewell of that beloved object, yet the impression of the man, that hath
been dear unto us, living an after life in our memory, there putteth us in mind
of farther obsequies due unto the deceased. And namely of the performance of   5
whatsoever we may judge shall make to his living credit, and to the effecting of
his determinations prevented by the stroke of death. By these meditations (as
by an intellectual will) I suppose myself executor to the unhappily deceased author of this poem, upon whom knowing that in his lifetime you bestowed many
kind favours, entertaining the parts of reckoning and worth which you found in   10
him, with good countenance and liberal affection: I cannot but see so far into
the will of him dead, that whatsoever issue of his brain should chance to come
abroad, that the first breath it should take might be the gentle air of your liking; for since his self had been accustomed thereunto, it would prove more
agreeable and thriving to his right children than any other foster countenance   15
whatsoever. At this time seeing that this unfinished tragedy happens under my
hands to be imprinted, of a double duty, the one to yourself, the other to the deceased, I present the same to your most favorable allowance, off'ring my utmost
self now and ever to be ready, at your Worship's disposing.

EDWARD BLOUNT

Walsingham: 1568–1630; Marlowe's patron.
1 *friend:* Marlowe.
6 *make:* contribute.
7 *determinations:* intentions.
8 *intellectual will:* "Intellectual presumably means apprehensible by the mind only, immaterial; but
   the further meaning may also be intended, a will concerning his intellectual possessions" (Martin).
10 *parts of reckoning:* qualities of his good reputation.
15 *thriving:* causing to thrive.
17 *of:* out of.
18 *allowance:* approbation, approval.
Blount: (?–1631); printer and bookseller. His shops were in St. Paul's Churchyard.

THE ARGUMENT OF THE FIRST SESTIAD

Hero's description and her love's;
The fane of Venus, where he moves
His worthy love-suit, and attains;
Whose bliss the wrath of Fates restrains
For Cupid's grace to Mercury: 5
Which tale the author doth imply.

On Hellespont, guilty of true love's blood,
In view and opposite two cities stood,
Sea-borderers, disjoined by Neptune's might:
The one Abydos, the other Sestos hight.
At Sestos Hero dwelt; Hero the fair,   5
Whom young Apollo courted for her hair,
And offered as a dower his burning throne,

Sestiad: invented by Chapman, from Hero's home, Sestos, on the model of Homer's *Iliad* (and Virgil's *Aeneid*). Chapman is the great Elizabethan translator of Homer; he divided Marlowe's 818-line poem into two "Sestiads," and wrote the verse Arguments to both, as well as adding four of his own Sestiads in continuation of the narrative.

1 *love's:* beloved's (Leander's).

2 *fane:* church.

5 *Cupid's:* Roman boy-god of love (or erotic desire), son of Venus and (in one version) Mars or (in another) Mercury. *Mercury:* Roman messenger god, son of Jupiter (Jove) and Maia, also known as Hermes. He invented the lyre and thus has connections to lyric poetry; he is also the god of thieves and liars, with connections to language and rhetoric, as well as the god of the intellect, with connections to philosophy ("hermetic"). With Cupid, Mercury appears in the poem's inset tale of lines 386–484.

6 *imply:* include.

1–4 A prologue to the complete narrative, partially told by Marlowe, with the rest told by Chapman, and emphasizing the idea of tragic separation between the sexes. Cf. Musaeus, *Hero and Leander* 27–29, translated by Chapman (1616): "Two towns there were, that with one sea were wall'd, / Built near, and opposite; this Sestus call'd, / Abydus that" (Shephard, ed.)

1 *Hellespont:* Ancient name for the Dardanelles, the strait (thirty-seven miles long, four miles wide) that joins the Aegean Sea and the Sea of Marmara, the very boundary between Europe and Asia and thus the point of intersection in the westward *translation of empire* (*translatio imperii*) and the *translation of learning* (*translatio studii*). See Ovid, *Heroides*, "Leander to Hero" 141. In classical mythology, Helle, daughter of Athamas, king of Thebes, joined her brother Phryxus in trying to flee persecution from their stepmother Ino on a golden ram; she became faint and drowned, and so the strait was named after her. Phryxus arrived in Colchis, where he sacrificed the ram but retained its fleece, thereby creating the Golden Fleece. Leander is famous for swimming the Hellespont to visit Hero—a feat imitated famously by the Romantic author Byron in the nineteenth century.

3 *sea-borderers:* Thomas Nashe quotes this phrase with reference to Marlowe in *Nashe's Lenten Stuffe* (1599; see McKerrow, ed. 3:199). *Neptune's might:* power of the Roman god of the sea; brother to Jupiter, god of the sky, and Pluto, god of the underworld. Neptune appears in lines 639–710.

4 *Abydos:* on the Asian coast of the Hellespont, a town opposite Sestos. *Sestos:* town on the European coast of the Hellespont, opposite Abydos. *hight:* called; named.

6 *Apollo {. . .} hair:* Marlowe's invention.

7 *dower:* dowry.

Where she should sit for men to gaze upon.
The outside of her garments were of lawn,
The lining purple silk, with gilt stars drawn;   10
Her wide sleeves green, and bordered with a grove,
Where Venus in her naked glory strove
To please the careless and disdainful eyes
Of proud Adonis that before her lies.
Her kirtle blue, whereon was many a stain,   15
Made with the blood of wretched lovers slain.
Upon her head she ware a myrtle wreath,
From whence her veil reached to the ground beneath.
Her veil was artificial flowers and leaves,
Whose workmanship both man and beast deceives.   20
Many would praise the sweet smell as she passed,
When 'twas the odour which her breath forth cast;
And there for honey bees have sought in vain,
And beat from thence, have lighted there again.
About her neck hung chains of pebble-stone,   25
Which lightened by her neck, like diamonds shone.
She ware no gloves, for neither sun nor wind
Would burn or parch her hands, but to her mind
Or warm or cool them, for they took delight
To play upon those hands, they were so white.   30
Buskins of shells all silvered used she,
And branched with blushing coral to the knee,
Where sparrows perched, of hollow pearl and gold,
Such as the world would wonder to behold:
Those with sweet water oft her handmaid fills,   35
Which as she went would chirrup through the bills.
Some say, for her the fairest Cupid pined,
And looking in her face, was strooken blind.
But this is true, so like was one the other,
As he imagined Hero was his mother;   40

---

9 *lawn:* a kind of fine linen.

10 *gilt:* a thin layer of gold.

15 *kirtle:* a gown or skirt.

18 *myrtle:* the flower sacred to Venus; the myrtle wreath is a sign of the Ovidian poet of love, in rivalry with the Virgilian poet of empire, who wears the laurel wreath. See text and notes at *OE* 1.1.34 and *OE* 3.1.34 and in the introduction.

20 *workmanship {. . .} deceives:* the motif of trompe l'oeil, taken to an extra degree, since the sense of smell is also deceived; a conventional trope of artistic rivalry.

26 *lightened:* made bright.

31 *Buskins:* boots worn by actors of Greek and Roman tragedies. See *OE* 3.1.14, 31 and introduction.

33 *sparrows:* figures of desire.

40 *mother:* Venus.

And oftentimes into her bosom flew,
About her naked neck his bare arms threw,
And laid his childish head upon her breast,
And with still panting rocked, there took his rest.
So lovely fair was Hero, Venus' nun,   45
As Nature wept, thinking she was undone,
Because she took more from her than she left,
And of such wondrous beauty her bereft:
Therefore, in sign her treasure suffered wrack,
Since Hero's time hath half the world been black.   50
Amorous Leander, beautiful and young
(Whose tragedy divine Musaeus sung)
Dwelt at Abydos; since him dwelt there none
For whom succeeding times make greater moan.
His dangling tresses that were never shorn,   55
Had they been cut, and unto Colchos borne,
Would have allured the vent'rous youth of Greece
To hazard more than for the Golden Fleece.
Fair Cynthia wished his arms might be her sphere;
Grief makes her pale, because she moves not there.   60
His body was as straight as Circe's wand;

---

45 *Venus' nun:* MacLure cites Stephen Gosson's *The School of Abuse* (1587), describing London prostitutes: "Other there are which [. . .] live a mile from the Cittie like Venus Nunnes in a Cloyster at Newington [. . .] where [. . .] they [. . .] spende their dayes in double devotion" (E7). MacLure also cites Shakespeare, *As You Like It* 4.1.101: "though Hero had turn'd nun." Gill adds that the text of Musaeus in Latin reads *"Veneris erat sacerdos,"* where the "regular Elizabethan translation for *sacerdos* was 'nun.'"

46 *she:* Nature.

47 *she {. . .} her {. . .} she:* Hero [. . .] Nature [. . .] Hero.

48 *her:* Nature.

49 *wrack:* destruction.

50 *black:* dark or ugly.

52 *Musaeus:* a fifth-century Greek poet who originally authored *Hero and Leander;* in the Renaissance, he was confused with the legendary founder of poetry by the same name.

55 *tresses:* braids of hair.

56 *Colchos:* a city on the Black Sea, home of Jason and Medea.

58 *Golden Fleece:* See note to line 1. Jason was the leader of the Argonauts, who sailed in the ship Argo to recover the Golden Fleece from the king of Colchis, Aeetes, after which he married Aeetes's daughter, Medea.

59 *Cynthia:* goddess of the moon; Raleigh's name for Queen Elizabeth I. The reference evokes Cynthia's love for the shepherd Endymion.

61 *Circe:* An enchantress ruling the island of Aeaea; daughter of the sun and the nymph Perseis. In Homer's *Odyssey* (book 9), she uses her magic wand to turn Odysseus's men into animals. For the Renaissance, she is a figure for the power of desire to bring about a degenerative transformation into a lower (bestial) identity.

Jove might have sipped out nectar from his hand.
Even as delicious meat is to the taste,
So was his neck in touching, and surpassed
The white of Pelops' shoulder. I could tell ye   65
How smooth his breast was, and how white his belly,
And whose immortal fingers did imprint
That heavenly path with many a curious dint,
That runs along his back, but my rude pen
Can hardly blazon forth the loves of men,   70
Much less of powerful gods: let it suffice
That my slack muse sings of Leander's eyes,
Those orient cheeks and lips, exceeding his
That leapt into the water for a kiss
Of his own shadow, and despising many,   75
Died ere he could enjoy the love of any.
Had wild Hippolytus Leander seen,
Enamoured of his beauty had he been;
His presence made the rudest peasant melt,
That in the vast uplandish country dwelt,   80

---

62 *Jove:* Jupiter, ruling god of the Roman pantheon; husband to his sister Juno but famous for
his lechery and hedonism. The reference is to Ganymede, the boy-god who bore Jove's cup of
nectar, divine drink of the gods.

65 *Pelops' shoulder:* in Ovid's *Metamorphoses* (6.404–11), Pelops is killed by his father Tantalus.
Tantalus cut Pelops's body up, cooked him, and served him to the gods for dinner; only the goddess Demeter ate, consuming his shoulder, but the gods later reconstructed him and replaced his
shoulder with one made of ivory. *I could tell ye:* the first appearance of Marlowe's personal voice (a
rarity in his canon), prompted by Leander's beauty.

68 *curious:* ornate, exquisitely beautiful. *dint:* indentation made by an assault, usually military.
Cf. Spenser, *FQ* 1.1.1: "Y cladd in mightie armes and silver shielde,/ Wherein old dints of
deepe wounds did remaine."

69 *rude:* rustic. "Uneducated, unlearned; ignorant; lacking in knowledge or book-learning" (*OED*).
Spenser's signature word for his poetry, pastoral as well as epic. Cf. Marlowe's dedicatory epistle
to Mary Sidney Herbert: "rudi calamo" (rude reed).

70 *blazon:* emblazon, make known, or trumpet; "To describe in proper heraldic language" (*OED*);
but also announcing the poet's blazon or Petrarchan description of the beloved's body parts, here
those not of the female but of the male. Cf. Spenser, *FQ* 1.Pr.1.8: "To blazon broad emongst her
[the Muse's] learned throng."

72 *slack:* weak, feeble. Marlowe's "slack muse" is another Ovidian signature: "Love slacked my
muse" (*OE* 1.22).

73 *orient:* radiant, glowing, associating Leander's cheek with the rising of the sun in the east.

73–76 *his { . . .} any:* Narcissus, who fell in love with his own face when he looked into a pool. See
Ovid, *Metamorphoses* 3.339–510.

77 *wild Hippolytus:* in Greek mythology, a chaste hunter who rejected love and all women and was
punished by Aphrodite when Phaedra, his stepmother, wife to his father, Theseus, fell in love
with him.

79 *rudest:* see note to line 69.

80 *uplandish:* rural, uncivilized, wild.

The barbarous Thracian soldier, moved with nought,
Was moved with him, and for his favour sought.
Some swore he was a maid in man's attire,
For in his looks were all that men desire,
A pleasant smiling cheek, a speaking eye,   85
A brow for love to banquet royally;
And such as knew he was a man would say,
"Leander, thou art made for amorous play:
Why art thou not in love, and loved of all?
Though thou be fair, yet be not thine own thrall."   90

The men of wealthy Sestos, every year,
For his sake whom their goddess held so dear,
Rose-cheeked Adonis, kept a solemn feast.
Thither resorted many a wand'ring guest
To meet their loves; such as had none at all   95
Came lovers home from this great festival.
For every street like to a firmament
Glistered with breathing stars, who where they went
Frighted the melancholy earth, which deemed
Eternal heaven to burn, for so it seemed,   100
As if another Phaethon had got
The guidance of the sun's rich chariot.
But far above the loveliest Hero shined,
And stole away th' enchanted gazer's mind;
For like sea-nymphs' inveigling harmony,   105
So was her beauty to the standers by.
Nor that night-wand'ring, pale and watery star
(When yawning dragons draw her thirling car
From Latmus' mount up to the gloomy sky,
Where crowned with blazing light and majesty,   110

---

81 *Thracian:* of the city Thrace, located in Greece. "The Thracians were notorious for their savagery
   in war; compare Horace's 'bello furiosa Thrace' (*Odes,* II.xvi.5)" (MacLure).
93 *Rose-cheeked Adonis:* see Shakespeare, *Venus and Adonis* 3: "rose-cheek't Adonis."
98 *Glistered:* glistened, glittered, sparkled.
101 *Phaethon:* son of Apollo, god of the sun. Phaethon tried to drive his father's chariot of the sun,
    but lost control of the horses. The chariot crashed back to earth and would have set the world on
    fire if Jove had not killed Phaethon with a thunderbolt. See Ovid, Metamorphoses 2.1–400. For
    the Renaissance, a symbol of (youthful) pride, arrogance, and over-reaching.
105 *sea-nymphs {. . .} harmony:* the Sirens, who sang songs to tempt sailors to shipwreck (see Homer,
    Odyssey, book 12). *inveigling:* seductive, beguiling, alluring.
107 *star:* the moon.
108 *yawning:* opening wide. *thirling:* whirling.
109 *Latmus:* In a cave on Mt. Latmus, Jove put the shepherd Endymion to eternal sleep, but
    Cynthia the moon goddess visited him and became his beloved.

She proudly sits) more over-rules the flood
Than she the hearts of those that near her stood.
Even as, when gaudy nymphs pursue the chase,
Wretched Ixion's shaggy-footed race,
Incensed with savage heat, gallop amain   115
From steep pine-bearing mountains to the plain:
So ran the people forth to gaze upon her,
And all that viewed her were enamoured on her.
And as in fury of a dreadful fight,
Their fellows being slain or put to flight,   120
Poor soldiers stand with fear of death dead-strooken,
So at her presence all surprised and tooken
Await the sentence of her scornful eyes;
He whom she favours lives, the other dies.
There might you see one sigh, another rage,   125
And some (their violent passions to assuage)
Compile sharp satires, but alas too late,
For faithful love will never turn to hate.
And many seeing great princes were denied,
Pined as they went, and thinking on her died.   130
On this feast day, O cursed day and hour,
Went Hero thorough Sestos, from her tower
To Venus' temple, where unhappily,
As after chanced, they did each other spy.
So fair a church as this had Venus none: 135
The walls were of discoloured jasper stone,
Wherein was Proteus carved, and o'erhead
A lively vine of green sea agate spread;
Where by one hand, light-headed Bacchus hung,
And with the other, wine from grapes outwrung.   140

---

111 *over-rules:* rules over.

114 *Ixion:* the king of Thessaly who attempted to seduce Juno. Through intercourse with a phantasm of Juno, centaurs were created; they had the head and shoulders of a man and the four legs of a horse. Jove punished Ixion by chaining him to a revolving wheel of fire in Hades.

115 *amain:* with hasty speed.

133–57 *Venus' temple {. . .} altar stood:* perhaps modeled on the splendidly extravagant palace of Cleopatra in Lucan, *Pharsalia* 10.111–46. Martin cites "Apuleius, *The Golden Ass*, Adlington's translation, 1566"; MacLure cites "Ovid's description of the palace of the sun and of the web of Arachne (*Metamorphoses*, II.1ff.; VI.103ff.)" and Spenser's House of Busirane at *FQ* 3.11.28–46 (see also Gill).

136 *discoloured:* multicolored.

137 *Proteus:* the seagod (see Homer, *Odyssey*, book 4) who could easily change his shape and appearance. A Renaissance symbol of illusion, deception, and false appearance.

138 *lively:* lifelike.

139 *Bacchus:* god of wine and of tragedy.

Of crystal shining fair the pavement was;
The town of Sestos called it Venus' glass.
There might you see the gods in sundry shapes,
Committing heady riots, incest, rapes:
For know, that underneath this radiant floor   145
Was Danae's statue in a brazen tower,
Jove slyly stealing from his sister's bed,
To dally with Idalian Ganymede,
Or for his love Europa bellowing loud,
Or tumbling with the Rainbow in a cloud;   150
Blood-quaffing Mars, heaving the iron net
Which limping Vulcan and his Cyclops set;
Love kindling fire, to burn such towns as Troy;
Sylvanus weeping for the lovely boy
That now is turned into a cypress tree,   155
Under whose shade the wood-gods love to be.
And in the midst a silver altar stood;
There Hero sacrificing turtles' blood,
Vailed to the ground, vailing her eyelids close,
And modestly they opened as she rose: 160
Thence flew Love's arrow with the golden head,

---

142 *Venus' glass:* the phrase reproduces "Venus looking glas" (the erotic magic mirror made by
   Merlin the magician for Britomart's father, King Ryence) at *FQ* 3.1.8.9.
146 *Danae:* Jupiter pursued the mortal Danae and came to her in the form of a shower of gold.
147 *sister:* Juno, Jove's wife.
148 *Idalian Ganymede:* either from Mt. Ida, where Ganymede was carried off by Jupiter to become
   his cupbearer, or from Idalium, a town in Cyprus near a grove sacred to Venus. For the former,
   see the opening scene to *Dido, Queen of Carthage.*
149 *Europa:* Jupiter wooed Europa, and then in the shape of a magnificent bull he carried her off.
150 *And {. . .} cloud:* "In his capacity as rain-god, Jupiter (surnamed Pluvius) would have {. . .] reason to be hidden in the clouds with Iris, messenger to the gods, who was usually portrayed as a
   rainbow" (Gill).
151–52 *Mars {. . .} Cyclops:* Vulcan, assisted by the Cyclops, used a net to trap his wife Venus in
   the act of adultery with Mars. See Ovid, *Metamorphoses* 4.171–89 (derived originally from
   Homer's *Odyssey,* book 8).
151 *quaffing:* drinking deeply and perhaps in large amount.
153 *Troy:* the original city of epic in Homer, Virgil, Spenser, and others; see introduction. The Trojan War was fought over the beauty of Helen: "Throughout his career as a writer, Marlowe was
   fascinated by [Helen of Troy]" (Gill).
154 *Sylvanus:* old rustic god of the woods who loved the boy Cyparissus (Ovid, *Metamorphoses*
   10.120–42; Spenser, *FQ* 1.6.7–33, esp. stanza 17). Cyparissus accidentally killed the stag of
   Apollo, who was so disturbed he metamorphosed the boy into the cypress tree.
157 *in the midst {. . .} stood:* cf. Spenser, *FQ* 2.8.53: "And in the midst thereof a silver seat."
158 *turtles:* turtle doves, birds of Venus who were figures of life-long fidelity in love.
159 *Vailed {. . .} vailing:* lowering in a reverent way.
161 *Love's arrow {. . .} golden head:* Cupid's gold and lead arrows. Cupid uses gold arrows to rouse
   love and lead arrows to extinguish it. See Ovid, *Metamorphoses* 1.470–71.

And thus Leander was enamoured.
Stone still he stood, and evermore he gazed,
Till with the fire that from his count'nance blazed,
Relenting Hero's gentle heart was strook: 165
Such force and virtue hath an amorous look.

It lies not in our power to love, or hate,
For will in us is overruled by fate.
When two are stripped, long ere the course begin,
We wish that one should lose, the other win;   170
And one especially do we affect
Of two gold ingots like in each respect.
The reason no man knows: let it suffice,
What we behold is censured by our eyes.
Where both deliberate, the love is slight: 175
Who ever loved, that loved not at first sight?

He kneeled, but unto her devoutly prayed;
Chaste Hero to herself thus softly said:
"Were I the saint he worships, I would hear him,"
And as she spake those words, came somewhat near him.   180
He started up, she blushed as one ashamed;
Wherewith Leander much more was inflamed.
He touched her hand, in touching it she trembled:
Love deeply grounded hardly is dissembled.
These lovers parled by the touch of hands;   185
True love is mute, and oft amazed stands.
Thus while dumb signs their yielding hearts entangled,
The air with sparks of living fire was spangled,
And Night, deep-drenched in misty Acheron,
Heaved up her head, and half the world upon   190

---

166 *virtue:* power.
171 *affect:* prefer.
172 *ingots:* "A mass (usually oblong or brick-shaped) of cast metal, esp. of gold or silver, and (in modern use) of steel; these last are of various shapes" (*OED*).
173 *no man knows:* cf. Spenser, *FQ* 2.6.15.5, Spenser's parody of the Sermon on the Mount, referring to the lilies of the field: "how, *no man knows,/* They spring, they bud."
174 *censured:* judged.
176 *Who {. . .} sight?:* Quoted by Shakespeare in *As You Like It* 3.5.82 in an allusion to Marlowe's death.
184 *hardly:* with difficulty.
185 *parled:* spoke.
186 *amazed:* bewildered, stunned.
189 *Acheron:* a river in Hades, the classical underworld.

Breathed darkness forth (dark night is Cupid's day).
And now begins Leander to display
Love's holy fire, with words, with sighs and tears,
Which like sweet music entered Hero's ears,
And yet at every word she turned aside,   195
And always cut him off as he replied.
At last, like to a bold sharp sophister,
With cheerful hope thus he accosted her.

"Fair creature, let me speak without offence,
I would my rude words had the influence   200
To lead thy thoughts, as thy fair looks do mine,
Then shouldst thou be his prisoner, who is thine.
Be not unkind and fair; misshapen stuff
Are of behaviour boisterous and rough.
O shun me not, but hear me ere you go,   205
God knows I cannot force love, as you do.
My words shall be as spotless as my youth,
Full of simplicity and naked truth.
This sacrifice (whose sweet perfume descending
From Venus' altar to your footsteps bending)   210
Doth testify that you exceed her far,
To whom you offer, and whose nun you are.
Why should you worship her? her you surpass
As much as sparkling diamonds flaring glass.
A diamond set in lead his worth retains;   215
A heavenly nymph, beloved of human swains,
Receives no blemish, but oft-times more grace,
Which makes me hope, although I am but base,
Base in respect of thee, divine and pure,
Dutiful service may thy love procure;   220
And I in duty will excel all other,
As thou in beauty dost exceed Love's mother.
Nor heaven, nor thou, were made to gaze upon;
As heaven preserves all things, so save thou one.
A stately builded ship, well-rigged and tall,   225

---

197 *sophister:* sophist or one who uses reason speciously; at Cambridge University in Marlowe's day, a second- or third-year student.
203 *stuff:* "persons, with special reference to their material or physical appearances" (Martin).
210 *bending:* inclining, turning.
214 *flaring:* gaudy, glaring.
216 *swains:* young men; often with pastoral connotations, shepherds.
223 *to gaze upon:* merely to gaze upon.

The ocean maketh more majestical:
Why vowest thou then to live in Sestos here,
Who on Love's seas more glorious wouldst appear?
Like untuned golden strings all women are,
Which long time lie untouched, will harshly jar.   230
Vessels of brass oft handled, brightly shine;
What difference betwixt the richest mine
And basest mould, but use? for both, not used,
Are of like worth. Then treasure is abused,
When misers keep it; being put to loan,   235
In time it will return us two for one.
Rich robes themselves and others do adorn,
Neither themselves nor others, if not worn.
Who builds a palace and rams up the gate,
Shall see it ruinous and desolate.   240
Ah simple Hero, learn thyself to cherish,
Lone women like to empty houses perish.
Less sins the poor rich man that starves himself
In heaping up a mass of drossy pelf,
Than such as you: his golden earth remains,   245
Which, after his decease, some other gains;
But this fair gem, sweet in the loss alone,
When you fleet hence, can be bequeathed to none.
Or if it could, down from th' enamelled sky
All heaven would come to claim this legacy,   250
And with intestine broils the world destroy,
And quite confound nature's sweet harmony.
Well therefore by the gods decreed it is,
We human creatures should enjoy that bliss.
One is no number; maids are nothing then,   255
Without the sweet society of men.
Wilt thou live single still? one shalt thou be,
Though never-singling Hymen couple thee.
Wild savages, that drink of running springs,
Think water far excels all earthly things: 260
But they that daily taste neat wine, despise it.
Virginity, albeit some highly prize it,
Compared with marriage, had you tried them both,
Differs as much as wine and water doth.

---

244 *drossy pelf:* ill-gotten wealth or worthless possessions.
255 *One {. . .} number:* a definition from Aristotle, *Metaphysics* 1080a6. See Chapman at 5.
    323–40.
258 *Hymen:* god of marriage. *never-singling:* never separating.

Base bullion for the stamp's sake we allow,   265
Even so for men's impression do we you.
By which alone, our reverend fathers say,
Women receive perfection every way.
This idol which you term Virginity
Is neither essence subject to the eye,   270
No, nor to any one exterior sense,
Nor hath it any place of residence,
Nor is 't of earth or mould celestial,
Or capable of any form at all.
Of that which hath no being, do not boast;   275
Things that are not at all, are never lost.
Men foolishly do call it virtuous;
What virtue is it that is born with us?
Much less can honour be ascribed thereto,
Honour is purchased by the deeds we do.   280
Believe me, Hero, honour is not won,
Until some honourable deed be done.
Seek you for chastity, immortal fame,
And know that some have wronged Diana's name?
Whose name is it, if she be false or not,   285
So she be fair, but some vile tongues will blot?
But you are fair (aye me) so wondrous fair,
So young, so gentle, and so debonair,
As Greece will think, if thus you live alone,
Some one or other keeps you as his own.   290
Then, Hero, hate me not, nor from me fly,
To follow swiftly blasting infamy.
Perhaps thy sacred priesthood makes thee loth,
Tell me, to whom mad'st thou that heedless oath?"

"To Venus," answered she, and as she spake,   295
Forth from those two tralucent cisterns brake
A stream of liquid pearl, which down her face
Made milk-white paths, whereon the gods might trace
To Jove's high court. He thus replied: "The rites
In which love's beauteous empress most delights,   300

---

265 *bullion:* usually unrefined precious metals (gold, silver), but also in any form uncoined.
270 *essence:* In Aristotelian terminology, something real, substantial, existing.
273 *mould:* "form, with reference perhaps to Platonic 'ideas'" (Martin).
284 *Diana:* Roman moon goddess of the hunt and a figure of virginity.
296 *tralucent:* translucent.
298 *trace:* go, walk.

Are banquets, Doric music, midnight revel,
Plays, masques, and all that stern age counteth evil.
Thee as a holy idiot doth she scorn,
For thou in vowing chastity hast sworn
To rob her name and honour, and thereby   305
Commit'st a sin far worse than perjury,
Even sacrilege against her deity,
Through regular and formal purity.
To expiate which sin, kiss and shake hands,
Such sacrifice as this, Venus demands."   310

Thereat she smiled, and did deny him so,
As put thereby, yet might he hope for mo.
Which makes him quickly reinforce his speech,
And her in humble manner thus beseech:

"Though neither gods nor men may thee deserve,   315
Yet for her sake whom you have vowed to serve,
Abandon fruitless cold virginity,
The gentle queen of love's sole enemy.
Then shall you most resemble Venus' nun,
When Venus' sweet rites are performed and done.   320
Flint-breasted Pallas joys in single life,
But Pallas and your mistress are at strife.
Love, Hero, then, and be not tyrannous,
But heal the heart that thou hast wounded thus,
Nor stain thy youthful years with avarice;   325
Fair fools delight to be accounted nice.
The richest corn dies, if it be not reaped;
Beauty alone is lost, too warily kept."
These arguments he used, and many more,
Wherewith she yielded, that was won before.   330
Hero's looks yielded, but her words made war;
Women are won when they begin to jar.
Thus having swallowed Cupid's golden hook,
The more she strived, the deeper was she strook.

---

301 *Doric:* solemn, majestic, heroic ("perhaps Marlowe's error for Lydian" [Orgel]).
303 *idiot:* ignorant person.
312 *put:* put away, put off. *mo:* more.
321 *Flint-breasted Pallas:* Pallas Athene, represented as a beautiful virgin clad in armor.
326 *nice:* coy.
330 *that:* that which.
332 *jar:* dispute, argue.

Yet evilly feigning anger, strove she still,   335
And would be thought to grant against her will.
So having paused a while, at last she said:
"Who taught thee rhetoric to deceive a maid?
Aye me, such words as these should I abhor,
And yet I like them for the orator."   340

With that, Leander stooped, to have embraced her,
But from his spreading arms away she cast her,
And thus bespake him: "Gentle youth, forbear
To touch the sacred garments which I wear.
Upon a rock, and underneath a hill,   345
Far from the town (where all is whist and still,
Save that the sea, playing on yellow sand,
Sends forth a rattling murmur to the land,
Whose sound allures the golden Morpheus
In silence of the night to visit us)   350
My turret stands, and there God knows I play
With Venus' swans and sparrows all the day.
A dwarfish beldam bears me company,
That hops about the chamber where I lie,
And spends the night (that might be better spent)   355
In vain discourse and apish merriment.
Come thither." As she spake this, her tongue tripped,
For unawares "Come thither" from her slipped,
And suddenly her former colour changed,
And here and there her eyes through anger ranged.   360
And like a planet, moving several ways
At one self instant, she poor soul assays,
Loving, not to love at all, and every part
Strove to resist the motions of her heart.
And hands so pure, so innocent, nay such   365
As might have made heaven stoop to have a touch,
Did she uphold to Venus, and again
Vowed spotless chastity, but all in vain.
Cupid beats down her prayers with his wings,

---

335 *evilly:* with difficulty; reluctantly.
346 *whist:* silent.
349 *Morpheus:* god of sleep.
351 *turret:* small tower.
353 *beldam:* old woman.
356 *apish:* silly.
361 *planet {. . .} ways:* "In the Ptolemaic system, each of the planets was conceived to move in its
 own orbit, while being carried about by the motion of the other 'spheres'" (MacLure).

Her vows above the empty air he flings; 370
All deep enraged, his sinewy bow he bent,
And shot a shaft that burning from him went,
Wherewith she strooken, looked so dolefully,
As made Love sigh, to see his tyranny.
And as she wept, her tears to pearl he turned, 375
And wound them on his arm, and for her mourned.
Then towards the palace of the Destinies
Laden with languishment and grief he flies,
And to those stern nymphs humbly made request,
Both might enjoy each other, and be blest. 380
But with a ghastly dreadful countenance,
Threat'ning a thousand deaths at every glance,
They answered Love, nor would vouchsafe so much
As one poor word, their hate to him was such.
Hearken awhile, and I will tell you why. 385

Heaven's winged herald, Jove-born Mercury,
The self-same day that he asleep had laid
Enchanted Argus, spied a country maid,
Whose careless hair, instead of pearl t' adorn it,
Glistered with dew, as one that seemed to scorn it. 390
Her breath as fragrant as the morning rose,
Her mind pure, and her tongue untaught to glose,
Yet proud she was (for lofty Pride that dwells
In towered courts is oft in shepherds' cells),
And too too well the fair vermilion knew, 395
And silver tincture of her cheeks, that drew
The love of every swain. On her this god
Enamoured was, and with his snaky rod
Did charm her nimble feet, and made her stay,

---

370 *above the empty air:* Gill suggests that "Cupid flings the vows so far away that they pass right through the sphere of air," which had "three [. . .] divisions" and was "located between the spheres of earth and fire."

373 *dolefully:* full of grief, sorrow.

377 *the Destinies:* the three Fates.

386–484 The digressive myth of Mercury (the Roman Hermes) and the country maid is Marlowe's invention.

388 *Argus:* a hundred-eyed giant whom the jealous Juno sent to guard Io, a mortal girl metamorphosed into a cow by Jove, who loved her. Mercury slays Argus at Jove's command. See Ovid, *Metamorphoses* 1.668–88.

392 *glose:* deceive through flattery.

396 *tincture:* tint.

398 *snaky rod:* the caduceus or snake-wreathed magic rod of Mercury/Hermes.

The while upon a hillock down he lay,   400
And sweetly on his pipe began to play,
And with smooth speech her fancy to assay,
Till in his twining arms he locked her fast,
And then he wooed with kisses, and at last,
As shepherds do, her on the ground he laid,   405
And tumbling in the grass, he often strayed
Beyond the bounds of shame, in being bold
To eye those parts which no eye should behold.
And like an insolent commanding lover,
Boasting his parentage, would needs discover   410
The way to new Elysium; but she,
Whose only dower was her chastity,
Having striv'n in vain, was now about to cry,
And crave the help of shepherds that were nigh.
Herewith he stayed his fury, and began   415
To give her leave to rise; away she ran,
After went Mercury, who used such cunning,
As she, to hear his tale, left off her running.
Maids are not won by brutish force and might,
But speeches full of pleasure and delight.   420
And, knowing Hermes courted her, was glad
That she such loveliness and beauty had
As could provoke his liking, yet was mute,
And neither would deny, nor grant his suit.
Still vowed he love; she, wanting no excuse   425
To feed him with delays, as women use,
Or thirsting after immortality—
All women are ambitious naturally—
Imposed upon her lover such a task
As he ought not perform, nor yet she ask.   430
A draught of flowing nectar she requested,
Wherewith the king of gods and men is feasted.
He ready to accomplish what she willed,
Stole some from Hebe (Hebe Jove's cup filled)
And gave it to his simple rustic love;   435
Which being known (as what is hid from Jove?)
He inly stormed, and waxed more furious

---

402 *her fancy to assay:* to try or test her love. *fancy:* imagination; mind.
411 *Elysium:* in classical mythology, the region of the afterlife reserved for the blest; paradise.
425 *wanting no excuse:* "availing herself of any pretext" (Martin).
426 *as women use:* as women usually do.
434 *Hebe:* Jove's cupbearer before Ganymede.

Than for the fire filched by Prometheus,
And thrusts him down from heaven; he wand'ring here,
In mournful terms, with sad and heavy cheer,   440
Complained to Cupid. Cupid for his sake,
To be revenged on Jove did undertake,
And those on whom heaven, earth, and hell relies,
I mean the adamantine Destinies,
He wounds with love, and forced them equally   445
To dote upon deceitful Mercury.
They offered him the deadly fatal knife
That shears the slender threads of human life;
At his fair feathered feet the engines laid,
Which th' earth from ugly Chaos' den upweighed.   450
These he regarded not, but did entreat
That Jove, usurper of his father's seat,
Might presently be banished into hell,
And aged Saturn in Olympus dwell.
They granted what he craved, and once again   455
Saturn and Ops began their golden reign.
Murder, rape, war, lust and treachery
Were with Jove closed in Stygian empery.
But long this blessed time continued not:
As soon as he his wished purpose got,   460
He reckless of his promise did despise
The love of th' everlasting Destinies.
They seeing it, both Love and him abhorred,
And Jupiter unto his place restored.
And but that Learning, in despite of Fate,   465
Will mount aloft, and enter heaven gate,
And to the seat of Jove itself advance,
Hermes had slept in hell with Ignorance.
Yet as a punishment they added this,

---

438 *Prometheus:* famous for his power of intellect (his name means "foresight"), Prometheus secretly
stole fire from Jove, who eventually punished him by binding him to a rock in the Caucasus
mountains, where a vulture eternally devoured his liver.

440 *terms:* state, condition. *cheer:* demeanor.

444 *adamantine:* firm, unyielding, immutable. "The Fates' decrees are called iron dooms ('ferrea
decreta') by Ovid, *Metamorphoses,* XV.781" (MacLure).

450 *upweighed:* raised.

452 *his father's:* Saturn's.

456 *Ops:* Saturn's wife.

458 *Stygian empery:* the domain of hell, encircled by the river Styx.

460 *he:* Mercury.

465 *Learning:* Hermes is the patron of learning.

That he and Poverty should always kiss.   470
And to this day is every scholar poor;
Gross gold from them runs headlong to the boor.
Likewise the angry Sisters, thus deluded,
To venge themselves on Hermes, have concluded
That Midas' brood shall sit in Honour's chair,   475
To which the Muses' sons are only heir:
And fruitful wits that inaspiring are
Shall discontent run into regions far.
And few great lords in virtuous deeds shall joy,
But be surprised with every garish toy,   480
And still enrich the lofty servile clown,
Who with encroaching guile keeps learning down.
Then muse not Cupid's suit no better sped,
Seeing in their loves the Fates were injured.

The end of the first Sestiad

THE ARGUMENT OF THE SECOND SESTIAD

Hero of love takes deeper sense,
And doth her love more recompense;
Their first night's meeting, where sweet kisses
Are th' only crowns of both their blisses;
He swims t'Abydos, and returns;   5
Cold Neptune with his beauty burns,
Whose suit he shuns, and doth aspire
Hero's fair tow'r and his desire.

By this, sad Hero, with love unacquainted,   485 [2.1]
Viewing Leander's face, fell down and fainted.
He kissèd her, and breathed life into her lips,
Wherewith, as one displeased, away she trips.
Yet as she went, full often looked behind,

---

473 *Sisters:* the Fates.
475 *Midas' brood:* the rich, and perhaps rich fools. When Midas chose Pan over Apollo in a musical
    contest, Apollo turned Midas's ears into those of an ass. See Ovid, *Metamorphoses* 11.85–193.
480 *surprised:* captivated.
481 *clown:* rustic bumpkin, boor, fool.
483 *sped:* succeeded.

1 *of love takes deeper sense:* feels love more deeply.
7 *aspire:* aspire to.
485 *this:* her being shot with Cupid's arrow (372–73). *By:* at.

And many poor excuses did she find   490
To linger by the way, and once she stayed,
And would have turned again, but was afraid,
In offering parley, to be counted light.
So on she goes, and in her idle flight,
Her painted fan of curled plumes let fall,   495 [2.11]
Thinking to train Leander therewithal.
He being a novice, knew not what she meant,
But stayed, and after her a letter sent,
Which joyful Hero answered in such sort,
As he had hope to scale the beauteous fort   500
Wherein the liberal Graces locked their wealth,
And therefore to her tower he got by stealth.
Wide open stood the door, he need not climb,
And she herself before the pointed time
Had spread the board, with roses strewed the room,   505 [2.21]
And oft looked out, and mused he did not come.
At last he came; O who can tell the greeting
These greedy lovers had at their first meeting?
He asked, she gave, and nothing was denied;
Both to each other quickly were affied.   510
Look how their hands, so were their hearts united,
And what he did she willingly requited.
(Sweet are the kisses, the embracements sweet,
When like desires and affections meet,
For from the earth to heaven is Cupid raised,   515 [2.31]
Where fancy is in equal balance peised.)
Yet she this rashness suddenly repented,
And turned aside, and to herself lamented,
As if her name and honour had been wronged
By being possessed of him for whom she longed;   520
Ay, and she wished, albeit not from her heart,
That he would leave her turret and depart.
The mirthful god of amorous pleasure smiled
To see how he this captive nymph beguiled;
For hitherto he did but fan the fire,   525 [2.41]

---

493 *parley:* a discussion, particularly between enemies or opposing forces. *light:* too forward, immodest.
494 *idle flight:* she wants to give the appearance of flight but really wants to be caught.
496 *train:* entice.
504 *pointed:* appointed.
510 *affied:* affianced, engaged, betrothed.
516 *peised:* poised, weighed.

And kept it down that it might mount the higher.
Now waxed she jealous, lest his love abated,
Fearing her own thoughts made her to be hated.
Therefore unto him hastily she goes,
And, like light Salmacis, her body throws   530
Upon his bosom, where with yielding eyes
She offers up herself a sacrifice,
To slake his anger, if he were displeased.
O what god would not therewith be appeased?
Like Aesop's cock, this jewel he enjoyed,   535 [2.51]
And as a brother with his sister toyed,
Supposing nothing else was to be done,
Now he her favour and good will had won.
But know you not that creatures wanting sense
By nature have a mutual appetence,   540
And wanting organs to advance a step,
Moved by love's force, unto each other leap?
Much more in subjects having intellect
Some hidden influence breeds like effect.
Albeit Leander, rude in love, and raw,   545 [2.61]
Long dallying with Hero, nothing saw
That might delight him more, yet he suspected
Some amorous rites or other were neglected.
Therefore unto his body hers he clung;
She, fearing on the rushes to be flung,   550
Strived with redoubled strength; the more she strived,
The more a gentle pleasing heat revived,
Which taught him all that elder lovers know.
And now the same 'gan so to scorch and glow,
As in plain terms (yet cunningly) he craved it;   555 [2.71]
Love always makes those eloquent that have it.
She, with a kind of granting, put him by it,
And ever as he thought himself most nigh it,

---

530 *Salmacis:* a water nymph who wooed the youth Hermaphroditus when he bathed in his spring.
   When he ignored her, she asked the gods to join them together. The gods granted the wish
   and created the hermaphrodite. See Ovid, *Metamorphoses* 4.274–388. See Spenser, *FQ* 3.12.46
   (1590 edition).
533 *slake:* reduce.
535 *Aesop's cock:* In the fable, a rooster, while scratching at dirt, finds both a jewel and a barley corn,
   but chooses the lesser over the greater object. Thus, Leander fails to recognize Hero's value.
539 *creatures wanting sense:* inanimate objects.
540 *appetence:* appetite, desire; natural tendency, affinity (Gill).
541 *organs:* means, instruments.
545 *rude:* inexperienced, untaught.

Like to the tree of Tantalus she fled,
And, seeming lavish, saved her maidenhead.   560
Ne'er king more sought to keep his diadem,
Than Hero this inestimable gem.
Above our life we love a steadfast friend,
Yet when a token of great worth we send,
We often kiss it, often look thereon,   565 [2.81]
And stay the messenger that would be gone:
No marvel, then, though Hero would not yield
So soon to part from that she dearly held.
Jewels being lost are found again, this never,
'Tis lost but once, and once lost, lost for ever.   570

Now had the Morn espied her lover's steeds,
Whereat she starts, puts on her purple weeds,
And red for anger that he stayed so long,
All headlong throws herself the clouds among.
And now Leander, fearing to be missed,   575 [2.91]
Embraced her suddenly, took leave, and kissed
Long was he taking leave, and loth to go,
And kissed again, as lovers use to do.
Sad Hero wrung him by the hand, and wept,
Saying, "Let your vows and promises be kept."   580
Then standing at the door, she turned about,
As loth to see Leander going out.
And now the sun, that through th' horizon peeps,
As pitying these lovers, downward creeps,
So that in silence of the cloudy night,   585 [2.101]
Though it was morning, did he take his flight.
But what the secret trusty night concealed,
Leander's amorous habit soon revealed:
With Cupid's myrtle was his bonnet crowned,
About his arms the purple riband wound   590

---

559 *Tantalus:* king of Lydia and a son of Jupiter. After stealing nectar from the gods to give it to
men, Tantalus was punished in hell by suffering extreme hunger and thirst while the fruit of a
tree was just out of reach.
561 *diadem:* crown.
571 *Morn {. . .} steeds:* "It was the function of Aurora, goddess of the dawn, to precede the horse-
drawn chariot of the sun-god through the skies; but no myth relates her as a lover to either Phoebus Apollo or his father, Hyperion" (Gill). Orgel suggests that Marlowe might be "conflating
two stories about the parentage of Phaethon, in one of which he is the child of Aurora and
Cephalus, in the other of Apollo and Clymene."
589 *Cupid's myrtle:* sacred to Venus.
590 *riband:* ribbon.

Wherewith she wreathed her largely spreading hair;
Nor could the youth abstain, but he must wear
The sacred ring wherewith she was endowed
When first religious chastity she vowed;
Which made his love through Sestos to be known,   595 [2.111]
And thence unto Abydos sooner blown
Than he could sail; for incorporeal Fame,
Whose weight consists in nothing but her name,
Is swifter than the wind, whose tardy plumes
Are reeking water, and dull earthly fumes.   600
Home when he came, he seemed not to be there,
But like exiled air thrust from his sphere,
Set in a foreign place; and straight from thence,
Alcides-like, by mighty violence,
He would have chased away the swelling main,   605 [2.121]
That him from her unjustly did detain.
Like as the sun in a diameter
Fires and inflames objects removed far
And heateth kindly, shining lat'rally,
So beauty sweetly quickens when 'tis nigh,   610
But being separated and removed,
Burns where it cherished, murders where it loved.
Therefore even as an index to a book,
So to his mind was young Leander's look.
O none but gods have power their love to hide,   615 [2.131]
Affection by the count'nance is descried.
The light of hidden fire itself discovers,
And love that is concealed betrays poor lovers.
His secret flame apparently was seen,
Leander's father knew where he had been,   620
And for the same mildly rebuked his son,
Thinking to quench the sparkles new begun.
But love resisted once, grows passionate,
And nothing more than counsel lovers hate.
For as a hot proud horse highly disdains   625 [2.141]
To have his head controlled, but breaks the reins,

---

591 *she:* Hero.
600 *reeking:* steaming.
604 *Alcides:* Hercules. See note to line 782.
607–09 *sun {. . .} lat'rally:* Here, the sun's rays are believed to be closest from the horizon
   ("lat'rally"), when they are actually more direct and warmer at noon.
619 *apparently:* obviously, clearly.

Spits forth the ringled bit, and with his hooves
Checks the submissive ground: so he that loves,
The more he is restrained, the worse he fares.
What is it now, but mad Leander dares?   630
"O Hero, Hero!" thus he cried full oft,
And then he got him to a rock aloft,
Where having spied her tower, long stared he on 't,
And prayed the narrow toiling Hellespont
To part in twain, that he might come and go,   635 [2.151]
But still the rising billows answered "No."
With that he stripped him to the ivory skin,
And crying, "Love, I come," leapt lively in.
Whereat the sapphire-visaged god grew proud,
And made his capering Triton sound aloud,   640
Imagining that Ganymede, displeased,
Had left the heavens; therefore on him he seized.
Leander strived, the waves about him wound,
And pulled him to the bottom, where the ground
Was strewed with pearl, and in low coral groves   645 [2.161]
Sweet singing mermaids sported with their loves
On heaps of heavy gold, and took great pleasure
To spurn in careless sort the shipwrack treasure.
For here the stately azure palace stood
Where kingly Neptune and his train abode.   650
The lusty god embraced him, called him love,
And swore he never should return to Jove.
But when he knew it was not Ganymede,
For under water he was almost dead,
He heaved him up, and looking on his face,   655 [2.171]
Beat down the bold waves with his triple mace,
Which mounted up, intending to have kissed him,
And fell in drops like tears because they missed him.
Leander being up, began to swim,
And, looking back, saw Neptune follow him;   660
Whereat aghast, the poor soul 'gan to cry,

---

627 *ringled:* ringed.
628 *Checks:* paws, stamps.
630 *What {. . .} dares:* What is it now that Leander dares not to do?
634 *toiling:* raging, stirred up.
639 *sapphire-visaged god:* Neptune.
640 *Triton:* a sea god, son of Neptune, who blows a trumpet.
642 *Ganymede:* cupbearer to Jove.
644–48 See Spenser, *FQ* 3.4.18–22.
649 *azure:* a deep blue.

"O let me visit Hero ere I die."
The god put Helle's bracelet on his arm,
And swore the sea should never do him harm.
He clapped his plump cheeks, with his tresses played,   665 [2.181]
And smiling wantonly, his love bewrayed.
He watched his arms, and as they opened wide
At every stroke, betwixt them would he slide,
And steal a kiss, and then run out and dance,
And as he turned, cast many a lustful glance,   670
And threw him gaudy toys to please his eye,
And dive into the water, and there pry
Upon his breast, his thighs, and every limb,
And up again, and close beside him swim,
And talk of love. Leander made reply,   675 [2.191]
"You are deceived, I am no woman, I."
Thereat smiled Neptune, and then told a tale,
How that a shepherd, sitting in a vale,
Played with a boy so fair and kind,
As for his love both earth and heaven pined;   680
That of the cooling river durst not drink,
Lest water-nymphs should pull him from the brink;
And when he sported in the fragrant lawns,
Goat-footed satyrs and up-staring fauns
Would steal him thence. Ere half this tale was done,   685 [2.201]
"Aye me," Leander cried, "th' enamoured sun,
That now should shine on Thetis' glassy bower,
Descends upon my radiant Hero's tower.
O that these tardy arms of mine were wings!"
And as he spake, upon the waves he springs.   690
Neptune was angry that he gave no ear,
And in his heart revenging malice bare:
He flung at him his mace, but as it went,
He called it in, for love made him repent.
The mace returning back, his own hand hit,   695 [2.211]
As meaning to be venged for darting it.
When this fresh bleeding wound Leander viewed,
His colour went and came, as if he rued
The grief which Neptune felt. In gentle breasts
Relenting thoughts, remorse and pity rests.   700

---

663 *Helle:* drowned in the Hellespont. See note to line 1.
666 *bewrayed:* revealed.
684 *upstaring:* a seventeenth-century variant reads "up-starting."
687 *Thetis' glassy bower:* the sea.

And who have hard hearts and obdurate minds,
But vicious, harebrained, and illit'rate hinds?
The god, seeing him with pity to be moved,
Thereon concluded that he was beloved.
(Love is too full of faith, too credulous,   705 [2.221]
With folly and false hope deluding us.)
Wherefore Leander's fancy to surprise,
To the rich Ocean for gifts he flies.
'Tis wisdom to give much, a gift prevails,
When deep persuading oratory fails.   710

By this, Leander being near the land,
Cast down his weary feet, and felt the sand.
Breathless albeit he were, he rested not
Till to the solitary tower he got,
And knocked, and called, at which celestial noise   715 [2.231]
The longing heart of Hero much more joys
Than nymphs and shepherds when the timbrel rings,
Or crooked dolphin when the sailor sings.
She stayed not for her robes, but straight arose,
And drunk with gladness to the door she goes,   720
Where seeing a naked man, she screeched for fear,
Such sights as this to tender maids are rare,
And ran into the dark herself to hide.
Rich jewels in the dark are soonest spied:
Unto her was he led, or rather drawn,   725 [2.241]
By those white limbs, which sparkled through the lawn.
The nearer that he came, the more she fled,
And seeking refuge, slipped into her bed.
Whereon Leander sitting, thus began,
Through numbing cold, all feeble, faint and wan: 730

"If not for love, yet, love, for pity sake,
Me in thy bed and maiden bosom take,
At least vouchsafe these arms some little room,
Who, hoping to embrace thee, cheerly swum.

---

702 *hinds:* fools, boors.
717 *timbrel:* a small drum similar to a tambourine.
718 *crooked dolphin {. . .} sings:* "It was thought that dolphins were charmed by the human voice:
   when the bard Arion was in danger of drowning, one of the dolphins who had been attracted by
   his singing bore him to land on its back" (Gill).
726 *lawn:* sheer fabric of her garment.

This head was beat with many a churlish billow,   735 [2.251]
And therefore let it rest upon thy pillow."
Herewith affrighted Hero shrunk away,
And in her lukewarm place Leander lay,
Whose lively heat, like fire from heaven fet,
Would animate gross clay, and higher set   740
The drooping thoughts of base declining souls
Than dreary Mars carousing nectar bowls.
His hands he cast upon her like a snare;
She, overcome with shame and sallow fear,
Like chaste Diana when Actaeon spied her,   745 [2.261]
Being suddenly betrayed, dived down to hide her.
And as her silver body downward went,
With both her hands she made the bed a tent,
And in her own mind thought herself secure,
O'ercast with dim and darksome coverture.   750
And now she lets him whisper in her ear,
Flatter, entreat, promise, protest and swear,
Yet ever as he greedily assayed
To touch those dainties, she the Harpy played,
And every limb did as a soldier stout   755 [2.271]
Defend the fort, and keep the foeman out.
For though the rising ivory mount he scaled,
Which is with azure circling lines empaled,
Much like a globe (a globe may I term this,
By which love sails to regions full of bliss),   760
Yet there with Sisyphus he toiled in vain,
Till gentle parley did the truce obtain.
Wherein Leander on her quivering breast,
Breathless spoke something, and sighed out the rest;
Which so prevailed, as he with small ado   765 [2.281]
Enclosed her in his arms and kissed her too.
And every kiss to her was as a charm,

---

735 *billow:* a large swell.
739 *fet:* fetched.
742 *dreary:* bloody.
744 *sallow:* sickly.
745 *Actaeon:* turned into a stag and killed by his own dogs for watching Diana bathe.
754 *she the Harpy played:* "withdrew the dainties" (Orgel).
758 *empaled:* enclosed, surrounded.
761 *Sisyphus:* condemned in hell to rolling a rock up a mountain for eternity.
763–74 Brooke first moved these lines to this position, since they appear to be out of place in the
   early quarto editions, where they appear after the present line 784.

And to Leander as a fresh alarm,
So that the truce was broke, and she alas
(Poor silly maiden) at his mercy was.   770
Love is not full of pity (as men say)
But deaf and cruel where he means to prey.
Even as a bird, which in our hands we wring,
Forth plungeth, and oft flutters with her wing,
She trembling strove; this strife of hers (like that   775 [2.291]
Which made the world) another world begat
Of unknown joy. Treason was in her thought,
And cunningly to yield herself she sought.
Seeming not won, yet won she was at length,
In such wars women use but half their strength.   780
Leander now, like Theban Hercules
Entered the orchard of th' Hesperides,
Whose fruit none rightly can describe but he
That pulls or shakes it from the golden tree.
And now she wished this night were never done,   785 [2.301]
And sighed to think upon th' approaching sun,
For much it grieved her that the bright daylight
Should know the pleasure of this blessed night,
And them like Mars and Erycine displayed,
Both in each other's arms chained as they laid.   790
Again she knew not how to frame her look,
Or speak to him who in a moment took
That which so long, so charily she kept,
And fain by stealth away she would have crept,
And to some corner secretly have gone,   795 [2.311]
Leaving Leander in the bed alone.
But as her naked feet were whipping out,
He on the sudden clinged her so about
That mermaid-like unto the floor she slid;
One half appeared, the other half was hid.   800
Thus near the bed she blushing stood upright,
And from her countenance behold ye might
A kind of twilight break, which through the hair,

768 *fresh alarm:* call to arms.
770 *silly:* helpless, defenseless, and therefore deserving of pity.
782 *Hesperides:* the nymphs who guarded the tree where the golden apples of immortality grew.
    Hercules, as one of his twelve labors, tried to obtain the golden apples.
789 *Erycine:* Venus.
793 *charily:* carefully, cautiously.
794 *fain:* readily, gladly.

As from an orient cloud, glimpse here and there.
And round about the chamber this false morn   805 [2.321]
Brought forth the day before the day was born.
So Hero's ruddy cheek Hero betrayed,
And her all naked to his sight displayed,
Whence his admiring eyes more pleasure took
Than Dis, on heaps of gold fixing his look.   810
By this Apollo's golden harp began
To sound forth music to the Ocean,
Which watchful Hesperus no sooner heard,
But he the day's bright-bearing car prepared,
And ran before, as harbinger of light,   815 [2.331]
And with his flaring beams mocked ugly Night,
Till she, o'ercome with anguish, shame, and rage,
Danged down to hell her loathsome carriage.

Desunt nonnulla

George Chapman, *Continuation of Hero and Leander*

To My Best Esteemed and Worthily
Honoured Lady, the Lady Walsingham,
One of the Ladies of her Majesty's
Bed-chamber.

I present your ladyship with the last affections of the first two lovers that ever
Muse shrined in the temple of memory; being drawn by strange instigation to
employ some of my serious time in so trifling a subject, which yet made the

---

804 *glimpse:* shines (for "glyms," meaning "gleams"). There is, however, a textual variant that reads
   "glimpsed," which would mean "glimmered" or "shined intermittently."
810 *Dis:* Pluto, god of wealth (and the Underworld).
813 *Hesperus:* the evening star.
818 *danged:* hurled, threw.
Desunt nonnulla: some [sections] are lacking.

Lady Walsingham: Audrey, wife to Sir Thomas Walsingham.
2 *drawn:* "moved by traction; dragged" (*OED*). *strange:* "Unfamiliar, abnormal, or exceptional to a
   degree that excites wonder or astonishment" (*OED*). *instigation:* "The action of instigating or goad-
   ing; an urging, spurring, or setting on; incitement, stimulation" (*OED*). This phrasing gives us our
   first explanation as to why Chapman decided to continue Marlowe's poem; the second occurs at
   3.195.

first author, divine Musaeus, eternal. And were it not that we must subject our
accounts of these common received conceits to servile custom, it goes much   5
against my hand to sign that for a trifling subject, on which more worthiness of
soul hath been showed, and weight of divine wit, than can vouchsafe residence
in the leaden gravity of any money-monger, in whose profession all serious
subjects are concluded. But he that shuns trifles must shun the world; out of
whose reverend heaps of substance and austerity I can, and will ere long, single   10
or tumble out as brainless and passionate fooleries as ever panted in the bosom
of the most ridiculous lover. Accept it therefore, good madam, though as a trifle,
yet as a serious argument of my affection: for to be thought thankful for all free
and honourable favours is a great sum of that riches my whole thrift intendeth.

Such uncourtly and silly dispositions as mine, whose contentment hath   15
other objects than profit or glory, are as glad, simply for the naked merit of
virtue, to honour such as advance her, as others that are hired to commend
with deepliest politic bounty.

It hath therefore adjoined much contentment to my desire of your true honour to hear men of desert in court add to mine own knowledge of your noble dis-   20
position how gladly you do your best to prefer their desires, and have as absolute
respect to their mere good parts, as if they came perfumed and charmed with
golden incitements. And this most sweet inclination, that flows from the truth
and eternity of noblesse, assure your ladyship, doth more suit your other orna-
ments, and makes more to the advancement of your name, and happiness of your   25
proceedings, than if (like others) you displayed ensigns of state and sourness in
your forehead, made smooth with nothing but sensuality and presents.

This poor dedication (in figure of the other unity betwixt Sir Thomas and
yourself) hath rejoined you with him, my honoured best friend, whose continuance of ancient kindness to my still-obscured estate, though it cannot in-   30
crease my love to him, which hath ever been entirely circular, yet shall it encourage my deserts to their utmost requital, and make my hearty gratitude
speak; to which the unhappiness of my life hath hitherto been uncomfortable
and painful dumbness.

By your ladyship's vowed in most wished service.
GEORGE CHAPMAN

THE ARGUMENT OF THE THIRD SESTIAD

Leander to the envious light
Resigns his night-sports with the night,
And swims the Hellespont again;

---

8 *money-monger:* seeker after profit.
9 *concluded:* included.
15 *silly:* unsophisticated.
31 *circular:* "Chapman's favorite adjective, meaning perfect, archetypally complete, as a circle is.
Compare III.246, below" (MacLure).

Thesme, the deity sovereign
Of customs and religious rites,   5
Appears, improving his delights
Since nuptial honours he neglected;
Which straight he vows shall be effected.
Fair Hero, left devirginate,
Weighs, and with fury wails her state;   10
But with her love and woman's wit
She argues, and approveth it.

New light gives new directions, fortunes new,
To fashion our endeavours that ensue;
More harsh (at least more hard) more grave and high
Our subject runs, and our stern muse must fly;
Love's edge is taken off, and that light flame,   5
Those thoughts, joys, longings, that before became
High unexperienced blood, and maids' sharp plights,
Must now grow staid, and censure the delights,
That being enjoyed ask judgement; now we praise,
As having parted: evenings crown the days.   10

And now ye wanton loves and young desires,
Pied vanity, the mint of strange attires,
Ye lisping flatteries and obsequious glances,
Relentful musics and attractive dances,
And you detested charms constraining love,   15
Shun love's stol'n sports by that these lovers prove.

By this the sovereign of heaven's golden fires,
And young Leander, lord of his desires,
Together from their lovers' arms arose:
Leander into Hellespontus throws   20
His Hero-handled body, whose delight
Made him disdain each other epithet.
And as amidst th' enamoured waves he swims,
The god of gold of purpose gilt his limbs,   *He calls Phoebus*
That this word gilt including double sense,   25   *the God of Gold*
The double guilt of his incontinence   *since the virtue*
Might be expressed, that had no stay t'employ   *of his beams*
The treasure which the love-god let him joy   *creates it.*

---

4 *Thesme:* law, rite.
6 *improving:* reproving, condemning.
12 *Pied:* parti-colored.
14 *Relentful:* soft, languishing.
24 *Phoebus* (margin): Apollo, the sun. *virtue* (margin): power.

In his dear Hero, with such sacred thrift
As had beseemed so sanctified a gift;   30
But like a greedy vulgar prodigal
Would on the stock dispend, and rudely fall
Before his time, to that unblessed blessing,
Which for lust's plague doth perish with possessing.
Joy graven in sense, like snow in water, wastes;   35
Without preserve of virtue nothing lasts.
What man is he that with a wealthy eye
Enjoys a beauty richer than the sky,
Through whose white skin, softer than soundest sleep,
With damask eyes the ruby blood doth peep,   40
And runs in branches through her azure veins,
Whose mixture and first fire his love attains;
Whose both hands limit both love's deities,
And sweeten human thoughts like paradise;
Whose disposition silken is and kind,   45
Directed with an earth-exempted mind—
Who thinks not heaven with such a love is given?
And who like earth would spend that dower of heaven,
With rank desire to joy it all at first?
What simply kills our hunger, quencheth thirst,   50
Clothes but our nakedness, and makes us live,
Praise doth not any of her favours give:
But what doth plentifully minister
Beauteous apparel and delicious cheer,
So ordered that it still excites desire,   55
And still gives pleasure freeness to aspire,
The palm of bounty ever moist preserving:
To love's sweet life this is the courtly carving.
Thus Time, and all-states-ordering Ceremony
Had banished all offence: Time's golden thigh   60
Upholds the flowery body of the earth
In sacred harmony, and every birth

---

40 *damask:* a deep rose color.
43 *limit:* hold.
57 *moist:* fruitful.
58 *carving:* adornment.
60 *Time's golden thigh:* "Time's *order* is the harmony of creation, a harmony expressed in terms of the musical scale by Pythagoras. Chapman combines this tradition with the legend that Pythagoras had a golden thigh, to make a striking image" (MacLure).

Of men and actions makes legitimate,
Being used aright. *The use of time is Fate.*

Yet did the gentle flood transfer once more   65
This prize of love home to his father's shore,
Where he unlades himself of that false wealth
That makes few rich, treasures composed by stealth;
And to his sister, kind Hermione
(Who on the shore kneeled, praying to the sea   70
For his return), he all love's goods did show,
In Hero seised for him, in him for Hero.
His most kind sister all his secrets knew,
And to her singing like a shower he flew,
Sprinkling the earth, that to their tombs took in   75
Streams dead for love to leave his ivory skin,
Which yet a snowy foam did leave above,
As soul to the dead water that did love;
And from thence did the first white roses spring
(For love is sweet and fair in every thing)   80
And all the sweetened shore as he did go,
Was crowned with od'rous roses white as snow.
Love-blest Leander was with love so filled,
That love to all that touched him he instilled.
And as the colours of all things we see   85
To our sight's powers communicated be,
So to all objects that in compass came
Of any sense he had, his senses' flame
Flowed from his parts with force so virtual,
It fired with sense things mere insensual.   90

Now (with warm baths and odours comforted)
When he lay down he kindly kissed his bed,
As consecrating it to Hero's right,
And vowed thereafter that whatever sight
Put him in mind of Hero, or her bliss,   95
Should be her altar to prefer a kiss.

Then laid he forth his late enriched arms,
In whose white circle Love writ all his charms,

---

67 *unlade:* to remove or rid a burden.
69 *Hermione:* Leander's sister (Chapman's invention). In book 4 of the *Odyssey,* Hermione is the beautiful daughter of Helen and Menelaus.
72 *seised:* settled, established, legally possessed by.
89 *virtual:* powerful.
96 *prefer:* proffer, offer.

And made his characters sweet Hero's limbs,
When on his breast's warm sea she sidling swims.   100
And as those arms (held up in circle) met,
He said: "See, sister, Hero's carcanet,
Which she had rather wear about her neck,
Than all the jewels that do Juno deck."

But as he shook with passionate desire   105
To put in flame his other secret fire,
A music so divine did pierce his ear,
As never yet his ravished sense did hear:
When suddenly a light of twenty hues
Brake through the roof, and like the rainbow views   110
Amazed Leander; in whose beam came down
The goddess Ceremony, with a crown
Of all the stars, and heaven with her descended;
Her flaming hair to her bright feet extended,
By which hung all the bench of deities,   115
And in a chain, compact of ears and eyes,
She led Religion. All her body was
Clear and transparent as the purest glass:
For she was all presented to the sense:
Devotion, Order, State, and Reverence   120
Her shadows were; Society, Memory;
All which her sight made live, her absence die.
A rich disparent pentacle she wears,
Drawn full of circles and strange characters;
Her face was changeable to every eye,   125
One way looked ill, another graciously;
Which while men viewed, they cheerful were and holy,
But looking off, vicious and melancholy.
The snaky paths to each observed law
Did Policy in her broad bosom draw;   130
One hand a mathematic crystal sways,
Which gathering in one line a thousand rays
From her bright eyes, Confusion burns to death,
And all estates of men distinguisheth.
By it Morality and Comeliness   135

---

99 *characters:* letters.
102 *carcanet:* necklace.
112 *Ceremony:* a goddess who represents principles of law, measure, and form (Chapman's invention). The invention is inspired by Spenser.
123 *disparent pentacle:* a magical multicolored, five-pointed star.
131 *mathematic:* prismatic, geometric.

Themselves in all their sightly figures dress.
Her other hand a laurel rod applies,
To beat back Barbarism and Avarice
That followed, eating earth and excrement
And human limbs, and would make proud ascent   140
To seats of gods, were Ceremony slain.
The Hours and Graces bore her glorious train,
And all the sweets of our society
Were sphered and treasured in her bounteous eye.
Thus she appeared, and sharply did reprove   145
Leander's bluntness in his violent love;
Told him how poor was substance without rites,
Like bills unsigned, desires without delights;
Like meats unseasoned; like rank corn that grows
On cottages, that none or reaps or sows;   150
Not being with civil forms confirmed and bounded,
For human dignities and comforts founded,
But loose and secret, all their glories hide;
Fear fills the chamber, darkness decks the bride.

She vanished, leaving pierced Leander's heart   155
With sense of his unceremonious part,
In which with plain neglect of nuptial rites,
He close and flatly fell to his delights;
And instantly he vowed to celebrate
All rites pertaining to his married state.   160
So up he gets, and to his father goes,
To whose glad ears he doth his vows disclose.
The nuptials are resolved with utmost power,
And he at night would swim to Hero's tower,
From whence he meant to Sestos' forked bay   165
To bring her covertly, where ships must stay,
Sent by his father, throughly rigged and manned,
To waft her safely to Abydos' strand.
There leave we him, and with fresh wing pursue
Astonished Hero, whose most wished view   170
I thus long have forborne, because I left her
So out of count'nance, and her spirits bereft her.
To look on one abashed is impudence,

---

142 *The Hours and Graces:* "The Hours are goddesses of the seasons, hence symbols of the order of
    natures; the Graces are emblematic of civility and order too. Compare *The Faerie Queene* VI.x.23"
    (MacLure).
158 *close:* secretly. *flatly:* plainly, without ceremony.
170 *Astonished:* overwhelmed.

When of slight faults he hath too deep a sense.
Her blushing het her chamber; she looked out,   175
And all the air she purpled round about;
And after it a foul black day befell,
Which ever since a red morn doth foretell,
And still renews our woes for Hero's woe.
And foul it proved, because it figured so   180
The next night's horror, which prepare to hear:
I fail, if it profane your daintiest ear.

Then thou most strangely-intellectual fire,
That proper to my soul hast power t' inspire
Her burning faculties, and with the wings   185
Of thy unsphered flame visit'st the springs
Of spirits immortal; now (as swift as Time
Doth follow Motion) find th' eternal clime
Of his free soul, whose living subject stood
Up to the chin in the Pierian flood,   190
And drunk to me half this Musaean story,
Inscribing it to deathless memory:
Confer with it, and make my pledge as deep,
That neither's draught be consecrate to sleep.
Tell it how much his late desires I tender   195
(If yet it know not), and to light surrender
My soul's dark offspring, willing it should die
To loves, to passions, and society.
Sweet Hero left upon her bed alone,
Her maidenhead, her vows, Leander gone,   200
And nothing with her but a violent crew
Of new come thoughts that yet she never knew,
Even to herself a stranger, was much like
Th' Iberian city that war's hand did strike
By English force in princely Essex' guide,   205
When peace assured her tow'rs had fortified,

---

175 *het:* heated.
183–98: Further phrasing on Chapman's motivation in continuing Marlowe's poem.
189 *his:* Marlowe's. *living subject:* bodily manifestation.
190 *Pierian flood:* spring or well of the Muses. The line evokes the myth of Tantalus; see note to line 1.559.
195 *his late desires I tender:* the precise phrasing for Chapman's motivation. The word "tender" has two primary senses: "respect" (Martin, citing *OED*); and "*Law:* A formal offer duly made by one party to another" (*OED*).
204 *Iberian city:* Cadiz, Spain. In 1596, Robert Devereaux, earl of Essex, captured the city in a famous military victory, celebrated (for example) by Spenser in *Prothalamion* (145–62).

And golden-fingered India had bestowed
Such wealth on her, that strength and empire flowed
Into her turrets, and her virgin waist
The wealthy girdle of the sea embraced;   210
Till our Leander, that made Mars his Cupid,
For soft love-suits, with iron thunders chid,
Swum to her towers, dissolved her virgin zone,
Led in his power, and made Confusion
Run through her streets amazed, that she supposed   215
She had not been in her own walls enclosed,
But rapt by wonder to some foreign state,
Seeing all her issue so disconsolate,
And all her peaceful mansions possessed
With war's just spoil, and many a foreign guest   220
From every corner driving an enjoyer,
Supplying it with power of a destroyer.
So fared fair Hero in th' expugned fort
Of her chaste bosom, and of every sort
Strange thoughts possessed her, ransacking her breast   225
For that that was not there, her wonted rest.
She was a mother straight, and bore with pain
Thoughts that spake straight, and wished their mother slain;
She hates their lives, and they their own and hers:
Such strife still grows where sin the race prefers.   230
Love is a golden bubble full of dreams,
That waking breaks, and fills us with extremes.
She mused how she could look upon her sire,
And not show that without, that was intire.
For as a glass is an inanimate eye,   235
And outward forms embraceth inwardly,
So is the eye an animate glass that shows
In-forms without us. And as Phoebus throws
His beams abroad though he in clouds be closed,
Still glancing by them till he find opposed   240
A loose and rorid vapour that is fit
T' event his searching beams, and useth it
To form a tender twenty-coloured eye,
Cast in a circle round about the sky:

---

223 *expugned:* vanquished, captured.
232 *extremes:* from the Latin (*in extremis*) for dire hardships.
234 *intire:* inward, within.
238 *In-forms:* forms within us.
241 *rorid:* dewy.
242 *event:* vent, give forth.

So when our fiery soul, our body's star   245
(That ever is in motion circular),
Conceives a form, in seeking to display it
Through all our cloudy parts, it doth convey it
Forth at the eye, as the most pregnant place,
And that reflects it round about the face.   250
And this event uncourtly Hero thought
Her inward guilt would in her looks have wrought;
For yet the world's stale cunning she resisted,
To bear foul thoughts, yet forge what looks she listed,
And held it for a very silly sleight,   255
To make a perfect metal counterfeit:
Glad to disclaim herself proud of an art
That makes the face a pander to the heart.
Those be the painted moons, whose lights profane
Beauty's true heaven, at full still in their wane.   260
Those be the lapwing faces that still cry,
"Here 'tis," when that they vow is nothing nigh.
Base fools, when every moorish fowl can reach
That which men think the height of human reach.
But custom that the apoplexy is   265
Of bedrid nature and lives led amiss,
And takes away all feeling of offence,
Yet brazed not Hero's brow with impudence;
And this she thought most hard to bring to pass,
To seem in count'nance other than she was,   270
As if she had two souls, one for the face,
One for the heart, and that they shifted place
As either list to utter or conceal
What they conceived; or as one soul did deal
With both affairs at once, keeps and ejects   275
Both at an instant contrary effects;
Retention and ejection in her powers
Being acts alike; for this one vice of ours,
That forms the thought, and sways the countenance,
Rules both our motion and our utterance.   280

These and more grave conceits toiled Hero's spirits;
For though the fight of her discursive wits

---

261 *lapwing:* deceitful.
263 *moorish fowl:* ordinary (marsh) bird.
265 *apoplexy:* a loss of consciousness caused by pressure on the brain.
266 *bedrid:* diseased.
273 *list:* wished.

Perhaps might find some little hole to pass
Through all these worldly cinctures, yet (alas)
There was a heavenly flame encompassed her,   285
Her goddess, in whose fane she did prefer
Her virgin vows; from whose impulsive sight
She knew the black shield of the darkest night
Could not defend her, nor wit's subtlest art:
This was the point pierced Hero to the heart.   290
Who heavy to the death, with a deep sigh
And hand that languished, took a robe was nigh,
Exceeding large, and of black cypress made,
In which she sat, hid from the day in shade,
Even over head and face down to her feet;   295
Her left hand made it at her bosom meet;
Her right hand leaned on her heart-bowing knee,
Wrapped in unshapeful folds 'twas death to see;
Her knee stayed that, and that her falling face,
Each limb helped other to put on disgrace.   300
No form was seen, where form held all her sight;
But like an embryon that saw never light,
Or like a scorched statue made a coal
With three-winged lightning, or a wretched soul
Muffled with endless darkness she did sit: 305
The night had never such a heavy spirit.
Yet might an imitating eye well see
How fast her clear tears melted on her knee
Through her black veil, and turned as black as it,
Mourning to be her tears. Then wrought her wit   310
With her broke vow, her goddess' wrath, her fame,
All tools that enginous despair could frame;
Which made her strew the floor with her torn hair,
And spread her mantle piecemeal in the air.

---

284 *worldly cinctures:* ideas from moral philosophy.
286 *fane:* church.
287 *impulsive:* penetrating.
293 *cypress:* "a fabric of a kind originally brought from Cyprus, especially Cypress lawn, used, when black, for mourning garments" (Martin).
297 *heart-bowing:* toward which her heart bowed.
299 *that, and that:* her hands.
301 *No {. . .} sight:* "Her true shape or form could not be seen, although what could be seen was a form, a vague one such as is figured in the comparisons that follow" (Martin).
302 *embryon:* embryo.
307 *imitating:* reflecting, endeavoring.
312 *enginous:* crafty, subtle, wily.

Like Jove's son's club, strong passion strook her down,   315
And with a piteous shriek enforced her swoon.
Her shriek made with another shriek ascend
The frighted matron that on her did tend;
And as with her own cry her sense was slain,
So with the other it was called again.   320
She rose, and to her bed made forced way,
And laid her down even where Leander lay;
And all this while the red sea of her blood
Ebbed with Leander; but now turned the flood,
And all her fleet of sprites came swelling in,   325
With child of sail, and did hot fight begin
With those severe conceits she too much marked,
And here Leander's beauties were embarked.
He came in swimming painted all with joys,
Such as might sweeten hell; his thought destroys   330
All her destroying thoughts; she thought she felt
His heart in hers with her contentions melt,
And child her soul that it could so much err,
To check the true joys he deserved in her.
Her fresh heat blood cast figures in her eyes,   335
And she supposed she saw in Neptune's skies
How her star wandered, washed in smarting brine
For her love's sake, that with immortal wine
Should be embathed, and swim in more heart's-ease
Than there was water in the Sestian seas.   340
Then said her Cupid-prompted spirit: "Shall I
Sing moans to such delightsome harmony?
Shall slick-tongued Fame, patched up with voices rude,
The drunken bastard of the multitude
(Begot when father Judgement is away,   345
And, gossip-like, says because others say,
Takes news as if it were too hot to eat,
And spits it slavering forth for dog-fees meat),
Make me, for forging a fantastic vow,

---

315 *Jove's son's:* Hercules'.
320 *called again:* recalled.
323 *blood:* feeling, enthusiasm, emotion.
326 *With {. . .} sail:* sails filled (pregnant) with wind.
330 *his thought:* the thought of him.
335 *fresh heat:* freshly heated.
336 *Neptune's skies:* the sea.
348 *dog-fees meat:* the meat from game given to hunting dogs.

Presume to bear what makes grave matrons bow?   350
Good vows are never broken with good deeds,
For then good deeds were bad; vows are but seeds,
And good deeds fruits; even those good deeds that grow
From other stocks than from th' observed vow.
That is a good deed that prevents a bad: 355
Had I not yielded, slain myself I had.
Hero Leander is, Leander Hero:
Such virtue love hath to make one of two.
If then Leander did my maidenhead get,
Leander being myself I still retain it.   360
We break chaste vows when we live loosely ever;
But bound as we are, we live loosely never.
Two constant lovers being joined in one,
Yielding to one another, yield to none.
We know not how to vow, till love unblind us,   365
And vows made ignorantly never bind us.
Too true it is that when 'tis gone men hate
The joys as vain they took in love's estate;
But that's since they have lost the heavenly light
Should show them way to judge of all things right.   370
When life is gone, death must implant his terror;
As death is foe to life, so love to error.
Before we love, how range we through this sphere,
Searching the sundry fancies hunted here:
Now with desire of wealth transported quite   375
Beyond our free humanity's delight;
Now with ambition climbing falling towers,
Whose hope to scale our fear to fall devours;
Now rapt with pastimes, pomp, all joys impure:
In things without us no delight is sure.   380
But love, with all joys crowned, within doth sit:
O goddess, pity love, and pardon it!"

This spake she weeping, but her goddess' ear
Burned with too stern a heat, and would not hear.
Aye me, hath heaven's strait fingers no more graces   385
For such as Hero, than for homeliest faces?
Yet she hoped well, and in her sweet conceit
Weighing her arguments, she thought them weight,
And that the logic of Leander's beauty,

---

385 *strait:* miserly, ungenerous.
388 *weight:* weighty.

And them together, would bring proofs of duty.   390
And if her soul, that was a skilful glance
Of heaven's great essence, found such imperance
In her love's beauties, she had confidence
Jove loved him too, and pardoned her offence.
Beauty in heaven and earth this grace doth win,   395
It supples rigour, and it lessens sin.
Thus her sharp wit, her love, her secrecy,
Trooping together, made her wonder why
She should not leave her bed, and to the temple.
Her health said she must live; her sex, dissemble.   400
She viewed Leander's place, and wished he were
Turned to his place, so his place were Leander.
"Aye me," said she, "that love's sweet life and sense
Should do it harm! my love had not gone hence
Had he been like his place. O blessed place,   405
Image of constancy! Thus my love's grace
Parts nowhere, but it leaves something behind
Worth observation. He renowns his kind.
His motion is like heaven's, orbicular,
For where he once is, he is ever there.   410
This place was mine; Leander, now 'tis thine;
Thou being myself, then it is double mine,
Mine, and Leander's mine, Leander's mine.
O see what wealth it yields me, nay yields him!
For I am in it, he for me doth swim.   415
Rich, fruitful love, that, doubling self-estates,
Elixir-like contracts, though separates.
Dear place, I kiss thee, and do welcome thee,
As from Leander ever sent to me."

The end of the third Sestiad

THE ARGUMENT OF THE FOURTH SESTIAD

Hero, in sacred habit decked,
Doth private sacrifice effect;
Her scarf's description, wrought by Fate;

---

392 *imperance:* commanding power.
402 *Turned to:* turned into, but also returned to.
409 *orbicular:* circular, spherical.
413 *mine:* for a similar pun on "wealth," see Shakespeare, "The Phoenix and Turtle," line 36.

Ostents that threaten her estate;
The strange, yet physical events,   5
Leander's counterfeit presents;
In thunder Cyprides descends,
Presaging both the lovers' ends.
Ecte the goddess of remorse
With vocal and articulate force   10
Inspires Leucote, Venus' swan,
T'excuse the beauteous Sestian;
Venus, to wreak her rites' abuses,
Creates the monster Eronusis,   *Eronusis,*
Inflaming Hero's sacrifice   15   *Dissimulation*
With lightning darted from her eyes;
And thereof springs the painted beast,
That ever since taints every breast.

Now from Leander's place she rose, and found
Her hair and rent robe scattered on the ground;
Which taking up, she every piece did lay
Upon an altar, where in youth of day
She used t' exhibit private sacrifice.   5
Those would she offer to the deities
Of her fair goddess and her powerful son,
As relics of her late-felt passion;
And in that holy sort she vowed to end them,
In hope her violent fancies that did rend them   10
Would as quite fade in her love's holy fire,
As they should in the flames she meant t' inspire.
Then put she on all her religious weeds,
That decked her in her secret sacred deeds:
A crown of icicles, that sun nor fire   15
Could ever melt, and figured chaste desire;
A golden star shined in her naked breast,
In honour of the queen-light of the east;
In her right hand she held a silver wand,

---

4 *Ostents:* omens.
6 *counterfeit:* portrait.
7 *Cyprides:* Venus, who was born on the island Cyprus.
8 *presaging:* foreshadowing.
9 *Ecte:* the name means "pity" (Chapman's invention).
11 *Leucote:* derived from *leukotas,* whiteness.
13 *wreak:* avenge but also bring about.
14 *Eronusis:* as the marginal gloss indicates, the name means "dissimulation" (Chapman's invention).
5 *exhibit:* offer, present.
18 *queen-light {. . .} east:* Venus.

On whose bright top Peristera did stand,   20
Who was a nymph, but now transformed a dove,
And in her life was dear in Venus' love;
And for her sake she ever since that time
Choosed doves to draw her coach through heaven's blue clime.
Her plenteous hair in curled billows swims   25
On her bright shoulder; her harmonious limbs
Sustained no more but a most subtle veil
That hung on them, as it durst not assail
Their different concord; for the weakest air
Could raise it swelling from her beauties fair;   30
Nor did it cover, but adumbrate only
Her most heart-piercing parts, that a blest eye
Might see (as it did shadow) fearfully
All that all-love-deserving paradise.
It was as blue as the most freezing skies,   35
Near the sea's hue, for thence her goddess came.
On it a scarf she wore of wondrous frame,
In midst whereof she wrought a virgin's face,
From whose each cheek a fiery blush did chase
Two crimson flames, that did two ways extend,   40
Spreading the ample scarf to either end,
Which figured the division of her mind,
Whiles yet she rested bashfully inclined,
And stood not resolute to wed Leander.
This served her white neck for a purple sphere,   45
And cast itself at full breadth down her back.
There (since the first breath that begun the wrack
Of her free quiet from Leander's lips)
She wrought a sea in one flame full of ships;
But that one ship where all her wealth did pass   50
(Like simple merchants' goods) Leander was;
For in that sea she naked figured him;
Her diving needle taught him how to swim,
And to each thread did such resemblance give,
For joy to be so like him it did live.   55

---

20 *Peristera:* the name is Greek for "dove" (Chapman's invention).

27 *subtle:* fine, delicate, of fine texture.

29 *different concord:* "concord of differing parts" (Martin).

37–44 "This description of Hero's scarf, unlike Marlowe's of her garments (I.9–20), is emblematic, 'figuring' a mental state" (MacLure).

38–40 Cf. Shakespeare, *Much Ado About Nothing* 4.1.159–64 for a similar description, of the virgin blush of a character named "Hero": "A thousand blushing apparitions / To start into her face, a thousand innocent shames / In angel whiteness beat away those blushes, / And in her eye there hath appear'd a fire, / To burn the errors that these princes hold / Against her maiden truth."

Things senseless live by art, and rational die
By rude contempt of art and industry.
Scarce could she work but in her strength of thought
She feared she pricked Leander as she wrought,
And oft would shriek so, that her guardian, frighted,   60
Would staring haste, as with some mischief cited.
They double life that dead things' griefs sustain;
They kill that feel not their friends' living pain.
Sometimes she feared he sought her infamy,
And then as she was working of his eye,   65
She thought to prick it out to quench her ill;
But as she pricked, it grew more perfect still.
Trifling attempts no serious acts advance;
The fire of love is blown by dalliance.
In working his fair neck she did so grace it,   70
She still was working her own arms t' embrace it;
That, and his shoulders, and his hands were seen
Above the stream, and with a pure sea green
She did so quaintly shadow every limb,
All might be seen beneath the waves to swim.   75

In this conceited scarf she wrought beside
A moon in change, and shooting stars did glide
In number after her with bloody beams,
Which figured her affects in their extremes,
Pursuing Nature in her Cynthian body,   80
And did her thoughts running on change imply;
For maids take more delights when they prepare
And think of wives' states, than when wives they are.
Beneath all these she wrought a fisherman,
Drawing his nets from forth that ocean,   85
Who drew so hard, ye might discover well
The toughened sinews in his neck did swell;
His inward strains drave out his bloodshot eyes,
And springs of sweat did in his forehead rise;
Yet was of nought but of a serpent sped,   90

---

61 *as {. . .} cited:* "as if summoned by some untoward accident" (Martin).
71 *still:* constantly.
74 *quaintly:* ingeniously.
76 *conceited:* imaginatively wrought; full of conceits or imaginative images.
79 *affects:* emotions, passions.
80 *Nature {. . .} body:* nature personified as the moon.
90 *Yet {. . .} sped:* Yet only caught a serpent.

That in his bosom flew and stung him dead.
And this by fate into her mind was sent,
Not wrought by mere instinct of her intent.
At the scarf's other end her hand did frame,
Near the forked point of the divided flame,   95
A country virgin keeping of a vine,
Who did of hollow bulrushes combine
Snares for the stubble-loving grasshopper,
And by her lay her scrip that nourished her.
Within a myrtle shade she sat and sung,   100
And tufts of waving reeds about her sprung,
Where lurked two foxes, that while she applied
Her trifling snares, their thieveries did divide:
One to the vine, another to her scrip,
That she did negligently overslip;   105
By which her fruitful vine and wholesome fare
She suffered spoiled, to make a childish snare.
These ominous fancies did her soul express,
And every finger made a prophetess,
To show what death was hid in love's disguise,   110
And make her judgement conquer destinies.
O what sweet forms fair ladies' souls do shroud,
Were they made seen and forced through their blood;
If through their beauties, like rich work through lawn,
They would set forth their minds with virtues drawn,   115
In letting graces from their fingers fly,
To still their eyas thoughts with industry;
That their plied wits in numbered silks might sing
Passion's huge conquest, and their needles leading
Affection prisoner through their own-built cities,   120
Pinioned with stories and Arachnean ditties.
Proceed we now with Hero's sacrifice:
She odours burned, and from their smoke did rise
Unsavoury fumes, that air with plagues inspired,
And then the consecrated sticks she fired,   125
On whose pale flame an angry spirit flew,
And beat it down still as it upward grew.

---

99 *scrip:* a shepherd's bag or satchel.
105 *overslip:* ignore.
114 *lawn:* fine linen.
117 *eyas:* fledgling hawk; youthful, full of energy.
121 *Arachnean:* elaborately woven. When the weaver Arachne challenged Athene to a weaving contest, the goddess turned her into a spider for her arrogance. See note to 1.133–57.

The virgin tapers that on th' altar stood,
When she inflamed them burned as red as blood:
All sad ostents of that too near success,   130
That made such moving beauties motionless.
Then Hero wept; but her affrighted eyes
She quickly wrested from the sacrifice,
Shut them, and inwards for Leander looked,
Searched her soft bosom, and from thence she plucked   135
His lovely picture, which when she had viewed,
Her beauties were with all love's joys renewed.
The odours sweetened, and the fires burned clear,
Leander's form left no ill object there.
Such was his beauty that the force of light,   140
Whose knowledge teacheth wonders infinite,
The strength of number and proportion,
Nature had placed in it to make it known
Art was her daughter, and what human wits
For study lost, entombed in drossy spirits.   145
After this accident (which for her glory
Hero could not but make a history)
Th' inhabitants of Sestos and Abydos
Did every year with feasts propitious
To fair Leander's picture sacrifice;   150
And they were persons of especial prize
That were allowed it, as an ornament
T' enrich their houses, for the continent
Of the strange virtues all approved it held;
For even the very look of it repelled   155
All blastings, witchcrafts, and the strifes of nature
In those diseases that no herbs could cure.
The wolfy sting of Avarice it would pull,
And make the rankest miser bountiful.
It killed the fear of thunder and of death;   160
The discords that conceits engendereth
'Twixt man and wife it for the time would cease;
The flames of love it quenched, and would increase;
Held in a prince's hand it would put out
The dreadful'st comet; it would ease all doubt   165

---

130 ostents: omens. *success:* event.
153 *continent:* contents.
154 *approved:* agreed, testified.
165 *doubt:* fear.

Of threatened mischiefs; it would bring asleep
Such as were mad; it would enforce to weep
Most barbarous eyes; and many more effects
This picture wrought, and sprung Leandrian sects,
Of which was Hero first, for he whose form   170
(Held in her hand) cleared such a fatal storm,
From hell she thought his person would defend her,
Which night and Hellespont would quickly send her.
With this confirmed, she vowed to banish quite
All thought of any check to her delight;   175
And in contempt of silly bashfulness,
She would the faith of her desires profess:
Where her religion should be policy,
To follow love with zeal her piety;
Her chamber her cathedral church should be,   180
And her Leander her chief deity.
For in her love these did the gods forego;
And though her knowledge did not teach her so,
Yet did it teach her this, that what her heart
Did greatest hold in her self greatest part,   185
That she did make her god; and 'twas less naught
To leave gods in profession and in thought,
Than in her love and life; for therein lies
Most of her duties and their dignities.
And rail the brain-bald world at what it will,   190
That's the grand atheism that reigns in it still.
Yet singularity she would use no more,
For she was singular too much before:
But she would please the world with fair pretext;
Love would not leave her conscience perplexed.   195
Great men that will have less do for them, still
Must bear them out, though th' acts be ne'er so ill;

---

169 *This picture wrought, and sprung Leandrian sects:* the line self-consciously models the marvel of
   Marlowe's poem: its ability to create response poems.
176 *silly:* naïve.
178 *policy:* expediency.
182 *forego:* precede.
185 *self:* own.
186 *naught:* wicked.
190 *brain-bald:* brainless.
193 *singular:* alone.
196 *less:* lower-class men.
197 *bear them out:* support them.

Meanness must pander be to excellence;
Pleasure atones falsehood and conscience.
Dissembling was the worst (thought Hero then)   200
And that was best, now she must live with men.
O virtuous love, that taught her to do best
When she did worst, and when she thought it least.
Thus would she still proceed in works divine,
And in her sacred state of priesthood shine,   205
Handling the holy rites with hands as bold
As if therein she did Jove's thunder hold,
And need not fear those menaces of error,
Which she at others threw with greatest terror.
O lovely Hero, nothing is thy sin,   210
Weighed with those foul faults other priests are in,
That having neither faiths, nor works, nor beauties,
T' engender any scuse for slubbered duties,
With as much count'nance fill their holy chairs,
And sweat denouncements 'gainst profane affairs,   215
As if their lives were cut out by their places,
And they the only fathers of the Graces.

Now as with settled mind she did repair
Her thoughts to sacrifice her ravished hair
And her torn robe, which on the altar lay,   220
And only for religion's fire did stay,
She heard a thunder by the Cyclops beaten,
In such a volley as the world did threaten,
Given Venus as she parted th'airy sphere,
Descending now to chide with Hero here.   225
When suddenly the goddess' waggoners,
The swans and turtles that in coupled feres
Through all worlds' bosoms draw her influence,
Lighted in Hero's window, and from thence
To her fair shoulders flew the gentle doves,   230
Graceful Aedone that sweet pleasure loves,

---

199 *atones:* reconciles.
202–03 "Hero was taught by 'virtuous love' to be most herself when she was doing what the world calls wrong, and what seemed to her most trivial" (MacLure).
210–17: Chapman's attack on the English clergy. See also 6.109–23.
213 *scuse:* excuse. *slubbered:* botched.
216 *cut out:* determined.
224 *parted {. . .} sphere:* left the heavens.
227 *feres:* mates, companions.
231 *Aedone:* derived from *hedone,* meaning pleasure.

And ruff-foot Chreste with the tufted crown;
Both which did kiss her, though their goddess frown.
The swans did in the solid flood, her glass,
Proin their fair plumes; of which the fairest was   235
Jove-loved Leucote, that pure brightness is,
The other bounty-loving Dapsilis.
All were in heaven, now they with Hero were,
But Venus' looks brought wrath, and urged fear.
Her robe was scarlet, black her head's attire,   240
And through her naked breast shined streams of fire,
As when the rarefied air is driven
In flashing streams, and opes the darkened heaven.
In her white hand a wreath of yew she bore,
And breaking th' icy wreath sweet Hero wore,   245
She forced about her brows her wreath of yew,
And said, "Now, minion, to thy fate be true,
Though not to me; endure what this portends;
Begin where lightness will, in shame it ends.
Love makes thee cunning; thou art current now   250
By being counterfeit: thy broken vow
Deceit with her pied garters must rejoin,
And with her stamp thou count'nances must coin:
Coyness, and pure deceits, for purities,
And still a maid wilt seem in cozened eyes,   255
And have an antic face to laugh within,
While thy smooth looks make men digest thy sin.
But since thy lips (lest thought forsworn) forswore,
Be never virgin's vow worth trusting more."

When Beauty's dearest did her goddess hear   260
Breathe such rebukes 'gainst that she could not clear,
Dumb sorrow spake aloud in tears and blood
That from her grief-burst veins in piteous flood

---

232 *ruff-foot:* feather-footed. *Chreste:* derived from both *chrestos,* meaning good, and *crista,* meaning tuft.
235 *Proin:* dress, preen.
237 *Dapsilis:* abundant, liberal, bounteous.
250–51 *thou {. . .} counterfeit:* "Hero has entered the world as current coin [= legal tender], but through infidelity to her vows, in respect of which she is counterfeit" (Martin).
252 *pied garters:* "the variegated colour symbolizing deceit" (MacLure).
253 *And {. . .} coin:* "Hero must use the mould of Deceit in coining her false facial expressions" (Martin).
254 *for:* instead of.
256 *antic:* grotesque, incongruous.

From the sweet conduits of her favour fell.
The gentle turtles did with moans make swell   265
Their shining gorges; the white black-eyed swans
Did sing as woeful epicedians,
As they would straightways die: when pity's queen,
The goddess Ecte, that had ever been
Hid in a wat'ry cloud near Hero's cries,   270
Since the first instant of her broken eyes,
Gave bright Leucote voice, and made her speak
To ease her anguish, whose swol'n breast did break
With anger at her goddess, that did touch
Hero so near for that she used so much.   275
And thrusting her white neck at Venus, said:
"Why may not amorous Hero seem a maid,
Though she be none, as well as you suppress
In modest cheeks your inward wantonness?
How often have we drawn you from above,   280
T' exchange with mortals rites for rites in love?
Why in your priest then call you that offence
That shines in you, and is your influence?"
With this the Furies stopped Leucote's lips,
Enjoined by Venus, who with rosy whips   285
Beat the kind bird. Fierce lightning from her eyes
Did set on fire fair Hero's sacrifice,
Which was her torn robe, and enforced hair;
And the bright flame became a maid most fair
For her aspect: her tresses were of wire,   290   *Description and*
Knit like a net, where hearts all set on fire   *creation of*
Struggled in pants and could not get released;   *Dissimulation*
Her arms were all with golden pincers drest,
And twenty-fashioned knots, pulleys, and brakes,
And all her body girdled with painted snakes.   295
Her down parts in a scorpion's tail combined,
Freckled with twenty colours; pied wings shined
Out of her shoulders; cloth had never dye,
Nor sweeter colours never viewed eye,

---

264 *favour:* countenance.
267 *epicedians:* singers of epicedes (funeral elegies).
271 *broken:* weeping.
275 *that she used:* what Venus herself did.
288 *enforced:* torn out.
294 *brakes:* harnesses; "probably toothed instruments, such as those used for crushing flax or hemp"
    (MacLure).

In scorching Turkey, Cares, Tartary,   300
Than shined about this spirit notorious;
Nor was Arachne's web so glorious.
Of lightning and of shreds she was begot;
More hold in base dissemblers is there not.
Her name was Eronusis. Venus flew   305
From Hero's sight, and at her chariot drew
This wondrous creature to so steep a height
That all the world she might command with sleight
Of her gay wings; and then she bade her haste,
Since Hero had dissembled, and disgraced   310
Her rites so much, and every breast infect
With her deceits; she made her architect
Of all dissimulation, and since then
Never was any trust in maids nor men.

O it spited   315
Fair Venus' heart to see her most delighted,
And one she choosed, for temper of her mind,
To be the only ruler of her kind,
So soon to let her virgin race be ended;
Not simply for the fault a whit offended,   320
But that in strife for chasteness with the moon,
Spiteful Diana bade her show but one
That was her servant vowed, and lived a maid.
And now she thought to answer that upbraid,
Hero had lost her answer; who knows not   325
Venus would seem as far from any spot
Of light demeanour as the very skin
'Twixt Cynthia's brows? Sin is ashamed of sin.
Up Venus flew, and scarce durst up for fear
Of Phoebe's laughter, when she passed her sphere;   330
And so most ugly clouded was the light,
That day was hid in day, night came ere night,
And Venus could not through the thick air pierce,

---

300 *Cares:* Caria, located in southwest Asia Minor.
302 *Arachne.* See note to 4.121.
304 *hold:* held, contained.
311 *infect:* infected.
316 *her:* Hero. *delighted:* causing delight.
317 *she choosed:* whom she had chosen.
324 *upbraid:* accusation, charge.
328 *Cynthia:* Diana, the moon and figure of chastity.
330 *Phoebe:* the moon, sister to Phoebus Apollo, the sun.

Till the day's king, god of undaunted verse,
Because she was so plentiful a theme   335
To such as wore his laurel anademe,
Like to a fiery bullet made descent,
And from her passage those fat vapours rent,
That being not throughly rarefied to rain,
Melted like pitch as blue as any vein;   340
And scalding tempests made the earth to shrink
Under their fervour, and the world did think
In every drop a torturing spirit flew,
It pierced so deeply, and it burned so blue.
Betwixt all this and Hero, Hero held   345
Leander's picture, as a Persean shield;
And she was free from fear of worst success.
The more ill threats us, we suspect the less;
As we grow hapless, violence subtle grows,
Dumb, deaf, and blind, and comes when no man knows.   350

The end of the fourth Sestiad

THE ARGUMENT OF THE FIFTH SESTIAD

Day doubles her accustomed date,
As loth the night, incensed by Fate,
Should wrack our lovers; Hero's plight
Longs for Leander and the night;
Which ere her thirsty wish recovers,   5
She sends for two betrothed lovers,
And marries them, that (with their crew,
Their sports and ceremonies due)
She covertly might celebrate
With secret joy her own estate;   10
She makes a feast, at which appears
The wild nymph Teras, that still bears
An ivory lute, tells ominous tales,
And sings at solemn festivals.

---

334 *the {. . .} verse:* Apollo, god of the sun and of poetry.
336 *anademe:* wreath.
346 *Persean:* Perseus used a mirror-shield to protect himself from the snaky-haired Gorgon, Medusa;
    if one looked at her, one was turned to stone.
347 *worst success:* failure.

1 *date:* duration, length.
12 *Teras:* the name means "sign" or "portent" (Chapman's invention).

Now was bright Hero weary of the day,
Thought an Olympiad in Leander's stay.
Sol and the soft-foot Hours hung on his arms,
And would not let him swim, foreseeing his harms:
That day Aurora double grace obtained   5
Of her love Phoebus; she his horses reined,
Set on his golden knee, and as she list
She pulled him back; and as she pulled, she kissed,
To have him turn to bed; he loved her more,
To see the love Leander Hero bore.   10
Examples profit much; ten times in one,
In persons full of note, good deeds are done.

Day was so long, men walking fell asleep;
The heavy humours that their eyes did steep
Made them fear mischiefs. The hard streets were beds   15
For covetous churls, and for ambitious heads,
That spite of nature would their business ply.
All thought they had the falling epilepsy,
Men grovelled so upon the smothered ground,
And pity did the heart of heaven confound.   20
The gods, the Graces, and the Muses came
Down to the Destinies, to stay the frame
Of the true lovers' deaths, and all world's tears:
But Death before had stopped their cruel ears.
All the celestials parted mourning then,   25
Pierced with our human miseries more than men.
Ah, nothing doth the world with mischief fill,
But want of feeling one another's ill.
With their descent the day grew something fair,
And cast a brighter robe upon the air.   30
Hero, to shorten time with merriment,
For young Alcmane and bright Mya sent,
Two lovers that had long craved marriage dues

---

2 *Olympiad:* four years, the time between the Olympic games.
3 *Sol:* the sun.
5 *Aurora:* the dawn.
6 *Phoebus:* the sun.
12 *full of note:* important, noteworthy.
14 *humours:* fluids.
16 *churls:* rude people.
32 *Alcmane:* Chapman borrows the name from a Spartan poet of the seventh century BCE. *Mya:* an ancient Spartan poetess.

At Hero's hands; but she did still refuse,
For lovely Mya was her consort vowed   35
In her maid's state, and therefore not allowed
To amorous nuptials, yet fair Hero now
Intended to dispense with her cold vow,
Since hers was broken, and to marry her.
The rites would pleasing matter minister   40
To her conceits, and shorten tedious day.
They came; sweet Music ushered th' odorous way,
And wanton Air in twenty sweet forms danced
After her fingers; Beauty and Love advanced
Their ensigns in the downless rosy faces   45
Of youths and maids, led after by the Graces.
For all these Hero made a friendly feast,
Welcomed them kindly, did much love protest,
Winning their hearts with all the means she might,
That when her fault should chance t' abide the light, 50
Their loves might cover or extenuate it,
And high in her worst fate make pity sit.

She married them, and in the banquet came,
Borne by the virgins; Hero strived to frame
Her thoughts to mirth. Aye me, but hard it is   55
To imitate a false and forced bliss.
Ill may a sad mind forge a merry face,
Nor hath constrained laughter any grace.
Then laid she wine on cares to make them sink;
Who fears the threats of Fortune, let him drink.   60

To these quick nuptials entered suddenly
Admired Teras with the ebon thigh,
A nymph that haunted the green Sestian groves,
And would consort soft virgins in their loves,
At gaysome triumphs and on solemn days,   65
Singing prophetic elegies and lays,
And fing'ring of a silver lute she tied
With black and purple scarfs by her left side.
Apollo gave it, and her skill withal,

---

44 *After her fingers:* as Music played.
50 *abide:* endure, bear, suffer.
62 *ebon:* here it means ivory, but Chapman uses it incorrectly.
64 *consort:* accompany.

And she was termed his dwarf, she was so small.   70
Yet great in virtue, for his beams enclosed
His virtues in her; never was proposed
Riddle to her, or augury, strange or new,
But she resolved it; never slight tale flew
From her charmed lips without important sense,   75
Shown in some grave succeeding consequence.

This little sylvan with her songs and tales
Gave such estate to feasts and nuptials,
That though oft times she forewent tragedies,
Yet for her strangeness still she pleased their eyes,   80
And for her smallness they admired her so,
They thought her perfect born, and could not grow.

All eyes were on her: Hero did command
An altar decked with sacred state should stand
At the feast's upper end, close by the bride,   85
On which the pretty nymph might sit espied.
Then all were silent; everyone so hears,
As all their senses climbed into their ears;
And first this amorous tale that fitted well
Fair Hero and the nuptials she did tell.   90

THE TALE OF TERAS

Hymen, that now is god of nuptial rites,
And crowns with honour love and his delights,
Of Athens was a youth so sweet of face,
That many thought him of the female race;
Such quick'ning brightness did his clear eyes dart,   95
Warm went their beams to his beholder's heart.
In such pure leagues his beauties were combined,

---

70 dwarf: "a very curious detail, possibly suggested by Marlowe's 'dwarfish beldame' (1.353)"
   (MacLure).
73 *augury:* omen.
77 *sylvan:* one who lives in the woods.
78 *estate:* esteem.
79 *forewent:* preceded.
91–426: "The source of the story is Servius' commentary on *Aeneid,* I.655, but Chapman probably found it retold in Cartari's *Imagines Deorum,* 'De Iunone'. See the Leyden edition of 1581,
   pp. 133–4" (MacLure).

That there your nuptial contracts first were signed.
For as proportion, white and crimson, meet
In beauty's mixture, all right clear and sweet,   100
The eye responsible, the golden hair,
And none is held without the other fair,
All spring together, all together fade:
Such intermixed affections should invade
Two perfect lovers, which being yet unseen,   105
Their virtues and their comforts copied been
In beauty's concord, subject to the eye;
And that, in Hymen, pleased so matchlessly,
That lovers were esteemed in their full grace
Like form and colour mixed in Hymen's face;   110
And such sweet concord was thought worthy then
Of torches, music, feasts, and greatest men.
So Hymen looked, that even the chastest mind
He moved to join in joys of sacred kind;
For only now his chin's first down consorted   115
His head's rich fleece, in golden curls contorted;
And as he was so loved, he loved so too,
So should best beauties, bound by nuptials, do.
Bright Eucharis, who was by all men said
The noblest, fairest, and the richest maid   120
Of all th' Athenian damsels, Hymen loved
With such transmission, that his heart removed
From his white breast to hers, but her estate
In passing his was so interminate
For wealth and honour, that his love durst feed   125
On nought but sight and hearing, nor could breed
Hope of requital, the grand prize of love;
Nor could he hear or see, but he must prove
How his rare beauty's music would agree
With maids in consort; therefore robbed he   130
His chin of those same few first fruits it bore,
And, clad in such attire as virgins wore,
He kept them company, and might right well,
For he did all but Eucharis excel
In all the fair of beauty; yet he wanted   135

---

101 *responsible:* correspondingly beautiful, responsible for the effect of beauty.
119 *Eucharis:* the name means "gracious," "pleasing."
122 *transmission:* transference, transport.
124 *interminate:* endless, limitless.
128 *prove:* attempt, test.

Virtue to make his own desires implanted
In his dear Eucharis, for women never
Love beauty in their sex, but envy ever.
His judgement yet (that durst not suit address,
Nor past due means presume of due success)   140
Reason gat Fortune in the end to speed
To his best prayers: but strange it seemed indeed
That Fortune should a chaste affection bless;
Preferment seldom graceth bashfulness.
Nor graced it Hymen yet; but many a dart   145
And many an amorous thought enthralled his heart
Ere he obtained her; and he sick became,
Forced to abstain her sight, and then the flame
Raged in his bosom. O what grief did fill him:
Sight made him sick, and want of sight did kill him. 150
The virgins wondered where Diaetia stayed,
For so did Hymen term himself a maid.
At length with sickly looks he greeted them:
'Tis strange to see 'gainst what an extreme stream
A lover strives; poor Hymen looked so ill,   155
That as in merit he increased still
By suff'ring much, so he in grace decreased.
Women are most won when men merit least:
If merit look not well, love bids stand by;
Love's special lesson is to please the eye.   160
And Hymen soon recovering all he lost,
Deceiving still these maids, but himself most,
His love and he with many virgin dames,
Noble by birth, noble by beauty's flames,
Leaving the town with songs and hallowed lights,   165
To do great Ceres Eleusina rites
Of zealous sacrifice, were made a prey
To barbarous rovers that in ambush lay,

---

142 *To {. . .} prayers:* as he most wished.

151 *Diaetia:* apparently Chapman's invention. The word appears to fashion a feminine singular of *daetarius,* a house-servant, and one who usually serves food (given the root of "diet"). The implication could be that Hymen had the figure of a woman (maid-servant) from not eating enough and/or that the maid-servant who serves him food has been mysteriously absent and therefore he has not been fed and looks "sickly" (undernourished).

166 *To {. . .} rites:* to perform the Eleusinian mysteries, performed to honor the goddess Demeter (Ceres) at Eleusis.

168–200 "The capture of the Athenian maidens by 'barbarous rovers' and their liberation by Hymen is reminiscent of *The Faerie Queene,* VI.xi" (MacLure), where the hero of Courtesy, Calidore, rescues his beloved, Pastorella, from brigands.

And with rude hands enforced their shining spoil,
Far from the darkened city, tired with toil.   170
And when the yellow issue of the sky
Came trooping forth, jealous of cruelty
To their bright fellows of this under-heaven,
Into a double night they saw them driven,
A horrid cave, the thieves' black mansion,   175
Where weary of the journey they had gone,
Their last night's watch, and drunk with their sweet gains,
Dull Morpheus entered, laden with silken chains,
Stronger than iron, and bound the swelling veins
And tired senses of these lawless swains.   180
But when the virgin lights thus dimly burned,
O what a hell was heaven in! how they mourned
And wrung their hands, and wound their gentle forms
Into the shapes of sorrow! Golden storms
Fell from their eyes; as when the sun appears,   185
And yet it rains, so showed their eyes their tears.
And as when funeral dames watch a dead corse,
Weeping about it, telling with remorse
What pains he felt, how long in pain he lay,
How little food he ate, what he would say;   190
And then mix mournful tales of others' deaths,
Smothering themselves in clouds of their own breaths;
At length, one cheering other, call for wine,
The golden bowl drinks tears out of their eyne,
As they drink wine from it; and round it goes,   195
Each helping other to relieve their woes:
So cast these virgins beauty's mutual rays,
One lights another, face the face displays;
Lips by reflection kissed, and hands hands shook,
Even by the whiteness each of other took.   200

But Hymen now used friendly Morpheus' aid,
Slew every thief, and rescued every maid.
And now did his enamoured passion take
Heart from his hearty deed, whose worth did make
His hope of bounteous Eucharis more strong;   205
And now came Love with Proteus, who had long

---

171 *yellow {. . .} sky:* the stars.
178 *Morpheus:* god of sleep.
206 *Proteus:* shape-shifting god of disguise and trickery.

Juggled the little god with prayers and gifts,
Ran through all shapes, and varied all his shifts
To win Love's stay with him, and make him love him;
And when he saw no strength of sleight could move him   210
To make him love, or stay, he nimbly turned
Into Love's self, he so extremely burned.
And thus came Love with Proteus and his pow'r,
T' encounter Eucharis: first like the flow'r
That Juno's milk did spring, the silver lily,   215
He fell on Hymen's hand, who straight did spy
The bounteous godhead, and with wondrous joy
Offered it Eucharis. She, wondrous coy,
Drew back her hand: the subtle flow'r did woo it,
And drawing it near, mixed so you could not know it.   220
As two clear tapers mix in one their light,
So did the lily and the hand their white.
She viewed it, and her view the form bestows
Amongst her spirits: for as colour flows
From superficies of each thing we see,   225
Even so with colours forms emitted be,
And where Love's form is, Love is; Love is form.
He entered at the eye, his sacred storm
Rose from the hand, Love's sweetest instrument;
It stirred her blood's sea so, that high it went,   230
And beat in bashful waves 'gainst the white shore
Of her divided cheeks; it raged the more,
Because the tide went 'gainst the haughty wind
Of her estate and birth. And as we find
In fainting ebbs the flow'ry Zephyr hurls   235
The green-haired Hellespont, broke in silver curls
'Gainst Hero's tower, but in his blast's retreat,
The waves obeying him, they after beat,
Leaving the chalky shore a great way pale,
Then moist it freshly with another gale: 240
So ebbed and flowed the blood in Eucharis' face,
Coyness and Love strived which had greatest grace.
Virginity did fight on Coyness' side,

---

207 *Juggled:* cozened, artfully coaxed.
215 *spring:* bring about. The lily was created (and changed from purple to white) when a drop of
   Juno's breast-milk fell on the earth, after Jupiter gave her the infant Hercules to nurse.
221 *tapers:* candles.
224 *Amongst {. . .} spirits:* in her mind.
235 *Zephyr:* the West Wind.

Fear of her parents' frowns, and female pride
Loathing the lower place more than it loves   245
The high contents desert and virtue moves.
With Love fought Hymen's beauty and his valour,
Which scarce could so much favour yet allure
To come to strike, but fameless, idle stood:
Action is fiery valour's sovereign good.   250
But Love once entered, wished no greater aid
Than he could find within; thought thought betrayed;
The bribed, but incorrupted garrison
Sung "Io Hymen." There those songs begun,
And Love was grown so rich with such a gain,   255
And wanton with the ease of his free reign,
That he would turn into her roughest frowns
To turn them out; and thus he Hymen crowns
King of his thoughts, man's greatest empery:
This was his first brave step to deity.   260

Home to the mourning city they repair,
With news as wholesome as the morning air
To the sad parents of each saved maid;
But Hymen and his Eucharis had laid
This plat, to make the flame of their delight   265
Round as the moon at full, and full as bright.

Because the parents of chaste Eucharis
Exceeding Hymen's so, might cross their bliss,
And as the world rewards deserts, that law
Cannot assist with force, so when they saw   270
Their daughter safe, take vantage of their own,
Praise Hymen's valour much, nothing bestown,
Hymen must leave the virgins in a grove
Far off from Athens, and go first to prove,
If to restore them all with fame and life,   275
He should enjoy his dearest as his wife.
This told to all the maids, the most agree:
The riper sort, knowing what 'tis to be
The first mouth of a news so far derived,

---

246 *contents:* pleasure, contentment, satisfaction.
248–49 *Which {. . .} strike:* which even Love's support could scarcely tempt to strike a blow.
265 *plat:* plot.
274 *prove:* learn, discover.
279 *so far derived:* from so far away.

And that to hear and bear news brave folks lived,   280
As being a carriage special hard to bear
Occurrents, these occurrents being so dear,
They did with grace protest they were content
T' accost their friends with all their complement
For Hymen's good; but to incur their harm,   285
There he must pardon them. This wit went warm
To Adolesche's brain, a nymph born high,
Made all of voice and fire, that upwards fly:
Her heart and all her forces' nether train
Climbed to her tongue, and thither fell her brain,   290
Since it could go no higher, and it must go;
All powers she had, even her tongue, did so.
In spirit and quickness she much joy did take,
And loved her tongue, only for quickness' sake;
And she would haste and tell. The rest all stay;   295
Hymen goes one, the nymph another way,
And what became of her I'll tell at last.
Yet take her visage now: moist-lipped, long-faced,
Thin like an iron wedge, so sharp and tart
As 'twere of purpose made to cleave Love's heart;   300
Well were this lovely beauty rid of her.
And Hymen did at Athens now prefer
His welcome suit, which he with joy aspired:
A hundred princely youths with him retired
To fetch the nymphs; chariots and music went,   305
And home they came: heaven with applauses rent.
The nuptials straight proceed, whiles all the town
Fresh in their joys might do them most renown.
First gold-locked Hymen did to church repair,
Like a quick off'ring burned in flames of hair;   310
And after, with a virgin firmament,
The godhead-proving bride attended went
Before them all; she looked in her command,
As if form-giving Cyprias' silver hand

---

281 *carriage:* burden.
282 *Occurents:* news.
285 *incur their harm:* risk harming themselves.
287 *Adolesche:* the name means "talker" or "chatterer" (Chapman's invention).
291 *it must go:* it had to keep moving.
310 *quick:* living.
312 *godhead-proving:* capable of turning her husband into a god.
314 *Cyprias:* Venus (from her birthplace, Cyprus).

Gripped all their beauties, and crushed out one flame;   315
She blushed to see how beauty overcame
The thoughts of all men. Next before her went
Five lovely children decked with ornament
Of her sweet colours, bearing torches by,
For light was held a happy augury   320
Of generation, whose efficient right
Is nothing else but to produce to light.
The odd disparent number they did choose,
To show the union married loves should use,
Since in two equal parts it will not sever,   325
But the midst holds one to rejoin it ever,
As common to both parts: men therefrom deem
That equal number gods do not esteem,
Being authors of sweet peace and unity,
But pleasing to th' infernal empery   330
Under whose ensigns wars and discords fight,
Since an even number you may disunite
In two parts equal, nought in middle left
To reunite each part from other reft;
And five they hold in most especial prize,   335
Since 'tis the first odd number that doth rise
From the two foremost numbers' unity,
That odd and even are: which are two and three,
For one no number is, but thence doth flow
The powerful race of number. Next did go   340
A noble matron that did spinning bear
A housewife's rock and spindle, and did wear
A wether's skin, with all the snowy fleece,
To intimate that even the daintiest piece
And noblest-born dame should industrious be;   345
That which does good disgraceth no degree.

And now to Juno's temple they are come,
Where her grave priest stood in the marriage room.
On his right arm did hang a scarlet veil,
And from his shoulders to the ground did trail,   350
On either side, ribands of white and blue;

---

315 *crushed out:* created, formed.
321 *efficient right:* correct purpose, true function.
342 *rock:* distaff, the staff from which thread is drawn in spinning by hand.
343 *wether:* a sheep or goat.
344 *piece:* girl.

With the red veil he hid the bashful hue
Of the chaste bride, to show the modest shame,
In coupling with a man, should grace a dame.
Then took he the disparent silks, and tied   355
The lovers by the waists, and side to side,
In token that thereafter they must bind
In one self sacred knot each other's mind.
Before them on an altar he presented
Both fire and water, which was first invented,   360
Since to ingenerate every human creature,
And every other birth produced by Nature,
Moisture and heat must mix: so man and wife
For human race must join in nuptial life.
Then one of Juno's birds, the painted jay,   365
He sacrificed, and took the gall away;
All which he did behind the altar throw,
In sign, no bitterness of hate should grow
'Twixt married loves, nor any least disdain.
Nothing they spake, for 'twas esteemed too plain   370
For the most silken mildness of a maid
To let a public audience hear it said
She boldly took the man; and so respected
Was bashfulness in Athens, it erected
To chaste Agneia, which is shamefastness,   375
A sacred temple, holding her a goddess.
And now to feasts, masques, and triumphant shows
The shining troops returned, even till earth's throes
Brought forth with joy the thickest part of night,
When the sweet nuptial song, that used to cite   380
All to their rest, was by Phemonoe sung,
First Delphian prophetess, whose graces sprung
Out of the Muses' well: she sung before
The bride into her chamber, at which door
A matron and a torch-bearer did stand;   385
A painted box of comfits in her hand
The matron held, and so did other some
That compassed round the honoured nuptial room.
The custom was that every maid did wear,
During her maidenhead, a silken sphere   390

---

355 disparent: varied, multicolored.
375 *Agneia:* the name means "purity" or "chastity."
381 *Phemonoe:* a priestess of Apollo. She shows up prominently in Lucan, *Pharsalia* 5.102–97.
390 *sphere:* belt.

About her waist, above her inmost weed,
Knit with Minerva's knot, and that was freed
By the fair bridegroom on the marriage night,
With many ceremonies of delight.
And yet eternized Hymen's tender bride   395
To suffer it dissolved so sweetly cried.
The maids that heard so loved and did adore her,
They wished with all their hearts to suffer for her.
So had the matrons, that with comfits stood
About the chamber, such affectionate blood,   400
And so true feeling of her harmless pains,
That every one a shower of comfits rains,
For which the bride-youths scrambling on the ground,
In noise of that sweet hail her cries were drowned.
And thus blest Hymen joyed his gracious bride,   405
And for his joy was after deified.

The saffron mirror by which Phoebus' love,
Green Tellus, decks her, now he held above
The cloudy mountains, and the noble maid,
Sharp-visaged Adolesche, that was strayed   410
Out of her way, in hasting with her news,
Not till this hour th' Athenian turrets views;
And now brought home by guides, she heard by all
That her long kept occurrents would be stale,
And how fair Hymen's honours did excel   415
For those rare news, which she came short to tell.
To hear her dear tongue robbed of such a joy
Made the well-spoken nymph take such a toy,
That down she sunk; when lightning from above
Shrunk her lean body, and for mere free love,   420
Turned her into the pied-plumed Psittacus,
That now the parrot is surnamed by us,
Who still with counterfeit confusion prates

---

391 *weed:* garment.
392 *Minerva's knot:* a symbol of chastity.
395 *eternized:* deified.
400 *affectionate blood:* feelings of affections; passion.
407 *saffron mirror:* the moon.
408 *Tellus:* Earth.
418 *take {. . .} toy:* take such offense, feel so slighted.
420 *free love:* indiscriminate energy, appetite, or desire.
421 *Psittacus:* a parrot.

Nought but news common to the common'st mates.
This told, strange Teras touched her lute, and sung   425
This ditty that the torchy evening sprung.

Epithalamion Teratos

Come, come, dear Night, Love's mart of kisses,
Sweet close of his ambitious line,
The fruitful summer of his blisses,
Love's glory doth in darkness shine.   430
O come, soft rest of cares, come Night,
Come naked Virtue's only tire,
The reaped harvest of the light,
Bound up in sheaves of sacred fire.
   Love calls to war,   435
   Sighs his alarms,
   Lips his swords are,
   The field his arms
Come, Night, and lay thy velvet hand
On glorious Day's outfacing face,   440
And all thy crowned flames command
For torches to our nuptial grace.
   Love calls to war,
   Sighs his alarms,
   Lips his swords are,   445
   The field his arms.
No need have we of factious Day,
To cast in envy of thy peace
Her balls of discord in thy way:
Here Beauty's day doth never cease;   450
Day is abstracted here,
And varied in a triple sphere.
Hero, Alcmane, Mya so outshine thee,

---

426 *sprung:* brought about.
427–63 Chapman's *Epithalamion Teratos* is inspired by the marriage poetry of Spenser, especially the 1595 *Epithalamion.* See introduction.
428 *line:* activities, proceedings.
432 *tire:* attire, clothing.
440 *outfacing face:* "face that outfaces others" (Martin).
451 *abstracted:* "reduced to its essence (?)" (MacLure).
453 *thee:* Day.

Ere thou come here let Thetis thrice refine thee.
   Love calls to war,   455
   Sighs his alarms,
   Lips his swords are,
   The field his arms.
The evening star I see:
Rise, youths, the evening star   460
Helps Love to summon war;
Both now embracing be.
Rise, youths, Love's right claims more than banquets, rise.
Now the bright marigolds that deck the skies,
Phoebus' celestial flowers, that (contrary   465
To his flowers here) ope when he shuts his eye,
And shut when he doth open, crown your sports.
Now Love in Night, and Night in Love exhorts
Courtship and dances. All your parts employ,
And suit Night's rich expansure with your joy.   470
Love paints his longings in sweet virgins' eyes:
Rise, youths, Love's right claims more than banquets, rise.
Rise, virgins, let fair nuptial loves enfold
Your fruitless breasts: the maidenheads ye hold
Are not your own alone, but parted are;   475
Part in disposing them your parents share,
And that a third part is, so must ye save
Your loves a third, and you your thirds must have.
Love paints his longings in sweet virgins' eyes:
Rise, youths, Love's right claims more than banquets, rise. 480

Herewith the amorous spirit that was so kind
To Teras' hair, and combed it down with wind,
Still as it comet-like brake from her brain,
Would needs have Teras gone, and did refrain
To blow it down: which staring up dismayed   485
The timorous feast, and she no longer stayed,
But bowing to the bridegroom and the bride,
Did like a shooting exhalation glide
Out of their sights; the turning of her back
Made them all shriek, it looked so ghastly black.   490
O hapless Hero, that most hapless cloud
Thy soon-succeeding tragedy foreshowed.
Thus all the nuptial crew to joys depart,

---

454 *let {. . .} thee:* attempting to make her son Achilles immortal, Thetis dipped him in the Styx
(or in another story, attempted to burn away his mortality).

But much-wronged Hero stood hell's blackest dart;
Whose wound because I grieve so to display,   495
I use digressions thus t' increase the day.

The end of the fifth Sestiad

THE ARGUMENT OF THE SIXTH SESTIAD

Leucote flies to all the winds,
And from the Fates their outrage binds,
That Hero and her love may meet.
Leander (with Love's complete fleet
Manned in himself) puts forth to seas,   5
When straight the ruthless Destinies
With Ate stir the winds to war
Upon the Hellespont; their jar
Drowns poor Leander; Hero's eyes,
Wet witnesses of his surprise,   10
Her torch blown out, grief casts her down
Upon her love, and both doth drown;
In whose just ruth the god of seas
Transforms them to th' Acanthides.

No longer could the Day nor Destinies
Delay the Night, who now did frowning rise
Into her throne; and at her humorous breasts
Visions and Dreams lay sucking: all men's rests
Fell like the mists of death upon their eyes,   5
Day's too-long darts so killed their faculties.
The winds yet, like the flow'rs, to cease began,
For bright Leucote, Venus' whitest swan,
That held sweet Hero dear, spread her fair wings,
Like to a field of snow, and message brings   10
From Venus to the Fates, t' entreat them lay
Their charge upon the winds their rage to stay,
That the stern battle of the seas might cease,
And guard Leander to his love in peace.

---

2 *from {. . .} binds:* "in the name of the Fates, commands the winds to remain calm" (Orgel).

7 *Ate:* a figure of Discord; she is important in Spenser, *FQ,* book 4, the Legend of Friendship (see 4.1.19).

10 *surprise:* overthrow.

13 *just ruth:* proper compassion.

14 *Acanthides:* the thistle-warps (a species of bird) into which Hero and Leander finally metamorphose; originally, they were goldfinches.

3 *humorous:* moist, possibly capricious.

The Fates consent (aye me, dissembling Fates),   15
They showed their favours to conceal their hates,
And draw Leander on, lest seas too high
Should stay his too obsequious Destiny;
Who like a fleering slavish parasite,
In warping profit or a traitorous sleight,   20
Hoops round his rotten body with devotes,
And pricks his descant face full of false notes,
Praising with open throat, and oaths as foul
As his false heart, the beauty of an owl;
Kissing his skipping hand with charmed skips,   25
That cannot leave, but leaps upon his lips
Like a cock-sparrow, or a shameless quean
Sharp at a red-lipped youth, and nought doth mean
Of all his antic shows, but doth repair
More tender fawns, and takes a scattered hair   30
From his tame subject's shoulder; whips, and calls
For every thing he lacks; creeps 'gainst the walls
With backward humbless, to give needless way:
Thus his false fate did with Leander play.

First to black Eurus flies the white Leucote,   35
Born 'mongst the negroes in the Levant sea,
On whose curled head the glowing sun doth rise,
And shows the sovereign will of Destinies,
To have him cease his blasts, and down he lies.
Next, to the fenny Notus course she holds,   40
And found him leaning with his arms in folds
Upon a rock, his white hair full of show'rs,
And him she chargeth by the fatal pow'rs
To hold in his wet cheeks his cloudy voice.
To Zephyr then that doth in flow'rs rejoice;   45

---

18 *obsequious:* compliant, fawning, but also evoking obsequies (funeral rites).
19 *fleering:* grinning, smirking.
20 *warping:* weaving.
21 *devotes:* acts of devotion.
22 *pricks* [. . .] *descant face:* writes his melody.
24 *owl:* for the Elizabethans, sinister, deceitful, and stupid.
27 *quean:* whore.
29 *repair:* furbish up.
33 *humbless:* humbleness.
35 *Eurus:* the East Wind.
36 *Levant sea:* the eastern Mediterranean or the Far East or Orient.
40 *fenny Notus:* a wet South Wind.
45 *Zephyr:* the West Wind.

To snake-foot Boreas next she did remove,
And found him tossing of his ravished love,
To heat his frosty bosom hid in snow,
Who with Leucote's sight did cease to blow.
Thus all were still to Hero's heart's desire,   50
Who with all speed did consecrate a fire
Of flaming gums and comfortable spice,
To light her torch, which in such curious price
She held, being object to Leander's sight,
That nought but fires perfumed must give it light.   55
She loved it so, she grieved to see it burn,
Since it would waste and soon to ashes turn;
Yet if it burned not, 'twere not worth her eyes,
What made it nothing gave it all the prize.
Sweet torch, true glass of our society: 60
What man does good, but he consumes thereby?
But thou wert loved for good, held high, given show;
Poor virtue loathed for good, obscured, held low.
Do good, be pined; be deedless good, disgraced:
Unless we feed on men, we let them fast.   65
Yet Hero with these thoughts her torch did spend:
When bees makes wax, Nature doth not intend
It shall be made a torch, but we that know
The proper virtue of it make it so,
And when 'tis made we light it; nor did Nature   70
Propose one life to maids, but each such creature
Makes by her soul the best of her free state,
Which without love is rude, disconsolate,
And wants love's fire to make it mild and bright,
Till when, maids are but torches wanting light.   75
Thus 'gainst our grief, not cause of grief we fight;
The right of nought is gleaned, but the delight.
Up went she, but to tell how she descended,
Would God she were not dead, or my verse ended!
She was the rule of wishes, sum and end   80
For all the parts that did on love depend.

---

46 *Boreas:* the North Wind.
47 *ravished love:* Orithyia, daughter of the king of Athens, who was carried off by Boreas.
53 *curious price:* peculiar or high esteem.
64 *pined:* starved, neglected.
77 *The {. . .} delight:* instead of the essential meaning of things—the cause—we think only about
   the pleasing effects. MacLure calls the line "an almost impenetrable gnomic utterance."
80 *rule:* standard.

Yet cast the torch his brightness further forth;
But what shines nearest best, holds truest worth.
Leander did not through such tempests swim
To kiss the torch, although it lighted him;   85
But all his pow'rs in her desires awaked,
Her love and virtues clothed him richly naked.
Men kiss but fire that only shows pursue;
Her torch and Hero figure show and virtue.

Now at opposed Abydos nought was heard   90
But bleating flocks, and many a bellowing herd
Slain for the nuptials, cracks of falling woods,
Blows of broad axes, pourings out of floods.
The guilty Hellespont was mixed and stained
With bloody torrents that the shambles rained;   95
Not arguments of feast, but shows that bled,
Foretelling that red night that followed.
More blood was spilt, more honours were addressed,
Than could have graced any happy feast.
Rich banquets, triumphs, every pomp employs   100
His sumptuous hand: no miser's nuptial joys.
Air felt continual thunder with the noise,
Made in the general marriage violence;
And no man knew the cause of this expense,
But the two hapless lords, Leander's sire,   105
And poor Leander, poorest where the fire
Of credulous love made him most rich surmised.
As short was he of that himself he prized
As is an empty gallant full of form,
That thinks each look an act, each drop a storm,   110
That falls from his brave breathings; most brought up
In our metropolis, and hath his cup
Brought after him to feasts; and much palm bears
For his rare judgement in th' attire he wears;
Hath seen the hot Low Countries, not their heat,   115
Observes their rampires and their buildings yet;
And for your sweet discourse with mouths is heard
Giving instructions with his very beard;
Hath gone with an ambassador, and been

---

98 *addressed:* offered.
109 *form:* outward ceremony.
111 *brought up:* mentioned, discussed.
116 *rampires:* ramparts.

A great man's mate in travelling, even to Rhene;   120
And then puts all his worth in such a face
As he saw brave men make, and strives for grace
To get his news forth. As when you descry
A ship with all her sail contends to fly
Out of the narrow Thames with winds unapt,   125
Now crosseth here, then there, then this way rapt,
And then hath one point reached; then alters all,
And to another crooked reach doth fall
Of half a bird-bolt's shoot, keeping more coil
Than if she danced upon the ocean's toil: 130
So serious is his trifling company,
In all his swelling ship of vacantry.
And so short of himself in his high thought
Was our Leander in his fortunes brought,
And in his fort of love that he thought won,   135
But otherwise he scorns comparison.

O sweet Leander, thy large worth I hide
In a short grave; ill-favoured storms must chide
Thy sacred favour: I in floods of ink
Must drown thy graces, which white papers drink,   140
Even as thy beauties did the foul black seas.
I must describe the hell of thy dis-ease,
That heaven did merit; yet I needs must see
Our painted fools and cockhorse peasantry
Still, still usurp, with long lives, loves, and lust,   145
The seats of Virtue, cutting short as dust

---

120 *Rhene:* the Rhineland.

123 *descry:* discern, discover.

129 *bird-bolt:* a small arrow used for shooting birds at close range. *keeping more coil:* causing more commotion.

132 *vacantry:* idleness.

137–43 *O {. . .} merit:* the opening phrasing in this address to Marlowe's Leander, "thy large worth I hide / In a short grave," very possibly alludes to one of Marlowe's most famous lines: "infinite riches in a little room" (*JM* 1.1.37). Cf. Shakespeare's two epitaphs on Marlowe: *As You Like It:* "A great reckoning in a little room" (3.3.15); and esp. *1 Henry IV:* "When that this body did contain a spirit, / A kingdom for it was too small a bound, / But now two paces of the vilest earth / Is room enough" (5.4.89–92). A. R. Humphreys, ed., *The First Part of King Henry IV,* 6th ed. (London : Methuen, 1974), cites *OE* 3.8, Ovid's epitaph on his fellow-poet Tibullus: "Yet better is't, than if Corcyra's isle / Had thee interred in ground most vile" (47–48). All three epitaphs seem to be in dialogue with one another.

138 *chide:* destroy.

139 *favour:* beauty.

144 *cockhorse:* upstart, cocky.

Her dear-bought issue. Ill to worse converts,
And tramples in the blood of all deserts.

Night close and silent now goes fast before
The captains and their soldiers to the shore,　　150
On whom attended the appointed fleet
At Sestos' bay, that should Leander meet,
Who feigned he in another ship would pass;
Which must not be, for no one mean there was
To get his love home, but the course he took.　　155
Forth did his beauty for his beauty look,
And saw her through her torch, as you behold
Sometimes within the sun a face of gold,
Formed in strong thoughts by that tradition's force
That says a god sits there and guides his course.　　160
His sister was with him, to whom he showed
His guide by sea, and said, "Oft have you viewed
In one heaven many stars, but never yet
In one star many heavens till now were met.
See, lovely sister, see, now Hero shines,　　165
No heaven but her appears; each star repines,
And all are clad in clouds, as if they mourned
To be by influence of earth outburned.
Yet doth she shine, and teacheth virtue's train,
Still to be constant in hell's blackest reign,　　170
Though even the gods themselves do so entreat them
As they did hate, and Earth as she would eat them."

Off went his silken robe, and in he leapt,
Whom the kind waves so licorously clept,
Thick'ning for haste one in another so,　　175
To kiss his skin, that he might almost go
To Hero's tow'r, had that kind minute lasted.
But now the cruel Fates with Ate hasted
To all the winds, and made them battle fight
Upon the Hellespont, for either's right　　180
Pretended to the windy monarchy.
And forth they brake, the seas mixed with the sky,
And tossed distressed Leander, being in hell,

---

162 *guide {. . .} sea:* Hero's torch.
166 *repines:* feels discontent.
174 *licorously:* greedily, lecherously. *clept:* embraced.
180 *either's right:* both their claims.

As high as heaven; bliss not in height doth dwell.
The Destinies sat dancing on the waves,   185
To see the glorious winds with mutual braves
Consume each other: O true glass, to see
How ruinous ambitious statists be
To their own glories! Poor Leander cried
For help to sea-born Venus; she denied;   190
To Boreas, that for his Atthaea's sake,
He would some pity on his Hero take,
And for his own love's sake, on his desires;
But Glory never blows cold Pity's fires.
Then called he Neptune, who through all the noise   195
Knew with affright his wracked Leander's voice,
And up he rose; for haste his forehead hit
'Gainst heaven's hard crystal; his proud waves he smit
With his forked sceptre, that could not obey;
Much greater powers than Neptune's gave them sway.   200
They loved Leander so, in groans they brake
When they came near him, and such space did take
'Twixt one another, loth to issue on,
That in their shallow furrows earth was shown,
And the poor lover took a little breath;   205
But the curst Fates sat spinning of his death
On every wave, and with the servile winds
Tumbled them on him. And now Hero finds,
By that she felt, her dear Leander's state.
She wept, and prayed for him to every Fate,   210
And every wind that whipped her with her hair
About the face, she kissed and spake it fair,
Kneeled to it, gave it drink out of her eyes
To quench his thirst; but still their cruelties
Even her poor torch envied, and rudely beat   215
The bating flame from that dear food it eat;
Dear, for it nourished her Leander's life,

---

186 *braves:* boasts.
187 *glass:* mirror.
188 *statists:* politicians.
191 *Atthaea:* Orithyia, wife of Boreas. Chapman coined the name from her title as princess of
Attica.
198 *crystal:* in the Ptolemaic universe, the crystalline sphere of the heavens. *smit:* struck.
208 *finds:* understands.
209 *By {. . .} felt:* by having felt the harsh winds.
214 *his:* the wind's.
216 *bating:* abating, extinguishing.

Which with her robe she rescued from their strife.
But silk too soft was such hard hearts to break,
And she, dear soul, even as her silk, faint, weak,   220
Could not preserve it; out, O out it went.
Leander still called Neptune, that now rent
His brackish curls, and tore his wrinkled face
Where tears in billows did each other chase,
And (burst with ruth) he hurled his marble mace   225
At the stern Fates; it wounded Lachesis
That drew Leander's thread, and could not miss
The thread itself, as it her hand did hit,
But smote it full and quite did sunder it.
The more kind Neptune raged, the more he rased   230
His love's life's fort, and killed as he embraced.
Anger doth still his own mishap increase;
If any comfort live, it is in peace.
O thievish Fates, to let blood, flesh, and sense
Build two fair temples for their excellence,   235
To rob it with a poisoned influence.
Though soul's gifts starve, the body's are held dear
In ugliest things; sense-sport preserves a bear.
But here nought serves our turns: O heaven and earth,
How most most wretched is our human birth!   240
And now did all the tyrannous crew depart,
Knowing there was a storm in Hero's heart
Greater than they could make, and scorned their smart.
She bowed herself so low out of her tow'r,
That wonder 'twas she fell not ere her hour   245
With searching the lamenting waves for him;
Like a poor snail, her gentle supple limb
Hung on her turret's top so most downright,
As she would dive beneath the darkness quite
To find her jewel; jewel! her Leander,   250
A name of all earth's jewels pleased not her
Like his dear name: "Leander, still my choice,
Come nought but my Leander; O my voice,

---

223 *brackish:* salty, distasteful.
225 *ruth:* pity, compassion.
226 *Lachesis:* one of the Fates. She spins thread to determine the length of life.
229 *smote:* struck, hit.
230 *rased:* demolished.
236 *it:* the antecedent is "excellence."
238 *sense-sport:* sports that please the senses; a reference to bear-baiting.

Turn to Leander: henceforth be all sounds,
Accents, and phrases that show all grief's wounds,   255
Analysed in Leander. O black change!
Trumpets do you with thunder of your clange,
Drive out this change's horror, my voice faints:
Where all joy was, now shriek out all complaints."
Thus cried she, for her mixed soul could tell   260
Her love was dead. And when the Morning fell
Prostrate upon the weeping Earth for woe,
Blushes that bled out of her cheeks did show
Leander brought by Neptune, bruised and torn
With cities' ruins he to rocks had worn,   265
To filthy usuring rocks, that would have blood,
Though they could get of him no other good.
She saw him, and the sight was much much more
Than might have served to kill her: should her store
Of giant sorrows speak? Burst, die, bleed,   270
And leave poor plaints to us that shall succeed.
She fell on her love's bosom, hugged it fast,
And with Leander's name she breathed her last.
Neptune for pity in his arms did take them,
Flung them into the air, and did awake them   275
Like two sweet birds, surnamed th' Acanthides,
Which we call thistle-warps, that near no seas
Dare ever come, but still in couples fly,
And feed on thistle-tops, to testify
The hardness of their first life in their last: 280
The first in thorns of love, and sorrows past;
And so most beautiful their colours show,
As none (so little) like them: her sad brow
A sable velvet feather covers quite,
Even like the forehead-cloths that in the night,   285
Or when they sorrow, ladies use to wear;
Their wings, blue, red, and yellow mixed appear;
Colours that, as we construe colours, paint

257 *clange:* a high, sharp sound.
260 *mixed:* confused.
265 *he:* Neptune.
271 *succeed:* follow afterward, live in our memories.
274–93 "The Ovidian metamorphosis is not in Museaus or any other ancient source, nor does
    Marlowe's poem seem to prepare for such a conclusion" (MacLure).
276 *Acanthides:* see note to Argument, line 14.
277 *thistle-warps:* see note to Argument, line 14.
285 *forehead-cloths:* perhaps worn to prevent wrinkles (MacLure).

Their states to life; the yellow shows their saint,
The devil Venus, left them; blue, their truth;   290
The red and black, ensigns of death and ruth.
And this true honour from their love-deaths sprung,
They were the first that ever poet sung.
　　　FINIS

Henry Petowe, *The Second Part of Hero and Leander, Containing their Further Fortunes*

To the Right Worshipful Sir Henry Guilford,
Knight, H. P. Wisheth All Increase of
Worship, and Endless Felicity.

Right worshipful: although presumption merit penance in dedicating such
rude and unpolished lines to the protection of so worthy a personage, yet I hope
your wonted favour and clemency will privilege me from blame, and accept of
the giver, as one who would hazard life to move your worship the least jot of
content. If it be thought a point of wisdom in that impoverished soul that by   5
taking sanctuary doth free himself from many dangers, then impute no blame
unto myself, that seek for safeguard, being round beset with many enemies. No
sooner had report made known my harmless muse's first progress, how she intended to make trial of her unfledged plumes, but (myself being present where
that babbling dame was prating) I heard injurious Envy reply to this effect: 10

　　Dares she presume to fly that cannot go?
　　We'll cut her plumes, said they; it shall be so.

Then with a snarl or two these ever meddling carpers betook them to their cabins. At the next rousing I expect no other favour than Envy's extremest fury,
which to withstand, if I may purchase your worship's safe protection, no better   15
guard will my fearful soul desire. To make the cause manifest unto your worthiness why Envy thus barketh at me, I entreat your wisdom to consider the
sequel. This history of *Hero and Leander,* penned by that admired poet Marlowe,
but not finished (being prevented by sudden death), and the same (though not

---

289 *yellow:* the color of envy and inconstancy.

4 *jot:* a small amount.
11 *go:* walk.

abruptly, yet contrary to all men's expectation) resting like a head separated   20
from the body, with this harsh sentence, *Desunt nonnulla;* I being enriched by a
gentleman, a friend of mine, with the true Italian discourse of those lovers' further fortunes, have presumed to finish the history, though not so well as divers
riper wits doubtless would have done: but as it is rude and not praiseworthy, so
neither do I expect praise nor commendations. This therefore is the cause of   25
their sudden enmity, that I being but a fly dare presume to soar with the eagle.
But however they dislike it, may your worthiness but grace this my first labour
with your kind acceptance, my heart shall enjoy the depth of his desire. And
your worship shall continually bind me in all serviceable duty to rest unto your
worship always devoted.   30

Your worship's most humbly to command,
HENRY PETOWE

To the Quick-Sighted Reader.

Kind gentlemen, what I would I cannot, but what I could with that little skill
I had, I have presumed to present to your favourable views: I am not ashamed
to beg your kind favours, because I find myself altogether insufficient to perform that which my good will hath taken in hand; yet with my soul I wish my
labours may merit your kind favours: if not for the toil herein taken, which I   5
confess have no way deserved the least jot of favour, yet for the subject's sake,
for Hero and Leander's sake. If neither of these purchase favour, the frowning
brows of sad discontent will banish my poor harmless muse into the vast
wilderness of eternal oblivion. I am assured, gentlemen, you will marvel what
folly or rather fury enforced me to undertake such a weighty matter, I being   10
but a slender Atlas to uphold or undergo such a massy burden; yet I hope you
will rather assist, and further me with the wings of your sweet favours, than
to hinder my forward endeavours with your dislikings, esteeming it as the first
fruits of an unripe wit, done at certain vacant hours. In which hope I rest captivated till I be freed by your liberal and kind censures.   15

Yours still, if mine ever,
HENRY PETOWE

When young Apollo, heaven's sacred beauty,
Gan on his silver harp with reverent duty
To blazon forth the fair of Tellus' wonder,

---

21 *Desunt nonnulla:* some sections are lacking. See Marlowe, HL, after line 818.
22 *true Italian discourse:* "merely corroborative detail intended to give artistic verisimilitude to an
   otherwise bald and unconvincing narrative" (Orgel).

15 *censures:* judgments.

3 *fair:* beauty. *Tellus:* Earth.

Whose fair all other fairs brought subject under,
Heaven gan to frown at earth's fragility,   5
Made proud with such adored majesty.
Hero the fair, so do I name this fair,
With whom immortal fairs might not compare,
Such was her beauty framed in heaven's scorn,
Her spotless fair caused other fairs to mourn;   10
Heaven frowned, Earth shamed, that none so fair as she,
Base-born of earth, in heaven might equal be.
Fell moody Venus pale with fretting ire;
"Aye me," quoth she, for want of her desire,
"Earth's basest mold, framed of the baser dust,   15
Strumpet to filth, bawd to loathed lust,
Worse than Medea's charms are thy enticements,
Worse than the mermaids' songs are thy allurements,
Worse than the snaky hag Tisiphone
To mortal souls is thy inveigling beauty!"   20
Thus she exclaims 'gainst harmless Hero's fair,
And, would the gods consent, her dangling hair,
Wherewith the busy air doth often play
(As wanton birds upon a sunshine day)
Should be transformed to snakes all ugly black,   25
To be a means of her eternal wrack.
But wanton Jove, sweet beauty's favourite,
Demands of Beauty beauty's worthy merit:
"If beauty's guerdon merit pain," quoth he,
"Your fair deserves no less as fair as she."   30
Then moody Juno frowning gan reply,
"I'll want my will, but strumpet she shall die!"
"Juno," quoth he, "we ought not tyrannize."
"On such," said she, "as you do wantonize!
But since our continent, the scope of heaven,   35
Contains her not unless from earth beriven,

---

11 *Earth shamed:* shamed by Earth.
12 *Base-born:* of low birth.
16 *Strumpet:* prostitute. *bawd:* whore.
17 *Medea:* the witch-princess of Colchis who helped Jason take the Golden Fleece from her father.
   See note to Marlowe, *HL,* line 1.
18 *mermaids:* sirens.
19 *Tisiphone:* One of the three Furies.
20 *inveigling:* persuading by flattery.
26 *wrack:* destruction.
29 *guerdon:* reward.
32 *I'll {. . .} will:* I might not have my way.
36 *beriven:* taken away.

I'll make a transformation of her hue,
And force the haughty mother Earth to rue
That her base womb dare yield such bastard fairs
That Jove must seek on earth immortal heirs.   40
I'll cause a second desperate Phaethon
To rule the fiery chariot of the sun,
That topsy-turvey heaven and earth may turn,
That heaven, earth, sea and hell may endless burn."
"Stay, headstrong goddess," Jove to Juno said,   45
"Can you do this without your husband's aid?"
With that she gan entreat it might be so,
But Jove would not sweet beauty overthrow;
But this he granted Juno, that Apollo
Should never more extol the fair of Hero.   50
His censure past, the ireful queen doth hie
To set a period to his harmony.
From forth his yielding arms she soon bereaves
Apollo's lute, whom comfortless she leaves,
Making a thousand parts of two gold strings;   55
Into Oblivion's cell the same she flings.

Quick-sighted spirits, this supposed Apollo,
Conceit no other but th'admired Marlowe;
Marlowe admired, whose honey-flowing vein
No English writer can as yet attain;   60
Whose name in Fame's immortal treasury
Truth shall record to endless memory;
Marlowe late mortal, now framed all divine,
What soul more happy than that soul of thine?
Live still in heaven thy soul, thy fame on earth   65
(Thou dead) of Marlowe's Hero finds a dearth.
Weep aged Tellus, all earth on earth complain,
Thy chief-born fair hath lost her fair again:
Her fair in this is lost, that Marlowe's want
Enforceth Hero's fair be wondrous scant.   70
O had that king of poets breathed longer,
Then had fair beauty's fort been much more stronger;
His golden pen had closed her so about,

---

41 *Phaethon:* son of Apollo who wrecked his father's chariot. See note to Marlowe, *HL,* line 101.
51 *hie:* hasten.
52 *period:* end.
54 *lute:* a stringed, pear-shaped musical instrument.
65 – 66 *thy {. . .} dearth:* earth is the object of *on* and the subject of *finds* (Orgel).

No bastard eaglet's quill the world throughout
Had been of force to mar what he had made,   75
For why they were not expert in that trade:
What mortal soul with Marlowe might contend,
That could 'gainst reason force him stoop or bend?
Whose silver charming tongue moved such delight
That men would shun their sleep in still dark night   80
To meditate upon his golden lines,
His rare conceits and sweet according rhymes.
But Marlowe, still admired Marlowe's gone,
To live with Beauty in Elysium,
Immortal Beauty, who desires to hear   85
His sacred poesies sweet in every ear:
Marlowe must frame to Orpheus' melody
Hymns all divine to make heaven harmony.
There ever live the prince of poetry,
Live with the living in eternity!   90

Apollo's lute bereaved of silver string,
Fond Mercury doth harshly gin to sing,
A counterfeit unto his honey note;
But I do fear he'll chatter it by rote.
Yet if his ill-according voice be such   95
That, hearing part, you think you hear too much,
Bear with his rashness and he will amend;
His folly blame, but his good will commend.
Yet rather discommend what I entreat;
For if you like it, some will storm and fret;   100
And then insulting eagles soaring high
Will prey upon the silly harmless fly—
Nil refert; for I'll pawn my better part,
Ere sweet-faced Beauty lose her due desert.

---

76 *For {. . .} trade:* because they were not skillful poets.
82 *according:* harmonizing.
84 *Elysium:* a place of happiness or paradise. See note on Marlowe, *HL,* line 411.
86 *poesies:* poetry.
87 *Orpheus:* legendary founder of poetry who used his art to move trees, tame wild beasts, and finally
   to rescue his wife Eurydice from the underworld. A figure for the civilizing power of poetry.
92 *Mercury:* Hermes, lower god of prose here (Petowe himself), to Apollo, higher god of poetry
   (Marlowe).
99 *discommend:* disapprove (opposite of commend).
103 *Nil refert:* it doesn't matter.

Avaunt base steel where shrill-tongued silver rings; 105
The chatt'ring pie may range when blackbirds sings:
Birds black as jet with sweet according voices,
Like to Elysium's saints with heavenly noises.
Why should harsh Mercury recount again
What sweet Apollo, living, did maintain? 110
Which was of Hero her all-pleasing fair,
Her pretty brows, her lip, her amber hair,
Her roseate cheek, her lily fingers white,
Her sparkling eyes that lend the day his light:
What should I say? Her all in all he praised, 115
Wherewith the spacious world was much amazed.
Leander's love and lovers' sweetest pleasure
He wrought a full discourse of beauty's treasure,
And left me nothing pleasing to recite,
But of unconstant Chance and Fortune's spite. 120
Then in this glass view Beauty's frailty,
Fair Hero and Leander's misery.

The virgin princess of the western Isle,
Fair Cambarina of the golden soil—
And yet not fair, but of a swarthy hue, 125
For by her gold her beauty did renew:
Renew as thus, that having gold to spare,
Men held it duty to protest and swear
Her fair was such as all the world admired it,
Her blushing beauty such, all men desired it. 130
The scornful queen made proud with fained praises,
Her black-framed soul to a higher rate she raises,
That men bewitched with her gold, not beauty,
A thousand knights as homage proffer duty.
If such a base deformed lump of clay, 135
In whom no sweet content had any stay,
No pleasure residence, no sweet delight,
Shelter from heat of day or cold of night;
If such a she so many suitors had,
Hero, whose angry frowns made heaven sad, 140
Hero, whose gaze gracing dark Pluto's cell,

---

105 *Avaunt:* go away.
106 *pie:* magpie.
124 *Cambarina:* Petowe's invention.
141 *Pluto's cell:* the Underworld, of which Pluto is god.

Pluto would deem Phoebus came there to dwell,
Hero, whose eyes heaven's fiery tapers stain,
Hero, whose beauty makes night day again,
How much more love merits so sweet a queen,   145
Whose like no outworn world hath ever seen.
Of sweet Leander's love to Hero's beauty,
Heaven, earth, and hell, and all the world is guilty;
Of Hero's kindness to her trusty fere,
By lost Apollo's tale it doth appear,   150
Recorded in the register of Fame:
The works of Marlowe do express the same.
But ere he gan of fickle chance to tell,
How bad chance 'gainst the better did rebel,
When love in love's sweet garden newly planted,   155
Remorseful Hero to Leander granted
Free liberty to yield the world increase;
Unconstant Fortune, foe to harmless peace,
Played such unruly pranks in love's despite
That love was forced from his true love's sight.   160

Duke Archilaus, cruel, void of pity,
Where Hero dwelt was regent of that city:
Woe worth that town where bloody homicides
And tyrants are elected city's guides;
Woe worth that country where unlawful lust   165
Sits in a regal throne: of force it must
Down to the low-laid bowels of the earth,
Like to a stillborn child's untimely birth.
Duke Archilaus loved, but whom loved he?
He courted Hero, but it would not be.   170
Why should he plant where other knights have sown?
The land is his, therefore the fruit his own.
Must it be thus? Alas, it is not so;
Lust may not force true lovers' overthrow.
Lust hath no limits, lust will have his will,   175
Like to a ravening wolf that's bent to kill,
The duke affecting her that was beloved
(Hero, whose firm-fixed love Leander proved)
Gave onset to the still-resisting fort;

---

142 *Phoebus:* Apollo, the sun.
149 *fere:* friend, companion, spouse.
161 *Duke Archilaus:* Petowe's invention.
178 *proved:* experienced.

But fearful hate set period to his sport.   180
Lust egged him on to further his desire,
But fell disdain enforced him to retire.
When Archilaus saw that thundering threats
Could not prevail, he mildly then entreats.
But all in vain; the doe had chose her make,   185
And whom she took she never would forsake.
The doe's sweet deer this hunter seeks to chase,
Harmless Leander, whose all-smiling face
Graced with unspotted fair to all men's sight
Would force the hounds retire, and not to bite: 190
Which when the duke perceived, another cur
Was forced from his den, that made much stir,
And Treason he was named, which held so fast
That fear's swift wings did lend some aid at last.
For force perforce Leander must depart   195
From Sestos, yet behind he left his heart.
His heart in Hero's breast Leander left;
Leander's absence Hero's joys bereft;
Leander's want the cruel duke thought sure
Some ease to discontent would soon procure.   200
Leander having heard his woeful doom,
Towards his weeping lady he doth come,
Dewing her cheeks with his distilling tears,
Which Hero dryeth with her dangling hairs;
They weeping greet each other with sweet kisses,   205
Kindly embracing, thus they gan their wishes:
"O that these folding arms might ne'er undo!"
As she desired, so wished Leander too;
Then with her hand she touched his sacred breast,
Where in his bosom she desires to rest.   210
Like to a snake she clung unto him fast,
And wound about him, which, snatched up in haste
By the prince of birds, borne lightly up aloft,
Doth writhe herself about his neck, and oft
About his wings displayed in the wind;   215
Or like as ivy on trees cling 'bout the rind;
Or like as crab-fish having caught in seas
His enemies, doth clasp him with his cleas.

---

185 *make:* mate.
195 *perforce:* by necessity; by force.
216 *rind:* bark.
218 *cleas:* claws.

So joined in one these two together stood,
Even as Hermaphroditus in the flood,   220
Until the duke did banish him away;
Then gan Leander to his Hero say.
"Let me go where the sun doth parch the green
In temperate heat, where he is felt and seen;
Or where his beams do not dissolve the ice;   225
In presence pressed of people mad or wise;
Set me in high, or else in low degree,
In clearest sky, or where clouds thickest be,
In longest night, or in the shortest day,
In lusty youth, or when my hairs be grey;   230
Go I to heaven, to earth, or else to hell,
Thrall or at large, alive whereso, I dwell,
On hill or dale, or on the foaming flood,
Sick or in health, in evil fame or good,
Thine will I be, and only with this thought: 235
Content thyself, although my chance be naught."
Thus parted these two lovers full of woes;
She stays behind, on pilgrimage he goes.
Leave we awhile Leander, wandering knight,
To Delphos taking all his speedy flight,   240
That by the oracle of Apollo
His further fortunes he may truly know.

True love quite banished, lust began to plead
To Hero like a scholar deeply read:
"The flaming sighs that boil within my breast,   245
Fair love," quoth he, "are cause of my unrest.
Unrest I entertain for thy sweet sake,
And in my tent choose sorrow for my make.
Why dost thou frown?" quoth he, and then she turned;
"O cool the fainting soul that flaming, burned,   250
Forced by desire to touch thy matchless beauty,
To whom thy servant vows all reverent duty."
With that her ireful brows clouded with frowns;
His soul already drenched in woe's sea drowns.
But floating on the waves, thus he gan say: 255
"Flint-hearted lady, canst thou be so coy?

---

220 *Hermaphroditus:* a youth wooed by Salmacis; they were transformed into a single body. See note
   on Marlowe, *HL,* line 530.
232 *Thrall:* enslaved. *at large:* free.
240 *Delphos:* Delphi, home to the famed Delphic oracle.
256 *coy:* unresponsive, unsympathetic.

Can pity take no place, is kind remorse
Quite banished, quite fled?" Then gan he to be hoarse,
Unable to exclaim against her longer,
Whose woe lament made Hero's heart more stronger,   260
Hero that gave no ear to her commander,
But ever weeps for her exiled Leander;
And weeping sore amongst her liquid tears,
These words she spake, wherewith her sorrow wears:
"The pillar perished is whereto I leant,   265
To my unhap, for lust away hath sent
Of all my joy the very bark and rind,
The strongest stay of my unquiet mind;
And I alas am forced without consent
Daily to mourn, till death do it relent.   270
O my Leander, he is banished,
From his sweet Hero's sight he is exiled!
O ye just heavens, if that heaven be just,
Rein the unbridled head of haughty lust;
Make him to stoop that forceth others bend,   275
Bereave his joys that reft me of my friend.
I want myself, for Hero wants her love,
And where Leander is my self doth move.
What can I more but have a woeful heart,
My mind in woe, my body full of smart,   280
And I myself myself always to hate,
Till dreadful death do ease my doleful state."

The angry duke lay listening to her words,
And till she ends no speech at all affords,
Until at length exclaiming 'gainst her kind,   285
Thus he breathed forth the venom of his mind:
"O timorous taunters that delights in toys,
Jangling jesters, deprivers of sweet joys,
Tumbling cock-boats tottering to and fro,
Growned of the graft whence all my grief doth grow;   290
Sullen serpents environed with despite,
That ill for good at all times doth requite;
As cypress tree that rent is by the root,
As well-sown seed for drought that cannot sprout,
As branch or slip bitter from whence it grows,   295

---

276 *reft*: bereft.
285 *kind*: nature.
289 *cock-boats*: ships' rowboats.
290 *Growned of*: grown from.

As gaping ground that rainless cannot close;
As filth on land to whom no water flows,
As flowers do fade when Phoebus rarest shows,
As Salamandra repulsed from the fire,
Wanting my wish, I die for my desire."   300
Speaking those words, Death seized him for his own,
Wherewith she thought her woes were overthrown;
Hero so thought, but yet she thought amiss:
Before she was beloved, now finds no bliss.
Duke Archilaus being sudden dead,   305
Young Euristippus ruled in his stead,
The next succeeding heir to what was his:
Then Hero's woes increased, and fled all bliss.

Look how the silly harmless bleating lamb,
Bereft from his kind make the gentle dam,   310
Left as a prey to butcher's cruelty,
In whom she finds not any drop of mercy;
Or like a warrior whom his soldiers flies
At his shrill echo of his foes' dread cries,
He all unable to withstand so many,   315
Not having wherewith to combat, nor any
Assured friend that dares to comfort him,
Nor any way for fear dares succour him;
But as a prey he yields to him he would not
If he had help, but, helpless, strive he could not.   320
So fared it with the meek distressed Hero,
That sweet Leander banished her fro,
She had no Hercules to defend her cause,
She had no Brandamour disdaining laws
To combat for her safety; this sweet Io   325
Had no kind Jove to keep her from her foe;
This Psyches had no Cupid, love was banished,
And love from love exiled, love needs must famish.

---

299 *Salamandra:* The salamander was believed to be able to live in fire.
306 *Young Euristippus:* Petowe's invention.
310 *make:* mate.
318 *succour:* relieve.
322 *That {. . .} fro:* since Leander was banished from her.
323 *Hercules:* see Marlowe, *HL,* line 781.
324 *Brandamour:* possibly Brandimarte. In Boiardo's *Orlando Innamorato* (and Ariosto's *Orlando Furioso*), Brandimarte is Orlando's friend and Fiordelisa's lover.
325 *Io:* priestess of Juno with whom Jupiter fell in love, to Juno's dismay. See note on Marlowe, *HL,* line 388.
327 *Psyches:* Psyche, loved by Cupid.

Wood Euristippus for his brother's death,
Like as a toiled huntsman wanting breath   330
Stormeth that bad chance in the game's pursuit
Should cause him panting rest as dead and mute;
Or like sad Orphey for Euridice,
Whom Cerberus bereft so hastily;
Like to the thundering threats of Hercules,   335
The world's admired prince, the great Alcides,
When Nessus got the height of his desire
By ravishing his fairest Deianire;
Such was his ire, and more if more may be,
Which he 'gainst Hero breathed spitefully.   340
"Thou damned hag—" thus gan he to exclaim,
"Thou base-born strumpet, one of Circe's train,
Durst thou presume, poor silly simple fly,
With venom's force to force an eagle die?
What though my brother Leander banished,   345
Must he by thee therefore be poisoned?
Die, cursed wretch!" With that he cast her from him,
And would not suffer her to look upon him.
The still amazed lady musing stood,
Admiring why the duke should be so wood.   350
Humbly she prostrates her at Anger's feet,
And with down-dropping tears like liquid sleet
She watereth the summer-thirsty ground,
Weeping so long she fell into a sound.
Again revived by the standers by,   355
She doth entreat them to resolve her why
Duke Euristippus wrongeth her so much
As to dishonour her with such a touch.
"Well know the gods my guiltless soul," quoth she;
"Was Archilaus poisoned by me?   360
If so, just heavens and immortal powers,
Rain vengeance down in all-consuming showers;

---

329 *Wood:* mad.
330 *toiled:* tired, exhausted.
333 *Orphey:* Orpheus. See note to line 87.
334 *Cerberus:* the doglike guard of Hades.
335–388 *Hercules {. . .} Deianire:* Hercules's wife Deianira was carried off by Nessus, a centaur. When Hercules gave the centaur his death wound, Nessus gave Deianira a cloak saturated in poisoned blood, telling her it would strengthen her husband's love for her. When she became jealous of Hercules's love for Iole, she gave him the cloak, causing his horrific death.
350 *Admiring:* wondering.
354 *fell {. . .} sound:* fainted.
358 *touch:* charge, accusation.

And cause that Hero that was counted fair
Like a mad hellish fury to despair."
The more she weeps, the more the heavens smile,   365
Scorning that beauty should take any soil,
Juno commanded Argus to defend her,
But Jupiter would not so much befriend her.
Argus stark dead, sweet Hero might not live,
For of her life the duke will her deprive.   370
Her doom was thus: ere three months' date took end,
If she found none that would her cause defend,
Untimely death should seize her as a prey,
And unresisting life should death obey.
Meantime within a rock-framed castle strong   375
She was imprisoned traitors vile among,
Where discontented when she should have rested,
Her food bad fare, with sighs and tears she feasted;
And when the breathless horses of the sun
Had made their stay, and Luna had begun   380
With cheerful smiling brows to grace dark night,
Clad in black sable weeds for want of light,
This all alone sad lady gan to play,
Framing sweet music to her welladay,
Th'effect whereof this sonnet plainly shows,   385
The fountain whence springs Hero's heavy woes.

HERO'S LAMENTATION IN PRISON

Night's mourning black and misty veiling hue
Shadows the blessed comfort of the sun,
At whose bright gaze I wonted to renew
My lifeless life when life was almost done.   390
Done is my life, and all my pleasure done,
For he is gone in whom my life begun:
Unhappy I, poor I, and none as I;
But pilgrim he, poor he, that should be by.

---

367 *Argus:* Juno's hundred-eyed guard of Io, killed by Mercury. See note to Marlowe, *HL*, line 388.
380 *Luna:* the moon.
384 *welladay:* grief, lament.
387–430 *Hero's Lamentation in Prison.* Cf. Florimell's lamentation in the prison of Proteus's rocky
    undersea cave for her lover Marinell (*FQ* 4.12.5–11).

My love exiled, and I in prison fast,   395
Out-streaming tears break into weeping rain;
He too soon banished, I in dungeon cast,
He for me mourneth, I for him complain.
He's banished, yet lives at liberty,
And I exiled, yet live in misery: 400
He weeps for me far off, I for him here;
I would I were with him, and he more near.

But this imprisoning cave, this woeful cell,
This house of sorrow and increasing woe,
Grief's teary chamber where sad care doth dwell,   405
Where liquid tears like top-filled seas do flow,
Beating their waves 'gainst still relentless stone,
Still still they smile on me, and I still moan:
I weep to stone, and stone of stone I find;
Cold stone cold comfort yields, O most unkind.   410

Oft have I read that stone relents at rain,
And I implete their barren womb with store;
Tears streaming down, they wet and wet again,
Yet pitiless they harden all the more;
And when my longing soul looks they should sunder,   415
I touch the flinty stone and they seem stronger.
They strong, I weak; alas, what hope have I?
Hero wants comfort, Hero needs must die.

When the melodious shrill-tongued nightingale
With heavy cheer had warbled this sad tale,   420
Night's drowsy god an ivory canopy
Curtains before the windows of fair beauty.
Drowned thus in sleep, she spent the weary night;
There leave I Hero in a heavy plight.
Now to the woeful pilgrim I return,   425
Whose passions force the gentle birds to mourn;
They see Leander weep, with heavy note

---

412 *implete:* fill. *store:* great quantity.
419–20 *When {. . .} tale:* cf. Shakespeare, *Rape of Lucrece:* "By this, lamenting Philomele had ended /
   The well-tun'd warble of her nightly sorrow" (1079–80). See also Lucrece's complaint to
   Philomele at 1128–48. *nightingale:* Philomela; see note to Raleigh, "The Nymph's Reply" (line
   7) to "The Passionate Shepherd" and to the dedication to Mary Sidney Herbert.

They faintly sing, as when they sing by rote:
While he gan descant on his misery,
The pretty fowls do make him melody.   430

LEANDER'S COMPLAINT OF HIS RESTLESS ESTATE

Bright heaven's immortal moving spheres,
  and Phoebus all divine,
Rue on low Earth's unfained tears
  that issue from Earth's eyne.
Eyes were these no-eyes, whilst eye's eyesight lasted,   435
But these dark eyes' clear sight sad sorrow wasted.

What creature living lives in grief
  that breathes on Tellus' soil,
But heavens pity with relief,
  save me, a slave to spoil?   440
Spoil do his worst, spoil cannot spoil me more;
Spoil never spoiled so true a love before.
The stricken deer stands not in awe
  of black grim ireful Death,
For he finds herbs that can withdraw   445
  the shaft, to save his breath.
The chased deer hath soil to cool his heat,
The toiled steed is up in stable set.

The silly owls lurk in the leaves,
  shine sun or night's queen weather;   450
The sparrow shrouds her in the eaves
  from storms of huffing weather.
Fowls comfort find, Leander finds no friend;
Then comfortless, Leander's life must end.

---

429 *descant:* "To play or sing an air in harmony with a fixed theme; gen. to warble, sing harmo-
  niously" (*OED*).
434 *eyne:* plural of eye.
438 *Tellus:* Earth.
440 *spoil:* destruction.
449 *silly:* innocent.
450 *night's queen:* the moon.
451 *her:* herself.

By this it pleased the smiling brows of heaven,   455
Whose deadly frowns him erst of joy beriven,
To set a period to Leander's toil.
Having enjoyed that long desired soil,
When he had viewed the stately territories,
And Delphos' sacred high erected towers,   460
Unto Apollo's oracle he goes,
In hope to find relief for many woes;
He craves long looked-for rest, or else to die,
To whom the oracle gan thus reply:

THE ORACLE

He loveth thine that loves not thee,   465
His love to thine shall fatal be.
Upon suspect she shall be slain
Unless thou do return again.

These harsh according rhymes to mickle pain
Did but renew Leander's woes again;   470
Yet as he might, with Fortunes sweet consent,
He gins return all dangers to prevent.
Within short time at Sestos he arriveth;
On love's light wings desire Leander driveth,
Desire that longs to view a blessed end   475
Of Love and Fortune that so long contend.
This back-retired pilgrim lived secure,
And in unknown disguise he did endure
Full two months space, until the time drew nigh
To free fair Hero, or enforce her die.   480
The date outworn of the prefixed day
When combatants their valour should display,
All things prepared, as blazing fame reported,
'Twere wonder to behold how men resorted;

---

455 *this:* this time.
456 *him {. . .} beriven:* bereaved him of joy.
457 *period:* end.
467 *suspect:* suspicion.
469 *mickle:* much.
481 *date outworn:* time passed.

Knights neighbouring by, and ladies all divine,   485
Darting day's splendour from their sunlike eyne:
Spectatum veniunt, veniunt spectentur ut ipsae,
But wanting fair, they come to gaze on beauty,
Beauty, fair heaven's beauty, world's wonder,
Hero, whose beauty keeps all beauty under.   490
This fair-faced beauty from a foul-faced cell,
A loathsome dungeon like to night's dark hell,
At the fell duke's command in open view,
Was sent for, on whose never-spotted hue
Earth's mortal souls do feed and gaze upon her;   495
So long they gaze that they do surfeit on her.
For when this earth's admired immortal sun
To peep from under sable hold begun,
Like as the piercing eye of cloudy heaven,
Whose sight the black thick clouds have quite beriven,   500
But by the huffing winds being overblown,
And all their black expelled and overthrown,
The day doth gin be jocund, secure, playing,
The fair of heaven his beauty so displaying:
So when the fairest Hero did begin   505
(Whilom yclad in darkness' black-tanned skin)
To pass the noisome portal of the prison,
Like to the gorgeous Phoebus newly risen,
She doth illuminate the morning day,
Clad in a sable mantle of black say,   510
Which Hero's eyes transformed to fair white,
Making the low'ring morn dark pure light.
As many mortal eyes beheld her eyes
As there are fiery tapers in the skies;

---

485 *Knights {. . .} ladies:* Petowe's imitation of the important programmatic line of Spenser's chivalric epic, *The Faerie Queene:* "And sing of Knights and gentle Ladies deeds" (1.Pr.1.5)—itself indebted to the opening of Ariosto's *Orlando Furioso* and originally of Virgil's *Aeneid.* The following knightly tournament fought for Hero's hand recalls the tournament fought for the hand of
Florimell in *The Faerie Queene,* book 4, canto 4 (published 1596).
487 *Spectatum {. . .} ipsae:* "They come as spectators, and to be watched themselves (Ovid, *Ars Amatoria,* I 99)" (Orgel).
488 *wanting fair:* lacking beauty.
503 *jocund:* high-spirited.
506 *whilom:* formerly.
507 *noisome:* offensively disgusting, harmful.
510 *say:* "A cloth of fine texture resembling serge; in the 16th c. sometimes partly of silk, subsequently entirely of wool" (*OED*).

As many eyes gazed on fair Hero's beauty   515
As there be eyes that offer heaven duty;
As many servitors attended on her
As Venus servants had to wait upon her.
Though by the stern duke she was dishonoured,
Yet of the people she was honoured;   520
Mongst whom exiled Leander all unseen
And all unknown attended on his queen.
When to the near-adjoining palace gate,
The place appointed for the princely combat,
They did approach, there might all eyes behold   525
The duke in armour of pure beaten gold,
Mounted upon a steed as white as snow,
The proud duke Euristippus, Hero's foe;
Hero being seated in rich majesty,
A servile handmaid to captivity,   530
From whence she might behold that gentle knight
That for her sake durst hazard life in fight;
For this was all the comfort Hero had,
So many eyes shed tears to see her sad.
Her handmaid Hope persuaded her some one   535
Undaunted knight would be her champion.
Yet since her lord Leander was not nigh,
She was resolved either to live or die;
But her Leander, careful of his love,
Intending love's firm constancy to prove   540
(If to his lot the honour did befall)
Withdrew himself into the palace hall,
Where he was armed to his soul's content,
And privily conducted to a tent,
From whence he issued forth at trumpet's sound,   545
Who, at the first encounter, on the ground
Forced the mazed duke sore panting lie,
Drowned in the river of sad ecstasy.
At length reviving he doth mount again,
Whom young Leander in short time had slain.   550
The duke quite dead, this all unknown young knight
Was forthwith made the heir of Sestos right,
The Princess Hero set at liberty,
Kept by the late dead duke in misery,

---

537 *nigh:* near.
548 *ecstasy:* unconsciousness.

Whose constancy Leander gan to prove,   555
And now anew begins to court his love.

"To walk on ground where danger is unseen
Doth make men doubt, where they have never been.
As blind men fear what footing they shall find,
So doth the wise mistrust the stranger's mind.   560
I strange to you, and you unknown to me,
Yet may not love twixt us two grafted be?
What I have done for Hero's love was done;
Say then you love, and end as I begun.
I hazard life to free thy beauty's fair   565
From tyrant's force and hellish soul despair:
Then, sacred fair, balance my good desert;
Enrich my soul with thy affecting heart."

Hero replied: "To rue on all false tears
And forged tales, wherein craft oft appears,   570
To trust each feigned face and forcing charm
Betrays the simple soul that thinks no harm.
Not every tear doth argue inward pain,
Not every sigh warrants men do not feign,
Not every smoke doth prove a present fire,   575
Not all that glisters golden souls desire,
Not every word is drawn out of the deep,
For oft men smile when they do seem to weep:
Oft malice makes the mind to pour forth brine,
And envy leaks the conduits of the eyne.   580
Craft oft doth cause men make a seeming show
Of heavy woes where grief did never grow.
Then blame not those that wisely can beware
To shun dissimulation's dreadful snare.
Blame not the stopped ears 'gainst sirens' song,   585
Blame not the mind not moved with falsehood tongue;
But rest content and satisfied with this:
Whilst true Leander lives, true Hero's his."

"And thy Leander lives, sweet soul," said he,
"Praising thy all-admired chastity.   590
Though thus disguised, I am that banished knight
That for affecting thee was put to flight.

---

555 *prove:* test.

Hero, I am Leander, thy true fere,
As true to thee as life to me is dear."

When Hero all amazed gan revive, 595
And she that then seemed dead was now alive,
With kind embracements kissing at each strain,
She welcomes him, and kisses him again.
"By thee my joys have shaken off despair;
All storms be past, and weather waxeth fair; 600
By thy return Hero receives more joy
Than Paris did when Helen was in Troy.
By thee my heavy doubts and thoughts are fled,
And now my wits with pleasant thoughts are fed."

"Feed, sacred saint, on nectar all divine, 605
While these my eyes," quoth he, "gaze on thy eyne.
And ever after may these eyes beware
That they on strangers' beauty never stare:
My wits I charm henceforth they take such heed,
They frame no toys my fancies new to feed. 610
Deaf be my ears to hear another voice,
To force me smile, or make my soul rejoice;
Lame be my feet when they presume to move
To force Leander seek another love.
And when thy fair, sweet fair, I gin disgrace, 615
Heaven to my soul afford no resting place."
What he to her, she vowed the like to him,
All sorrows fled, their joys anew begin.
Full many years those lovers lived in fame,
That all the world did much admire the same. 620
Their lives' spent date, and unresisted death
At hand to set a period to their breath,
They were transformed by all divine decrees
Into the form and shape of two pine trees,
Whose nature's such, the female pine will die 625
Unless the male be ever planted by:
A map for all succeeding times to come
To view true love, which in their loves begun.

FINIS

Qualis vita, finis ita

---

621 *spent date:* time ended.
630 *Qualis {. . .} ita:* "As the life is, so is its end" (Orgel).

EPITAPH ON SIR ROGER MANWOOD

IN OBITUM HONORATISSIMI VIRI
ROGERI MANWOOD MILITIS QUAESTORII
REGINALIS CAPITALIS BARONIS

Noctivagi terror, ganeonis triste flagellum,
Et Jovis Alcides, rigido vulturque latroni,
Urna subtegitur. Scelerum gaudete nepotes!
Insons, luctifica sparsis cervice capillis
Plange! fori lumen, veneranda gloria legis,   5
Occidit: heu, secum effoetas Acherontis ad oras
Multa abiit virtus. Pro tot virtutibus uni,
Livor, parce viro; non audacissimus esto
Illius in cineres, cuius tot millia vultus
Mortalium attonuit: sic cum te nuntia Ditis   10
Vulneret exsanguis, feliciter ossa quiescant,
Famaque marmorei superet monumenta sepulchri.

ON THE DEATH OF THE MOST HONORABLE MAN
ROGER MANWOOD, THE MILITARY ATTORNEY
AND BARON OF THE QUEEN'S EXCHEQUER

Terror of night-stalkers, flayer of prodigals,
Jovian Hercules, raptor of robbers,
Lies urn-interred. Rejoice, Offspring of crime:
Lament, you innocents, with mournful hair strewn back.
The bright sun of the court, the glory of worshipped law, has fallen.   5

Manwood: d. 1592. Canterbury jurist. See Introduction.
2 *Jovian:* Jove-like; offspring of Jove. *Hercules:* half-mortal of heroic strength who famously performed his gigantic Twelve Labors.

Great goodness now is gone to barren shores of Acheron.
Spare him, Envy, for his many virtues,
Do not profane his ashes whose face awed
Thousands of men; so that, Great Sir, when Death
Arrives with final scythe your bones lie peaceful   10
And your fame outlives your marble marker.

---

6 *Acheron:* land of the dead in the classical underworld.
7 *Envy:* the addressee of *OE* 1.15.

The Dedicatory Epistle to Mary Sidney Herbert

ILLUSTRISSIMAE HEROINAE OMNIBUS & ANIMI, & CORPORIS DOTIBUS ORNATISSIMAE, MARIAE PENBROKIAE COMITISSAE

Laurigera stirpe prognata Delia; Sydnaei vatis Apollinei genuina soror; Alma
literatum parens, ad cuius immaculates amplexus, confugit virtus, barbarici &
ignorantiae impetu violata, ut olim a Threicio Tyranno Philomela; Poetarum
nostri temporis, ingeniorumque omnium foelicissime pullulantium, Musa;
Dia proles, quae iam rudi calamo, spiritus infundis elati furoris, quibus ipse   5
misellus, plus mihi videor praestare posse, quam cruda nostra indoles proferre
solet: Dignare Posthumo huic Amyntae, ut tuo adoptivo filio patrocinari:
Eoque magis quod moribundus pater, illius tutelam humillime tibi legaverat.
Et licet illustre nomen tuum non solum apud nos, sed exteras etiam nationes,
latius propagatum est, quam aut unquam possit aeruginosa Temporis vetustate   10
aboleri, aut mortalium encomiis augeri, (quomodo enim quicquam possit esse
infinito plus?) multorum tamen camaenis, quasi siderum diademate redimita
Ariadne, noli hunc purum Phoebi sacerdotem, stellam alteram coronae tuae
largientem, aspernari: sed animi candore, quem sator hominum, atque deorum,
Iupiter, praenobili familiae tuae quasi haereditarium alligavit, accipe, & tuere.   15
Sic nos, quorum opes tenuissimae, littorea sunt Myrtus Veneris, Nymphaeque
Peneiae semper virens coma, prima quaque poematis pagina, Te Musarum
dominam, in auxilium invocabimus: tua denique virtus, quae virtutem ipsam,
ipsam quoque aeternitatem superabit.

Honoris tui studiosissimus, C. M.

Mary Sidney Herbert (1561–1621), poet and dramatist, and a great patron of letters; sister to
Sir Philip Sidney and Sir Robert Sidney, aunt of Lady Mary Wroth (see Introduction). After
Thomas Watson (b.? 1557–92), the author of *Amintae Gaudia,* died (perhaps of plague), Mar-
lowe wrote this Latin dedication to Herbert for the volume.

TO THE MOST ILLUSTRIOUS WOMAN, ADORNED
WITH ALL GIFTS OF MIND AND BODY, MARY,
COUNTESS OF PEMBROKE

Delia, born of a race of poets, lawful sister of Sidney, the Priest of Apollo. She
was the nurturing mother of letters to whose sinless embrace virtue took refuge, violated by the blows of barbarism and ignorance, just as Philomela once
fled the Thracian tyrant; O Muse most happy to inspire the new, young, and
gifted poets of our time; Divine offspring, who inspires my rude reed with   5
high, creative madness which I, by myself, am too wretched a writer to attain
without you; consider it as noble an endeavor to be patroness to this posthumous Amyntas as you would to adopt a son, especially because his father as he
lay dying humbly beseeched you and committed to your care the safety of this
child. And even though your glorious name is spread rather widely both here   10
and abroad so that it can never disappear by the relentless movement of time
or be made even greater by the praises of mere mortals (for how can infinity
increase?), nevertheless, being crowned with as many poems as Aridane was
with stars, do not spurn this poor priest of Phoebus as he adds yet this new
star to your crown: but with the clarity of mind which the creator of men and   15
gods, Jupiter, has assigned to your family, receive him and keep him safe. Thus
I, whose very slim ability is owed to the seashore myrtle of Venus and
Daphne's always-greening hair, on the first and every page of these poems will
beg your favor, chosen-lady of the Muses. In the very end, it will be your virtue which will surpass both virtue itself and even eternity.

Most desirous to do thee honor, C. M.

---

1 *Delia:* Marlowe's name for Herbert, borrowed from Samuel Daniel and his sonnet sequence *Delia.*
  Apollo: god of poetry.
3 *Philomela:* the nightingale.
4 *Thracian tyrant:* Tereus. Philomela was once a princess of Athens, so beautiful that her brother-
  in-law, Tereus, raped her. After she communicated with her sister Procne (Tereus's wife) by sending her a tapestry depicting the crime, the sisters plotted revenge. They served Tereus his son,
  Itys, in a pie, and after revealing their plot to him, he chased them and they turned into birds,
  Philomela becoming the nightingale.

INDEX

Page numbers in **boldface** denote descriptions of figures in classical mythology important to this edition.

Abydos, 18, 194, 196, 210, 214, 226, 238, 262
Accius, 64, 66
Achelous, 114–15, 117
Acheron, 22, 23, **201**, 290
Achilles, 13, 23, 45, 53, 59, **68**, 81–82, 92, 98–99, 123, 258
Acis, 10
Actaeon, 13, **218**
Actium, 172
Adonis, 123, **163**, 195, 198
Adriatic Sea, 14, 87
Aeaea, 196
Aeetes, 196
Aegean (Carpathian) Sea, 47, 81, 174, 197
Aegyptos, 68
Aeneas, 10, 13, **36**, 49, 64, 88, 90, 92, 100, 123, 131, 177
Aesop, 212
Aesope, 115
Aetna, 130, 172, 188
Aetolia, 115
Africa, 87, 96, 178, 182, 192
Agamemnon, 45, 53, 68, 77, **81**, 89, 133
Agave, 189
Agrippa, 172
Aiora, festival of, 95
Ajax, 45, 68
Alba, 177, 188
Alcides. *See* Hercules
Alcinous, 56
Alcmaeon, 56
Alcmane, 245, 257
Alcmena, 61
Alexander the Great, 146
Almo, 190
Alpheus, 114–15
Alps, 95, 177–78, 180, 186, 188

Amazon, 73
Americas, 149
Amphiarus, 56
Amphion, 131
Amphitryon, 61
Amulius, 114
Amymone, 54
Amyntas, 23, 291–92
Anchises, 88
Andromache, 53
Andromeda, 110
Anio, 114–15, 189
"Another of the Same Nature, Made Since," 4–5, 12, 160–62
Antony, Mark, 16, 172, 179
Anubis, 90
Aonian harp, 34, 100
Apelles, 62
Aphrodite. *See* Venus
Apis, 91
Apollo, 15, 20, 24, 34, 37, 43, 62, 68, 75, 87, 100, 108, 111, 121, 123, 130, 161, 172–73, 192, 194, 198, 200, 210, 213, 220, 222, 243–44, 246, 255, 269, 271–74, 276, 283, 291–92
Apuleius, *Golden Ass, The,* 199
Arachne, 13, 76, 199, 237, 243
Araris, 185
Aratus, 66; *Phaenomena,* 64
Arcadia, 46, 115
Arethusa, 114
Argo, 64, **86**, 163, 196
Argolis, 114
Argonauts, 64, 66, 86, 163, 196
Argos (land), 54, 68
Argus, 70, 112, 207, 280
Ariadne, 46
Ariminum, 177–78

293